DATE DUE

APR 0 9 1994	
NOV 2 2 1994	
DEC - 6 1994	
OCT 5 1996	
NOV 1 4 1996	
OCT 1 4 1997	
APR 1 4 1999	
FEB - 1 2000	
APR 0 3 2000	
APR 1 0 2000	
APR 1 0 2000	
APR 1 1 2000	

BRODART   Cat. No. 23-221

60

Sixty Years of Southwestern Archaeology

60

SIXTY YEARS OF

a history of the

SOUTHWESTERN

pecos conference

ARCHAEOLOGY

Richard B. Woodbury

University of
New Mexico Press

Library of Congress Cataloging-in-Publication Data
Woodbury, Richard B. (Richard Benjamin), 1917–
Sixty years of southwestern archaeology : a history of the Pecos
Conference / Richard B. Woodbury.
    p.   cm.
Includes bibliographical references and index.
ISBN 0–8263–1411–2
1. Pecos Conference.   2. Southwest, New—Antiquities.   3. Indians
of North America—Southwest, New—Antiquities.
4. Archaeology—Southwest, New—History—20th century.
I. Title.   II. Title: 60 years of southwestern archaeology.
                                        F798.W66   1993
        92–21420   979'.0072079—dc20
            CIP

© 1993 by Richard B. Woodbury.

*Designed by
Linda M. Tratechaud*

To Madeleine Kidder
and A. V. Kidder

CONTENTS

FIGURES

TABLES

FOREWORD

The invitation to write the foreword to Richard Woodbury's insightful and exhaustive history of the Pecos Conference is a distinct honor. It comes at a time when I normally would say no to such requests and would be tempted to respectfully decline, but the caprice of history dictates otherwise. I was one of the five students fortunate enough to attend the first meeting at Pecos in 1927 and am one of the few remaining participants in that initial Conference, held among the piñons of north-central New Mexico.

As I reflect on the changes in Southwestern prehistory from my vantage point of sixty-five years in archaeology, two events of stellar significance impress me. The development of tree-ring studies by Dr. A. E. Douglass was a technological breakthrough bringing into focus the important dimension of time, which is central to archaeological studies everywhere. But the main credit must go to the other event, the creation of the prestigious and well-known Pecos Conference, which has done more than all else to bring Southwesternists together intellectually and philosophically to consider seriously the meaning of their labors.

This evaluation may come as a shock to some readers of these introductory pages, so a further word of explanation is necessary. From the time of the earliest explorations of the Southwest by the Wetherills, Nordenskiöld, Bandelier, Cushing, and Fewkes until the time of Hewett, Cummings, Kidder, Morris, Judd, and a host of others during the first decades of this century, one important dimension of research was missing: the opportunity for them to come together to discuss mutual problems. In retrospect, the explanation of this is simple, for those early days were times of discovery, of fact finding, of learning what the archaeological resources really were. The time was not yet right for the kind of experience so lucidly discussed in this volume.

By the 1920s, the accumulated findings of myriad investigators resulted in a jumble of confusing, often contradictory ideas; there was much specific knowledge but of only a few places. Lacking was an overall plan that would bring the scattered information into a cohesive structure. Luckily, this void and the need to develop a bonding process for the accumulated data were recognized by leaders in the field at the time, notably A. V. Kidder. As Woodbury reports in detail, Kidder reviewed this thought with Neil Judd, then working at Pueblo Bonito. A positive response encouraged Kidder to proceed with plans for the first-ever gathering of workers in the Southwestern field. Because that gathering was something that had never been tried before, Kidder must have had misgivings about the outcome of the venture.

Under Kidder's able leadership and after much debate, often acrimonious, something positive did result: the first codification of the sum and substance of what was known about Southwestern archaeology at the time, the Basketmaker-Pueblo or Pecos Classification. Admittedly imperfect, because it did not accommodate the archaeology of southern Arizona and other remains in the mountainous zone of Arizona and New Mexico, it soon became the target of attacks and suggestions for modification. It nevertheless provided a central and defensible rallying point that gave structure to the whole field of Southwestern archaeology. Of almost greater importance is the fact that the Pecos Conference of 1927 and its successors provided the opportunity for people of diverse interests and inclinations to convene face to face to air their problems. The Conference came to be seen as an annual event not to be missed. Its survival for more than sixty years, with a few uncertain episodes along the way, is eloquent testimony to the value of the meetings for the participants.

Through time the Conference evolved into a rich tradition among Southwestern archaeologists of holding meetings in August at the end of most field sessions. It thus served as a forum where from the podium the latest findings, ideas, and interpretations could be informally presented and debated. But more than that, it provided the occasion for people with kindred interests to fraternize and exchange views, who otherwise might not have had the opportunity to do so. This led to a cohesiveness in the research effort that pushed Southwestern archaeology ahead of that in other regions. Indeed, it was the model for the development of other regional conferences.

The informality of the meetings, in contrast to the tightly structured national meetings, remains a distinct advantage in spite of several attempts to change it. In my view, therein lies the real value of the Conference. It worked positively in 1927, and it continues to do so today. Little wonder that attendees of recent years reflect on Conferences they participated in with the same warm glow and hint of nostalgia as those who attended fifty years ago.

Without wishing to anticipate or repeat Woodbury's incisive analysis of the Pecos Conference's birth, adolescence, and adulthood, I want to reflect on one significant change in the character of the Conferences that has been for the good. Although students were excluded from the 1927 Conference for both intellectual and logistical reasons, five were in attendance, as explained by Woodbury. Today, on the other hand, students are welcomed, not only for what they can learn but also for what they contribute. It is they who must provide the continuity and the leadership for tomorrow. Because of them and because of the general growth of archaeology as an academic discipline, the numbers of attendees at Conferences have increased from the initial 45 or so in 1927 to more than 300 in recent times. This change must be seen as beneficial, though the increased numbers have caused some losses of informality and freedom of communication as well as an increase in logistical problems. A particular lament from this old-timer, who was fortunate enough to be present at the 1927 Conference, is that the consensus about the interpretation of Southwestern archaeology that characterized the first session has been largely missing in later meetings. This shortcoming is not caused by any lack of pressing problems in Southwestern archaeology, but rather by the diversity of minds and the attendant differences in importance placed on the issues of the day. After all, the declaration of the first Conference, helpful as it was through the years, has been greatly modified and expanded, even rejected in part. Clearly, the motives for holding the Conference have changed since 1927.

Woodbury has favored us and generations to come with an accurate and detailed account of the history of the Pecos Conference. A careful perusal of it cannot fail to impress us with the importance that this institution has had and continues to hold for students of Southwestern archaeology.

Emil W. Haury
2 May 1991
Tucson

PREFACE

We glorify the present only when it has become the past.

—John Stewart Collis, *The Worm Forgives the Plough*, Book I

This chronicle of the Pecos Conference, from 1927, when it was begun by A. V. Kidder, to an arbitrary cut-off date of 1988, necessarily includes much about the archaeology and related activity in the Southwest during those six decades, but it does not pretend to be a complete history of Southwestern archaeology. That would have to start at least a half century earlier and include much that is omitted here. The Pecos Conference was the occasion when, summer after summer, anyone and everyone could report their own research activities and learn what others had been doing. Therefore, recounting each Conference's events and looking at changes in interests and emphases through the years brings in a good deal of archaeological history from which a general panorama of archaeology in the Southwest emerges. It also offers a close-up view of how a small conference is planned and run, as well as of the personal networks and rivalries that have always been just below the surface of Southwestern (or any other) archaeology.

Among anthropological organizations the Pecos Conference is unique in having no memberships, no officers, no office or headquarters, no treasury, and no publications. Every year a host institution volunteers—or is persuaded—to organize the next year's meeting, a mailing list is passed on, and an interim committee appointed for program and local arrangements. Universities and colleges, museums, the National Park Service, and other organizations have been remarkably generous in shouldering the burden in both time and money. (The many locations of the Conference are shown in Figure 15.1 and Table 15.1.) It is not surprising that sometimes there have been disagreements on the meeting format, particularly on the question of extempore versus formal reports, and in the early years there were arguments about the role of students (speaking or only listening). Conference attendance has grown from about fifty at the start to several hundred in recent years, yet a considerable degree of informality has been maintained, one of the attributes most valued by conferees. In reporting in *Science* on the first Conference in 1927, A. V. Kidder, the founder, wrote:

> The purposes of the meeting were: to bring about contacts between workers in the Southwestern field; to discuss fundamental problems of Southwestern history [including prehistory], and to formulate plans for coordinated attacks upon them; to pool knowledge of facts and techniques, and to lay foundations for a unified system of nomenclature.

These purposes, held to year after year, have been achieved to a substantial degree and have continued to guide the Pecos Conference today—although there have been few "coordinated attacks" and much "pool[ing of] knowledge and facts."

A comment in a letter from Theodore R. Frisbie (5 November 1981) reflects the hold the Pecos Conference has on many of us:

> As a student in the 1950[s]–1960s, I sensed a sort of charismatic quality about the meetings—something which transcends "tradition." I don't believe it was what various faculty said, but rather a reading between the lines. Perhaps this stemmed from the fact that great decisions used to be made as Southwestern archaeology took shape, sweeping concepts put forth.

My history of the Pecos Conference came about through the urging of Albert H. Schroeder and Emil W. Haury, and my enthusiastic, indeed rash assent to their suggestion. Like many undertakings, "if I'd only known" what I was committing myself to I might have had second thoughts, yet the writing has been a continuing pleasure as colleagues generously responded to inquiry after inquiry. What began as a modest effort grew and grew, thanks to the steady accumulation of information and records from many people and places. Perhaps novels are written by a single person, but any historical account depends on myriad sources and much generous assistance, as I record in the acknowledgments. Sources range from letters about a coming year's program and mimeographed handouts to formal reports in newsletters and professional journals, enriched by personal recollections. The significant will be found alongside the trivial, both intended to bring alive the Conferences, their many individual participants, the changing flow of research interests, and the issues and problems of the day.

More than three centuries ago Thomas Hobbes provided a justification for chronicling the Pecos Conference when he wrote, "Out of our conceptions of the past, we make the future." On a lighter note Washington Irving said in his *Knickerbocker's History of New York:* "That I have not written a better history of the days of the patriarchs is not my fault—had any other person written one as good I should not have attempted it at all. That many will hereafter spring up and surpass me in excellence I have very little doubt." Until then, however, I offer the story of the Pecos Conference's origin, survival, and growth as a glimpse of the archaeological enterprise that has made Southwestern archaeology such an extensive, varied, and fascinating resource for understanding the past.

16 May 1991
Shutesbury, Massachusetts

Note: The term *Papago* follows historic usage in cited letters and memoranda rather than the more recent designation *Tohono O'odham.*

Acknowledgments

So many people have provided such invaluable help during my writing that it seems unfair to single out a few at the expense of the many. Nevertheless, several friends and colleagues have done so much in supplying information records, comments, and criticisms that I will begin with them. Emil W. Haury and Albert H. Schroeder, especially, have provided constant encouragement, as well as quantities of useful information and advice. In addition, they read and improved many of these chapters. Others who have been particularly helpful in many ways are Katharine Bartlett, David M. Brugge, Carol A. Gifford, Douglas R. Givens, Marjorie T. Lambert, Stewart Peckham, Watson Smith, Raymond H. Thompson, and Nathalie F.S. Woodbury.

For some years abundant details of the Conference are available from notes taken by Lee Correll, Edward B. Danson, James C. Gifford and Carol A. Gifford, Elaine Bluhm Herold, Sharon F. Urban, and Pat Wheat. For their labors I am deeply grateful. I am also indebted to many who kept correspondence, announcements, programs, and photographs and filed them where they could be retrieved, particularly in the Pecos Conference Archives of the Laboratory of Anthropology (Santa Fe), the Department of Anthropology and the Arizona State Museum Archives at the University of Arizona (Tucson), and the Library of the Museum of Northern Arizona (Flagstaff). The planners and hosts of future Conferences are urged to deposit records of all kinds in the Pecos Conference Archives. There were many informative responses to my 1978 questionnaire and also to Robert Euler's 1969 letter, the replies to which he made available to me.

In 1988 the organizing committee of the Pecos Conference held at Dolores, Colorado, that year generously contributed a substantial sum from the proceeds of the Conference, to help with photocopying and other incidental costs involved in the preparation of this history. Their thoughtfulness is greatly appreciated. The staff of the University of New Mexico Press has been extremely helpful throughout the editing and production of this book and I am extremely grateful to them.

Twice, and unfortunately only twice, the entire Conference was recorded on tape, the skilled work of John L. Champe; later the tapes were generously given to the Pecos Conference Archives by Flavia Champe. The aging and fragile tapes were expertly transferred to cassettes in 1987 by Jaap van Heerden. They were transcribed with the help of Sue Ruiz. These tapes make the records for the 1959 and 1960 Conferences unique.

Many to whom I am indebted for their published reports on the Pecos Conferences will not be listed here, as their names appear in the references, along with the indefatigable Anonymous. Other friends and colleagues who have generously supplied valued information, recollections, and comments include the following: Leland J. Abel, John Adair, William Y. Adams, Barbara Kidder Aldana, Richard J. Ambler, E. Wyllys Andrews V, Jeanne Armstrong, Galen R. Baker, Bryant Bannister, Homer G. Barnett, Hans Bart, Harry W. Basehart, Ronald J. Beckwith, Robert E. Bell, John V. Bezy, Richard A. Bice, Vorsila L. Bohrer, Donald D. Brand, Beatriz Braniff, David A. Breternitz, J. O. Brew, Richard H. Brooks, Jeton Brown, Carol Burke, Joseph B. Casagrande, Robert G. Chenhall, Henry B. Collins, Susan M. Collins, J. Ferrell Colton, Linda S. Cordell, Edward B. Danson, Al Dart, E. Mott Davis, Hester A. Davis, William E. Davis, Jeffrey S. Dean, Frederica de Laguna, Charles C. Di Peso, Alfred E. Dittert, Keith A. Dixon, David E. Doyel, Bertha P. Dutton, Fred Eggan, Florence Hawley Ellis, Nigel Elmore, Robert C. Euler, Clifford Evans, N. Kenyon Fairy, Jim D. Feagins, Gloria J. Fenner, William N. Fenton, Edwin N. Ferdon, Jr., Bobbie Ferguson, T. J. Ferguson, Richard E. Fike, Don D. Fowler, Theodore R. Frisbie, Faith Kidder Fuller, Rex E. Gerald, Dennis Gilpin, Kathleen Grate, Linda Gregonis, James B. Griffin, George J. Gumerman, Alfred K. Guthe, Jonathan Haas, Hulda E. Haury, Julian D. Hayden, Alden C. Hayes, Mark S. Henderson, James J. Hester, James N. Hill, William Curry Holden, Kathie Hubenschmidt, Bruce Huckell, Calvin H. Jennings, Jesse D. Jennings, Frederick Johnson, A. Trinkle Jones, W. James Judge, Brian Kenny, John L. Kessell, Charles H. Lange, Frederick W. Lange, Steven A. LeBlanc, Mark Leone, Alexander J. Lindsay, Jr., Martin A. Link, June Lipe, William D. Lipe, Robert H. Lister, Karen Lominac, Ron Marshall, F. Joan Mathien, Thomas R. McGuire, David J. Meltzer, Jimmy H. Miller, Daniela Moneta, Elizabeth A. Morris, Larry Nordby, Timothy J. O'Leary, Ernest W. Ortega, Nancy J. Parezo, David A. Phillips, Jr., Lloyd M. Pierson, Peter J. Pilles, Fred Plog, Willow Roberts Powers, Ann Rasor,

Charles L. Redman, Erik K. Reed, James S. Reed, Marion J. Riggs, Carroll L. Riley, John B. Rinaldo, John M. Roberts, William J. Robinson, Arthur H. Rohn, Bobbie Ross, Catherine Ross, Richard Rudasill, Dean Saitta, Curtis F. Schaafsma, Douglas W. Schwartz, Mike Shannon, Patricia Shannon, Harry L. Shapiro, Jack E. Smith, Robert F. G. Spier, James N. Spuhler, Michael B. Stanislawski, Peter L. Steere, Robert L. Stephenson, Omer C. Stewart, Dee Ann Story, Ben K. Swartz, Jr., Clara Lee Tanner, Walter W. Taylor, Helga Teiwes, Chester A. Thomas, David Hurst Thomas, Elisabeth Tooker, Jim Trott, Christy G. Turner II, Herman J. Viola, R. Gwinn Vivian, Patty Jo Watson, Waldo R. Wedel, Fred Wendorf, Joe Ben Wheat, Rex A. Wilson, Thomas C. Windes, Arnold M. Withers, Anne I. Woosley, and H. Marie Wormington.

To any whose names have been accidentally omitted I apologize, and I accept responsibility for errors due to sometimes ignoring comments and criticisms.

PART ONE

CREATION OF THE PECOS CONFERENCE

Southwestern Archaeology in the 1920s

Pecos, N.M. July 3, 1927
My dear Dr. Douglass:—
   Am sitting on a dirt-pile, hence the pencil—I'm sure as a fellow field-man you will make allowances.
   I am most grateful for the preliminary report on the Pecos beam material. It is disappointing that there is no prehistoric material, but the data are of the greatest value to me as establishing highly important points in the history of Pecos. . . .
   With many thanks—Oh! by the way—I had been meaning to write to ask if it would be possible for you to be at Pecos Aug 29–Sept 2 when we are having a conference of Southwestern field-workers—almost all . . . will be here, and it would be the greatest pleasure to have you.

Most sincerely,
A. V. Kidder

   With some two dozen letters to colleagues, several containing similar offhand invitations, Kidder gathered together at the pueblo ruin of Pecos, New Mexico, an archaeological force that changed the course of Southwestern archaeology. The Conference endorsed what came to be called the Pecos Classification and began a tradition of late summer field conferences that, with some gaps in the early years, has continued to the present day—a potent stimulus in communicating and evaluating new information and ideas concerning archaeology in the American Southwest. The history of these Conferences, as it unfolds in these pages, reflects the growth of a discipline rich with dynamic and colorful characters, with serious confrontations about the methods of interpreting the prehistoric record, with intriguing discoveries in often rough but magnificent terrain, and with great advances decade by decade in understanding the lives of the ancient Native Americans of the Southwest.

By 1927 A. V. Kidder, then forty-two years old, was recognized by many as the leader of Southwestern archaeological research, although his ideas had not yet been adopted by some of his elders. He had first visited the Southwest as a green easterner, still an undergraduate at Harvard, in the summer of 1907. His visit was the result of a lucky accident and a growing dislike for the courses, especially chemistry, that were required in preparation for medical school, then his choice of a career. The accident was seeing an announcement "that three men who had specialized in anthropology [he had had only one course at this time] might be accepted as volunteers on an expedition to the cliff-dwelling country under the auspices of the Archaeological Institute of America" (Kidder 1960).

He and two others were accepted and joined Edgar Lee Hewett, director of the School of American Archaeology (later School of American Research), at Bluff City, Utah. Hewett gave them sketchy instructions for making "an archaeological survey" and left them on their own for the next six weeks. Later in the summer they went with Hewett to map cliff ruins at Mesa Verde, Colorado, and then to excavate for a few weeks at Puye, a ruin on the Pajarito Plateau of New Mexico. This impressive introduction to Southwestern archaeology determined the direction of Kidder's life.

After graduating from Harvard the next year he returned to the Southwest. He began graduate work in 1909, continued summer archaeological research, and in 1914 received his Ph.D. from Harvard with a dissertation on Southwestern ceramics. He had been rapidly developing his talents for the systematic collection and recording of information—in contrast to the somewhat random and often poorly recorded work of his mentors—and for following description with analysis and synthesis.

In 1915 the Department of Archaeology at Phillips Academy in Andover, Massachusetts, selected Kidder to direct a large, long-term program of excavation in the Southwest. He promptly chose the large ruined pueblo of Pecos (see Bandelier 1881) at the eastern margin of the region of prehistoric settled villages in New Mexico and directed excavations there for ten seasons. Midway, he prepared a summary of all that was then known of Southwestern archaeology, the first regional synthesis for any part of the New World. It was published in 1924 as *An Introduction to the Study of Southwestern Archaeology,* a landmark in the discipline. As Gordon R. Willey has written, "It is a rarity in that it introduces systematics to a field previously unsystematized, and, at the same time, it is vitally alive and unpedantic. It might well be said that Kidder put the classification of potsherds into Southwestern archaeology without removing or obscuring the people who made the pottery" (Willey 1967: 299).

ARCHAEOLOGICAL ACTIVITIES IN THE 1920S   At the time of the first Pecos Conference there was an amount of archaeological activity in the Southwest that would have seemed impossible only a few decades before. Serious investigations had started more than a half century before, but careful, systematic excavation and orderly recordkeeping had only recently begun to replace the casual methods that emphasized digging for specimens, with little or no record of provenience or associations.

Only a decade had passed since Nels C. Nelson of the American Museum of Natural History had introduced to the Southwest the systematic application of the long-established geological concept of stratigraphy. With this technique it was possible to define with precision a local sequence of styles of pottery decoration and thus achieve a basis for determining chronological changes. Kidder had quickly adopted Nelson's technique and at Pecos had been applying it brilliantly to elucidate the long history of the pueblo.

Archaeological research was expanding beyond the Four Corners area where Arizona, Colorado, New Mexico, and Utah meet and where impressive remains of cliff dwellings and open masonry sites had first attracted the attention of nineteenth-century explorers, soldiers, ranchers, and eventually archaeologists. But the cultural manifestations in other parts of the Southwest that would later be known as Hohokam, Mogollon, Hakataya, and Sinagua were as yet little known or altogether unrecognized. The conspicuous, attractive, and numerous remains of the Four Corners area—mostly within the San Juan drainage—continued to hold the attention of most archaeologists as well as of the reading public.

Information on some two dozen separate archaeological efforts during 1927 is available from the reports on field work in North America that appeared in *American Anthropologist* annually for some years, from

Teocentli (an informal archaeological newsletter), and from other publications. Most of this 1927 research was probably reported and discussed at the Conference held at Kidder's field camp, a pattern that has continued through all subsequent Pecos Conferences. A summary here of work in progress in 1927 provides a perspective on the state of Southwestern archaeological research at the time, with its gradually increasing quality and geographic diversity.

In Nevada, M. R. Harrington had terminated his work the previous year at Pueblo Grande de Nevada "with the feeling that we should have spent at least one more season at the site. . . . We had not finished the largest and best preserved house unit—60 out of 100 rooms dug." He had done this work for the Museum of the American Indian-Heye Foundation of New York City, and for that museum he continued in 1927 with "reconnaissance of Pueblo sites in Nevada for several months and then . . . excavating some dry caves on the Pyramid Lake reservation, Washoe County" in the far western part of the state. (This and most of the following information on 1927 work is from Guthe 1928. Some details are from *Teocentli*, nos. 3 and 4, 1927.)

In Utah, A. A. Kerr, who had succeeded Byron Cummings at the University of Utah when Cummings moved to the University of Arizona, continued an "archaeological survey of the territory between Cottonwood Wash and Whiskers Draw" in the San Juan drainage in the southeastern corner of the state. He reported that "no excavations were undertaken" but also said "some one hundred and fifty specimens of pottery . . . were added to the collection." J. O. Brew, in referring to Kerr's work, said many years later that "it can only be described as 'pot-hunting' " (Brew 1946: 23). Kerr, it should be added, did not attend the Pecos Conference, and it seems unlikely that he was invited.

Not far to the east, in southern Colorado, Earl Morris's major summer work was in September and October, excavating a large Basketmaker III village in the La Plata Valley for the University of Colorado Museum. In July and August he first "made a few trial excavations of the ruins adjoining the Aztec Ruin National Monument" (where he had been custodian since 1923 and where he had started digging in 1916). Then, with Harry L. Shapiro of the American Museum of Natural History, he excavated burials at Mitten Rock and Tocito, in the Chuska Mountains of extreme northwestern New Mexico, another part of the San Juan drainage. Clark Wissler, head of anthropology at the American Museum, reported that this work "gave a good return of skeletons and pottery." Morris ended field work that year by returning to Canyon de Chelly and Canyon del Muerto in October and November to collect sections of roof beams for Douglass to use in developing his tree-ring sequence.

One of the most important excavation programs ever undertaken in New Mexico had been largely completed the previous summer: Neil Judd's work at Pueblo Bonito, the enormous "apartment house" in Chaco Canyon. He started in 1921, under the joint sponsorship of the Smithsonian Institution (he was on the U. S. National Museum staff) and the National Geographic Society. But in 1927 Judd came back to Chaco for one more summer, to begin preparing reports on the work, reports that he hoped would be "completed within the year." In fact, it was not until 1964 that the third and last of his monumental reports on his Chaco work was published. However, he did have the satisfaction in the spring of 1927 of seeing in print at last his "Archeological Observations North of the Rio Colorado" (Judd 1926), reporting his field work of 1915 through 1920. In writing of his return to Chaco Canyon in 1927, Judd said that he further studied the stairways and "so-called 'roads'" leading out of Chaco Canyon, which he believed had been built to aid in the task of transporting the many huge logs needed for roofing rooms and kivas at Pueblo Bonito and other large towns of the canyon. (Today the roads are thought by most archaeologists to have been built for a more complex purpose: to serve in Chaco Canyon's wider economic activities, exchange networks extending for many hundreds of miles, and probably also for ceremonial or ritual purposes.)

That summer the major work in Chaco Canyon was the excavation by Frank H.H. Roberts in June and July of Shabik'eschee, a large Basketmaker III village on the mesa top south of Chaco Canyon, discovered by him the previous summer when he was still working for Judd on the Chaco program. This was the first "pure" (that is, single phase, short-term occupation) Basketmaker III site excavated (Roberts 1929), and it aided greatly in defining this time period that summer at the first Pecos Conference and subsequently.

One important excavation program completed in southern New Mexico in 1927 was the work at the Swarts Ruin by Harriet and Burton Cosgrove, carried out with the encouragement and advice of A. V. Kidder (Cosgrove and Cosgrove 1932). The Mimbres culture, which the Swarts site exemplified, had been curiously neglected even after Walter Hough and Jesse Walter Fewkes of the Smithsonian had published reports on the area in 1907 and 1914. It was only in the 1920s that it finally began to excite interest, particularly because of the finely painted decorations on its pottery—people, insects, and birds, singly and in scenes, sometimes realistic and sometimes modified into decorative patterns. In the summer of 1927 two other Mimbres sites less than ten miles from Swarts were also excavated: Cameron Creek by Wesley Bradfield, who spent six weeks there for the San Diego Museum, and Galaz Ruin, excavated by the Southwest Museum, Los Angeles. In another two years Kidder's advice and encouragement would result in Paul H. Nesbitt excavating yet another Mimbres site, the Mattocks Ruin, a few miles north of Swarts. The Mimbres culture was suddenly receiving long-deserved attention.

Farther southeast in New Mexico and beyond into Texas, research in 1927 was expanding the area that could be called "Southwestern." The Cosgroves explored caves near Las Cruces and El Paso, finding well-preserved bags, baskets, and wooden objects, interpreted as belonging to the Basketmaker period. In May, Frank Roberts had investigated cave sites, also near El Paso, for the Bureau of American Ethnology, which he had just joined.

In the Big Bend region of Texas, still farther east, Victor J. Smith of the West Texas Historical and Scientific Society, who was searching for prehistoric sites, added 17 rock shelters, open camp sites, and pictograph sites to the 118 he had already recorded. Also on the periphery of what was then regarded as the Southwest, Monroe Amsden of the Southwest Museum carried out reconnaissance in northeastern Sonora, searching for the western limits of the Casas Grandes cultural sphere.

Charles Amsden also traveled over "the region from the Santa Fe Railroad to the Mexican border" that summer to collect sherds from some one hundred sites "to form the nucleus of our 'sherd library' " at the Southwest Museum. The idea of a "sherd library" to put on record the kinds of pottery characteristic of each site across a large region, and to identify areal differences, had originated in 1910 when Kidder, with Samuel J. Guernsey, began systematic collecting of sherds from northeastern Arizona and the Santa Fe area; soon after this Nelson began a similar project in the Galisteo Basin (Kidder and Shepard 1936: xxiv). Amsden's work with Kidder in northeastern Arizona as a camp helper when he was about fifteen years old perhaps had given him the idea that he was now putting into practice on his own in 1927. The use of sherds as important clues to the ages and relationships of sites was not new, of course. In 1915 Alfred L. Kroeber, carrying on ethnographic research at Zuni, had also collected sherds from nearby ruins and determined their relative ages from the changing proportions of different kinds of decoration (see Kroeber 1916). Leslie Spier immediately expanded on this work with brilliant results (Spier 1917). In the 1970s Keith W. Kintigh reexamined Spier's ceramic collections, preserved in the American Museum of Natural History, and confirmed the accuracy and importance of Spier's interpretations. He then added his own conclusions about population movements in the Zuni area (Kintigh 1985). This is an impressive reminder of how valuable well-documented sherd collections can still be after a half century.

One of the most energetic field workers in the Southwest in the 1920s was Byron Cummings, director of the Arizona State Museum in Tucson and head of the University of Arizona's archaeology department. In 1927 he or his students worked in several parts of Arizona. They dug a site near Bylas on the San Carlos Apache Reservation, investigated Vandal Cave in the Lukachukai Mountains (the actual field work being done by Emil W. Haury and E. J. Hand), and dug a pithouse village in the Tanque Verde Mountains east of Tucson (reported by Haury in 1928 in his master's thesis, University of Arizona).

Work in southern Arizona was also undertaken by Harold S. Gladwin for the Southwest Museum, Los Angeles, at the Casa Grande and Adamsville sites near Coolidge. Omar A. Turney, of the Turney Museum in Phoenix, dug at the site of La Ciudad, then at the edge of the city but now engulfed by it, and continued his search for prehistoric irrigation canals, the work for which he was best known. Finally, also in Arizona but far to the north, Noel Morss, a Harvard undergraduate (and later an attorney and talented amateur archaeologist) carried out reconnaissance of the Moenkopi Wash for the Peabody Museum of Harvard University.

It is interesting to note how much of this research was done by museums, universities, and other research centers outside of the Southwestern states, particularly by institutions on the east and west coasts, in Los Angeles, Washington, New York, and Cambridge. As late as 1953 Walter W. Taylor felt justified in saying:

> From the very beginning, exploitation of the Southwestern field
> was in the hands primarily of eastern institutions and under the
> direction of men who came west to dig. Even after 1930 when
> local organizations became increasingly active, they simply
> continued the trends already inaugurated [Taylor 1954: 565].

This situation was soon to change, although slowly at first, and was in marked contrast to the present time, when vigorous research centers exist in all of the Southwestern states and work by outside institutions is proportionately less important.

In the 1920s Southwestern archaeology was not only expanding its attention beyond the Four Corners area into southern Arizona and New Mexico, Texas, and Nevada, but also enlarging its horizons in other ways. "Two discoveries of the moment stimulated the archaeological community to begin to think in larger stretches of time and other environmental conditions than they were accustomed to studying" (Haury, letter to Woodbury, 18 September 1981). The first discovery was the finding of grinding tools in place below the tusk and partial skull of a mammoth and in association with the bones of horse and bison at Double Adobe in the Sulphur Spring Valley of southeastern Arizona. Cummings, with his students Lyndon L. Hargrave, John C. McGregor, and Emil W. Haury, investigated the find in November 1926 and verified the genuineness of the association. Conventional thinking was seriously strained by finding man-made tools as old as the long-extinct mammoth and horse, especially implements used to process food by grinding. Nevertheless, archaeologists recognized and began to accept the evidence for a very early food-gathering subsistence economy contemporary with a big-game-hunting economy (see Thompson 1983).

The second, and more famous, discovery was near the little town of Folsom, in northeastern New Mexico. In 1926 Jesse D. Figgins and other paleontologists of the Colorado Museum of Natural History (now the Denver Museum of Natural History) were excavating the bones of an extinct species of bison when they found a chipped projectile point embedded in clay surrounding the rib. Realizing the implications of this association, Figgins notified archaeologists that winter but received only skeptical responses. In the summer of 1927 he found another point in situ with the bison bones, stopped all digging, and wired several leading institutions to send representatives to examine the find. From the American Museum of Natural History came the famous paleontologist Barnum Brown, and Frank Roberts and A. V. Kidder came from the Smithsonian Institution and Phillips Academy, Andover. All three agreed on the authenticity of the association, and the long-held conviction that the New World was occupied by humans only quite recently began at last to crumble. In the summer of 1927 many doubters were not yet persuaded, but a new viewpoint was in the wind (see Wormington 1957).

Another new horizon in Southwestern archaeology was opening up in the 1920s—the possibility of precise dating of prehistoric sites from the tree rings in beams and charcoal. A. E. Douglass, the astronomer, had become interested in the relationships of the sun, climate, and plant growth in 1894 when he joined the staff of Lowell Observatory in Flagstaff. In 1911 he found that tree rings in the Flagstaff and Prescott areas, fifty miles apart, were nearly identical in pattern. In 1918 he received from Earl Morris beam sections from the Aztec Ruin and Pueblo Bonito whose ring patterns matched each other, proving them to be approximately contemporary, thus linking the two sites chronologically, although an age in calendar years could not be determined. As Judd later wrote (see Guthe 1930: 362–363):

> One of our early and quite natural desires was to determine, absolutely, the age of Pueblo Bonito. Unexpected inspiration came from a conference on cyclic phenomena, held in December, 1922, at the Carnegie Institution of Washington, at which Dr. A. E. Douglass, Director of the Steward Observatory, University of Arizona, presented certain conclusions from his study of tree rings. What most impressed me at the moment was his statement that cross identification of annual growth rings in timber from Pueblo Bonito and Aztec showed the latter to be twenty years younger than the former. That was my stimulus. If the relative ages of these two prehistoric ruins could be determined from a few ceiling beams, then their actual ages should be ascertainable, provided an unbroken, year-to-year sequence could be established extending from living trees back, and connecting with, the annual growth rings in ceiling timbers from either ruin. It meant wood samples from a succession of Pueblo villages, each slightly older than the other, until Pueblo Bonito itself was reached. Assured of Dr. Douglass's cooperation, the Research Committee of the National Geographic Society in 1923 sent into the field a beam-collecting expedition.

When the American Museum of Natural History withdrew its support of Douglass's work, the National Geographic Society connection arranged by Judd became the basis for acquiring the gradually expanding sequence of matching ring series from the present back to prehistoric times. By 1927 records from some thirty ruins had contributed to a master sequence of tree-ring patterns extending back to about A.D. 1400, with a separate, earlier, "floating" sequence that could not yet be connected to it. However, the promise of dating sites by the tree-ring method had now been demonstrated, and in 1929 the sequence would be joined, to reach back unbroken to A.D. 700.

NEW SOUTHWESTERN RESEARCH CENTERS   With increased archaeological data, new techniques, lengthening time perspectives, "the intellectual ferment and high activity of that time set the stage" (Haury, letter to Woodbury, 18 September 1981) for a significant expansion of archaeological research centers at the end of the 1920s and the beginning of the 1930s.

On 1 August 1927 a meeting of citizens was held in Flagstaff to consider founding a local museum. Harold S. Colton was on the planning committee, not surprisingly, as he and Mrs. Colton had long been coming to Flagstaff from the University of Pennsylvania (where he was on the zoology faculty) to spend their summers vacationing and, since 1915, in archaeological survey and excavation. In 1928 the Northern Arizona Society of Science and Art was founded, having as one of its principal aims the creation of a local museum. Dr. Colton was elected president of the board of trustees, and soon after the nucleus of the future Museum of Northern Arizona was established.

Also in 1928 Gila Pueblo, in Globe, Arizona, came into existence, the result of Harold S. Gladwin's passionate interest in archaeology. That interest began in 1924 when A. V. Kidder showed him that what looked like "a prairiedog's burrow" was actually an archaeological site. As he wrote, "Sure enough, the mound was covered with sherds, and by the time we had a collection, my future course was set" (dust jacket of Gladwin's *History of the Ancient Southwest,* 1957). Gila Pueblo was a combination of residence, research laboratory, year-round seminar with a stream of archaeological visitors, and storehouse of sherds and survey records that Gladwin and his wife were accumulating. They created Gila Pueblo by excavating and rebuilding a pueblo ruin that they had purchased for the purpose.

Closer to Kidder's work at Pecos and directly involving him in its creation was the ambitious and unique Laboratory of Anthropology at Santa Fe—intended to promote "anthropological research, public education, the welfare of the native races of the Southwest, and publication." Tradition has it that when the John D. Rockefeller, Jr., family visited Mesa Verde in 1924 and Rockefeller described his ideas for a research center to Jesse L. Nusbaum, then director of the park, Nusbaum suggested Santa Fe as the best possible location, but when Rockefeller visited Hewett in Santa Fe no plans or action eventuated.

Then in 1926, tradition continues, the Rockefellers were conducted on a tour of the Indian pueblos by Kenneth Chapman, who described the Indian Arts Fund, which was buying and preserving the best contemporary Pueblo art. Chapman was asked to draw up a statement of the goals of the museum for the fund's collections and for research with them. The next year Hewett and Herman C. Bumpus of the American Association of Museums, who was also a trustee of Brown University and former director of the American Museum of Natural History, "arrived at a general understanding about future work in the Santa Fe area, including the proposed Archeological Laboratory and Museum" (Stocking 1982).

Soon after this a group of archaeologists from eastern institutions, "some with a long history of professional antagonism to Hewett" (Stocking 1982), began plans to take the direction of the proposed laboratory and museum away from Hewett. They met at the Yale Club in New York on 1 June 1927 to plot the end run that would accomplish this. By incorporating in New Mexico they provided a ready-made vehicle for Rockefeller support. Not surprisingly, Jesse L. Nusbaum, Kidder's long-time friend and a key figure in steering Rockefeller support to Santa Fe, would be appointed the laboratory's first director, causing him to give up his position at Mesa Verde National Park. In the 1930s Kidder's friend Kenneth Chapman became the second director, and the second chairman of the board of trustees was another friend, Carl A. Guthe.

Kidder's concern for the projected new institution in Santa Fe was undoubtedly mainly due to his hope, as leader of the "new archaeology" of that time, that up-to-date anthropological research would be carried out there, rather than the outmoded research approach that Hewett exemplified. Hewett, by far the senior, was not "a rival" but rather "the problem."

Yet another important research center was established a few years later, but part of the same pattern of easterners creating the means within the Southwestern states for expanded archaeological (and other) research. This was the Amerind Foundation, located at Dragoon in the southeastern corner of Arizona. It grew out of the interests of William Shirley Fulton, president of a Connecticut brass foundry, and his wife Rose Hayden Fulton, interests that developed out of their visits to Arizona and New Mexico from 1919 onward. The collections of Indian materials, both prehistoric and recent, that they brought back were eventually housed in their ranch home in Texas Canyon, near Dragoon, following Fulton's retirement in 1931.

By 1934 the Fultons were excavating a pit-house village near the ranch, under the aegis of their old friend, George G. Heye, of the Museum of the American Indian, in New York. Adding a three-room museum to their home in 1936, the Fultons were launched on the creation of a research center, which they incorporated the following year. That same year the first full-time trained archaeological staff member was added: Carr Tuthill, a University of Arizona student recommended by Emil Haury.

These new institutions, although developing from the interests of "outsiders," provided a local basis for research that greatly strengthened archaeological work in the decade that followed the first Pecos Conference. They reflect the rapid changes that made the Pecos Conferences' review of past work and blueprint for future research so timely and uniquely appropriate. Their importance to the Southwest is emphasized in a comment by Harold S. Gladwin (1936: 256): "Each one of these institutions began a type of investigation which had not theretofore been emphasized, archaeological surveys in which as many sites as possible were visited, surface indications were described, and collections made of sherds and flints, without excavation."

THE ORIGINS AND PLANNING OF THE FIRST CONFERENCE   The idea of the Pecos Conference—a meeting held at the field camp of a major archaeological program by serious researchers in archaeology but welcoming those from allied fields and conducted in an informal manner over a two- or three-day period—has generally been credited to Kidder, in the absence of specific statements to the contrary. But in Kidder's invitation to Morris in March 1927 he mentioned a preliminary discussion in Neil Judd's office at the U. S. National Museum in the autumn of 1926. Kidder and Judd were close friends, and in view of the fact that Judd had held a series of what he called "symposia" at his Chaco Canyon field headquarters, it may have been his suggestion to continue the meetings, in at least modified form, at Pecos (the work in Chaco having come to an end). If so, Kidder proved receptive to the idea. Judd has written of his Chaco Canyon meetings in *Men Met Along the Trail*:

> Once firmly settled at Pueblo Bonito in 1921, we began the annual practice of inviting certain co-workers in other disciplines to spend two or three days in camp with us in consultation on matters of mutual interest. . . . Our idea seemed such a good one that it was repeated in 1923 and 1925. But we found that the

distance from the railroad and the limitations of our facilities were too great. Then, in 1927, Kidder inaugurated his famous Pecos Conference, and we were content to end ours [Judd 1968: 129–130].

There is an obvious difference between the Pueblo Bonito symposia and the Pecos Conference of 1927: Judd invited specialists in several nonarchaeological fields whose knowledge would help him and his archaeological staff understand the past of Chaco Canyon, whereas Kidder included mostly archaeologists active in the Southwest, to discuss a broad range of problems extending far beyond his work at Pecos. The relation of the earlier meetings to the later cannot be defined with complete certainty, but there is at least some continuity of ideas and of individual participants.

Details of the planning of the first Pecos Conference are sketchy. When Kidder was interviewed on tape a few years before his death by Gordon R. Willey, J. O. Brew, and Fay-Cooper Cole, Willey asked him, "Whose idea was the Pecos Conference? Was it yours?" Kidder replied, "Yes, it was. But I can't remember how it happened to be hatched." Brew asked him, "Did you invite a certain number of people to come at a given time?" Kidder responded, "Yes, I wrote around some months in advance. I don't remember how I made up the list." One example of this "writing around" is in a letter to Clark Wissler (Wissler papers, Ball State University, Muncie, Indiana; letter supplied by courtesy of James Reed with letter to Woodbury of 25 May 1982):

> January 28, 1927
> I have been talking over Southwestern matters this autumn and winter with Morris and Judd and Roberts, and we all feel strongly that our work would be advanced if all Southwesternists could arrive at an understanding in regard to the underlying problems, the methods of accumulating and presenting data, and (last, but in some ways most important) a standardized nomenclature for artifacts, decorative motifs, and periods of culture. We have considered the possibility of attempting to hold a field conference during the coming summer, and I believe we could get together either at Pueblo Bonito or at Pecos the majority of active workers in this field.
>
> I am writing you, who have so much experience with conferences of one sort and another, for your opinion as to whether the

project is worth the time entailed; also as to whether you think that Bonito or Pecos would be the better place. I may add that I am not contemplating attempting to raise any money from any source for the meeting. Do you think there is any possibility of your being able to come? If [Harry L.] Shapiro would be in the Southwest, I would hope that he might be able to help us out with Physical Anthropology.

Although Emil W. Haury recalls that Dean Cummings received an invitation (Haury was Cummings's student at the time), only four other personal invitations have come to light. One is to Frederick Webb Hodge of the Southwest Museum, Los Angeles. Another is to A. E. Douglass, quoted at the beginning of the chapter. The third is to Earl H. Morris, who at that time was on the staff of S. G. Morley of the Carnegie Institution of Washington, working on a multiyear project of excavation and restoration at Chichen Itza in Yucatan. However, he spent his summers back in the Southwest where his archaeological career had begun and would end. On 31 March 1927 Kidder wrote to Morris:

> This is a little premature, but I want to get a bid for your time in as early as possible. Roberts and Judd and I are planning to have a get-together of as many field workers in Southwestern archaeology as possible at Pecos for two or three days, beginning August 29th, to thrash out at leisure the various questions of problems, method, and nomenclature which we discussed in a preliminary way in Judd's office this autumn [1926, that is]. I hope very much that you can arrange your affairs in such a way as to be there, as the whole project could hardly be a success in your absence [Lister and Lister 1968: 85].

The fourth surviving invitation was by postcard to Odd Halseth, dated 4 August:

> We are trying to have an informal conference on Southwestern subjects here on Aug 29–31 inclusive. Judd, Morris, Amsden, Kroeber, Chap[man], Roberts, Hodge, Nusbaum, etc will attend. I hope you can manage to come. If you can will you bring a bedroll & if possible a tent. Awfully sorry to have missed you at Puyé Tuesday. Drop me a line on the attached card. Hastily A. V. K.

By this time Pecos obviously had been chosen over Chaco Canyon, probably with Judd's agreement in view of the problems of housing and feeding a sizable group for even a few days. Kidder also announced in the June issue of *Teocentli* that "there is being planned for August 29–September 1 a conference at Pecos on the general problems of Southwestern Archaeology and all Teocentlis are most cordially invited." Kidder presumably wrote a couple of dozen personal letters, perhaps more, to individuals whom he was particularly desirous of having present. Most of those asked probably came, although a few absences are noted in chapter 2. By any standards many of those attending would be considered the leaders of Southwestern research at that time, and Kidder's own leadership virtually assured important results.

2

THE FIRST PECOS ROSTER

It is now time to consider who came to the first Pecos Conference, why they were there, and what interests had brought them there. In his report that fall in *Science,* Kidder (1927) included a list of those present. However, neither it nor the same list, repeated the next year in a shorter report in *American Anthropologist* (Kidder 1928), is really complete. An even less complete list was published by the Listers in their biography of Earl Morris. Here I have supplemented Kidder's list by using the identifications that accompany photographs of the 1927 participants taken by Burton Cosgrove, T. T. Waterman, and Emil Haury (files of the Arizona State Museum, the Southwest Museum, and the Laboratory of Anthropology). In Waterman's picture thirty-four people are present, in Cosgrove's only thirty-one. In Haury's, taken from closer range, half a dozen people at the ends of the line are cut off but many of those shown are clearer. With a mimeographed list of identifications for Cosgrove's photograph there is also a list titled "not in the picture," containing sixteen names, including one repetition. This adds up to forty-six individuals, but there were yet others present at Pecos, younger family members not rounded up for the group photographs, and wives of whom we have no record of attendance.

In the discussion of participants that follows I have arbitrarily divided the roster into (1) "hard-core" members of the Conference, professionals or serious amateurs actively engaged in Southwestern archaeology, a group that had five husband-wife teams (virtually the only way a woman could engage in field archaeology in the 1920s); (2) members of the Carnegie Institution of Washington's Maya program, good friends of the Kidders as well as colleagues in Kidder's

Table 2.1. Participants in the 1927 Pecos Conference

Active Southwesternists

Charles Amsden	Odd S. Halseth	Ann Axtell Morris
Kenneth M. Chapman	Mark R. Harrington	Earl H. Morris
Harold S. Colton	Edgar L. Hewett	Jesse L. Nusbaum
Mary-Russell Ferrell	Walter Hough	Frank Pinkley
Colton	Neil M. Judd	Etienne B. Renaud
C. Burton Cosgrove	Alfred V. Kidder	Frank H. H. Roberts, Jr.
Harriet S. Cosgrove	Madeleine Kidder	Linda B. Roberts
Byron Cummings	Harry P. Mera	
Andrew E. Douglass		

The Carnegie Group

Frances R. Morley	Edith Bayles Ricketson	Oliver G. Ricketson, Jr.
Sylvanus G. Morley		

From Other Specialities or Interests

Lansing B. Bloom	Thomas F. McIlwraith	Herbert J. Spinden
Erna Gunther (Spier)	James A. B. Scherer	Joseph B. Thoburn
Percy Jackson	Henry D. Skinner	Thomas T. Waterman
Alfred L. Kroeber	Leslie Spier	

Students and Beginners

Monroe Amsden	Emil W. Haury	Harry L. Shapiro
Clara Lee Fraps (Tanner)	Hulda Penner (Haury)	Robert Wauchope
Charlotte D. Gower	Paul S. Martin	

new Maya activities; (3) those interested in one or another area of archaeology or anthropology, but not Southwesternists; and (4) students and beginners (Table 2.1). And finally, three of the couples brought children. This pattern that marked the first Conference attendance has continued to the present.

Most of the biographical information that follows comes from obituaries (particularly in *El Palacio, American Antiquity,* and *American Anthropologist*), a few newspaper clippings, several festschriften, and the forewords or introductions to monographs and books, none of which is specifically referenced here. A few other biographical sources are identified where cited.

It is worthwhile to say a few words about each of the participants in order to provide a better basis for understanding their interests and the contributions they may have made to the Conference, and also to demonstrate the rather close network of friendship and collaboration that characterized Southwestern archaeology then—and still does, to a lesser degree, today.

THE CORE SOUTHWESTERN GROUP   *Charles Avery Amsden* (Fig. 2.1) entered Harvard after graduating from the high school in his hometown, Farmington, New Mexico. After receiving his A.B. in 1922 he joined the U.S. Diplomatic Service. In 1912 Kidder had met Charley Amsden's father, a Farmington banker, who cashed his traveler's checks and then showed him his collection of prehistoric pottery. Two years later, Charley, then fifteen, became a camp helper on Kidder's expedition to northeastern Arizona for the Peabody Museum, Harvard University. Later, after his health broke down while he was serving as consul in Agua Prieta, Sonora, Amsden joined Kidder again, this time at Pecos, working particularly on the classification of pottery (Amsden 1931). He joined the Southwest Museum in Los Angeles in 1927 as curator and became its secretary and treasurer the next year. In the 1930s he was on the staff of the Peabody Museum's Awatovi Expedition to the Hopi country. His major archaeological publication *Prehistoric Southwesterners from Basketmaker to Pueblo* (Amsden 1949), appeared eight years after his death, with an affectionate introduction by Kidder. Amsden's most highly acclaimed publication, however, was *Navaho Weaving* (1934), a scholarly study that quickly became a standard reference work and was reprinted in 1949.

Kenneth Milton Chapman (Fig. 2.2) came to Las Vegas, New Mexico, in 1899 as a "health seeker" after working in St. Louis, Chicago, and Milwaukee as a commercial artist, illustrator, and engraver. Although without a college degree, he was soon hired as an art instructor at Las Vegas Normal School by Edgar L. Hewett, its president. In 1909, when the Museum of New Mexico, Santa Fe, was founded, Chapman joined its staff as executive secretary, with duties that included putting in exhibits, lecturing, and doing archaeological research. He taught in the early field schools of the School of American Research, Santa Fe, which Hewett directed, and increasingly found his major interest in the study of Southwestern pottery, modern as well as prehistoric. In 1926 Mr. and Mrs. John D. Rockefeller, Jr., were so impressed with the Pueblo pottery already purchased by the new Indian Arts Fund

2.1 Charles A. Amsden, 1929. Southwest Museum negative no. N16201, photo by Fred K. Hinchman.

that they provided the means for Chapman to travel throughout the Southwest and add to its collections. Their interest eventually led to the creation of the Laboratory of Anthropology, as has already been described.

It was Chapman with whom Kidder first visited the ruins of Pecos Pueblo—a site that so impressed Kidder that in 1915 he chose it for his long-term excavation program. It is safe to say that "Chap" could hardly have been kept away from the 1927 Conference, as he was keenly interested in what Kidder was doing and was one of the large circle of colleagues with whom the Kidders enjoyed especially close bonds of friendship. Chapman's interest was mainly in recent Indian pottery, rather than archaeology, but it is interesting to see how similar the discussion and analysis of pottery design are in his *Pottery of Santo Domingo Pueblo* (1936) and in his study of the black-on-white wares of Pecos (Chapman 1931). After Chapman's death in 1968 his *Pottery of San Ildefonso Pueblo* was published (1970), and John Gaw Meem points out in his introduction that it was Chapman who "influenced Julian Martinez . . . and his wife Maria . . . to use native designs and their traditional black polished ware technique in making their pottery, thereby sparking a revival of excellence in . . . Indian pottery."

Harold Sellers Colton (Fig. 2.3) was accompanied at the first Pecos Conference by his wife, *Mary-Russell Ferrell Colton* (Fig. 2.4), and their son *J. Ferrell Colton,* then thirteen years of age. The Coltons had begun spending their summers in and around Flagstaff in 1913, and in 1916 they became interested in the archaeology of the area. This interest led to increasingly systematic surveys and eventually to excavation and publication. Harold Colton was a professor of zoology at the University of Pennsylvania until he retired in 1926, to move permanently to Flagstaff with his family. Mary-Russell Colton, a talented artist, was interested in both her own painting and that of others, and also in the arts and crafts of the Hopi Indians, whose pueblos are within easy visiting distance of Flagstaff. Less than a month before the 1927 Pecos Conference, Flagstaff citizens had begun planning for the museum that was founded a year later, under the Northern Arizona Society of Science and Art, which reflected in its name the Coltons' dual interests. From 1928 onward the Coltons' careers were devoted to the museum and to research in northern Arizona.

As of 1927 Harold Colton had had little opportunity to meet other Southwesternists, although he knew some of them through his par-

2.2 Kenneth M. Chapman, 1929. Courtesy Museum of New Mexico, negative no. 28131.

ticipation in meetings of the American Anthropological Association. Colton has recorded in his unpublished autobiography that he learned of the conference Kidder was planning, and although not personally invited drove from Flagstaff to Pecos in his 1922 Buick with his wife and her artist friend Isabelle Bronson Cartwright of Philadelphia. They camped across the wash from Kidder's excavations, and Colton attended the daily sessions. These were of great importance to Colton, as it was a chance to meet nearly all the important Southwestern archaeologists and learn of their research (Miller 1991: 84). With his background as a zoological systematist, Harold Colton played a considerable role in the development of nomenclature for Southwestern pottery, a binomial system inspired by the Linnaean system. Such a system was discussed at Pecos in 1927 and later generally agreed on and made use of.

Harriet Silliman Cosgrove (Fig. 2.5) and *Cornelius Burton Cosgrove* (Hattie and Burt to their host of friends) developed an interest in archaeology soon after they moved from Kansas to Silver City, New Mexico, in 1909 and started a highly successful hardware business. Concerned over the extensive looting of Mimbres sites in the surrounding area for the pottery that was in demand by art museums and private collectors, they realized that although it could not be stopped by any means at their disposal, it could perhaps be partly counteracted by protecting at least one site. In 1919 they purchased such a site and in 1920 spent their summer vacation visiting Frederick Hodge at Hawikuh and Neil Judd at Pueblo Bonito to learn about archaeological techniques. Their abilities were quickly recognized. In 1922 they carried out an archaeological survey of the Mimbres region at the request of Chapman, Wesley Bradfield, and Lansing B. Bloom of the New Mexico State Museum, which led later to Bradfield's excavations at the Cameron Creek site. With encouragement and advice from Kidder they began serious excavation at their Swarts Ruin in 1924 and completed the work in 1927. During this period they became members of the research staff of the Peabody Museum. In 1925 they sold their hardware business and moved to Cambridge, to work on the materials they had excavated and to write a report. Their rise from amateur to professional status was rapid but not unique at a time when formal training was scarce, paid professional positions few, and archaeology widely regarded as a better avocation than vocation.

Byron Cummings (Fig. 2.6), called "the Dean," received an A.M. degree from Rutgers in 1892 but had already begun his professional career teaching at the Syracuse, New York, High School in 1887–88.

2.3 Harold S. Colton, probably in Tucson in 1967. Arizona State Museum negative no. 15271, photo by Helga Teiwes.

2.4 Mary-Russell Ferrell Colton, self-portrait. Museum of Northern Arizona negative no. 82.0106.

2.5 Harriet S. Cosgrove, Pecos Conference, Flagstaff, 1953. Museum of Northern Arizona negative no. 74.1318, photo by A. O. Brodie.

In 1893 he became instructor in Greek and Latin at the University of Utah, and two years later he was a full professor and department head. By 1906 he was dean of arts and science but resigned that position in 1915 in protest over the university's administrative policies. Immediately he was invited to the University of Arizona, Tucson, as head of its new department of archaeology and director of the Arizona State Museum. Soon after this he also became dean of men and dean of the College of Letters, and in 1921 and 1927–28 he was acting president.

Cummings's interest in archaeology had begun in 1906 as a result of a holiday trip through Nine Mile Canyon in central Utah. Nearly every year after this until his retirement in 1938 he carried out field explorations in one part or another of the Southwest, but particularly in Arizona. He was an extremely popular teacher and regularly took students with him on his summer expeditions. "Even at 70 few student helpers could wield a shovel as long and as efficiently as he, and none could equal him on a cross-country hike" (Judd 1954a). But he was an explorer and a teacher more than a systematic researcher or writer; others wrote up much more of his field work than he did. Nonetheless, in 1927 he was one of the leading figures in Southwestern archaeology, both loved and respected, and it was appropriate that he brought with him to Pecos two of his students from the university, one of whom was to come as close as anyone ever did to taking the places of both Cummings and Kidder. It was typical of Cummings's kindness that he invited a young woman from Kansas, who was visiting in Tucson at the time, to occupy the fifth seat in the car.

Andrew Ellicott Douglass (Fig. 2.7), a few years Cummings's junior, was an equally well-known and respected figure in the Southwest. In 1927 he was close to reaching the goal of a tree-ring sequence against which wood and charcoal specimens could be matched to provide absolute dates for many ruins, back through twelve centuries (and eventually much earlier). An astronomer interested in the effects of sunspot cycles on the earth's weather, Douglass had first worked with living trees, the sequoias in California and Ponderosa pines in Arizona. He was asked by Clark Wissler in 1919 whether the contemporaneity of Pueblo Bonito and Aztec Ruin could be determined from beam samples, and when this proved possible, dating soon became a major goal of tree-ring studies. The breakthrough would come in 1929, but at the 1927 Conference "he reported his research on the climate of the southwest and gave the results of his study of tree-rings in their relation to the dating of pueblo and cliff-house ruins. He ap-

2.6 Byron Cummings. Arizona State Museum negative (unnumbered), photo by Tad Nichols.

pealed for the help of all field-workers in the gathering of further materials for this all-important investigation" (Kidder 1927).

Several of those at the Conference had been collecting wood specimens for Douglass for some years; they included Colton, Cummings, Haury, Kidder, Morris, and Oliver Ricketson. "By the end of July, 1927, my 'small beam' sequence at Wupatki had extended into a very considerable, but quite independent, tree-ring record which I assumed to belong somewhere in the large gap between Chaco dating and modern trees" (Douglass 1935). Douglass was on the brink of giving Southwestern archaeologists a new and invaluable technique for dating archaeological sites as well as for reconstructing past climates. There are few more dramatic examples of apparently unrelated fields—in this case astronomy and climatology—aiding archaeological research. A comprehensive biography of Douglass provides a full record of his remarkable career and his contributions to archaeology (Webb 1983).

Odd Sigurd Halseth, like many of his colleagues, came to archaeology more by chance than design. A Norwegian seaman, he left his ship in San Francisco early in World War I and enlisted in the Air Section of the Signal Corps (in 1920 this became the Air Service and in 1926 the Air Corps), where he developed an interest in the uses of aerial photography. No one now seems to know how he came to work for the San Diego Museum of Man early in the 1920s, but this job would have brought him into contact with archaeology, through its founder and director, Edgar Lee Hewett. Soon after this Halseth moved to Santa Fe to work for Hewett, becoming resident curator of Puye Ruins. Hewett was excavating the site for the School of American Archaeology (later the School of American Research) and also building a small museum adjacent, to educate the traveling public. Halseth soon left Puye and moved to Phoenix, where he took charge of the Arizona Museum, which opened in November 1927 with both civic and private support. The next spring and summer he was pleased to have visits by Kidder and Monroe Amsden, by George Vaillant on his way to Mexico, and by Bradfield heading for the Mimbres area for a summer of digging (*Teocentli,* June 1928). By 1930 he was "a recognized authority on prehistoric Arizona irrigation canals" (Judd 1968: 83) and was director of what had become the Phoenix City Museum. He worked closely that year with Judd in the aerial photographic survey of prehistoric canals along the Salt and Gila rivers. Emil Haury has written of Halseth that "anyone who knew him never failed to be stimulated by the ideas that flowed from his versatile mind . . . [and in discussion] he

2.7 Andrew E. Douglass, Forestdale Valley, 1929. Courtesy of Laboratory of Tree-Ring Research, University of Arizona.

often injected ideas that were calculated to stir things up" (*Teocentli,* October 1966). His participation at Pecos in 1927 doubtless lived up to this description.

Mark Raymond Harrington's (Fig. 2.8) archaeological career began in 1899, when he was seventeen years old and still in high school. He was given a job by Frederick W. Putnam at the American Museum of Natural History, New York, and was soon assisting in the excavation of village sites and rock shelters in Westchester County and on Long Island. He started college with a scholarship to the University of Michigan, but then transferred to Columbia University, where his courses in anthropology included one by Adolph Bandelier, whose classic report on the ruins of Pecos had been published in 1881, the year before Harrington was born. With his B.A. and M.A. in hand, Harrington hoped for a job at the American Museum of Natural History, but when none was available he went to work for Covert's Indian Store on Fifth Avenue. His first collecting trip for the store, to the Iroquois, was so successful that he was hired by a wealthy collector, George G. Heye, for whom he made archaeological and ethnological collections for the next twenty years—a substantial contribution to what became the Museum of the American Indian, New York. His research at Pueblo Grande de Nevada, ending in 1926, has already been mentioned. When he came to Pecos in 1927 he was only a year and a half away from ending this phase of his career and joining the Southwest Museum as director of research (later curator), where he continued until his retirement in 1964. His interest in the Southwest is reflected in a short report he wrote in 1927 for *Teocentli:* "I attended the Pecos Archeological Conference, where I learned a lot, after which Jess Nusbaum was kind enough to take Dr. Hough, my son and myself on a spectacular tour, which ended up at Mesa Verde, following which I had the added pleasure of visiting Morris at Aztec, and Judd at Pueblo Bonito."

Edgar Lee Hewett (Fig. 2.9), only five years younger than Cummings, was another major figure in the archaeology of the Southwest, active in 1927 in a wide range of administrative and research responsibilities. Hewett was born on an Illinois farm; later his family moved to Chicago, then to Missouri. He was a student at Tarkio College in Missouri, and became a country school teacher after graduation. Within a few years he became a superintendent of schools, first in Missouri and then in Colorado. Next he was director of the training department at the State Normal School, Greeley, Colorado. In 1898 he became the first president of the Las Vegas Normal University, New Mexico (of

2.8 Mark R. Harrington, at Gypsum Cave, Nevada, 1920. Southwest Museum negative no. N6497.

which Frank Roberts' father was a later president, and which became New Mexico Highlands University). Hewett was early influenced by the writings of Lewis H. Morgan (especially his *Houses and House-Life of the North American Aborigines,* 1881), of Daniel Brinton, and of John Wesley Powell. About 1900 he came to know well the circle of Smithsonian anthropologists that included Powell, Alice G. Fletcher, William H. Holmes, and Jesse W. Fewkes. By 1896 he had already begun his first field work, excavation on the Pajarito Plateau, a few miles west of Santa Fe, and in 1898 he introduced archaeology and anthropology courses at the school in Las Vegas.

Hewett began his graduate work in 1903 at the University of Geneva, Switzerland, receiving his doctoral degree in 1908 for a dissertation, "Les communautés anciennes dans le désert américain," which first defined the main prehistoric cultural areas of the Southwest (Elliott 1987: 16). It is considered to have had an important influence on Kidder's 1924 *Introduction;* an English translation will be published by the Archaeological Society of New Mexico. In 1907 the Archaeological Institute of America, New York, appointed him director of its new School of American Archaeology (now the School of American Research), established in Santa Fe. The year before he had played a significant role in the development and passage of the Antiquities Act, the first national step toward the protection of archaeological sites and materials. In 1917 he founded the San Diego Museum of Man and was its first director, continuing until 1929; he also taught at the State Teachers College, San Diego, even while remaining extremely active in his New Mexico responsibilities.

Although his strong interest and involvement in archaeological field work continued throughout his life, Hewett was more often "an administrator, builder, promoter of civic works, and educator" (Schwartz 1981: 256). For example, in 1926 he inaugurated a museum with visitor facilities at the Puye cliff dwellings and arranged that the Indian Detours of the Santa Fe Railroad—Fred Harvey system regularly stop there. (It was this museum that Odd Halseth helped build and manage.) The same year as the 1927 Pecos Conference he created the department of archaeology and anthropology at the University of New Mexico and became its chairman, while from 1932 onward he also held a chair of archaeology at the University of Southern California. Hewett's archaeological research focused on the northwest Rio Grande, and his first major report in 1906 dealt with the Jemez Plateau, but increasingly his publications were either brief summaries or popular interpretations for a broader audience.

2.9 Edgar Lee Hewett, 1932. Photo by Jack Adams, courtesy Museum of New Mexico, negative no. 7373.

After 1909 Hewett (called "El Toro" behind his back) was more and more occupied with "creating a number of organizations supporting education and research, and providing inspiration to Indian craftsmen, students, scholars, and an expanding public interest in anthropology, a public he helped create" (Schwartz 1981: 256). But in 1927 Hewett had just lost a major struggle: the control of the Laboratory of Anthropology in Santa Fe would not be his, but instead was held by the group that was so strongly represented at the Pecos Conference, the friends and colleagues of A. V. Kidder. It is surprising that he accepted Kidder's invitation to attend the 1927 Pecos Conference, but it was the only one to which he ever came, as far as the records indicate.

Walter Hough (Fig. 2.10) at sixty-eight was the senior statesman of the first Pecos Conference, with his active field work some years behind him. His first archaeological research was in 1896 as an assistant to Fewkes, ten years after he had joined the U.S. National Museum as a copyist, under Otis T. Mason. He became an assistant curator in 1894 and by 1923 had become head curator of anthropology. The following year he served as president of the American Anthropological Association (AAA). Beginning in 1901 he visited the Southwest and made both ethnological and archaeological collections, his most important publications pioneering in the archaeology of what eventually came to be known as the Mogollon (Hough 1907). His ethnological interests included many aspects of technology—pottery making, fire making, and so on—and what today would be called ecology, the interaction of the prehistoric and historic Indians with their environment.

It is interesting to note that while president of the AAA Hough appointed a committee made up of Kidder, Morris, and Judd (chairman) "to inquire into the subject of illegal excavations in ruins on the public domain." Their report (Judd 1924) describes a situation that sounds painfully modern: "an order for one thousand pieces of prehistoric pottery," received by a trading post in New Mexico, which the trader was working to fill. They concluded that no federal effort was being made to enforce the 1906 Antiquities Act, although lengthy correspondence with the secretary of the interior produced some hope of improvement. This committee is another example of the close working relations among many of the participants in the first Pecos Conference.

Neil Merton Judd (Fig. 2.11) began his lifelong interest in archaeology while a freshman at the University of Utah in 1907, when he went with his uncle, Byron Cummings, on an exploring trip in the Four Corners region. That summer he first met A. V. Kidder, then a

2.10 Walter Hough, about 1932. Smithsonian Institution negative no. 31315-E.

Harvard senior on his own first archaeological field trip. The following summer Judd met Kidder again, and also Jesse Nusbaum, when he accompanied Cummings in excavating on Alkali Ridge, in southern Utah, under the overall direction of Hewett and the field supervision of Kidder. Judd, Nusbaum, and Kidder remained close, lifelong friends from those first years onward. In 1910 Judd assisted Hewett on an expedition to the Rito de los Frijoles (now part of Bandelier National Monument).

In June 1911 Judd joined the staff of the U.S. National Museum, where he remained until his retirement in 1949. From "Aide, Division of Ethnology" under William H. Holmes, he advanced to become curator of the Division of Archeology. His early associates at the museum included Cosmos and Victor Mindeleff, who had studied Hopi and Zuni architecture in such detail that their reports are still indispensable. Another Smithsonian associate was W. H. Jackson, whose photographic record of the West began in 1870 with the Hayden Survey, and who in the 1920s revisited Chaco Canyon as the guest of Judd's Pueblo Bonito expedition. Following the excavation and repair of the famous site of Betatakin in northeastern Arizona, Judd began in 1921 the long-term program at Pueblo Bonito that was just closing in 1927 when he came to the Pecos Conference.

Judd had been closely involved with Douglass in the development of tree-ring dating and in the field trips that secured the essential beam samples from which the ring sequence was assembled. Judd was extremely forward looking for the 1920s in his interest in prehistoric environmental problems—an ecologist ahead of his time. At Pueblo Bonito Judd brought together on several occasions a group of natural scientists, nonarchaeologists, to consider problems of prehistoric groundwater, forest cover, farming, climate, and erosional cycles. Like Kidder, he placed great emphasis on the importance of detailed and complete publication of data, as well as interpretations and conclusions. In 1927, with his work in Chaco Canyon just completed, he was one of the most knowledgeable archaeologists in the Southwest, particularly on the ceramics and architecture of the "Great Pueblo" period.

Alfred Vincent Kidder (Fig. 2.12) and *Madeleine Appleton Kidder* (Fig. 2.13) were completing their ninth (and next-to-last) season at Pecos when the Conference visitors came to spend three days at their field camp. Although only forty-two years old, A. V. Kidder had emerged as the leader of the "new" Southwestern archaeology, nationally as well as locally admired for his accomplishments and innovations, recognized for his scientific leadership and administrative abilities,

2.11 Neil M. Judd in Chaco Canyon in the 1920s. Photo (c) National Geographic Society.

and enormously liked as a person. His life and career have been sketched elsewhere (Woodbury 1973); a more detailed study of Kidder has been made by Douglas Givens (1992). It is important to note here that at Pecos Kidder first applied on a large scale and with great success the stratigraphic concepts just introduced to the Southwest by Nels C. Nelson, and that he pioneered in using the systematic classification of pottery as a clue to chronology and regional relationships.

Although he did not teach at a university until after his retirement, Kidder trained many future archaeologists at Pecos. His administrative talents were manifested in his work as vice chairman (1925–26) and chairman (1926–27) of the Division of Anthropology and Psychology of the National Research Council, and his years as secretary (1920–27) of the AAA and concurrently as its treasurer (1922–26). From 1927 to 1935 he was chairman of the board of directors of the Laboratory of Anthropology and later served with Frank Roberts and A. L. Kroeber on the committee that wrote the constitution and bylaws of the Society for American Archaeology, which came into existence in 1934.

Even though by 1927 he was committed professionally to the Maya area, Kidder's interest in Southwestern archaeology and his love of field work in the Southwest were not displaced. His Maya career was the result of his lifelong friendship with S. G. Morley, who had begun a long-term program of Maya research in 1914 under the auspices of the Carnegie Institution of Washington. Kidder visited the work at Chichen Itza, Yucatan, in 1925 as a consultant to the Carnegie, became a research associate in 1926, and in 1927 accepted the position of director of Carnegie's entire archaeological program, with Morley remaining field director in Yucatan. Kidder was soon making plans for an expanded, multipurpose, interdisciplinary program, of which Morley's work would be only one important facet. It is ironic that by the time Kidder made one of his great and enduring contributions to Southwestern archaeology, the First Pecos Conference and its Pecos Classification, he had already ended his formal archaeological work in the Southwest. He was, nevertheless, destined to return many summers for visits to the field camps of friends and colleagues, to discuss their research with them, and to spend many winters completing the reports on Pecos. As he wrote so poignantly in his final volume on Pecos,

> In 1924 I thought I knew a good deal about the Southwest in general, and Pecos, in particular. The pages . . . of the present

2.12 A. V. Kidder at Awatovi about 1939. Arizona State Museum negative no. 7892, photo by Phillip Hobler.

2.13 Madeleine A. Kidder. Arizona State Museum negative no. 27873, photo by Helga Teiwes.

belated contribution show how very wrong I was. But, I flatter myself, I was not nearly as wrong as he who advised me, just 50 years ago, to take up work in another field because, he said: "The Southwest is a sucked orange." I only wish I could return to that wonderful country and wet my lips once again in the rich juice of a fruit which a half-century of research has little more than begun to tap [Kidder 1958: 322].

Kidder once confided that it was Fewkes who advised him that the Southwest was "a sucked orange" (R. H. Thompson, letter to Woodbury, 5 September 1989).

During the summer of 1927 at Pecos, as in previous summers, Madeleine Kidder played an important role, supervising the field camp and its activities, and also washing and sorting the potsherds that poured from the excavations by the thousands. Later A. V. (Ted) Kidder wrote, "I doubt if any other human being has handled so much broken pottery" (Kidder 1931: 15). In addition, with the assistance of a Scotch nurse who came with the family from Cambridge each summer, she looked after the Kidder children. During the 1927 Pecos Conference the two oldest, Alfred (then sixteen) and Randolph (fifteen) came back from the ranch where they had been enjoying life as junior cowboys and worked washing dishes and chopping firewood. The younger three, Faith, Barbara, and Jimmy, were sent off during the Conference with the nurse to the Cowles's hunting and fishing camp in what is now the Pecos Wilderness Area (Aldana 1983). As Faith Kidder Fuller once remarked, this was essential because she, even if not the others, had "been making a nuisance of myself," climbing trees around the camp to watch the grownups and engaging in childish pranks. The Pecos Conference, though informal, was a time for serious business and hard work.

Alfred (Alfie) was little interested in archaeology in 1927, but when he entered Harvard in 1929 he turned to it. After receiving his Ph.D. in anthropology from that university in 1937, he was appointed to the faculty. His major interest was Andean archaeology, and in 1950 he moved to the University of Pennsylvania. Besides his teaching, field work, and writing, he moderated for several years the CBS television show "What in the World?" in which a group of anthropologists were asked to identify and comment on archaeological and ethnological specimens.

Harry Percival Mera was a relative newcomer to the Southwest in 1927, having left his medical practice in Abilene, Kansas, in 1922 to move to Santa Fe, where he became county health officer. But ever since a visit in 1905, while practicing medicine in Detroit, he had developed a deepening interest in the Southwest and its peoples. As health officer in the 1920s he visited the New Mexico pueblos frequently, and also began an archaeological survey and collection of sherd samples that by 1929 had grown to over two thousand sites, the nucleus of the continuing Laboratory of Anthropology site records.

Mera's growing interest in the pottery of the living Indians led him to join, and soon lead, a group of Santa Feans whose collecting efforts laid the foundations of the Indian Arts Fund, a major collection of historic and recent pottery representing all the pueblos and their many styles. He wrote in 1926 that "I am endeavoring to build up a comparative file of potsherds from the pre- and post-Spanish sites of the Southwest" (*Teocentli*, December 1926). He noted further that he would "try and reduce the sherds to comparative formulas as regards form, paste, slip and decoration . . . to distinguish age, cultures, etc." (*Teocentli*, June 1927). Thus his interest in systematizing the way in which potsherds were "named" and described paralleled and contributed to the Pecos Conference effort to set up a binomial system of pottery classification, something not accomplished in 1927 but planned in detail in 1931 at the Globe Caucus. As his interests centered on the Rio Grande, he undoubtedly followed Kidder's work at Pecos with special attention, and in fact Kidder included Mera's terminology for the Pecos pottery, as well as preparing his own, in his monumental report published in 1936, *The Pottery of Pecos*, volume 2 (coauthored with Anna O. Shepard).

In the summer of 1927, *Earl Halstead Morris* (Fig. 2.14) and *Ann Axtell Morris* returned from their Carnegie Institution work at Chichen Itza on July 8 and went to their home in Aztec, New Mexico, where Earl was custodian of Aztec Ruin, a huge pueblo on the Animas River about fifteen miles above its junction with the San Juan. Earl Morris's interest in archaeology went back to his boyhood and his father's passion for collecting prehistoric pottery (although his livelihood came mainly from grading roads and moving earth, particularly for mining companies). Earl entered the University of Colorado in 1908, after working his way through high school as an expert fireplace and chimney mason. He left the university temporarily in 1912 to go to Quirigua, Guatemala, with Hewett and Morley and received his degree in 1914, with a major in psychology (these and many other details come from the biography of Earl Morris's Southwestern years by Lister and Lister 1968). That winter he went back to Quirigua, this time with Judd and Nusbaum to make glue molds of the large sculptured monuments for the Panama-California Fair in San Diego.

By this time, through the influence of Hewett, Morris's interests had turned from psychology wholly to archaeology. Although he received a fellowship to study for a Ph.D. at Columbia University, he stayed only a year, but during this time he met Wissler of the American Museum of Natural History, who asked him to join the program at Aztec Ruin, which would consist of both digging and restoration.

A couple of years before this, Ann Axtell of Omaha, Nebraska, had paid a visit to a cousin who ran a trading post near Shiprock, thirty miles west of Farmington, New Mexico. There she met Earl Morris, and in 1923 they were married. Ann had graduated from Smith College in Northampton, Massachusetts, in 1922 (a year before Edith Bayles [Ricketson]), had studied in France with the American School of Prehistoric Research, and was a talented artist. From 1923 onward she collaborated with her husband in his archaeological work both in Yucatan and in the Southwest. She wrote two popular books on their experiences, published in 1931 and 1934. One of their two daughters, Elizabeth Ann Morris, became a Southwestern and Plains archaeologist, earning her Ph.D. at the University of Arizona and teaching for many years at Colorado State University.

Earl Morris was an indefatigable digger, with a gift for spotting a rewarding site or a rich burial. From 1924 to 1929 he combined the winter's work in Yucatan with the summer spent working in the Southwest. But as Kidder wrote in his obituary of Morris, "Being often at Chichen during his five years there, I sensed, and he finally told me, that he itched to pull out. Morley realized this and in 1929, with characteristic generosity, most regretfully let him" (Kidder 1957: 392). Thereafter Morris's Southwestern work made up another segment of the Carnegie archaeological program. His Southwest digging made him familiar with almost every corner of the region; in August and September 1926, for example, he dug in the Mimbres country for the University of Colorado Museum, Boulder, securing 200 vessels. "From the Mimbres," he wrote (*Teocentli*, December 1926), "I crossed over into Arizona, went for a distance down the Gila Valley, then up the Tonto River and over the Mogollon Range to Camp Verde, Arizona . . . and examined and reported upon an extensive aboriginal salt mine for the American Museum of Natural History." Later that same year he went to Canyon de Chelly and built diversion dams to protect the White House ruin from destruction by floods. Then, "the pueblo was excavated. A large collection of pottery and other artifacts was

2.14 Earl H. Morris and Ann A. Morris, about 1940. Photo from Watson Smith Collection, Museum of Northern Arizona, negative no. 72.535.

recovered." The Morrises' 1927 work has already been mentioned, as well as Kidder's cordial invitation to the Pecos Conference.

Jesse Logan Nusbaum (Fig. 2.15) was described by Judd, when he first met him in 1908 and their friendship began, as Hewett's "chief photographer . . . , a tall, blue-faced individual who rode with a case of glass plates on one hip, his camera on the other. At home in the city he shaved three times a day, but out here among the cedars and pinons he could be himself . . . Nusbaum was raising a pair of low-slung side burns that gave his dark-skinned features . . . an elongated appearance precisely matching his horse's face" (Judd 1968: 22). Nusbaum, a native of Greeley, Colorado, was actually a handsomer individual than this humorous portrait indicates.

Nusbaum was a man of many talents reflected, for example, in his supervision of the construction of the Museum of Fine Arts in Santa Fe, with its auditorium modeled on the chapel of the Pecos mission, which he had excavated and restored in 1915 as a part of Kidder's Pecos program. He was the first staff member of the Museum of New Mexico, when it was founded by Hewett in 1909. He worked from then until 1913 to repair and restore the Palace of the Governors as its headquarters—a considerable responsibility, as this ancient building was the first capital of Spanish New Mexico and the oldest government building in continuous use in the United States. Judd also noted that when he first visited Frijoles Canyon in 1910 (Judd 1968: 142) the regular members of the staff of the School of American Research were there—Nusbaum, John P. Harrington, Chapman, and J. Percy Adams. In 1921 Nusbaum became superintendent of Mesa Verde National Park, Colorado, where he combined his engineering and archaeological talents in building its access road, excavating and repairing its ruins, and creating the facilities that a major tourist attraction would need. And in 1930 his administrative skills were put to use when he became first director of the new Laboratory of Anthropology. Later he returned to serve again as superintendent at Mesa Verde National Park, and then in the 1950s pioneered in the development of salvage archaeology with the surveys and excavations along the route of the El Paso Natural Gas Company's lines in New Mexico and Arizona (see Wendorf and others 1956).

Frank Pinkley, born in 1881, came to Phoenix in 1900 from Chillicothe, Ohio, because of a medical diagnosis of "the probability of tuberculosis," and spent several months living in the desert near Phoenix (in an area long since swallowed up by metropolitan sprawl), to put on weight and reduce the hazard of contracting the disease. He was

2.15 Jesse L. Nusbaum, Pecos Conference at Flagstaff, 1953. Museum of Northern Arizona negative no. 74.1338, photo by A. O. Brodie.

offered the position of caretaker of the federally owned Casa Grande ruin, near Coolidge, Arizona, and moved there in 1901, where he set up a tent as a home, office, and headquarters. He assisted Fewkes in the 1906–08 excavations there by the Smithsonian Institution (Fewkes 1912) and learned firsthand all that Fewkes could teach him about archaeology. Two years after the creation of the National Park Service in 1916, Casa Grande National Monument was established, with Pinkley as "resident custodian." When the broad administrative unit known as Southwestern National Monuments was set up in 1924, he was appointed superintendent, responsible for fourteen monuments in Arizona and New Mexico. Eventually, another fourteen were added, and for all of these, Pinkley had a detailed knowledge of not only their archaeology but their road-building problems, visitor facilities (and needs), staffs, and annual budgets. Although his administrative duties left little time for research, he did test digging in a ball court at Casa Grande, and in reporting on it to the Park Service he suggested that it was not a reservoir—a popular idea that persisted for a long time—but was probably used for "ceremony, games or festivals" (A. L. Schroeder, letter to Woodbury, 31 March 1982). Everyone familiar with the Southwestern National Monuments realized that in a real sense they were the creation of Frank Pinkley, rather than the distant Washington administration, and to his staff and many others in the Southwest he was the "Grand Old Man" of the National Park Service (Anonymous 1940c) until his sudden death in 1940. His daughter-in-law Jean M. Pinkley was a Park Service archaeologist, with a career in both administration and research that was cut short by her early death in February 1969.

Etienne Bernardeau Renaud was born near Paris in 1880, graduated in 1905 from the University of Paris, and in 1907 came to the United States. After teaching in the East, he came to the University of Colorado as a professor of romance languages and in 1920 earned his doctorate at the University of Denver, where he began teaching anthropology in 1924. Although he carried out extensive archaeological surveys of the High Plains and frequently visited Southwestern archaeological sites as well as modern pueblos, he was best known as a teacher, often adding summer school in Boulder to his regular duties in Denver. He is remembered as "a very inspiring and excellent teacher" (Katharine Bartlett, letter to Woodbury, September 1981), and among his students were Katharine Bartlett, who had a long archaeological career at the Museum of Northern Arizona, Flagstaff, with the Coltons; Charlie Steen and Dale S. King, who both became

National Park Service archaeologists; and Frank H.H. Roberts, Jr., who is discussed below. Although he had limited research interests in Southwestern archaeology, Renaud was an inveterate traveler and had doubtless visited the work in progress at Pecos. Also, as one of the few archaeologists at any Southwestern university, he would have been invited to the Conference by Kidder.

Frank Harold Hannah Roberts, Jr. (Fig. 2.16), was just beginning his distinguished archaeological career in the 1920s and in 1927 was also beginning his marriage with *Linda Butcher Roberts,* who had been a student of his four years earlier at Denver University. Frank Roberts was born in Ohio, but grew up mostly in Laramie, Denver, and then Las Vegas, New Mexico, his father teaching college history and civics in all three places and becoming president of Las Vegas Normal University in 1910. Roberts graduated from the University of Denver in 1919 and became a reporter and city editor for the Las Vegas *Daily Optic.* In 1921 he received an M.A. in political science at Denver University, but courses with Renaud turned his interests to archaeology. In 1923 and 1924 he was assistant curator at the Colorado State Museum, Boulder, and did archaeological field work in southwestern Colorado. As Judd later wrote, "Because pottery was our major problem [at Pueblo Bonito] in 1925, I offered Frank a job on the strength of his capable analysis of Piedra Valley pottery, vouched for by my long-time Harvard friend, A. V. Kidder" (Judd 1966: 1227).

In 1924 Roberts had begun work on his doctorate at Harvard, with a Hemenway Fellowship; among his fellow students were Oliver LaFarge, Burton Cosgrove, Harry Shapiro, George Vaillant, and Frans Blom, and it may be here that he first met Kidder, who was curator of North American archaeology at the Peabody Museum. In 1926 he received an offer to join the American Museum of Natural History, but declined it to accept Fewkes's offer of a position as archaeologist at the Bureau of American Ethnology, which remained his institutional affiliation throughout his career. He received his doctorate at Harvard in June 1927. His dissertation on the ceramics of Chaco Canyon was never published, although it was referred to years later in Judd's monumental report, *The Material Culture of Pueblo Bonito* (Judd 1954b: 177).

Following his work for Judd on the Chaco pottery, in which he was assisted in the field by Monroe Amsden, Roberts was ready in 1927 to plan and carry out an excavation of his own. With Judd's cooperation and with support from the Bureau of American Ethnology, he worked at Shabik'eschee, a Basketmaker village he had found the

2.16 Frank H. H. Roberts, Jr., 1960. Smithsonian Institution, National Anthropological Archives, negative no. 53521.

year before. The site proved of great importance in defining the "late" period of the Basketmaker (III, that is). Already in 1927 Roberts was emerging as an important younger leader in the Southwest.

THE CARNEGIE GROUP   In addition to the preceding Conference participants, all of whom were more or less actively engaged in Southwestern archaeological research at the time, there were others who had personal ties with the Kidders or who, despite other primary scholarly interests, found their way to Pecos that August. Among these we will mention first the members of "the Carnegie Group."

Sylvanus Griswold Morley, known as "Vay" (Fig. 2.17), and *Frances Rhoads Morley* were, like the Robertses, married in 1927. By then Vay Morley had already enjoyed a long career in Mesoamerica and had become the leading scholar of Maya hieroglyphs. But he also had close Southwestern ties. When he was ten years old his family had moved to Buena Vista, Colorado, and he had quickly developed a strong interest in archaeology, including that of Egypt. After earning a degree in civil engineering in 1904 he went to Harvard, where Frederick Ward Putnam and Alfred M. Tozzer persuaded him that the Maya field (Tozzer's primary interest) had more promise than the Egyptian— after all, Egyptian hieroglyphs had long since been deciphered and the culture history of the Nile Valley worked out in some detail. In 1909, a year after he received his M.A. degree (he never did earn a Ph.D.), he moved to Santa Fe and began working for Hewett on the staff of the School of American Archaeology. In 1914 he visited sites in northern Yucatan, Quirigua in Guatemala, and sites in the Usumacinta and Peten areas, the last two areas on a trip with Herbert J. Spinden.

Morley had first met Kidder when, as Harvard students, they had answered a call for volunteers for an archaeological expedition under Hewett, in the Southwest. Kidder wrote vividly of that summer in 1907 and the importance to them of Morley's prior field experience, since Kidder and the other undergraduate, John Gould Fletcher (who became a well-known poet), were tenderfeet in the extreme (Kidder 1960). Later that same summer they met Nusbaum at Mesa Verde and Chapman in Santa Fe.

When Morley, in 1913, presented to the Carnegie Institution of Washington a plan for a long-term study of the ancient Maya, his plan was selected against the competition of a proposal by the eminent British anthropologist, W.H.R. Rivers, for research in Oceania and one by A. E. Jenks for a research laboratory to study "ethnic heredity, environment and amalgamation." By 1925 the program had developed

2.17 *Sylvanus G. Morley. Courtesy of Museum of New Mexico, negative no. 10316.*

from Morley's initial almost singlehanded search for hieroglyphic inscriptions to the large-scale excavation and restoration of Chichen Itza that Kidder visited that year. In 1927 came Kidder's selection as director of Carnegie's entire archaeological program. Although Morley spent each winter in Yucatan, his home had been in Santa Fe since 1909, and about 1925 he acquired a permanent office in the Palace of Governors, provided by Hewett, who directed the museum that occupied most of the building. Morley, as part of the Santa Fe archaeological community and a long-time friend of the Kidders, and now also a formal colleague in the Carnegie program, was quite naturally invited by Kidder to come out to Pecos for the Conference.

Oliver Garrison Ricketson, Jr., and *Edith Bayles Ricketson* had met at Chichen Itza in 1925, where each had gone to work for Morley, she as his secretary, he as an archaeologist. Later that year they were married and in 1926 made Guatemala City their home. Oliver Ricketson had studied anthropology at Harvard but then changed to medical school, to which he returned after World War I service as a machinist's mate but never completed the degree. In 1920 he moved to Flagstaff, and then to Kayenta where he lived with John and Louisa Wetherill at the famous trading post they had established many years before. For a while Ricketson worked in Marsh Pass with the archaeologist Samuel J. Guernsey of Peabody Museum. (Guernsey, incidentally, a colleague and friend of A. V. Kidder, had recommended Kidder for the position at Phillips Academy, Andover, Massachusetts, which made possible Kidder's excavation of Pecos.)

In 1921 Ricketson met Morley and went with him to Yucatan as a mule skinner, returning the next year as a cartographer and draftsman. He worked with J. A. Jeançon, of the University of Colorado, in 1923, securing borings of roof beams for Douglass to use in creating his tree-ring sequence. It was Ricketson's idea to take borings from beams in Oraibi, the Hopi town considered by many to be the oldest continuously inhabited settlement of North America. He overcame local opposition by placing offerings of turquoise in each hole after the boring. In 1923 he turned again to Maya archaeology, joining the Carnegie Institution and working for Morley, first in Chichen Itza, and then in 1926 taking charge of the work at Uaxactun. In 1927 his staff included Monroe Amsden, no longer working for Judd in Chaco Canyon. Ricketson's study of Uaxactun was the basis for the dissertation that he submitted at Harvard in 1933.

Edith Bayles was born in Puerto Rico, where her father was a mining engineer. After graduating from Smith College in 1921, she went to Norway on a fellowship to study Norwegian literature. Becoming interested in archaeology during the summer travel in Europe, she began graduate study in Paris and took part in excavations of the American School of Prehistoric Research, which had recently been founded by George Grant MacCurdy and Charles Peabody and later was affiliated with the Archaeological Institute of America. In 1924 she went to the Santa Barbara Museum of Natural History as an assistant curator and the next year began working for Morley in Yucatan. Thereafter she devoted herself to Maya archaeology as a partner in her husband's work at Uaxactun and subsequently elsewhere in Guatemala.

OTHER INTERESTED PARTICIPANTS   Several other participants in the 1927 Conference were friends of the Kidders, had had previous interests in the Southwest, or came as friends or colleagues of other participants. It may be that they played a less active part in the daily discussions, but some at least may have contributed greater breadth to the Conference through the variety of their interests. Brief biographical sketches of these ten participants follow.

Lansing Bartlett Bloom graduated from Williams College in 1902 and from Auburn Theological Seminary in 1907. He served in Presbyterian missionary work in Utah, Montana, Mexico, and then from 1912 to 1917 in New Mexico, mainly at Jemez Pueblo. He had received an M.A. in history from Williams in 1912, and in 1917 history became his main interest; he moved to Santa Fe to be executive secretary of the State Historical Service. His association with the School of American Research began in 1913 (until 1917 the School of American Archaeology), and at the Museum of New Mexico he was assistant to the director, Hewett, from 1920 to 1929. He left to join the faculty of the University of New Mexico, Albuquerque.

In 1921 and 1922 he took part in the School of American Research's archaeological investigations of the Spanish mission at Jemez Pueblo and, from 1923 through 1925, of the Mission of San Buenaventura at Gran Quivira, where his fellow field workers included Halseth and Pinkley. During these years his historical interests were increasingly turning to the Spanish colonial period in the New World. In spite of lifelong poor health he made trips to Mexico and Spain, searching for documentary materials. In the Vatican archives he found and copied the 300 illustrations for Bandelier's manuscript work on the Franciscan missions, Pecos being among them. In Florence he secured photographs of the only complete manuscript of Sahagun's *History of Ancient*

Mexico. He held a long and distinguished editorship of the *New Mexico Historical Review,* to which he was also an important contributor.

Percy Jackson is one of the Conference participants about whom it has been difficult to secure information. He was probably there more as an observer than an active contributor. He is remembered as "a true gentleman of the old school . . . [who had] a scholar's, and intelligent layman's interest in anthropology" (Marjorie Lambert, letter to Woodbury, 8 November 1981). He was an easterner who had moved west, making his home in Colorado Springs. He also had a ranch (as a "hobby") at Wagon Mound, about sixty-five miles northeast of Pecos, across the Sangre de Cristo range. He was a good friend of many members of the Santa Fe Circle, which included archaeologists at the School of American Research; was a member of the board of regents of the Museum of New Mexico; and had visited Morley in Yucatan to see the work at Chichen Itza.

Alfred Louis Kroeber (Fig. 2.18) was one of the most versatile anthropologists and most admired scholars in the nation in 1927, and nine years later a volume of essays by distinguished colleagues would be issued to honor his sixtieth birthday (Lowie 1936). His important but brief contribution to Southwestern archaeology took place as an almost accidental by-product of his major study of Zuni Pueblo, published in 1917 as *Zuni Kin and Clan.* Picking up sherds from seventeen sites near Zuni, as he sometimes strolled away from the pueblo, he found that they could be seriated on the basis of color (black ware, black-on-red, and "three colors") and that the percentage of corrugated pottery decreased steadily to near zero, with modern Zuni at one end of the series and presumably with the most ancient sites in his group at the other end. This was just what Kidder had done with the pottery of the Pajarito Plateau ten years before, but Kroeber apparently reinvented the technique, not knowing of Kidder's work. It was on the basis of these experiments in seriation that Leslie Spier would build a more formal structure for seriation.

When Kroeber began research in Peruvian archaeology in 1922 he used this important new analytical tool to verify Max Uhle's chronology through a restudy at the University of California, Berkeley, of the Uhle grave pottery. In 1924 he applied this seriation technique to the Valley of Mexico, but did not continue to work in that area (where Kidder's student and friend George Vaillant began his chronological research in 1927). Kroeber's direct concern with Southwestern archaeology was behind him by 1927, but he continued to take a keen interest in all aspects of anthropology and doubtless recognized Kidder's work as of outstanding importance. There can be no doubt that he was welcome at Pecos in 1927 for both his sharp analytical mind and his great professional prestige.

Thomas Forsyth McIlwraith, born in Hamilton, Ontario, in 1899, attended McGill University, where his studies were interrupted by World War I, and received a master's degree from Cambridge University in 1924. He became the first anthropologist to be appointed to a Canadian university, when he was made a lecturer at the University of Toronto in 1925. He was best known in later years for his major study of the Bella Coola Indians of British Columbia, supported by the National Museum of Canada, a pioneering work in Canadian ethnology. Although the living Indians were his main interest, he also laid the foundations of archaeological research in Ontario through his position as associate director of archaeology at the Royal Ontario Museum. Popular with students and colleagues, McIlwraith was recalled by one acquaintance as "an inveterate conference goer, who loved conversation and was good company" (J. O. Brew, letter to Woodbury, 12 August 1981).

Although Pecos seems far from his home ground in Ontario, the Conference was apparently widely enough announced that McIlwraith learned of it. As a successor at the University of Toronto has said, "Sometimes this 'Harvard of the North' is a very isolated outpost, and attending meetings is about the only way to learn of the profession. Certainly the files indicate that McIlwraith also encouraged his faculty to take every advantage of professional meetings" (Maxine R. Kleindienst, letter to Woodbury, 20 October 81). Since McIlwraith was a research assistant to Wissler at the Yale Institute of Psychology in 1925, it is also possible that Wissler, knowing of his archaeological interests, told him about the Pecos Conference when it was announced in June 1927 (Reed 1980: 120–121, 366, 368).

James Augustin Brown Scherer came to the Pecos Conference from Los Angeles, where he was director of the Southwest Museum, which Charles Amsden had recently joined and where Harold S. Gladwin was an acting curator at the time. He had been president of the California Institute of Technology from 1903 to 1920; earlier, from 1892 to 1897, he had been an instructor in English at the Imperial Government School in Saga, Japan. A widely recognized authority on Japan, he later made Japanese-language broadcasts to that country for the U.S. Office of War Information in World War II. One of the most distinguished educators and administrators of his day, Scherer was also a scholar and world traveler, and in wide demand as a speaker.

2.18 A. L. Kroeber, about 1936. Photo from Lowie Museum of Anthropology, University of California, Berkeley.

What role he played in the Pecos Conference is not known, but at the least he would have been an interested and astute observer and doubtless would have been well briefed by Amsden on the train trip from California if they travelled together.

Henry Devenish Skinner remained a mystery for a long time during the preparation of this history. His existence was known only from a typed list with a photograph of the 1927 group, taken by C. B. Cosgrove and preserved in the files of the Arizona State Museum. Following the identifications of those in the picture, this list had at the end the names of those "not in the picture," and here was listed "Judge Skinner." My initial guess was that he was a local judge interested in the work at Pecos, invited by Kidder to come for the occasion, but gone by the time the picture was taken. This could not have been further from the facts. On writing to Ben K. Swartz, Jr., at Ball State University, Muncie, Indiana, to inquire about the Wissler correspondence that I learned was in the university archives, my interest was in letters that would shed light on Wissler's considerable role in Southwestern archaeology in the late 1920s. Swartz generously supplied copies of several letters of the period, one of which was written to Wissler from "Pecos Ruin, N.M.," on 12 August 1927, and signed H. D. Skinner. It said, in part,

> Thank you for your letter. I have had a great time here, as
> Dr. Kidder made me foreman at a site we have called Dick's
> Ruin. This afternoon I leave for the Mimbres, my address being
> c/o Cosgroves, Haywood, New Mexico. Then I return to
> Gallup to see the Indian festival. After that I propose, with your
> permission, to join Miss [Beatrice] Blackwood's party which is
> going to Canon de Chelly. Thereafter to San Francisco. . . . My
> time in the Southwest has been of the greatest use to me.

Further information came from several sources, including the 1950 *International Directory of Anthropologists*. Thanks to Timothy J. O'Leary, an indefatigable bibliographer at the Human Relations Area Files in New Haven, Connecticut, I learned of two 1974 volumes, one of essays presented to Skinner (edited by J. D. Freeman and W. R. Geddes) and one collecting some of his Pacific material culture papers spanning 1921 to 1972 (edited by Peter Gathercole and others). Both had extensive biographical introductions. Additional details of his career appear in *Prehistory at Cambridge and Beyond* by Grahame Clark (1989: 22–23).

Skinner was born in New Zealand in 1886 and by the age of eight was an enthusiastic collector of archaeological and ethnographical material. He read law in 1906 (hence, "Judge") but eventually turned back to anthropology. Discharged during World War I to recover from wounds received in the Gallipoli campaign, he studied anthropology at Cambridge University (1916–18), mainly with A. C. Haddon, the distinguished specialist on Oceania, and examined New Zealand collections there and in various British museums. In 1927–28 he studied Maori material in American museums with a Carnegie Traveling Fellowship. During 1927 he not only was at Pecos with Kidder, but took part in field work in Ohio with Shetrone and spent some time with the Cosgroves (as he mentioned to Wissler in the letter quoted above) and with Neil Judd at Pueblo Bonito.

Additional details came from James Reed's *Clark Wissler* where, citing examples of Wissler's active support of various young scholars' research while Wissler was at Yale, Reed wrote (1980: 123): "H. D. Skinner, affiliated with the Institute of Psychology which Wissler directed during 1926–1927, conducted a 'type study of diffusion and invention' in his investigation of stone implements in the Pacific area." Since Wissler was in close touch with Kidder on many matters, and had been invited to Pecos himself, it seems probable that Skinner's summer at Pecos was a direct result of Wissler's suggestion, as he would realize what a valuable field experience this would be for an archaeologist who had worked mainly from museum collections. Kidder's keen interest in the classification of stone implements would have been a further source of stimulation and training for Skinner.

While I was investigating this puzzle, Watson Smith of Tucson, to whom I had written in case his wide Southwestern experience had brought him in contact with a "Judge Skinner," was also solving the mystery. He knew Skinner, had visited him in New Zealand, and had seen his immense collection of Polynesian stone artifacts. Furthermore, Smith's wife, Lucy Cranwell, a palynologist born in New Zealand, had a presentation copy of *Anthropology of the South Seas: Essays Presented to H. D. Skinner* (Freeman and Geddes 1959). The title page had Skinner's signature, similar to the one on the letter to Wissler written thirty-two years before. Skinner died in 1978, and it is sad to reflect that during all these years no one who had been at Pecos in 1927 seems to have remembered him or been in touch with him at various conferences when the "founders" were honored.

Leslie Spier (Fig. 2. 19) and his wife *Erna Gunther* were on their way in August 1927 from the University of Washington, where both of them were on the anthropology faculty, to Norman, Oklahoma, where Spier had a visiting appointment at the university. With them were the two youngest "participants" at the Conference, Christopher (Kit), seventeen months old, and Robert (Rob), aged five. The latter became an anthropologist like his parents, receiving his Ph.D. at Harvard in 1954, and was a member of the faculty of the University of Missouri until his retirement. Long after the 1927 Conference Alfred Kidder recalled that while the Conference sessions were going on he had the additional and doubtless unwelcome chore of caring for these two small children.

Leslie Spier had studied engineering as an undergraduate, but while working for the New Jersey archaeological and geological survey in 1913 and 1914 he developed an interest in archaeology that led to graduate work at Columbia University under Franz Boas. Spier's major archaeological contribution, however, was not his work in New Jersey, important as that was at the time, but rather a result of the extensive survey of sites in the Zuni area that he conducted for the American Museum of Natural History the year after Kroeber's brief study of Zuni potsherds.

> In this pioneering study . . . Spier developed a chronology of the Zuni area ruins by ordering the proportions of different ceramic wares found in his stratigraphic trenches and random surface collections. He also discussed the evolution of architectural types that accompanied the ceramic changes and neatly laid out the settlement pattern sequence [Kintigh 1985: 3].

It was Kidder, coincidentally, who reviewed Spier's volume in 1919 for the *American Anthropologist,* and did so very enthusiastically. However, by the time Spier received his Ph.D. in 1920 his interests had shifted to ethnology, and from 1918 onward he carried out important research among the Havasupai, Wishram, Klamath, Maricopa, and others. His ethnological interests were always strongly oriented toward culture history and the distributional and historical dimensions of cultures.

Erna Gunther, who graduated from Barnard College in 1919, met Leslie Spier when they were graduate students at Columbia, and they were married in 1921. Gunther became a lecturer at the University of Washington, two years after Spier's appointment there, and she continued work on her Ph.D., receiving it in 1928. She became director of the Washington State Museum in 1929 as well as a professor at the

2.19 Leslie Spier, in Oklahoma in 1927. Photo courtesy of Robert F. G. Spier.

University of Washington. Her research interests were particularly the Northwest coast and sub-Arctic regions.

Herbert Joseph Spinden (Joe) was one of the participants whose presence is somewhat surprising, although he was a frequent visitor to Santa Fe and many of the participants were his good friends. He had received his Ph.D. at Harvard in 1909, two years after Kidder's first undergraduate exposure to Southwestern archaeology. Spinden's *Maya Art,* published in 1913, marked him as a leader in the field of Maya studies; it continues to be reprinted decades later. He was a curator of anthropology at the American Museum of Natural History (1909–21), curator of Mexican archaeology and ethnology at Peabody Museum (1921–25), and in 1927 was the newly appointed curator of anthropology at the Buffalo Museum of Arts and Science.

Spinden had traveled extensively in the Southwest between 1907 and 1920, and his hundreds of photographs remain an important record (housed in the Haffenreffer Museum, Brown University) of a Southwest that has long disappeared. His presence at Pecos in 1927 may have been less the result of a lingering interest in the Southwest than of his active interest in Morley's work and the Carnegie's Maya program that Kidder was joining. In addition, like many of those who came to Pecos in August 1927, he was one of the "subscribers" to Guthe's informal newsletter *Teocentli,* in which Kidder had announced the Conference. Also, Spinden was at the meeting in New York that June which planned how to wrest control of the proposed museum and laboratory in Santa Fe from Hewett. Finally, as one longtime friend commented, "I don't think that Joe Spinden's presence *anywhere* should be surprising" (Watson Smith, letter to Woodbury, 8 January 1983).

Joseph Bradfield Thoburn was a pioneer in Oklahoma history and archaeology, self-taught for the most part, and immensely successful in developing the Oklahoma Historical Society at the University of Oklahoma. But he was plagued throughout his career by scarcity of funds and by uncertain administrative support. He began serious field archaeology in Oklahoma about 1915, worked with Warren King Moorehead (of the same Phillips Academy that sponsored Kidder's work at Pecos) in an archaeological survey of the Arkansas River Valley, and worked briefly at the Deer Creek Site in northern Oklahoma with Fred H. Sterns. In 1917 he made a three-week field trip to New Mexico but apparently did no digging. Thoburn's position as the only serious archaeologist in Oklahoma at the time is reflected in a comment by Wissler in a letter of 3 November 1924 to A. V. Kidder, who was then chairman of the National Research Council's Committee on State Archaeological Surveys. Wissler said, "Keep in touch with Mr. Thoburn, since a little encouragement accomplishes a great deal with these State organizations," referring to the archaeological role of the state historical society. Thoburn corresponded extensively with Putnam, Holmes, Kidder, and many other archaeologists of his day, but within Oklahoma had no archaeological colleagues. He was a founder of Epworth University (later Oklahoma City University) and was active in water conservation and flood prevention programs. His excavations were mostly made possible by crews of student volunteers, and he published much less in archaeology than in Oklahoma history, but his contributions were a significant beginning for archaeology in the state. His field work was substantial enough to earn him the harassment of commercial dealers in antiquities (see Paul Lambert 1980).

Thoburn had original and unorthodox ideas about the origins of the American Indians: he believed that they came not from Asia but from a "racial swarming ground" in Mexico and Central America, from which population pressure generated a series of migrations, one for each of the major North American linguistic stocks. Still, it is not surprising that he would be invited to Pecos by Kidder, who was generous in support of archaeologists everywhere and tolerant of unorthodox views. In 1927 Thoburn was certainly the only person in Oklahoma who could appreciate the importance of the Conference (P. Lambert 1980; Kent Ruth, letter to Emil Haury, 11 October 1981). Incidentally, the journal of Charles F. Lummis (in the Southwest Museum) describes his visit on 1 September 1927 to Frijoles Canyon and the rest-house-with-museum managed by Halseth with Hewett, Thoburn, and Percy Jackson, further evidence of Thoburn's Southwestern ties.

Thomas Talbot Waterman is best remembered as the coauthor, with Kroeber, of *Source Book in Anthropology* (1920), the first and for many years the only volume of selected readings for students. At the University of California, Waterman had switched from postgraduate work for the ministry to the study of anthropology, as a result of a course on experimental linguistics with Pliny Earl Goddard and the experience of assisting Goddard in recording Indian languages in the field. After receiving a Ph.D. from Columbia University under Boas in 1913, he taught at the University of Washington, then at California, left there to work at the Heye Foundation in New York, and was successively at the Bureau of American Ethnology, the National Museum of Guatemala, and Fresno College. Still restless, he went to the University of Arizona in 1927 to teach there for a year, whence he moved to the University of Hawaii (where he remained!). He has been described as "first of all a brilliant, incisive, colorful teacher, rarely systematic and sometimes erratic, but extraordinarily stimulating [and also] . . . in his professional work, he loved concrete facts and sharply defined findings" (Kroeber 1937). Waterman came to Pecos with Cummings and the students from Tucson, perhaps invited by the Dean, perhaps also curious to see the widely known Pecos excavations and meet the distinguished group assembling there, and he was certainly welcome, as any guest of the Dean would have been. Waterman's important role at the Conference will be discussed shortly.

STUDENTS AND BEGINNERS   Finally, we must look at the group of students and beginners who attended the first Pecos Conference, for at least a few of whom it was an event long remembered as a major step in their progress toward professionalism. For some, on the other hand, their future interests turned entirely away from archaeology.

Monroe Amsden, like his older brother Charlie, was a native of Farmington, New Mexico, the base for much archaeological exploration in the Four Corners area. As a boy and a young man he worked for Judd at Chaco Canyon, where his tasks included pottery sorting and classification with Frank Roberts. In 1925 he went with Kidder and Morris to Canyon de Chelly to cook for a party that included William Claflin and Raymond Emerson and their wives, all friends and supporters of the Peabody Museum, and also Vaillant and Erich F. Schmidt, who in 1925 had been a pioneer in the study of the Lower Gila region (Schmidt 1928; see also Hohmann and Kelley 1988). Monroe, however, despite his varied talents, did not pursue an archaeological career like his brother Charlie, and as far as we know the 1927 Conference and his work for Ricketson, mentioned earlier, were his last appearances on the archaeological stage.

Clara Lee Fraps (Tanner) (Fig. 2.20), born in North Carolina in 1906, was one of the archaeology students who came to Pecos with Dean Cummings. She had received her B.A. that spring, and would receive her M.A. the next year. She joined the faculty at the University of Arizona in 1929, and her major interest turned from archaeology to Southwestern Indian arts and crafts, a subject in which she has continued to make notable contributions.

Charlotte Day Gower attended Smith College and received her M.A. from the University of Chicago in 1927. Her thesis on Antillean cul-

2.20 Clara Lee Fraps (Tanner). Courtesy of Clara Lee Tanner.

ture was published by the AAA (Gower 1927). Before then, as a student of Fay-Cooper Cole, she had dug in Hopewell sites in the Middle West, but her interests shifted to ethnology and in 1928 she received a research fellowship from the Social Science Research Council for a study of a Sicilian village (the other two anthropological fellows that year were Ruth Bunzel, to do research at Zuni, and Margaret Mead for research in Melanesia). It is probable that the only Pecos Conference participant that she already knew was her fellow graduate student Paul Martin, but as a student of Cole she would have been well informed of the archaeological work of Kidder, and Cole would have seen Kidder's announcement in *Teocentli*, as he was a contributor. Some years later, while she was teaching at Lingan University in China, Gower was imprisoned by the Japanese. In 1942 she was repatriated to the United States and joined the Marine Corps. She served in U.S. intelligence agencies from then until her retirement in 1964.

Emil Walter Haury (Fig. 2.21), like Fraps, came from Tucson to Pecos with the Dean, and like her had received his B.A. that spring at the University of Arizona and was to earn his M.A. the next year. Haury's interest in archaeology had been aroused while he was a student at Bethel College, in his hometown of Newton, Kansas, when Cummings visited the college campus to lecture. Haury talked with him about the possibility of joining his archaeological work in the Valley of Mexico at the famous site of Cuicuilco, but he was not able to do so immediately. Haury (letter to Woodbury, 8 April 1982) has written that

in the spring of 1925 . . . I re-established contact with him to see if he would be back in Arizona in the summer, and he wrote back that he would not be back and he made the comment, "I can think of no better place to be introduced to archeology than Mexico." Whereupon my father said, "Why don't you write him and ask him if you could join Cummings if we pay your way?" I did and Cummings replied: "If your family pays your way to Mexico, I want you to come and help me this summer since I'll be alone. I will take care of your keep here, pay your way back to Tucson, and give you a job in the Museum so you can go to school."

Two other students at Bethel College, Roland Richert and Waldo R. Wedel, were also stimulated by Cummings's visit, and both came to Tucson a couple of years after Haury. Both had long and distinguished archaeological careers, Richert in the National Park Service and Wedel

2.21 *Emil W. Haury, in Tesgi Canyon, 1928. Arizona State Museum negative (unnumbered), photo by Clay Lockett.*

at the U.S. National Museum (later the National Museum of National History). Haury went to Harvard to earn his Ph.D. (1934) while on the staff of Gila Pueblo, and then in 1937 succeeded Dean Cummings as head of the archaeology department at the University of Arizona. Haury's recollections of his and Fraps's role at the 1927 Conference are quoted below.

Paul Sidney Martin (Fig. 2.22) graduated from the University of Chicago in 1923 and did his first archaeological field work in Wisconsin in the summer of 1927. He reported on that excavation the same year in the *Wisconsin Archaeologist,* a pattern of promptness in publication that he was to continue throughout his entire career. In 1926 and 1927 he led field parties excavating in Illinois, part of the ongoing program that Cole had begun in 1925, when Illinois archaeology was almost wholly unknown. In December 1926 Martin went to Yucatan for six months' work at Chichen Itza with Morley, Maya archaeology being the specialty he had chosen. At the end of his third season in Yucatan, he was advised for medical reasons—following severe malaria and amoebic dysentery—to give up any further work in the tropics. His colleagues at Chichen Itza included Ann and Earl Morris, Edith and Oliver Ricketson, and Karl Ruppert (who had been a student of Cummings at Arizona, had worked with Judd in Chaco Canyon, and would be at the Pecos Conference in 1929, although not in 1927).

In the summer of 1927 Martin accepted a position with the State Historical Society of Colorado, which would begin in September with a visit to the Hovenweep area "with the idea of locating a possible site for work in 1928" (*Teocentli,* June 1928). He had returned to Denver from Yucatan in May and, as he wrote many years later, "soon . . . received a most kind invitation from Dr. A. V. Kidder to attend a conference of Southwestern archaeologists and ethnologists at Kidder's field station at Pecos, New Mexico. My superiors at Denver thought I should attend the conference. Needless to say, I would not have missed it for anything" (Martin 1974: 4). A better start for his career in the Southwest can hardly be imagined, and the conference should have been a source of great encouragement to a graduate student (he would receive his Ph.D. in 1929 from Chicago). Some of Martin's recollections of the 1927 Conference are quoted later. (I have followed Martin's letters in *Teocentli* and the Carnegie *Yearbooks* here, rather than the 1976 obituary by Longacre, which differs in some respects.)

Hulda Penner (Haury), a native of Newton, Kansas, was a teacher in a western Kansas school. In 1927 she was visiting a sister in Tucson and was invited by Cummings to join the trip to Pecos. She came to

2.22 Paul S. Martin, 1947. Courtesy of William A. Longacre.

Tucson permanently when she and Haury were married in 1928. She entered the university as a music major, but only completed her degree much later, after many years as a devoted partner and supporter of her husband's archaeological career.

Harry Lionel Shapiro has remarked of his presence at the Pecos Conference, "I was really an outsider" (telephone conversation with Woodbury, 13 February 1980). Having received his doctorate at Harvard only the year before (in physical anthropology with Earnest Hooton), he had immediately become an assistant curator in the anthropology department at the American Museum of Natural History, where he remained for a long career of research, writing, and administration. Kidder's letter to Wissler, quoted earlier, indicates that he was already recognized for his ability and knowledge. In the summer of 1927 Shapiro was accompanying Morris in the latter's work, to secure skeletal material for the museum's study collections. Morris had taken Shapiro to visit Judd at Chaco Canyon, and they had seen Roberts's work in progress at Shabik'eschee and had then proceeded to Pecos. But Shapiro had no particular interest in archaeology except as it related to his specialty. However, he was certainly interested in the ongoing disagreement as to whether "long-headed" Basketmakers were succeeded by "round-headed" Puebloans, or whether the introduction of a new cradling practice resulted in head deformation, with no genetic change at all. Some years later the question would be settled by another student of Hooton's, Carl C. Seltzer, who demonstrated that the change was indeed due to cradling methods (Seltzer 1944).

Robert (Bob) Wauchope became interested in archaeology as a boy in South Carolina and collected arrowheads enthusiastically. When he was about to graduate from high school he convinced his father that he should join an archaeological expedition. On the advice of a friend his father, a professor of English, wrote Kidder, and to the young man's delight Kidder agreed to take him on as a field assistant that summer, following his first semester of college. A half century later Alfred Kidder, the oldest of the Kidder children, wrote, "I am the first person who met Bob that summer. The Santa Fe railroad stops for water at Glorieta, New Mexico, not very far from Pecos. My mother and I went to Glorieta in the ancient 1914 Ford to see Bob off the train . . . I was fifteen [*sic*], and all I thought about was horses and cowboys. I remember my cowboy hat and boots and that I had been told that Bob was about my age so I walked up to him and said, 'You must be Mr. *Watch-ope*' " (Kidder II 1978). (He would learn that the name was actually pronounced "Walk-up"!) Bob Wauchope took an active part in the excavation of Forked Lightning Ruin that summer, and also began a lifelong friendship with the Kidders.

Alfred Kidder also recalled that Bob (then eighteen years old) was the "youngest person with any archaeological interest at the First Pecos Conference." Some of the Conference participants he met were to be his professional associates later, and the very next year the Cosgroves invited him to join them in their excavations at Stallings Island, Georgia, turning him to his long interest in Southeastern rather than Southwestern archaeology. Although he continued in college as an English major, after his graduation in 1931 he was encouraged by Kidder to choose archaeology as a career and to enter Harvard, which he did. His freshman year he became a member of the Carnegie staff and made major contributions throughout his career to Maya as well as Southeastern U.S. archaeology.

CHILDREN   To conclude this roll call of those at the 1927 Pecos Conference, we should list the children, some of whom have been mentioned already: a son of M. R. Harrington about whom we have no details; J. Ferrell Colton; five Kidders, Alfred (sixteen), Randolph (fifteen), Barbara (ten), Faith (seven), and James, the youngest; and the two Spier children, Robert (Rob) and Christopher. The three younger Kidders were "banished," as mentioned earlier, leaving a total of about fifty people present at the Pecos field camp during those memorable discussions.

COMPOSITION OF THE CONFERENCE   Contrary to an impression that has understandably grown up in recent years, the first Pecos Conference was not made up largely of patriarchs. As with recent Conferences, a substantial part of the group was fairly young. In fact, of the forty-four participants for whom we know their ages in 1927 (and excluding children), there were more under forty than over fifty. Their average age was 40.7, and the age distribution was as follows:

Age 18–29: 13 (C. Amsden, M. Amsden, Fraps, Gower, Haury, McIlwraith, Martin, A. Morris, Penner, E. Ricketson, L. Roberts, Shapiro, Wauchope).
Age 30–39: 8 (M.-R.F. Colton, Gunther, Halseth, M. Kidder, E. Morris, F. Roberts, O. Ricketson, Spier).
Age 40–49: 10 (Bloom, H. S. Colton, Harrington, Judd, A. V. Kidder, Nusbaum, Pinkley, Renaud, Skinner, Waterman).
Age 50–59: 8 (Chapman, C. B. Cosgrove, H. S. Cosgrove,

Kroeber, Mera, S. G. Morley, Scherer, Spinden).
Age 60–68: 5 (Cummings, Douglass, Hewett, Hough, Thoburn).

In contrast to the age distribution, the institutional affiliations of the participants are quite different from those of recent Conferences. A considerable majority came from outside the Southwest, although of course some of those based farthest away were already in the area for a summer of field work and simply added Pecos to their itineraries. Only 14 participants had an institutional base in the Southwestern states: Santa Fe (4), Tucson (5), Phoenix (1), Denver (2), and the National Park Service (2 locally based, although with national headquarters in Washington). From farther away there came 27: Los Angeles (2), Berkeley (1), Seattle (2), Toronto (1), Chicago (1), Buffalo (1), New York (2), Philadelphia (2), Washington (11), Cambridge (2), Columbia, South Carolina (1), and Norman, Oklahoma (1). The count for Washington is raised by including the Morleys (whose home was Santa Fe but who were affiliated with the Carnegie Institution, Washington) and the Ricketsons, who had a home in Guatemala.

It is clear from details in the biographical sketches of Conference participants that Kidder drew on a large personal network of friends and colleagues. A large majority of the 1927 conferees had close personal and professional connections with Kidder—considerably more than can be judged members of Hewett's personal network, or Judd's (Woodbury 1985b). There was apparently no one at the Conference who can be considered a "stranger," not known personally by some of the others, which must have made for both informality and an open exchange of agreements and disagreements.

Before turning to the events of the Conference itself, one more aspect of participation deserves comment. On the basis of a survey of who was interested in Southwestern archaeology at the time, not everyone who might have been expected was there. Nelson, for example, had returned to the American Museum of Natural History the previous month from a long trip to China, searching for Pleistocene human fossils and tools, and had plunged into the backlog of museum chores awaiting him. Fewkes of the U. S. National Museum was only half a year from retirement, and although he had been in the field the summer before, excavating Elden Pueblo near Flagstaff, "the infirmities of age [he was seventy-seven] at last began to retard his progress," as Hough wrote a few years later in his obituary (Hough 1931). Guernsey, who had worked with Kidder some years earlier, was now mainly occupied with creating museum models of archaeological ruins and modern pueblos, for which he became well known. Also, one former colleague has commented that Guernsey "wouldn't have been seen dead at" a conference (J. O. Brew, letter to Woodbury, 12 August 1981).

Guthe, Kidder's former associate at Pecos, was now directing the development of the new anthropology museum at the University of Michigan, and his recent archaeological work had been in the Philippines, not the Southwest. Hodge, who directed the excavation of the prehistoric and historic Zuni town of Hawikuh from 1918 to 1923, was invited, as we have seen. In 1932 he would become director of the Southwest Museum, and he was a friend and colleague of many of the participants. His absence can best be explained by the comment of an acquaintance that he was never a conference goer, by strong preference. Gladwin, for reasons unknown, did not come over to Pecos from the Southwest Museum with Amsden and Scherer, although he was a close friend of the Kidders and was active in Southwestern archaeology. But he, too, was by inclination not a conference goer; he attended the 1929 Conference but, as far as the records indicate, no others. Bradfield, Hewett's associate director of the San Diego Museum of Man, and before that on Hewett's staff at the museum in Santa Fe, was also absent, although he had dug that summer in the Cameron Creek site in southern New Mexico.

Bruce Bryan, who was long associated with the Southwest Museum and worked at the museum's excavation of the Galaz Site in 1927, has recalled that "Scherer invited Malcolm Rogers to attend—then discovered he didn't have the authority to issue invitations and had to retract. Naturally there was some embarrassment" (Bruce Bryan, letter to Woodbury, 1 February 1982). Rogers's version of the affair is contained in a letter he wrote to Halseth on 28 August 1927 (on file, Pueblo Grande Museum Archives).

> Director Scherer . . . balled everything up. After getting me all
> set for Pecos I received another letter about a week ago saying
> that he had failed to consult Dr. Kidder and that the doctor had
> informed him that they were cramped for space . . . (in the wide
> open spaces at that). . . . Of course this isn't the reason. . . . I
> can imagine what he did was to represent me as a promising
> young man (stressing the youth) under his tutelage, undergoing
> probationary training. . . . Next I got my Teocentli containing
> the invitation of Kidder extended to all Teocentlis and I believe

it did jar him some, for he wrote back saying he was making the supreme effort to procure me an invitation. I knew this was applesauce. . . . I haven't heard from him since of course. . . . It has been a great discouragement as we are all looking forward to visiting you. I did so want to have Ethel see Puyé and all the Santa Fé country. . . . I have about determined to turn "pot hunter" and go into that more remunerative field of our honorable profession.

Halseth wrote Rogers on 2 December 1927 on several matters, and included the comment, "Don't get sore at the Teocently; nor on Kidder, they are not responsible for the make-up of our L.A. friend. . . . Kidder would have been tickled to have you come to Pecos."

As we have already seen, Wissler, one of the leading anthropologists of the time, was invited by Kidder, but did not attend, perhaps because his duties in New York and New Haven did not permit the ten days to two weeks it required—at least three days each way by train and several days in the Southwest.

Charles Fletcher Lummis, writer, traveler, and enthusiastic promoter of the West, almost attended the Conference. His unpublished journal records that on Monday, 29 August 1927, he drove out to Pecos from Santa Fe with "Rev. Lansing Bloom" and McIlwraith ("his first trip West. A fine type, to whom we both took"). Cummings had already arrived, and "in breezed Jess Nusbaum after a 500 mile drive looking . . . as if he had just stepped out of a band box. . . . Kidder is going to have a 'round up of anthropologists' there tomorrow and for several days, has already roped some 35 people for the gathering. Hewett stopped for the first session. B. & I came back [to Santa Fe]" (Braun Research Library, Southwest Museum). Although intensely gregarious, Lummis was very busy in Santa Fe and may not have been urged to remain at Pecos.

Others not present who might have been expected include Noel Morss of the Peabody Museum; Frank Mitvalsky (later "Midvale") who was to work for Gladwin at Gila Pueblo and in 1927 was already active in the archaeology of the Salt River area (see Wilcox 1987); Anna O. Shepard, then at the San Diego Museum of Man, where her colleague Bradfield was encouraging her to undertake the technological studies of pottery for which she became famous (she coauthored with Kidder the monumental second volume of *The Pottery of Pecos,* published in 1936); Schmidt of the American Museum of Natural History, whose 1925 survey and stratigraphic excavation in the Lower

Gila area for the museum was a major contribution to a little-known area (see Hohmann and Kelley 1988); Jeançon of the Colorado State Museum, Denver, who was interested in both the archaeology and ethnography of the Southwest and whose report on the Chama Valley was published in 1923 by the Bureau of American Ethnology (Jeançon 1923); Karl Ruppert of the Carnegie program at Chichen Itza, who spent part of the summer of 1927 with the Cosgroves at the Swarts ruin; and Florence Hawley, who had received her B.A. at the University of Arizona that June, as had Haury (oral tradition has it that her mother felt Florence should not go on a long, unchaperoned auto trip). Finally, it is a pity that Beatrice M. Blackwood was not at the Conference, since her presence in the Southwest is indicated in the letter from Skinner to Wissler already quoted. Although she is best known for her research in New Guinea, she had strong interests in archaeology (Penniman 1976).

Even with the absences noted, which include several active archaeologists who could have made contributions to the discussions, it is clear that a substantial proportion of archaeologists then working in the Southwest did accept invitations to the Conference. With the addition of the Maya group and the others listed above whose Southwestern connections are not obvious, the total number probably strained to the limit the sleeping and commissary arrangements that the Kidders could provide. An even larger group might also have been less effective in accomplishing the purposes Kidder had in mind.

Although the number at the Conference may have been greater than ideal for a "working group," it is probable that some participants were more active than others. On a purely intuitive basis I would expect that about a dozen men did the greater part of the talking—Cummings, Halseth, Judd, A. V. Kidder, Kroeber, Morris, Nusbaum, Renaud, Roberts, Spier, Spinden, and Waterman.

3
Conferences at Pecos, 1927 and 1929

With the archaeological scene of the 1920s in the Southwest now set and the cast of characters assembling at Pecos introduced, it is time to raise the curtain on the events of 29 August to 1 September 1927. The record provides considerable detail concerning the setting and the activities of the first Pecos Conference.

First Pecos Conference, 1927   Barbara Kidder Aldana has recalled with affection the scene at Pecos, fixed vividly in her memory by the many summers she enjoyed there with her parents, sister, and brothers.

> It was a long way by Model-T from Rowe (a flag stop of the Santa Fe Railroad) to the campsite; it must be ten miles or so on a pretty rough dirt road, but at last we are at the turnoff by the church, the ancient beautiful ruined adobe mission church that marks the site of Pecos Pueblo. Across the flat dotted with prairie dog hills, down the arroyo, up the other side and there it is, our house, our dear adobe house of three rooms front and three rooms back with a double sleeping porch to one side. There were several tents with wooden floors and sides and fly roofs, and way to the back the two privies, "funnies" we called them, and the dining room-kitchen to complete the Campsite in the most lovely sweet-smelling red earth, juniper, pinyon, and tall pine country, with the most wonderful people in the world. . . .
>
> The Campsite was set up in a remote corner of Forked Lightning Ranch; at our backs several miles distant were the tracks of the Santa Fe and beyond them the line of the Pecos Mesa and La Escoba Park, the landmark of my summer life. To the front was

the great Arroyo del Pueblo and beyond lay the ruins and the road to Pecos, Glorieta and Santa Fe. . . .

The logistics of feeding so many staff plus frequent visitors all through the long summer must have been complex, but there in Pecos was The Store, Harrison's, now Adelo's, where supplies were bought and charged to the Expedition. A redolent, exciting store it was with everything that one could possibly desire in the way of food both fresh and canned, hardware and clothing, and out front was the gasoline tank to fuel up Old Blue, the 1911 vintage Model-T, and Black, which was newer and without as much character. . . .

I must tell of Jim and Bertha Vandegrift, handyman and cook, without whom we could not have functioned at all. Jim did everything that needed doing around camp, and Bertha cooked and cooked and cooked the most delicious meals on her huge wood stove in the corner of the kitchen-dining room. Her refrigerator was a big wooden sort of meat safe with screened sides, all hung about with burlap suspended from a basin of water at the top. . . . The visitors brought their own camping equipment but usually ate with us at the long, long dining room table with its equally long, long benches running down either side. Big people had iced tea. We had lemonade! [Aldana 1983: 244–248].

By 1927 Kidder was no longer digging at the main ruin of Pecos—work had been completed there the year before. He was investigating a smaller and older site, which he found to be immediately ancestral to the settlement of Pecos. Forked Lightning Ruin, as it was called (in place of the earlier name, Bandelier's Bend), actually underlay in part the expedition's long-established field camp, and its full extent was only brought to light through digging holes for tent posts. It was about a quarter mile south of Pecos, across the Arroyo del Pueblo. When the Pecos Conference convened, Emil Haury recalls that the Conference sessions were held under the piñons and junipers across the arroyo from Forked Lightning Ruin, toward the ruins of Pecos (Fig. 3.1).

Many came to Pecos by car, rather than train, but roads were not what they are today, and auto travel often involved breakdowns and delays. For the fiftieth anniversary of the Pecos Conference in 1977, Haury recounted some details of the trip from Tucson in 1927. At 9:30 a.m. on 27 August, the University of Arizona Lincoln that was

*3.1 The first Pecos Conference, 1927; standing (*left to right*): Oliver Ricketson, J. B. Tho-*
burn, C. Burton Cosgrove, E. B. Renaud, Jesse L. Nusbaum, Andrew E. Douglass, Harry L.
Shapiro, Neil M. Judd, Erna Gunther Spier, Sylvanus G. Morley, Kenneth M. Chapman,
Madeleine A. Kidder, Paul S. Martin, A. V. Kidder, Linda Roberts, Frank H.H. Roberts, Jr.,
Clara Lee Fraps (Tanner), Lansing Bloom, Hulda Penner (Haury), Byron Cummings, Wal-
*ter Hough, Mark R. Harrington, Leslie Spier, Frederick W. Hodge; sitting (*left to right*):*
Edith B. Ricketson, Frances R. Morley, Charles Amsden, Earl H. Morris, Ann A. Morris, A. L.
Kroeber, Charlotte Gower, Frank Pinkley, J.A.B. Scherer, Harriet S. Cosgrove. Photograph by
T. T. Waterman, Southwest Museum negative no. N24602.

available to Dean Cummings (as acting president) left Tucson, with the Dean, T. T. Waterman, Clara Lee Fraps, Hulda Penner, and Haury. They reached Deming, New Mexico, about 200 miles east of Tucson, at 7:30 p.m., having had two flat tires on the way. Haury, who did most of the driving, recalls that the car got about seven miles to the gallon, and "we had to make careful calculations between watering holes." Next morning they were off at 7 and at Las Cruces turned north up the Rio Grande, reaching San Marcial at noon. After dinner at the Harvey House, they continued to Santa Fe, arriving—after brake problems and another flat—at 8 in the evening and put up at the Montezuma Hotel. The next morning, 29 August, they drove out to Pecos and were shown around the ruins by Kidder. At 2 P.M. after they'd been served lunch, the first session began (E. W. Haury, notes in the Arizona State Museum files).

Hulda Haury has also recalled her impressions of that first Conference:

> Arriving at Dr. Kidder's Pecos Camp, after a long, warm and dusty drive from Tucson, the five of us . . . found the Conference already in informal discussion. Most were seated on the ground, some on chairs, in the shade of a cluster of juniper and piñon trees, an impressive group! Where were the casual field clothes that one would expect? After all, it *was* a field camp where sleeping, eating, laboratory work had to be done under the protection of simple frame structures, tents, and tarps. But here were staid, scholarly-looking individuals, the men in dress trousers, with [dress] shirts and even ties. The women wore what might be considered afternoon or street dresses. To be sure, there were a few exceptions: Dr. Kidder in his gray knickers, several men in khakis and boots, a couple of women in riding-type pants, shirts, and high boots with heavy socks turned down over the boot tops. Wide-brimmed felt hats were worn almost without exception. As I remember, Dr. Kidder's field hat—a felt—had seen a good many field seasons and already looked a near museum piece! Just like "Old Blue," his faithful Model-T Ford.
>
> Almost immediately, I was aware of the relaxed, informal atmosphere, yet permeated by an intense and high-level curiosity about the intent of the Conference, together with active participation in contributing and sharing of field experiences

and knowledge; in fact, a coming together of minds, working toward some common concepts and ideas.

Little was seen of Madeleine Kidder, but the sounds of busy footsteps on the wood floor, the rattle of pots and pans, the clinking of dishes and tableware as mealtime approached, and the delicious smells emanating from the kitchen, was explanation enough. With little help—only a local woman and the two young Kidder sons, Alfie and Randy, to fetch water and wood for the range—Mrs. Kidder was kept on the go from morning till night [Hulda Haury, letter to Woodbury, 22 July 1980].

Years later Madeleine Kidder recalled of her teenage son Alfie and Bob Wauchope that "during the conference they were both $1.00 a day dish washers" (M. Kidder, letter to Jean Pinkley, 10 January 1969).

In his report on the Conference, published in *Masterkey,* Charles Amsden described the scene as he had just seen it:

> The Conference met . . . on the very site of an early Pecos Pueblo. Here Dr. Kidder had established his field camp when the Pecos excavations were begun, on a mesilla overlooking the Pecos Valley. A thick growth of piñon and juniper furnishes abundant shade, and grass covers the slopes thickly. One's conception of the Southwest as an arid desert proves absurdly inaccurate at Pecos. Fortunately, though, the weather held true to the best desert traditions, and no drop of rain threatened to disrupt the meetings, which were held, morning and afternoon, out of doors. . . .
>
> Tents had been provided for some, others brought their own camp equipment. All took their meals at the camp "mess," and met under the cedars morning and afternoon for the serious business of the assembly, Dr. Kidder acting as chairman of the meetings [Amsden 1927: 15–16].

As Kidder reported in *Science* the following November, "the morning of Monday, August 29, was spent in inspecting the excavations in the pre-Pecos site at Bandelier Bend [Forked Lightning], and visiting the main Pecos ruin. Monday afternoon and the mornings and afternoons of Tuesday and Wednesday were devoted to the business of the meeting, less formal campfire gatherings being held each evening." This main business was "the classification of Southwestern culture-periods," a scheme of time periods intended to replace the ill-defined concepts then in use. It formalized the distinction of Basketmaker and Pueblo as the two main cultural configurations of the Southwest, the second growing out of the first; the geographical regions that were later found to be markedly different, and to which this scheme could not apply, were not then sufficiently known to be considered. Numbered subunits (Basketmaker I, II, III, and Pueblo I, II, III, IV, V) were defined mainly on the basis of the pottery and house types familiar in the San Juan drainage of the Colorado Plateau. With later refinements and additions the Pecos Classification continued to be useful for many years, and it is still used for the Anasazi culture in the northern part of the Southwest. The Conference also discussed terminology, especially for pottery. "A survey was made of the work now in progress or in contemplation," Kidder wrote. The problems of permits for digging on public land were discussed. And A. E. Douglass reported on his progress in dating ruins by tree rings. The contents of these discussions and the results of the Conference will be examined in more detail later.

Emil Haury also recalled in 1977 a few other details of the first day: how they went back to the Pecos ruin itself after supper and talked around a campfire, after which Neil Judd and Haury took Clara Lee and Hulda to the village of Pecos, to spend the night in the Erickson home. Presumably Judd and Haury then returned to Kidder's camp, but Haury adds in his rough notes of 1977, "Where did I stay?" The next morning Haury drove to Santa Fe to pick up the Morleys, taking them back after the day's sessions were over. On Wednesday, 31 August, Dean Cummings and his passengers left for Tucson, had two more flat tires, and spent the night in Lordsburg, almost to the Arizona line. Haury recalled, also, that the Conference was an exhilarating occasion for the "neophyte archaeologists," who had a chance to become acquainted with "the *greats* of the time." He concluded, "What a heady experience that was!" More recently Haury has also said that

> Clara Lee and I retain a common impression that the people in
> the 1927 Conference who were doing the talking were not only
> active archaeologists, but tackled the problems with dignity
> and maturity. There were differences of opinion [as detailed by
> Halseth, below], but they were resolved to the extent possible
> in a professional manner. . . . The four students, and here I in-

clude Charlotte Gower and Paul Martin, and the two of us, were too awed to open our mouths. It was a key learning experience [letter to Woodbury, 18 September 1981].

Additional recollections of the first Conference come from Odd Halseth, who wrote a statement for the 1963 Conference, to memorialize the death of A. V. Kidder earlier that summer.

Those of you who attended that meeting [in 1927] will remember the friendly spirit which prevailed around the Pecos camp fires, even when arguments sometimes reached climactic passages. The meeting laid a foundation for a tradition in Southwestern archeology, which Kidder himself referred to as the "Pecos Clan Spirit," and many of us have benefitted from the friendships which were cemented on that occasion.

Since this happened 36 years ago, it might be well to review briefly the status of Southwestern archeology at that time. It may not be too far amiss to say that it was just emerging from a metaphysical stage into an accelerated period of specialization in both perspective and technology. There were few schools teaching this specialty, but in several places faculties and training programs were geared to produce teachers who, in turn, produced archeological technicians.

At Harvard men like Putnam, Tozzer, and Dixon turned out men like Kidder and Morley, among others. Kroeber, Waterman, and Gifford built similar programs at Berkeley; Boas had a strong program going at Columbia, although his students seldom turned to archeology. Cole and Redfield were building up the department at Chicago, Cummings was going strong at Tucson and Renaud was starting a department in Denver.

Dr. Hewett presided over the School of American Research, as well as the museums in Santa Fe and San Diego, and while not connected with a university department, offered opportunities for students to participate in excavation work. In fact, Kidder, among others, began his archeological studies under Dr. Hewett's direction.

The only background available to students in the early twenties came from the writings of Bandelier, Holmes, Fewkes, Hough, Hodge, Mindeleff, Cushing and a few others. Their combined results in reporting were not yet clearly synthesized, however, and selection of sites and methods of excavation were still, to some degree, based more on museum prerogatives than upon planned research.

This is where Dr. Kidder's influence made the greatest impact on Southwestern archeology as we know it today. He was the sparkplug, even though his methods of seeking and getting cooperation were always low-voltage. His personality as well as his scholarship disarmed any rebel in camp, and though no one could be more generous and kind, his integrity of purpose and judgment never was compromised. . . . He also had a faculty of subtle communication which inspired as much as it taught; and though his good humor was always close to the surface, one never failed to feel his everlasting dignity in all he said and did. . . .

To give a purely personal impression of the first Pecos Conference, I must be excused for indulging in reminiscences. In the first place there was at the time considerable competition for acceptance of archeological classifications and terminology, particularly by those who were teaching. I remember Cummings complaining that his students were sometimes confused by the number of overlapping and conflicting terms then in use, and advocated one of his own. Renaud spoke up and said he was thankful that his students were smart enough to understand all of them and would probably come up with one of their own. Before this kind of discussion could reach a personal level, Kidder would interject a statement to the effect that what we placed on the hatrack was more important than the shape of the rack itself, and everyone got the point, I think.

There were also several heated discussions about what areas properly should be included within the so-called Pueblo Culture. The San Juan, Little Colorado, Rio Grande, Mimbres, and Chihuahua Basin were pretty well established, but the peripheral areas to the east, south and west needed clearer definitions. To the east we had the state of Texas, which some Southwesterners still considered a state of mind with which they would rather not be associated. The western periphery was mostly unknown, except for M. R. Harrington's work in Nevada, and the Upper and Lower Gila cultures had not yet been synthesized into a workable scheme.

In San Diego I had met Malcolm Rogers and seen his digs and carefully prepared notes, and suggested he be consulted on the western problem. Kroeber asked for Mac's address and stopped off to see him on his return home. He wrote me that it had been a most worthwhile visit.

There were also a few of us who felt that the Gila Basin problems should be investigated more fully before we made up a final map of Southwestern culture areas. Rogers and I had been through this area in 1922 and we both felt that the ecology of the whole desert region needed much more attention than it had so far received. It was this impression which eventually caused my move to Phoenix. Kidder agreed with my suggestion at the meeting, as he did with my later move, and through the years followed the archeology of this region with keen interest.

Those of you who were there remember that there was no standing on prerogatives at the early Pecos Conferences. I believe it was M. R. Harrington who showed up with an air mattress, the first seen in an archeological camp. Poor M. R. had to patch his bed every night before turning in. Ted and Madeleine ran a hospitable and comfortable camp and set a wonderful table, but an air mattress was just too much for all of us. Students who came with their teachers were asked for their opinions and were heard and noted for their contributions [Laboratory of Anthropology files].

When Paul Martin was asked by Gordon R. Willey in the early 1970s to look back and write about his archaeological career for *Archaeological Researches in Retrospect,* he mentioned the pleasure he felt at receiving Kidder's invitation to Pecos, as quoted earlier. He went on with additional recollections:

I would say that my being invited was pure luck as I was a greenhorn with only a little experience in the mounds of Illinois and the Mayan cities. Here I had a chance to meet all the eminent archaeologists and ethnologists of the time. I could mix freely and informally with them at meals and during our discussion times, as we lounged under the pinyon trees on the mesa and in our sleeping quarters. I was housed with A. L. Kroeber, T. T. Waterman, Joe Spinden, who had a leak in his air mattress [did Halseth mis-recall this as being Harrington's?] and swore at it every night, Earl Morris and Karl Ruppert! [Martin is incorrect on Ruppert, who was at the 1929 Conference, but not that of 1927.] Imagine my feelings of awe at being permitted to share bunk space with them. The excitement of those moments and of the conference are still as fresh in my mind now as they were in 1927.

Among other things, my superior in Denver, the President of the Historical Society, wanted me to seek advice on whether digging in southwestern Colorado was worthwhile. He also wanted to know whether there were sites that the Society (relatively poor) could afford to excavate [Martin 1974: 5].

The differences of opinion that Haury and Halseth mention did not, quite naturally, become part of the official record of the Conference. But recollection has survived in Santa Fe, as oral history, that Edgar Lee Hewett walked out of the Conference, saying that the proposed classification system would never work and would never be accepted by other archaeologists (Marjorie Lambert, conversation with Woodbury, 2 March 1980). Haury recalled the event: "Hewett was there for only part of the time the conference was in session, but I wasn't smart enough to realize at the time what the reason may have been. He was an individualist and nobody was going to push him around" (Emil Haury, letter to Woodbury, 31 March 1980). Hewett was also about to have a meeting of the Museum of New Mexico board of regents in Santa Fe, but his premature departure from the Pecos Conference probably had deeper roots than just skepticism about the usefulness of the Pecos Classification or a busy schedule. Behind it lay a long and sometimes bitter rivalry between Hewett and other archaeologists working in the Southwest. Hewett was ambitious to develop and direct institutions and activities, centered in the Santa Fe area, but also including southern California, while his scholarly contributions were becoming increasingly insubstantial. As early as 1910, A. M. Tozzer of Harvard University wrote about Hewett in a long letter to Gardiner Lang, a Boston financier, a letter that was not published until many years later. Following detailed comments on Hewett's weaknesses as a scholar, Tozzer concluded:

> As for Hewett's standing among the American archaeologists I can say, I think, with truth that with the exception of certain people connected with the Bureau of Ethnology and the Smithsonian at Washington together with personal friends in the west there is not a person connected with a scientific institution in the country which is doing work in American anthropology who approves of Hewett's work [Hinsley 1980].

A hint of Kidder's own feelings about Hewett occurs in an unusually blunt and uncomplimentary comment in the introduction to *The Pottery of Pecos,* volume 1: "In the above summary of Rio Grande archaeology I have been unable to evaluate the long series of excavations carried out by the School of American Research and the Museum of New Mexico because their results remain, practically speaking, unpublished" (Kidder 1931: 7 n. 5). Kidder was very rarely other than kindly, even overly generous, in his comments on the work of others.

Jesse Nusbaum's recollections are worth noting, also, since he worked for Hewett for many years and knew him well. In *Tierra Dulce: Reminiscences from the Jesse Nusbaum Papers* he is quoted as saying, in a short chapter on Hewett:

> Edgar L. Hewett was difficult in the earlier days . . . [ellipsis in original] always taking leads where he thought he'd get a following. He wanted things done fast, you'd do it and then he would leave for the Near East, Athens, or Rome and then casually take credit for your work. . . . As he grew older he became more fearful of change and improvement. He fought the ideas of younger men. Kidder at the Pecos Ruins had a hard time. Ideas other than his own were an anathema to Hewett and he opposed them [Nusbaum 1980: 21].

And he added a reminiscence: "I wasn't alone in my impression of Hewett. I recall one night sitting up until the small hours . . . with Sylvanus G. Morley, J. Eric Thompson, and Oliver Ricketson, Jr., . . . Dwight W. Rife . . . and Mr. Shufeldt. . . . This night Hewett's name came up distastefully several times regarding his relations with others" (Nusbaum 1980: 22–23).

Finally Nusbaum quoted a limerick sent him later by Eric Thompson, composed by Beatrice Blackwood of the Pitt-Rivers Museum of Oxford, who had been "a member of Hewett's archaeological field camp in the Jemez Canyon" (Nusbaum 1980: 22):

> *There was an old duffer called Hewett*
> *Who was head of the school—and he knew it.*
> *When anyone came, who knew naught of his fame*
> *He took out his trumpet, and blew it.*

As with the occasional frictions at Pecos in 1927, so the amusing and lighter incidents of the Conference did not become part of the official record. One such item was recalled in 1967 by Erna Gunther, however: "after a day's discussion of the Kiva Rob [Spier], who was then five years old and had sat patiently through much of it, turned to his father and said, 'But Leslie, what is a kiva?' " (Gunther, letter to R. H. Thompson, 15 May 1967). Kidder's own version of this discussion, published in his report in *Science*, reads:

> There was much discussion of the term "kiva" and of such parts of the kiva as the ventilating passage, the fire-screen or deflector, etc. It was agreed that ceremonial rooms varied so greatly in form and interior arrangement, and the types shaded into each other so imperceptibly that no valid distinction as to essential function could be drawn between, for instance, round and square, or between above-ground and subterranean examples. The following very broad definition was thereby adopted: A kiva is a chamber specially constructed for ceremonial purposes[Kidder 1927: 490].

A half century later, in spite of this succinct "definition" and Watson Smith's classic essay, "When Is a Kiva?" (Smith 1952b, 1990), Rob Spier's question is still being asked.

The best-known and most influential accomplishment of the 1927 Conference was the Pecos Classification, defining successive periods of Southwestern culture history. It may have been created by the conferees, prepared in rough form ahead of time and perfected by the conferees, or presented as an essentially complete statement to be endorsed at the Conference. Whichever of these guesses may be correct, the Classification was immediately influential and has continued so. Before looking at the evidence for its origin, I will sketch the nature of the Classification.

In his own account of the Conference, Kidder briefly recounts the sequence of events in the Southwest from nonagricultural, prepottery times to the historic period, and then describes the development of the Classification:

> The meeting attempted, as a basis for more precise definition of culture-stages, to arrive at agreement as to diagnostic culture-traits. A sub-committee prepared a chronological tabulation of elements, which was used during the subsequent discussions. Architecture was considered to be of much value as an index of growth; as were village types, sandals, pictographs, etc. Much

further information, both as to nature and distribution, was decided to be needed, however, before these categories can be used with full confidence. Pottery it was agreed, is at the present time the most abundant, convenient and reliable criterion, and the cooking wares the simplest type for preliminary chronological determinations [Kidder 1927: 490].

There follows a short "outline of development": (1) plain wares; (2) neck corrugations; (3) spiral corrugations with indentations over the entire vessel; (4) "a degeneration of the corrugated technique"; and (5) return to plain surfaces.

Kidder's report in *Science* presents the complete, but briefly characterized, list of time periods that has been known ever since as the Pecos Classification. But he includes more than a hint of divergent views that were only partially reconciled in the Conference's sessions:

During all the discussions leading to development of the above outlines, there kept arising questions of period nomenclature. Entire unanimity was not achieved but the following terms for chronologically sequent periods proved acceptable to the majority:

Basket Maker I, or Early Basket Maker—a postulated (and perhaps recently discovered) stage, pre-agricultural, yet adumbrating later developments.

Basket Maker II, or Basket Maker—the agricultural, atlatl-using, non-pottery making stage, as described in many publications.

Late Basket Maker, Basket Maker III, or Post-Basket Maker— the pit- or slab-house-building, pottery-making stage (the three Basket Maker stages are characterized by a long-headed population, which did not practice skull-deformation).

Pueblo I, or Proto-Pueblo—the first stage during which cranial deformation was practiced, vessel neck corrugation was introduced, and villages composed of rectangular living-rooms of true masonry were developed (it was generally agreed that the term pre-Pueblo, hitherto sometimes applied to this period, should be discontinued).

Pueblo II—the stage marked by widespread geographical extension of life in small villages; corrugation, often elaborate in technique, extended over the whole surface of cooking vessels.

Pueblo III, or Great Period—the stage of large communities, great development of the arts, and growth of intensive local specialization.

Pueblo IV, or Proto-Historic—the stage characterized by contraction of area occupied; by the gradual disappearance of corrugated wares; and, in general, by decline from the preceding cultural peak.

Pueblo V, or Historic—the period from 1600 A.D. to the present.

In his report for *Masterkey,* Amsden described the genesis of the Pecos Classification in this way:

> One of the most interesting and significant accomplishments of the Pecos Conference was agreement upon a recognition—perhaps tentative and subject to modification, but sufficiently clearly indicated to warrant scientific acceptance—of a division into periods of the development of the predominant cultures of the Southwestern region: the Basketmaker and its successor, the Pueblo [Amsden 1927: 16].

The origins of the Pecos Classification, always considered to be Kidder's own creation, were unequivocally credited to Waterman in remarks Kidder made at the 1948 Pecos Conference at Point of Pines, its twenty-first year, when the Conference "came of age." Kidder said, "The first Pecos Conference . . . is best known for its formulation of the Pecos Classification of Southwestern prehistory. This Classification came as a suggestion of the late T. T. Waterman, a fact which appears not to be generally known" (Haury 1949). Kidder added, however, that he accepted personal responsibility "for introducing the term Basketmaker I which . . . still only meets a theoretical requirement of the time scale." It seems probable, nevertheless, that Kidder and others contributed substantially to formulating the details of the Classification, even though Waterman's year in Tucson would have enabled him to learn much of what was then known about the Southwest. Kidder himself had used a general scheme of culturally defined chronological units in his *Introduction* in 1924. It appears in his discussion of the San Juan drainage, the area most fully described because it was, as he wrote, "in many ways the best known archaeologically of the major territorial divisions of the Southwest" (Kidder 1924: 47, 49). His classificatory units are:

- Sites with no pottery (Basket Maker sites)
- Sites with crude pottery (post–Basket Maker ruins)
- Sites with less-developed pottery (Pre-Pueblo ruins)
- Sites with well-developed pottery (Pueblo ruins)

It is difficult to say now just what Waterman's role really was, as Kidder's crediting him with it in his 1948 remarks may simply be one more example of Kidder's well-known generosity and modesty, traits that all his friends were familiar with, and which crop up again and again in his writing.

Regardless of how credit should be assigned, the Pecos Classification can be seen as building on Kidder's and his colleagues' prevailing ideas in the late 1920s, and the accomplishment of the Conference was not to create a wholly new system of time periods but to codify their criteria and secure agreement among Southwestern archaeologists. In his invitation to Earl Morris, Kidder had referred to "the various questions of problems, methods, and nomenclature which we discussed in a preliminary way in Judd's office," which sounds suspiciously like the initial plans for the Classification. Perhaps the most important point is that without Kidder's espousal of the Classification as agreed on and quickly published, Southwestern archaeologists would have continued to use various schemes.

Haury, asked about his recollections of the sources of the Classification, wrote:

> On the genesis of the Pecos Classification, both Clara Lee's and my memories are vague. We both recall extended discussions of the substance of different periods in the evolutionary picture which preceded the formulation of the period labels. Those discussions took up the major part of the Conference time. I suspect that although Kidder, as I recall, presented the Classification as we know it, it may have been formulated in a rump session between Roberts, possibly Waterman, Morris, and Kidder [and Judd?], but this is only a surmise. I can understand that Roberts may have had a hand in it, but the fact that he revamped the structure within a few years, leads me to believe that he might not have been altogether happy with the Pecos Conference formula [Emil Haury, letter to Woodbury, 18 September 1981].

Several years later Haury recalled in conversation that Waterman followed up the discussion of various traits—such as the first pottery, the earliest black-on-white decoration, the earliest black-on-red, and polychrome, and certain architectural traits—with comments on their potential value as time markers. Haury also recalled that Waterman may have suggested numbering the time units, with Kidder urging that an "unknown" Basketmaker I be included as a "period of development that adumbrated" the advanced basket making that was the earliest known yet. Haury also observed that "if Kidder said it, it must be true" (conversation with Woodbury, Wilderness Inn, Pecos, 14 August 1987). Frank Roberts's role in the origin of the Pecos Classification is described briefly, probably pretty much in his own words, in the Forty-fifth Annual Report of the Bureau of American Ethnology: "While at the conference he [Roberts] assisted in the drafting of a new outline of the sequence of cultural stages in southwestern prehistoric and early historic development of the sedentary Indian groups" (Dorsey 1930: 7).

The most reasonable conclusion may be that Kidder had gradually matured the general idea of the Classification over a period of years; that he discussed it in at least preliminary fashion with close friends and colleagues, such as Judd and Morris; that Waterman, as an outsider, was asked to take an impartial look at it; and that Kidder had the tact and acumen not to present it at the Conference as a fait accompli but rather to let the group work out mutually agreeable details in the course of a couple of days of informal discussion, including the relaxed atmosphere of the evening campfire. But even then it was not equally acceptable to all. Halseth recalled that Cummings expressed himself somewhat negatively on the proposal (quoted above). Hewett even walked out of the Conference, if tradition is correct, either to emphasize his objection to the Classification or simply to show that he had more important things to do elsewhere. Roberts probably had reservations, as Haury suggests, although he promptly began casting his introductory summaries to field reports in the Classification's terms (*Shabik'eschee Village* [Roberts 1929], *Early Ruins in the Piedra District* [Roberts 1930], and *The Ruins at Kiatuthlanna* [Roberts 1931]). Only in 1932 in *The Village of the Great Kivas* (Roberts 1932) did he modify the Pecos system by dividing both Pueblo III and Pueblo IV into early and late phases. During these years no one else was publishing such careful summaries of the status of Southwestern archaeology, and Roberts's use of the Classification did much to make it familiar and acceptable.

About a decade later Morris, an active participant in the 1927 Conference, wrote at some length concerning the Conference and particularly the Pecos Classification.

With the hope of bringing order into the [Southwest archaeo-
logical] situation Kidder, in August 1927, convened an archaeological conference at his camp at Pecos Ruin, New Mexico. The
meeting was widely attended. The many workers thus brought
together to a large extent threshed out their differences and
pretty generally agreed upon a system of nomenclature to cover
the Basket Maker-Pueblo cycle. . . .

The Pecos chronology has been so severely criticized that
perhaps I should also rake it over the coals, but I do not feel inclined to in a very serious way. Assuredly the system is far from
perfect, but with adaptations I have found it both usable and
useful. Its formal appearance in tabular presentation tends to
foster the impression that the various culture strata are like the
layers of a cake, each one of uniform thickness and definitely
set off from those above and below, thus imposing definite time
limits on the respective units. Nothing, I believe, was farther
from the intention of those who had most to do with drawing
up the table. I, for one, regarded it as an expression of the ideal-
ised norm of development from Basket Maker-Pueblo culture
in which all chronological connotations previous to 1540 were
relative [Morris 1939: 3–4].

Morris's role in designing the Pecos Classification was clearly recalled years later by Judd, who wrote:

In tribute to his experience and retentive memory, Earl Morris
was drafted at the first Pecos Conference in 1927 to supply much-
needed information regarding distribution of the Pre-Pueblos
and the Basketmakers. No one else could furnish that information in equal measure. Having travelled the length and breadth
of the Anasazi domain, peering into every nook and corner, he
knew where and how the Old People had lived [Judd 1969: 92].

Writing not long after the Conference, Kroeber commented that
with the Pecos Classification,

Kidder . . . was able to weld the prehistory of the most distinctive part of the [Southwest] area in a comprehensive and
continuous whole of two Basket Maker and five Pueblo periods. This fundamental work will no doubt be corrected in detail,
enriched and intensified, and certainly is in need of areal ex-

tension; but its framework promises to be permanent [Kroeber 1928: 375].

However, a systematic classification of Southwestern cultural development was by no means the only item that Kidder had on his ambitious agenda for this Conference. In his 1927 report in *Science* he listed four others, all of which received some serious attention during the sessions:

1. Nomenclature for architecture, geographical areas, pottery types and shapes, elements of ceramic decoration, and "a binomial ware-nomenclature" were all up for discussion, but apparently little if any consensus emerged, and these topics were postponed, "to be kept in mind by those present and gone into at a possible future gathering."

2. "A survey was made of work now in progress or in contemplation." This has become a firmly held tradition at subsequent Pecos Conferences, usually referred to now as "field reports." In 1927, Kidder stated, it became apparent that "certain central areas" of the Southwest "were under intensive study," but "the peripheral regions, with the exception of Nevada, are being neglected." Kidder went on to specify the areas that most needed additional attention—southwestern Arizona, Sonora, Chihuahua, and eastern New Mexico. And he pointed out that even in the central area, "the Little Colorado in general and the Hopi country in particular" needed more study. Chronologically, he said, Basket Maker III and Pueblo III were receiving much more attention than other periods of time. And he emphasized the need for more intensive rather than extensive work, with "each excavation a model of care and thoroughness." This observation perhaps was chiefly directed to the work of a few of his eminent seniors, who dug at many sites briefly, worked in different locations in rapid succession, and often issued only the most superficial reports on the work. Fewkes and Hewett come to mind as "hit and run" archaeologists of the time.

3. The problems of work on public lands, relations between field workers and National Park Service personnel, the "rights and duties of states and outside institutions," and the problems of unauthorized digging, which the Antiquities Act of 1906 had done disappointingly little to solve, were matters of concern.

4. There was a report by A. E. Douglass, whom many of the participants were assisting in the collection of beam samples.

G. E. Webb has written:

On the second day of the conference, Douglass presented a brief address entitled "Archaeological Side of Tree Rings and Climatic Records." He explained his technique, showing how the bridge method led to a gradual extension of the tree-ring chronology. He emphasized, however, that the gaps in the record prevented the calculation of absolute dates. To close these gaps, he appealed for continued and increased assistance from field workers to add to his archaeological wood specimens [Webb 1983: 134–135].

As if all this were not enough, yet another topic is mentioned by Amsden in his *Masterkey* report, a topic that Kidder does not specifically allude to in his 1927 report:

> The place of the Pueblo culture . . . in the great general plan of American civilization was discussed at length by the Conference, and many interesting points of contact between the Pueblo and the peoples of Mexico and Central America were brought out. Corn is the great link, for corn is exclusively American. . . . Maize had its origin, certainly, in the highlands of Mexico . . . but the true relationship of the various people to whom corn was life cannot yet be stated; a later conference, perhaps, will clear up the uncertainty which surrounds this vital question [Amsden 1927: 18].

Although both Kidder and Amsden referred in general terms to a future "conference," or "gathering," there does not appear to have been any agreement on a time or place, or any plan for reconvening the group. In more recent Pecos Conferences there has always been a serious effort to agree on who would host the next meeting, and to make at least minimal arrangements for continuity. In 1927, Amsden at least implied, the feeling was that another conference would be appropriate in the fairly distant future. He said, "At some later time they will meet again and measure progress from this first conference, as from a milestone at the beginning of the way."

To bring our consideration of the first Conference to a close, we should ask the difficult questions of what it accomplished and what long-term importance it had. Kroeber's evaluation of the 1927 Conference has been quoted above. A few other judgments have been expressed through the years. But the best contemporary indication of its impact (or lack of it) is in the letters to *Teocentli* that appeared in December 1927, for which Carl Guthe probably sent a reminder to readers in October. There were letters from eleven of the archaeologists who had been at the Pecos Conference a couple of months before. Of these, six made no mention of it at all, summarizing other activities of the past six months but omitting the meeting at Pecos: C. B. Cosgrove, Halseth, Judd, Kidder, Mera, and Oliver Ricketson. Cummings, on the other hand, wrote:

> Since I last sent in my report of my doings, I have been trying to guide the University of Arizona [as acting president] along the path of right living and to establish peace and amity among men. Archaeologically, I have enjoyed the conference at Pecos and a brief visit to Santa Fe.

Harrington also mentioned the Conference favorably, if briefly: "I attended the Pecos Archeological Conference, where I learned a lot." Morris was noncommittal: "After attending the Pecos Conference during the latter days of August, I immediately began seven weeks of digging." Renaud had the most enthusiastic comment of those who mentioned it: "Then drove to Santa Fe; later attended the Pecos Symposium, the best and most interesting and useful anthropological meeting I ever attended . . . I sent to France for publication . . . a short report on the Pecos meeting." (No copy of this report has been found.) Finally, Frank Roberts noted, "I spent the latter part of August in reconnaissance . . . and then attended the Pecos Conference." It would be unfair to read too much into these few and rather perfunctory personal comments, as *Teocentli* at that time seemed to elicit almost uniformly dry, terse, and impersonal statements of the writers' archaeological activities, with opinions and evaluations at a minimum. But "those present at the creation" do seem to have returned to ordinary routines with little awareness that they had participated in a historic event.

Kidder's own view, a decade later, was that formal classifications "are useful when our task is to reduce to order, and to bring meaning into, a mass of more or less disconnected data. But as archaeological findings group themselves to form a historical picture, systematic rigidities are better eschewed" (Kidder and Shepard 1936: xviii n. 3).

One relatively recent evaluation of the Pecos Conference is that of Florence and Robert Lister, in their biography of Morris. They say of those attending that after evaluating past accomplishments, they set about charting the future course of Southwestern archaeology. . . . The importance of this first Pecos Conference . . . cannot be overestimated. It set the guidelines for the future, the Pecos Classification which became the chart every Southwesterner consulted in assigning his ruin a place. There were faults in its rigidity, as future work revealed, and a decided overestimation of time involved which would be corrected by dendrochronological evidence. There was danger in the use of a system because it inadvertently would force the fitting of sites into a framework, sometimes without much evidence beyond one or two elements called "diagnostic." But it was a giant step forward. It did much to wipe out a terminological muddle in which more than one worker had been mired. . . . It was a series of astute surmises based upon a surprisingly small number of excavations, many of which were unpublished [Lister and Lister 1968: 85, 87].

Paul Martin, in his chapter for Gordon R. Willey's 1974 *Archaeological Researches in Retrospect,* added to the recollections already quoted: "the archaeologists present at the conference forged a synthesis that came to be called the 'Pecos Classification' and that even today has much value and is freely used by many workers in the field for a quick and handy reference to a culture stage. . . . Its supreme value was that it brought order out of chaos and placed cultures relative to one another in a rough lineal framework" (Martin 1974: 5). Only the year before, however, Martin and Fred Plog had mentioned, in *The Archaeology of Arizona* (1973: 28), "the Pecos Conference, the first conference of Southwestern workers to discuss the new ideas that were rocking the world. It is still held annually, although nowadays it is spiritless and given to mouthing old incantations; it needs a rebirth."

Not only in 1927 but down through the years, the Pecos Conference has been seen by many as almost inseparable from the man who convened it, guided its discussions, provided initiative, combined enthusiasm with skepticism in responding to the ideas of others, and added wit and charm to even the most businesslike statements. Writing in 1965, Haury commented on Kidder's central role in the Conference: "he was a man full of humility in his own accomplishments and it was this fact, I believe, as well as any other, that made the first Pecos

Conference so productive" (Emil Haury, letter to Robert Wauchope, 19 April 1965).

An indication of Kidder's view that the Conference was successful is his replication of it at Chichen Itza in 1930 and 1931, where he had taken charge of the Carnegie Institution's Maya program. Of the first "Chichen Conference," in January 1930, he writes: "there was held at the archaeological field station . . . at the ruins of Chichen Itza an informal conference of persons interested in development of researches bearing upon the history of man in the Yucatan peninsula . . . without agenda and in a purely preliminary way" (Kidder 1930).

Perhaps the strongest evidence of the importance of the first Pecos Conference, in addition to the continued use of the Classification it produced, is that the Conference has continued to the present day, in spite of lapses in the early 1930s and during World War II. In 1946 it was revived and has continued on an annual basis to the present, growing in size and complexity. The arguments as to its "ideal" or "proper" structure and organization; the discussions over informal versus formal presentations, over reports of current work versus syntheses of major areas or problems; and the disagreements over who should or should not participate: all attest to the concern Southwesternists have for it. Even Martin and Plog urged "rebirth," not euthanasia. As an organization with no headquarters, no governing board or executive committee, no continuing officers, no treasury, no members, and no charter or bylaws, the Pecos Conference has shown remarkable vitality. And it has preserved to a substantial degree its original function of making possible an exchange of current information and ideas on archaeological and other research in the Southwest, in an informal and relatively open setting. As one would expect, there have been changes through the years, swings of emphasis, innovations in format, and these, as well as the continuities, are discussed in the pages that follow.

THE SECOND PECOS CONFERENCE, 1929   No time or place for the next Pecos Conference had been settled on in 1927, contrary to the practice that developed later. There was, however, general agreement that another conference should take place, both to review archaeologists' success (or lack of it) in putting the Pecos Classification to use and to exchange information on recent field work. Kidder was not working at Pecos in 1928, so a conference there would not have been possible. But with the rapid progress in tree-ring dating made by the Second

Beam Expedition in 1928 and the breakthrough that came with the Third Beam Expedition in 1929, there was now a special reason for archaeologists to meet, hear the results, and discuss their implications.

When Judd and Douglass arrived at Show Low, Arizona, on 22 June 1929, Haury and Lyndon Hargrave, who had been excavating for charred beams at the Whipple Ruin there, were able to offer specimens that gave promise of "closing the gap." Douglass, with the assistance of many archaeologists, had developed a ring chronology extending back from living trees to about A.D. 1300, and there was a "floating" sequence of 585 years that was presumed earlier, but by how much was unknown. That night at Show Low it was determined that one of the new specimens, HH—39, did indeed overlap both sequences, thus providing a continuous chronology of more than 1,200 years (Haury 1962; see also Judd 1930). Now archaeologists would have the actual dates when roof beams had been cut at long-famous ruins. (One from Cliff Palace, Mesa Verde, was cut in A.D. 1073, for example, and dates from White House in Canyon de Chelly extended from 1060 to 1090.) It was also discovered that most Pueblo III sites were younger and their period of occupancy shorter than had been supposed. Previous estimates of the antiquity of Basketmaker materials were "cut . . . in half," as was the prevailing opinion on the age of Pueblo Bonito (Emil Haury, letter to Woodbury, 8 April 1984).

It is difficult now to recover the sense of excitement that these solid results of many years of patient work on tree-ring specimens brought to Southwestern archaeology, but the new information from Beam HH—39 and its promise for the future would be a central topic when the Pecos Conference met that summer.

There would be plenty to report at the Conference in August 1929 besides the news about tree-ring dating. "Archaeological Field Work in North America during 1929" (Guthe 1930) lists more than forty separate archaeological investigations in the Southwest. Their nature and geographical distribution suggest that archaeologists were paying at least some attention to the views expressed at the 1927 Conference on the need for more research in areas other than the best-studied "central" region. There were surveys of several poorly known areas, including (1) Judd's survey of irrigation canals along the Salt and Gila rivers, which were about to be obliterated by reclamation work; (2) continuation of Gila Pueblo's widespread surveys, bringing to 2,500 the number of sites from which the Gladwins had sherd collections; (3) reconnaissance by J. Alden Mason of both the Navajo

Mountain area and the Canadian River in the Texas Panhandle, for possible Pueblo-Panhandle connections; (4) a search by the Cosgroves in the mountains north of Silver City, New Mexico, for Mimbres extensions; (5) the start of a statewide archaeological survey by Reginald Fisher for the School of American Research and the University of New Mexico, under Hewett's direction; (6) continuation by Noel Morss for the Peabody Museum, Harvard University, of the study of the Fremont area of Utah; (7) exploration in Utah west of Moab by William Claflin, Raymond Emerson, and Henry Roberts for the Peabody Museum of "a hitherto unknown archaeological field"; and (8) continuing search by the Colorado Museum of Natural History for Folsom sites in Yuma County, Colorado.

In the months just before the 1929 Pecos Conference, excavation of sites in the better known parts of the Southwest included that by Morris in Antelope Cave, Canyon del Muerto, where Ann Morris made a systematic record of the pictographs; Morris's excavation in the La Plata—Mancos area for the Colorado Museum of Natural History; and Martin's work in Montezuma County, Colorado, in both "unit-type" and "rim-rock" sites. Continued enthusiasm for the Mimbres culture and its pottery is reflected in the excavations by Paul Nesbitt of Beloit College at the Mattocks Ruin and by Albert Jenks at the Galaz Ruin for the University of Minnesota and the Minneapolis Institute of Fine Arts.

Some of the peripheral or less known areas received increased attention, such as the Little Colorado drainage and the Hopi country, with Roberts's excavation of Kiatuthlanna on the Long H Ranch, forty-five miles west of Zuni; work by Cummings and his students at Turkey Hill, near Flagstaff; excavation of kivas at Wide Ruin (also known as Kintiel) and Kokopnyama by Hargrave for the Museum of Northern Arizona, Flagstaff. In Nevada Harrington dug at Mesa House. Caves in the Hueco area of southern New Mexico were dug by Cambridge University in cooperation with the Museum of the American Indian, New York. In southern Arizona Arthur Woodward examined "small compounds" just east of Casa Grande, for the Southwest Museum, Los Angeles, and Halseth began excavating Pueblo Grande, which was then "five miles east of Phoenix." In addition, Guthe's report of 1929 field work mentions one of the first systematic ceramic studies in the Southwest, that of Chaco Canyon pottery by Florence Hawley, then a student at the University of Arizona.

Archaeological training programs, so numerous in later decades, were making significant beginnings. The Laboratory of Anthropology archaeological fellows under Kidder's direction worked at Pecos and at Tsama Ruin near Abiquiu in the Chama Valley. The School of American Research and the University of New Mexico resumed work at Chetro Ketl in Chaco Canyon, with a six-week field school, and the same university continued its Jemez archaeological field school.

From Andover, Massachusetts, Kidder sent out a "Memorandum re proposed field conference," dated 2 February 1929. He said the three groups of the Laboratory of Anthropology's summer scholarship students would meet at Pecos the first week of August, and "it has been suggested that the last three days of the week might possibly be devoted to a second informal conference upon Southwestern problems, similar to the one held in 1927. I should be very pleased to have your opinions as to the desirability of holding such conference." He also asked to know who might attend and said that if a conference was decided on he would send out agenda suggestions later. Enthusiasm for a second conference was not unanimous. N. C. Nelson wrote to Kidder (21 February 1929), "As to my opinion about another informal conference at Pecos, it isn't worth much. I have only a superficial notion of what really happened at the last one. On general principles I shouldn't suppose that once in two years would be too often, provided you can get a fair-size bunch together." Nelson went on to say that he would not be in the Southwest that summer, anyway. Before that (6 February 1929) Hewett had written:

> My dear Dr. Kidder:
> I am in receipt of your memorandum of the 2nd ult. with reference to your proposed field conference at Pecos. Unhappily, I shall be completely tied up during that week with our field school at Battleship Rock. I doubt if I could get away for even an hours [*sic*] attendance at the conference.
> As always,
>
> Very sincerely yours
> [No signature on file copy]

Halseth, however, responded positively on 12 February 1929, saying in part:

> I wish to state most emphatically that another field conference will be more than desirable. These meetings, to my mind, are necessary and should be held at least once a year. As you have stated to me previously, there is nothing like personal contact to

clarify things and the field conferences certainly accomplish this better than any other medium of contact.

Kidder sent out a later notice, giving the dates as 22–24 August, asking for a response from those coming, "whether and when you will arrive by train or motor; and whether or not you can bring: (a) tent, (b) bedroll. The station for Pecos is Glorieta; mail to Pecos; telegrams to Glorieta."

The Second Pecos Conference was convened 22 August 1929 by Kidder at his field camp, site of the first Conference, and lasted to the 25th. In a report published in *Masterkey* (Anonymous 1929) it is described as "a congress of workers in archaeological and ethnological research," which was a departure from the overwhelmingly archaeological orientation of 1927. A look at the list of participants demonstrates this difference, although archaeologists are still a large majority (Table 3.1). Newcomers included C. Daryll Forde, A. I. Hallowell, Paul Kirchhoff, Gladys A. Reichard, Clark Wissler, and a group of four ethnology students with Laboratory of Anthropology summer fellowships (the first year of this program) working under the supervision of A. L. Kroeber. Folklore was represented by J. Frank Dobie, and there were three linguistics students in the Laboratory program, directed by Edward Sapir. In the years ahead there would be arguments as to whether the Pecos Conference was really an archaeological conference or whether it should include all anthropological research going on in the Southwest. As will be seen, the archaeologists continued to dominate the Conferences by a large majority, but many of them gave at least token agreement to the idea of a broader, more inclusive meeting, and in many Conferences at least a few ethnologists took part, and sometimes even linguists and physical anthropologists.

The second Conference, like the first, had a substantial influence on the future course of Pecos Conferences, not least in the composition of the participating group—their institutional affiliations, geographical distribution, professional status, and particular interests. Therefore, it is fortunate that the *Masterkey* report on the Conference lists the attendees (see Table 3.1) and that we also have a record of the Laboratory of Anthropology students, all of whom attended (A. V. Kidder, letter to Stanley Stubbs, 1952, Pecos Conference Archives, Laboratory of Anthropology). It will be noticed that all the ethnology students were men while three of the five archaeology students were women, contrary to the anthropological folklore that archaeology was not receptive to women students in the field.

Table 3.1. Participants in the 1929 Pecos Conference
(Affiliation as reported in *The Masterkey*)

Charles Amsden, Southwest Museum

Katharine Bartlett, University of Denver

Wesley Bradfield, Museum of New Mexico

Kenneth M. Chapman, Laboratory of Anthropology

C. U. Clark, Smithsonian Institution

Harold S. Colton, Museum of Northern Arizona

C. Burton Cosgrove, Peabody Museum, Harvard

Harriet S. Cosgrove, Peabody Museum, Harvard

J. Frank Dobie, University of Texas

C. Daryll Forde, University of California

Harold S. Gladwin, Gila Pueblo

Carl E. Guthe, University of Michigan

A. Irving Hallowell, University of Pennsylvania

Odd S. Halseth, Phoenix

Lyndon L. Hargrave, Museum of Northern Arizona

M. R. Harrington, Southwest Museum

Emil W. Haury, University of Arizona

Irwin Hayden, Southwest Museum

Frederick W. Hodge, New York City

J. A. Jeançon, Denver

Neil M. Judd, U.S. National Museum

A. V. Kidder, Phillips Academy

Paul Kirchhoff, American Museum of Natural History

A. L. Kroeber, University of California

Paul S. Martin, Field Museum

J. Alden Mason, University of Pennsylvania

Harry P. Mera, Indian Arts Fund [Santa Fe]

Frank Mitvalsky [later Midvale], Gila Pueblo

Sylvanus G. Morley, Carnegie Institution of Washington

Ann A. Morris, American Museum of Natural History

Earl H. Morris, Carnegie Institution of Washington

Noel Morss, Peabody Museum, Harvard

J. E. Pearce, University of Texas

Frank Pinkley, National Park Service

Gladys A. Reichard, Barnard College

E. B. Renaud, Colorado Museum of Natural History

Frank H. H. Roberts, Jr., Bureau of American Ethnology

Mrs. [Linda] Roberts

Henry B. Roberts, Peabody Museum, Harvard

Karl Ruppert, Carnegie Institution of Washington

Edward Sapir, University of Chicago

James A. B. Scherer, Southwest Museum

Richard M. Snodgrass, American Museum of Natural History

Matthew W. Stirling, Bureau of American Ethnology

Joyce Stock, University of California

William Duncan Strong, University of Nebraska

Floyd Studer, Amarillo, Texas

Joseph B. Thoburn, Oklahoma Historical Society

Clark A. Wissler, American Museum of Natural History

Arthur Woodward, Los Angeles [County] Museum

Table 3.1. Participants in the 1929 Pecos Conference
(continued)
(Affiliation as reported in *The Masterkey*)

J. F. Zimmerman, University of New Mexico

From the Laboratory of Anthropology summer training program: Ethnology, under A. L. Kroeber

Scudder McKeel, University of Chicago
Fred B. Kniffen, University of Chicago
Gordon MacGregor, Harvard University
Maurice A. Mook, Northwestern University

Archaeology, under A. V. Kidder

Eva Horner, University of Chicago
William Bowers, Harvard University
Isabel Kelly, University of California
Ssu Yung Liang, Harvard University
Frances E. Watkins, Denver University

Linguistics, under Edward Sapir

Harry Hoijer, University of Chicago
Berard Haile, Franciscan Mission, St. Michaels, Arizona
V. Riste, University of Chicago
William H. Sassman, University of Chicago

Note: Although not listed, Madeleine Kidder was, of course, at the conference, and probably also Frances Morley and Mary-Russell Ferrell Colton. C. U. Clark was a historian searching European archives for documents on the early history and ethnology of Mesoamerica. S. Daryll Forde was later Professor of Anthropology, University of London, and Director of the International African Institute.

As in 1927, the participants from Southwestern institutions (nineteen from Colorado, New Mexico, and Arizona) were in a minority. In comparison, fifty-one were from California, Oklahoma, Texas, Nebraska, Michigan, Illinois, Pennsylvania, New York, Massachusetts, and Washington, D.C. Southwestern institutions were growing, but no faster than the nationwide interest in the Southwest. Continuity with the 1927 Conference was provided by twenty-three participants in 1929 who had also been present two years before, including some of those most active in the field and probably with the most to say. But even among active Southwestern archaeologists there were newcomers—Wesley Bradfield (who died suddenly only three months later), Harold Gladwin, Hargrave, Irwin Hayden, Frank Mitvalsky, and Morss.

An insight into a somewhat surprising event during the 1929 Conference is provided in a letter from William Curry Holden, of Lubbock, Texas (letter to Woodbury, 28 April 1982), which said, in part:

I vividly recall [the 1929 Pecos Conference]. . . . The meeting was at Kidder's camp, and in the open with no accommodations whatever except the shade of a few cedar trees. The crews of the four or five institutions then running summer digs in New Mexico and Arizona came directly to the Pecos [Conference] with their bedrolls and equipment. The only place to sit was on a bedroll or the ground. Kidder, then in his mid 40's, presided in a most casual and offhand manner. No papers were read. The various groups just told what they had done and found. No record was made of the proceedings. All was most informal.

The only two people from Texas were Floyd V. Studer of Amarillo and myself. We were not invited. We just heard about the meeting and went. We were both interested in the slab stone culture along the Canadian River in the Texas Panhandle and to learn if there were a connection between it and the pueblo of New Mexico and Arizona. When we arrived we met Dr. Kidder and told him who we were and why we were there. He made no comment.

At noon he announced lunch would be served in the makeshift kitchen at his camp. A line formed and Kidder stood at the door. When Studer and I approached he took us by the arms and drew us to one side. Then told us that the meal was only for invited guests, and advised that we might find somewhere a place to eat in the little town of Pecos a short distance upstream. Studer and I, somewhat abashed at this breach of western hospitality, went to the town and got hamburgers, and returned to listen to the afternoon reports. We found no one interested in our Panhandle problem.

Later we attended other Pecos Conferences, and never did the Panhandle problem get attention at any sessions I was at. . . . The eastern boundary of the Pecos Conferences was the drainage of the Pecos River.

It may be that Kidder's uncharacteristic lack of hospitality arose from a combination of the heavy burden the invited Conference members put on the kitchen facilities and his surprise at Holden and Studer arriving unexpectedly. Oddly, Studer appears in the published list of attendees and Holden does not.

Details of the 1929 program can be gleaned from the short report in *Masterkey:*

> Regular morning and afternoon sessions were held, devoted
> to the more obscure phases of early Pueblo culture. Particular
> attention was given to the examination of pottery and other ob-
> jects excavated during the current summer. The archaeological
> branch of the work was represented by reports from 15 differ-
> ent institutions now active in the southwest. A survey of the
> ethnological fields was presented by Dr. A. L. Kroeber. . . .
> [Anonymous 1929:28]

In addition, there was the novelty of enlarged air photos of a number of archaeological sites, the results of Charles and Anne Lindberg's
interest and cooperation. The schedule of sessions each morning and
afternoon was recalled by Haury, in notes jotted down some years
later: "Aug. 22—met Judd at Glorieta Sta., to AVK camp by breakfast.
Conf. starts after lunch. Fr. 23—a.m., p.m. sessions. Stayed Pecos
River Camp. Sat. 24–5-a.m. session & p.m. too. Sun. 25 to Sta. Fe."

In his letter to *Teocentli* in December 1929, Halseth wrote in his usual
sprightly but perceptive vein: "saw a lot of you fellows at Pecos, where
all, I am sure, learned that we know a lot of things that 'ain't so,' but
where we also learned much that is new." Kenneth Chapman wrote
in the same issue, "I have been kept pretty closely in Santa Fe with
all sorts of plans for the Laboratory [of Anthropology]. The Pecos
Conference made up for the lack of contacts with those in the field."
Frank Roberts's letter to the same publication was the most enthusiastic of all: "During August I managed to break away from the diggings
[Kiatuthlanna] long enough to attend the second Pecos Conference,
which after all proved the high spot of the summer's experience."

For Carl Guthe the Conference was something of a homecoming,
as he had worked at Pecos with Kidder in 1916 and 1917, and in
1922 made his important study of pottery making in San Ildefonso
as part of the Pecos Program. He wrote in *Teocentli,* "I chose for my
vacation the latter half of August and the first half of September.
Mrs. Guthe, the three boys and I hooked a camping trailer behind
our car, and trundled [from Ann Arbor, Michigan] out to the Pecos
Conference, later renewing friendships in Santa Fe, the Mesa Verde,
and Canyon City."

A personal evaluation of the 1929 Conference is found in a letter from Halseth to Mrs. Dwight B. Heard (6 September 1929), mostly on other matters:

> The consensus of opinion at the Pecos meeting was largely this:
> [1] Much more survey work needs to be done in many areas before actual digging is undertaken. This to know what stock the inventory reveals, so to speak.
> [2] More careful work needs to be done on "Basketmaker 3" (Post B.M. and Pre-Pueblo), "Pueblo," and "Pueblo 2" cultures, to establish differences, if any.
> [3] More work is needed in peripheral areas.
> [4] The most important field to be attacked is that of the Gila and Salt in central Arizona. Particularly from Phoenix to the Colorado. (Kidder holds this view as to archaeology.)
> [5] The most important work to be done ethnologically, (Kroeber speaking) is among the Pimas, Papagos, Apaches, the Yuman tribes along the Colorado, as well as some of the northern tribes, like the Utes, and some in Old Mexico.
> [6] Several men were condemned, without the mention of names, which was unnecessary, for not publishing accounts of their work. Kidder made the pledge for himself and the staffs under him with the Carnegie Institution, the Peabody Museum and Andover, that they would not undertake more digging in a season than they could properly work up in a report during the winter, and that no shovel was to be put in the ground before the previous season's work was ready for publication.

Some shrewd observations on the Conference, frank and personal, are contained in a letter from Reichard to Elsie Clews Parsons, dated 25 August 1929 (see N.S.F. Woodbury 1991).

Several years later Frank Roberts (1935: 6) commented on the 1929 Conference and its evaluation of the Pecos Classification:

> The sessions of the second gathering were devoted mainly to a review of the original classification and to reports on excavations conducted subsequent to the first conference. Most of those attending the second conference expressed the belief that the classification had been of help to them in their studies. Some stated that they had difficulty in applying the criteria. This was especially true of one definite region. The consideration of this

perplexity served to emphasize a fact which had been becoming more and more apparent. Namely the remains in the southern and western portions of the area, the desert domain, were not Puebloan in type. Cosmos Mindeleff commented on this in 1896. . . . Kidder in 1915 separated Southwestern culture into two major divisions on the strength of the dissimilarities and he again pointed them out in 1924. . . . Nelson had recognized the distinction and again in 1919 indicated it on his diagrammatic chart [Nelson 1919: Fig. 1]. . . . The situation was not accorded the attention which it merited, actually was overlooked at the first conference, until Gladwin and others, beginning in 1927 . . . secured definite evidence that the types are different.

It was not until 1931, however, that action was taken by the Pecos Conference to add recognition of the non-Puebloan parts of the Southwest, and then it was in large part the effect of research carried on by Gila Pueblo under Gladwin's direction and discussed at his Globe conference or caucus in April 1931.

Since the first two Pecos Conferences and many subsequent ones were held at the field camps of archaeological programs, rather than at museums, hotels, or campuses, this account of the 1929 Conference can appropriately end with a reminder of how travel to or from a field camp in 1929 differed from travel today. In 1981 Haury (letter to Woodbury, 18 September 1981) recalled his trip with Judd after they left the Conference:

> As an incidental note, after the 1929 Pecos Conference, Hulda and I drove Neil Judd from Santa Fe to Chaco Canyon, where he wanted to check on certain architectural details that bothered him. We spent several days there while he did that. Just about at the end of our stay, the rains came. Chaco Wash was in flood, so we had to return to Gallup via Farmington, travelling late at night, with no chance of gassing our car, then an Overland Whippet. We got to Gallup about 2:00 a.m. with a teaspoon of gas left in the tank, walked into the Harvey House for a bite to eat, and I recall vividly how Neil Judd ordered an onion sandwich because it would put him to sleep.

PART TWO

PERSISTENCE: GATHERING "WHERE THE WIND COULD BLOW AWAY THE COBWEBS FROM ONE'S MIND"

4
The Early Years in New Mexico, 1931–41

Before the Pecos Conference of 1931 took place in Santa Fe, an important independent conference was held at Gila Pueblo. It deserves mention here because it was intended to and did have a significant influence on the 1931 Pecos Conference and the future of Southwestern archaeology. Gila Pueblo had been founded in Globe, Arizona, only a few years before by Harold S. Gladwin and Winifred MacCurdy (Gladwin), and it had quickly become a major center of research and innovative ideas in Southwestern archaeology (see Haury 1988). Gladwin was something of an enfant terrible and a brilliant iconoclast, but at the same time he was an indefatigable, systematic, and knowledgeable investigator, who made his ideas and data quickly available in his own privately printed *Medallion Papers*. The first ten of these, some very brief but all bristling with new and stimulating ideas, were published from 1928 through 1935 and included "A Method for Designation of Ruins in the Southwest" (Gladwin and Gladwin 1928a), "The Use of Potsherds in an Archaeological Survey of the Southwest" (Gladwin and Gladwin 1928b), "A Method for the Designation of Southwestern Pottery Types" (Gladwin and Gladwin 1930b), and four reports on "The Red-on-Buff Culture" of southern Arizona (Gladwin and Gladwin 1929a, 1929b, 1930a, 1935).

Gladwin welcomed archaeologists of every viewpoint to his research center, to use its growing collection of pottery and site data, and to discuss their (and Gladwin's) ideas in almost daily workshops. He is well described by A. V. Kidder, who had introduced him to archaeology, in a foreword to Gladwin's "Excavations at Snaketown, II: Comparisons and Theories":

> It is characteristic of Mr. Gladwin that, although he is aware of
> my strong disapproval of much of his reasoning and of my vio-

lent disagreement with most of his conclusions, he has nevertheless asked me to write the foreword to his book. . . . [His views
on] the rise of New World civilization . . . illustrate what seem
to me the weaknesses and strengths of Gladwin's work. On the
one hand he is, in my opinion, hasty and, in selection of evidence, not sufficiently critical; on the other he is untiringly avid
for information and fiercely intolerant of dogma [Kidder 1937].

As Frank Roberts said in his 1935 comments on the 1927 and 1929
Pecos Conferences (quoted earlier), the differences between the northern and southern, or the plateau and desert areas of the Southwest
had been seriously slighted in the Pecos Classification. Gladwin and
others had recognized that the Classification confused time units and
cultural units, rendering it less useful than intended. Gladwin set out
with his characteristic vigor and ability to remedy this. Gila Pueblo's
site surveys covered a vast area: "We have ranged as far north as Montana and as far south as Zacatecas, and from our wanderings we have
brought back the descriptions, the sherds, the stone chips and tools,
wood and charcoal for dating, and often photographs, from about ten
thousand sites" (Gladwin 1957: 8). But very soon his strongest interest
and greatest activity were focused on the desert south, and it was the
need to recognize, define, and describe this major region and correct
the flaws in the Pecos Classification that led him to invite a selected
group of archaeologists to a private conference at Gila Pueblo in 1931.

THE 1931 CAUCUS AT GILA PUEBLO   From 16 through 18 April 1931,
a group of twenty-six invited individuals met at Gila Pueblo, including Gladwin and members of his staff. It is noticeable that Kidder, Roberts, and Neil Judd were absent, perhaps due to other commitments rather than lack of invitations: Gladwin had no fear of
disagreement and, in fact, welcomed it as a means by which arguments could be developed and new understandings reached. Their
absence may have simply been the problem of travel; air travel in
1931 was uncertain and schedules limited, and the train trip from the
East Coast to Arizona took three days or so. Participants were all
from Southwestern and California institutions: Gila Pueblo; Laboratory of Anthropology; Los Angeles Museum of History, Science, and
Art; Museum of Northern Arizona, Flagstaff; San Diego Museum;
Southwest Museum, Los Angeles; Southwestern National Monuments Association; and University of Arizona. The School of American Research, Museum of New Mexico, Santa Fe, and the Carnegie
Institution were not represented.

The conference was planned to find solutions to the shortcomings in cultural and chronological classifications that had become apparent since the 1927 Pecos Conference. For example, the numbering of cultural stages implied a chronology that was not always demonstrable. Also, the major geographical areas of the Southwest needed to be divided into smaller areas, each characterized by a distinctive culture.

Three years later this approach had a full and definitive statement in the Gladwins' "Method for the Designation of Cultures and their Variations" (Gladwin and Gladwin 1934), a scheme consisting of "roots," "stems," and "branches," within the last of which temporal and geographical "phases" were established. But the most important consensus at the 1931 Gila Pueblo conference was on the definition of a Plateau area and a Desert area, differing in architecture, pottery, and disposal of the dead, with "the feeling of some members of the conference that the Desert group, particularly that section which is characteristic of the Gila Valley, could properly be designated as the 'Hohokam,' meaning the Ancient Ones, as used by the Pima at the present time."

Gladwin was choosing the term that Frank Russell (1908) had used in his important monograph, "The Pima Indians." However, when A. L. Kroeber published his influential "Native Culture of the Southwest" in 1928, he used the term *Gila-Sonora* to distinguish the area from *Pueblo*. Similarly, Kidder in his 1924 *Introduction to the Study of Southwestern Archaeology* avoided the term *Hohokam,* preferring to name most of his cultural units geographically, by drainages, in this case *Lower Gila.*

There is no reason to think that Gladwin intended his conference at Gila Pueblo to compete with or displace the Pecos Conference. Rather, he wished to have a relatively small group of Southwestern archaeologists discuss and approve his proposals for modification and amplification of the Pecos Classification and present these changes that summer for Pecos Conference approval. It was a well-orchestrated caucus with the outcome that Gladwin had planned.

SANTA FE, 1931 (THIRD PECOS CONFERENCE) The Third Pecos Conference, called at the time "The Third Biennial Pecos Conference" in a Laboratory of Anthropology report, differed in many ways from the first two, being held away from Kidder's Pecos field camp and having much more formal arrangements for invitations and program. This formality was mainly because the meeting was held in conjunction with the official opening and dedication of the Laboratory of Anthropology. The Laboratory files contain several lists of possible invitees, tentative programs, and details of arrangements such as luncheons and tours of the Laboratory's collections. As director of the Laboratory, Jesse Nusbaum had major responsibilities for all aspects of both the dedication ceremonies and the Conference. From at least as early as the beginning of July he and Kidder were busy with myriad details.

Although this Conference was unique in some ways, it also foreshadowed some of the arrangements that later became routine; for this reason, it is of interest to quote or paraphrase some of the surviving records of the planning in the summer of 1931. On 15 July a form letter was sent by Nusbaum to all those whose names Kidder had supplied. The letter was very specific about arrangements, as can be seen in a copy in the Laboratory files that happens to be addressed to Charles Amsden:

> On September second, third and fourth, there will be held at the Laboratory of Anthropology in Santa Fe an informal conference upon the problems of Southwestern archaeology. It is planned to devote the first day to discussion of general questions. On the second and third days, it is hoped that smaller groups will meet for consideration of more highly specialized matters.
>
> The Laboratory will make and confirm room reservations at local hotels and auto camps as you may desire. Please indicate on the attached form what accommodations you wish, returning promptly to this office.
>
> Automobile transportation between local hotels and camps, and the Laboratory (a distance of approximately one and three-quarters miles) will be provided by the Laboratory as required.
>
> Conferees will be guests of the Laboratory at noon-day luncheons on September third and fourth at Hotel La Fonda. The formal opening of the Laboratory is scheduled for the evening of September first, immediately preceding this conference.

With this letter went a mimeographed form to be returned by those wishing to have hotel or auto camp reservations made for them. Anyone who has stayed in Santa Fe in recent years will envy the schedule of rates listed in Table 4.1.

At the Orchard Auto Camp on the Old Santa Fe Trail, long replaced by Garrett's Desert Inn, Conference participants could choose among many options, including "Single, gas plate, no bath, $1.25 without bedding, $1.75 with bedding"; singles with stove, with stove and shower, or with stove and bathtub; doubles (specified as "two beds") "without bath $2.50 without bedding. Add $1.00 for bedding";

Table 4.1. Hotel Rates in Santa Fe in 1931

Hotel	Single		Double	
	With bath	Without	With bath	Without
La Fonda	$3.00	$2.50	$5.50	$4.00
(Fred Havey)				
De Vargas	3.00	2.00	5.00	3.00
El Fidel	2.00	1.50, 2.00	3.50	2.50

as well as doubles with shower and doubles with tub, again with or without bedding.

Among those receiving an invitation was Frank Roberts, who wrote Nusbaum on 20 July from Allantown, Arizona, where he was excavating, with a question that was to vex Pecos Conferences for many years to come:

> Dear Nusbaum:
>
> The notification for the Conference to be held in Santa Fe September 2, 3, and 4 has been received. I should like to ask what the plans are with respect to the archaeological students. Will they go to Santa Fe and be present at the meeting or will they conclude their work at that time and leave for home from Gallup? I think it would be to their advantage to attend the sessions if possible. We could bring them to Santa Fe in the station wagon and bring them back to Gallup from which point they could scatter to their respective homes. It may be that they would be willing to stand their own expenses in Santa Fe although I doubt very much if two of the boys could afford to do it.

The students, all of them members of the Laboratory of Anthropology's summer field training program, were (as listed later in a news story in the *Santa Fe New Mexican*) Carl F. Miller, University of Arizona; Dale S. King, University of Denver; Solon S. Kimball, Harvard University; and Ralph S. Brown, Harvard. The students with Ruth Benedict, mentioned below in Nusbaum's reply to Roberts, were John Gillen, Harvard; Sol Tax, University of Wisconsin, Milwaukee; Regina Flannery, University of Washington; Morris E. Opler, University of Chicago; and Paul Frank, University of Chicago. Nusbaum's reply to Roberts was prompt, written on 23 July:

Dear Roberts:

In reference to your letter of July 20:

When Kidder was here, we discussed the whole plan for the Field Conference and it was decided that your students and those of Dr. Benedict should come. Each of you has a Ford station wagon capable of moving your party of students to Santa Fe. . . . I should think you would plan to conclude your work with the group prior to their departure from Santa Fe, in order that they will be free to move homeward immediately after the conference here. We shall have to stand the expense of the students' stay here. . . . Please let us know explicitly how many will come and what day you will arrive, as it is necessary to arrange long ahead for hotel accommodations . . . as it is Fiesta time.

Dr. Kidder is anxious for all to attend the general conference the first day and is equally desirous of limiting the number in the potsherd conference in Mera's quarters downstairs to the group most vitally interested in this division of the work. He hopes to have about eighteen persons in this "star chamber" session. Morley's Carnegie Institution group will be assigned other quarters upstairs for his conference, and it is hoped that other groups will wish to divide up for conferences on various problems. You, naturally, will be taking an active part in the sherd conference, and I see no reason why your students who are actively interested in this part of the work could not well sit in as observers.

I am glad to know that your work is progressing well. . . . I trust that you will arrange to make a showing here, photographically and otherwise, of the season's work, and bring such sherd material as may logically come up for discussion in the conference. . . .

Wishing you the continued success which your work seriously merits, with kindest regards to Mrs. Roberts and yourself,

Sincerely yours
Jesse L. Nusbaum
Director

Whether Kidder and Nusbaum would have welcomed Roberts's and Benedict's students to the Conference if they had not been members of the Laboratory's summer training program can only be guessed at. But their presence nevertheless helped set a precedent that continued, although not without controversy: students were to be "admitted" but on a different basis than their mentors, coming as "observers" rather than full participants.

Invitations for the opening ceremonies on Tuesday evening, 1 September, posed additional problems for Nusbaum, who wrote Kidder on 18 July that

> Harry Mera and Chap [Kenneth Chapman] have suggested that
> Mrs. R. B. Alves and Mrs. G. Windsor Smith, both of El Paso,
> be extended invitations to attend the conference. . . . Stallings
> [William (Sid) Stallings, Jr.] knows them well and thinks that
> the invitation might lead to making the Laboratory [the] reposi-
> tory of their collections in the future. Mrs. Smith has one of
> the finest personal collections of Casa Grande [probably Casas
> Grandes, Chihuahua] pottery in private hands, and you unques-
> tionably know of the Alves Basket-maker material from the
> Guadalupes [mountains 100 miles east of El Paso]. What do you
> think of this inclusion in the invitation list? I shall await your
> further word.

Mrs. Smith and Mrs. Alves were invited. An undated typed "List of Acceptances Received to Date" for the opening ceremonies has fifty-one names on it, with five more written in later. Most of them are marked with cryptic checks, circles, and roman or arabic numerals—keys to details of the planning that cannot be deciphered now. Another typed list is headed "Invitations to Conference Sent to:" and also contains fifty-one names, a coincidence as the lists are not the same, even though many individuals are on both. Some differences in these lists may be due to the fact that one is a list of acceptances, the other of invitations sent, but there can be little doubt that Nusbaum, Kidder, and others had good reasons for each name on the invitation list. The names on a third and longer list are provided in Table 4.2. The struggles for control of the Laboratory and its financial resources were still fresh in the minds of all concerned, and invitations would have had political as well as scholarly or social implications. At this distance in time it is impossible to decide what purpose was served by each name, but as a whole they reflect the local and national constituencies of the new Laboratory, the personal network of Kidder and his colleagues, and the growing number of Southwesternists. That December, in *Teocentli,* Nusbaum commented that the Conference "was attended by an average of fifty of the seventy-four invited."

Table 4.2. Invitation List for the 1931 Pecos Conference, Santa Fe

Mrs. R. B. Alves (yes)	Earl H. Morris (yes)
Charles Amsden (yes)	Noel Morss
Katharine Bartlett (yes)	Dwight W. Morrow, Jr. (yes)
Ruth Benedict (yes)	N. C. Nelson (no)
Franz Boas (no)	Paul H. Nesbitt (yes)
K. M. Chapman (yes)	Jesse L. Nusbaum (yes)
Faye Cole [sic] (no)	Elsie Clews Parsons
Harold S. Colton (yes)	J. A. Pearce
Byron Cummings (yes)	Frank Pinkley
A. E. Douglass	W. W. Postlethwaite (yes)
F. H. Douglas (yes)	E. B. Renaud (no)
May Morrill Dunne	F. H. H. Roberts, Jr. (yes)
Fisher [Reginald?]	Henry Roberts (yes)
Harold Gladwin (no—wrote Kidder yes)	Malcolm Rogers (no)
Mrs. Goodwin (yes)	Ralph Roys (yes)
Carl E. Guthe (no)	Donald Scott
Odd S. Halseth (no [yes is crossed out])	Frank Setzler
Lyndon L. Hargrave (yes)	Anna Shepard (yes)
Florence Hawley (yes)	Mrs. G. Windsor Smith
M. R. Harrington (no)	F. G. Speck (no)
Emil Haury (yes [no is crossed out])	Leslie Spier (no)
Edgar L. Hewett (no)	W. S. Stallings (yes)
F. W. Hodge (no)	Matthew W. Stirling
E. A. Hooton	Julian Steward
Walter Hough	Gustav Stromsvik
Edgar Howard (yes)	S. A. Stubbs (yes)
J. A. Jeançon (yes)	Marjorie Trumbull
Neil M. Judd (yes)	Van Bergen (yes)
A. E. [sic] Kidder (yes)	George Woodbury (yes)
A. L. Kroeber (yes)	Arthur Woodward (yes)
Ralph Linton (no)	Frank Roberts' students—4
Winifred MacCurdy (no)	Dr. Benedict's students—5
Paul C. [sic] Martin (yes)	[added in longhand]
John McGregor (yes)	John Howells
H. P. Mera (yes)	Berard Haile
Frank Mitalski	Gladys Reichert [sic]
S. G. Morley (yes)	Ruth Underhill

Although the opening was the more prestigious event, Conference participants were treated well also. The Laboratory files include the menus for the luncheons on 3 and 4 September at La Fonda, for a "party of 50 to 60: each day, to be seated at tables of fours and sixes around the wall—New Mexico Room," with the added note by Nusbaum, "Phone Bourginon [?] Wed. a.m. exact no. to prepare for." Friday's menu consisted of "Melon Supreme, Radishes, Mixed Olives, Chicken Patty a la King, French Fried Potatoes, New Peas, Combination Salad, Apple Pie, Coffee." Arthur Woodward's comment in December in *Teocentli* was that "if anyone wants royal treatment, drop in at the Laboratory."

Still another of Nusbaum's responsibilities, handled with his usual efficiency and skill (perhaps experience managing archaeological field work, with crews, schedules, budgets, and all, is useful to archaeologists in other realms) was preparing the actual programs of the opening and the Conference. Several handwritten preliminary sketches exist indicating, for example, that the first day would be "General, semi-public" and the second and third days would be "Executive sessions," with the fourth day a meeting of the board of trustees of the Laboratory in the morning and "Canyon de Chelly Conference, afternoon of Sept. 5th." Nusbaum also noted on one memo that the Santa Fe Fiesta would begin at 9 p.m. on 5 September and continue on 6, 7, and 8 September "to conclusion."

The *Santa Fe New Mexican* announced the plans in detail on 29 August under a banner headline, "Open Anthropology Laboratory Today," and began its story as follows:

> With addresses in the main building by Governor Seligman, Dr. Clark Wissler and Dr. A. V. Kidder, and a reception in the spacious new director's residence, the Laboratory of Anthropology, Rockefeller-endowed [*sic*] center for the study of man in the Americas, will be officially opened to the public at 8 p.m.
>
> The first [and the last, as it turned out] completed unit of the great institution will be thrown open for public inspection, with scientists in the various departments to exhibit to the public work going on and rare treasures of the Indian Arts Fund and of the laboratory proper.
>
> Following the opening will be a three-day conference of anthropologists and archeologists, with scores of prominent men and women from all over the country in attendance. The

conference will be an invitation affair, bringing in persons specially interested in the discussions.

On the night of the opening, Governor Seligman of New Mexico delivered the "Address of Welcome"; Clark Wissler of the American Museum of Natural History, New York, spoke on "Anthropological Research in the Southwest"; and Kidder outlined the "History, Aims, and Purpose of the Laboratory of Anthropology." Unfortunately, no copies of these speeches have survived, as far as can be determined.

What was called the "Santa Fe Laboratory Conference" in the news story began on Wednesday, 2 September, with morning and afternoon sessions devoted to "a general conference of all field workers on the broader problems of anthropological research," chaired by Kidder. Thursday morning was devoted to three concurrent sessions: (1) the sherd conference, chaired by Kidder in the archaeological survey room; (2) a session on ethnological methods and practices, conducted by Benedict and Wissler, in the main conference room; and (3) the "Carnegie Institution group" in the library reading room, chaired by S. G. Morley. That noon, the program stated, "all conferees will be guests of Laboratory of Anthropology at luncheon, La Fonda Hotel." At 8 p.m. there was a "Showing of Laura Gilpin's 'Pictorial Lantern Slides of the Southwest.'" (Nearly fifty years later, when she was past the age of eighty, Gilpin was still giving lectures illustrated with her extraordinarily beautiful photographs.) Friday, the program stated, "Respective conferences will be continued to completion in designated rooms, 9:00 a.m. to 12 noon and 1:30 to 5:00 p.m.," with conferees again taken to La Fonda for luncheon. The evening was to be "open for final contacts and minor conferences" (whether at the Laboratory or the La Fonda bar is not specified). There appears to have been no session devoted to reports of recent field work, something which became an important part of later Conferences. Concurrent sessions on specialized topics never became common but took place intermittently.

On Saturday, following the Conference, the Laboratory's board of trustees met in the morning, and in the afternoon what had originally been called the Canyon de Chelly conference had now become a "Special Conference called at the request of Director Albright of the National Park Service to formulate plans for appropriate development of the archeological features in National Parks, National Monuments, and the Public domain; Jesse L. Nusbaum, chairman."

Although it is tempting and perhaps correct to say at the end of every Pecos Conference that "there will never be another one like this one," such a sentiment is probably even more appropriate than usual for the 1931 Conference, with its special events, hospitality, and its carefully chosen audience for the ceremonial opening of the Laboratory, all made possible by the then substantial Rockefeller-supported budget of the Laboratory.

The formal program and the news stories make no mention of what was almost certainly the most important archaeological achievement of the 1931 Conference. Roberts later summarized it as follows: "The results of the Gila Pueblo [April 1931] conference were presented to a larger group of Southwestern workers at the Laboratory of Anthropology, Santa Fé, New Mexico, in September of that year. The Santa Fé session, which took the place of the biennial Pecos conference of 1931, discussed and adopted the Globe recommendation" (Roberts 1935: 7). This meant that the Hohokam and Mogollon had achieved coordinate status with the Anasazi in the thinking of at least a substantial number of Southwesternists. Emil Haury (letter to Woodbury, 8 April 1982) recalled that there were, however, still skeptics: "I have a most vivid recollection about the general conservative attitude on the part of the conferees toward the new names being bandied about, Mogollon and Hohokam. . . . I was sitting next to Frank Roberts around the big table in the Laboratory of Anthropology when I reported on Roosevelt 9:6 and had occasion to use the word 'Hohokam.' He turned to me and said quietly, 'That's a lot of hokum.' "

A further insight into this event is provided by a letter (8 September 1931) to Gladwin from Haury, who was on the staff of Gila Pueblo from 1930 to 1937 and in September 1931 was en route to Cambridge, Massachusetts, where he would be studying at Harvard University for his Ph.D. degree. Pausing in the journey at Newton, Kansas, where his and his wife Hulda's parents lived, he wrote:

> My wire from Trinidad may have seemed to contain a little
> conceit in that the San Juan people had something else to think
> about except their own stamping ground. It was very noticeable
> that the "big shots" such as Morris, Judd, and Roberts had prac-
> tically nothing to say. [It should be recalled that none of them
> was at the April conference in Globe.] All major discussions
> centered about things which concern us vitally [the proposals
> coming from the Globe conference]. Of course, nothing defi-
> nite was accomplished, a fact which you predicted, but we have
> gained a point simply in being able to place emphasis on our

southern material. A definition of a phase was drawn up which runs something like this: A phase is a ware or complex of wares which is a recognizable expression of a major ceramic category. Does that meet your idea? It was also said that a phase should bear a geographic name.

After I had read the provisions of the plan, Colton said he found no fault, that he had misunderstood your letter. It seems to me that they are so involved in their own area that they cannot see over the edge of the saucer.

The conference was a very placid affair, less heat and less talk than in previous sessions.

A hint of the personal currents running beneath the "placid" surface of the 1931 Conference is provided in a short letter from Edgar L. Hewett to Nusbaum, dated 26 August 1931.

My dear Jess:

Terribly sorry but one of my usual congested programs, made some weeks ago and which I simply can't change, prevents my being at your opening and at the following conference and Board meeting. It's bad luck for me but no help for it, and so I am wishing you an auspicious time and sending you and Aileen [Mrs. Nusbaum] and the staff and such members of the Board as may come my heartiest felicitations and warm personal regards.

As always,

Faithfully yours,
Edgar L. Hewett

It would doubtless be too much to expect that after trying so vigorously to control the direction of Rockefeller support for archaeology and anthropology in Santa Fe, and losing to Kidder, Wissler, Morley, Judd, Nusbaum, and others, Hewett would have enjoyed attending the ceremonies opening the Laboratory, testimony to their triumph and his defeat. Hewett had not attended the 1929 Conference at Pecos (and had left the 1927 Conference early). According to the surviving attendance records of subsequent Conferences, he never attended another Pecos Conference, except perhaps those at Chaco Canyon following the University of New Mexico field school sessions.

It appears to have been Kidder's intention that annual conferences at the Laboratory of Anthropology would take the place of the Pecos

Conferences, as reported by George Stocking in his important article on the founding of the Laboratory (Stocking 1982: 6):

> In a letter to Zimmerman [president of the University of New Mexico] Kidder was at great pains to reassure him [and thus indirectly Hewett] that the new Laboratory would not undermine existing Southwestern institutions. Its proposed site surveys and annual field conferences (on the model of the Pecos Conference Kidder had organized in 1927) were to be coordinative rather than competitive.

As we shall see, it did not turn out that way: the next Conference at the Laboratory of Anthropology would not take place until 1946.

THE FIVE-YEAR GAP, 1932–36   By 1936 it would have seemed to most Southwesternists that the idea of an annual or biennial summer archaeological conference had been abandoned. Many archaeologists were active in the Southwest, but no one planned and held a conference on the Pecos model. Archaeological activity was, in fact, more intensive and extensive than ever before, as Roberts attested in one of his frequent summaries of the state of knowledge:

> Archaeological investigations in the Southwestern field proceed apace. New facts and fancies burst in such profusion that the trend of studies is well-nigh obscured by the complexity of information emanating from the area. . . . To many the archaeology of the Southwest now seems so involved, so cluttered with minutiae that it has become dull and stupid and can no longer be regarded as the source for a fascinating story of the cultural and material growth of a primitive people. Yet the new chapters being added are even more interesting than those with which most people are familiar. . . .
>   Because of the rapidly changing interpretations and a continual uncovering of more evidence it is practically impossible to present an up-to-date summary of the subject [although Roberts did just that]. Before an article can be set in type the unrolling panorama presents new scenes and a shifting viewpoint [Roberts 1937: 3].

Roberts then proceeds to discuss in characteristically clear and thoughtful paragraphs the changing ideas and interpretations of the preceding few years, as well as to report important new information. Of the twenty-two archaeological reports he cites, only four are earlier than 1931, a clear indication that publication was accompanying field work.

The vigor, variety, and intensity of Southwestern research are indicated in the annual summary, "Archaeological Field Work in North America," contributed to *American Anthropologist* by Carl Guthe through 1933 and then shifted to the new journal *American Antiquity*. A look at 1932 field work, for example, shows that in Arizona Roberts spent a second season at Allentown; King's Ruin in the Chino Valley forty miles north of Prescott was excavated under Byron Cummings's direction; Odd Halseth continued to excavate Pueblo Grande for the Phoenix Archaeological Commission; Haury, then assistant director of Gila Pueblo, dug in Canyon Creek, east of the Sierra Ancha; for the Museum of Northern Arizona, John McGregor dug pit houses in the Flagstaff area, searching for beam material to date the eruption of Sunset Crater; Lyndon Hargrave repaired rooms in the Walnut Canyon ruins; Katharine Bartlett continued the museum's site survey; Harold Colton investigated Hohokam influences in the Flagstaff area; and Earl Morris, with Carnegie funding, secured the tower in Mummy Cave from collapsing and continued adding timber sections to Douglass's tree-ring specimens.

In New Mexico, Deric Nusbaum expanded the sherd library of the Laboratory of Anthropology; the fifth Jemez Field School was held; students under Paul Reiter's direction continued work at Chetro Ketl and Casa Rinconada in Chaco Canyon; Harry Mera, of the Laboratory of Anthropology, studied upper Rio Grande Valley Biscuit Ware sites; Stanley Stubbs surveyed the Tesuque Valley; Stallings was in the second year of the Laboratory's Dendro-Archaeological Project; and Anna Shepard was continuing her studies of ceramic technology. Morris secured 400 more tree-ring samples from Basketmaker III through Pueblo III sites, from the Tohachi area north of Gallup and from the Chuska Mountains. Gila Pueblo's site survey concentrated on the area between Zuni, Chaco, and Acoma. For the University Museum of Pennsylvania and the Philadelphia Academy of Natural Sciences Alden Mason and Edgar B. Howard dug "Basketmaker" burials and investigated caves with extinct Pleistocene fauna associated with hearths in the Guadalupe Mountains.

In Texas Frank Setzler of the U.S. National Museum dug caves in the Big Bend area; W. C. Holden of Texas Technological College dug a village on the Canadian River that had Pueblo IV sherds associated with it; and E. B. Sayles added 800 sites to the Gila Pueblo survey of West Texas. In Utah Albert B. Reagan continued his work in the Uinta Basin and Nine Mile Canyon. Julian H. Steward of the University of Utah surveyed the Colorado River by boat from the mouth of the Fremont to Lee's Ferry and also explored canyons and mesas between the Paria and Kanab rivers. For the Peabody Museum, Harvard University, J. O. Brew continued the excavations at Alkali Ridge that he had begun the year before. All this in 1932!

By 1934 Gladwin and Haury had begun digging at Snaketown; Roberts was working at the Folsom site of Lindenmeier; Paul Martin was excavating at Lowry; M. R. Harrington had returned to Pueblo Grande de Nevada; Hewett was directing five excavation and restoration projects in Chaco Canyon and also work at Unshagi, at Bandelier's Puaray, at Kuaua, and at Quarai; Stubbs was digging at Pindi; Haury was running a six-week training dig at the Harris Site in the Mimbres country for the Laboratory of Anthropology's fellowship program; and Paul Nesbitt of Beloit College was excavating the Starkweather site near Reserve, New Mexico.

This and other work in the Southwest provided the basis for Roberts's comments on the rapidly expanding and changing scene that he summarized in 1937. But no conferences were held to disseminate this new information promptly, or to discuss new ideas and new interpretations of the data. It should be noted that Southwestern field work was no longer being done by Kidder, by Frederick Hodge, by Judd, or by C. Burton Cosgrove and Harriet Cosgrove, all of whom had been active at the time of the 1927 Pecos Conference. In part, however, their places were being taken by another generation, including Martin, Colton, McGregor, Haury, Sayles, Stallings, Nesbitt, and Steward (although the last turned from archaeology to ethnology in the next decade).

It is risky to generalize too broadly, but much of the field work going on in the 1930s seems at first glance to be little different in orientation from that of the 1920s—interesting sites, such as those selected by Roberts, Cummings, Halseth, Martin, McGregor, and others, were chosen to add needed details to the general picture. But their data were analyzed in somewhat different ways, benefiting from the new attention to pottery typology, to tree-ring dating, to relationships among the distinct cultural areas and subareas that were being defined, particularly by Gladwin and Colton. There was also a growing attention to the preservation and restoration of ruins that could continue to interest the general public, or be available for future research. Surveys were numerous, especially by the Museum of Northern Arizona, the Laboratory of Anthropology, and Gila Pueblo. These surveys were more systematic and thorough than in the past, with printed record forms, permanent sherd samples, and photographs; they served well as the basis for the planning of future field projects. Many of their data still have great research value. The attention being given to the Hoho-kam culture of southern Arizona was a particularly noticeable change from the areal limitation of interest at the time of the first Pecos Conference. In his 1937 review of the Southwest, Roberts pointed out that research was also addressing the relationships between major areas, an interest that foreshadows the rise of attention to the processes of culture change and regional interaction.

Dramatic indication of how Southwestern archaeology's entire conceptual base had changed in less than two decades comes from comparing the major categories within which Kidder placed the data of his 1924 *Introduction to the Study of Southwestern Archaeology* with those used by Roberts in 1937: Kidder categorized data according to the major river drainages—San Juan, Rio Grande, Upper Gila, and so forth—while Roberts used the categories of Anasazi, Hohokam, Mogollon, and Nomadic and Semi-nomadic Groups (the last awkwardly including both Folsom and the late prehistoric Athabascan and Shoshonean peoples). The first three Pecos Conferences undoubtedly hastened the adoption of new and different research approaches in the Southwest. But whether the lack of conferences in the following years slowed progress is more difficult to judge. Many active field workers visited each other's sites and kept up an extensive correspondence with colleagues, at least a partial substitute for the communication possible at a summer conference.

In part the suspension of the Pecos Conferences was also compensated for by the annual meetings of the Southwestern Division of the American Association for the Advancement of Science (AAAS). Comments in *Teocentli* show that they were welcomed as an important means of keeping up personal and professional contacts and for exchanging new archaeological information and ideas. In April 1936 the sixteenth meeting of the Southwestern Division was held in Flagstaff, with thirty-three anthropological papers read. The report published soon afterward indicates the extent of participation (Haury 1936a: 50). Donald Brand, University of New Mexico, arranged a symposium on prehistoric agriculture with speakers from all across the country. Other sessions had participants from ten Southwestern institutions.

However, the Depression of the 1930s was cutting funds for travel and field work. Arthur Woodward, for example, wrote in *Teocentli* (December 1932) "Well, the old man with the ax finally caught up with the personnel at the Los Angeles Museum and for the next few months we'll be operating on half-time and reduced pay. . . . Field work has become almost a thing of the past." Halseth said in the same issue, "To ease the budget as much as possible, I'm using chain-gang labor this season, but cannot recommend it highly." Matthew Stirling wrote, "Government economy is going to give members of this Bureau [of American Ethnology] a wonderful chance to catch up on their work [that is, by writing reports]. Field work is taboo for the coming season as well as the present." If anyone was making preliminary inquiries at this time about holding another Pecos Conference, the responses might well have been negative or at best uncertain.

Before the 1930s were over, however, a quite unforeseen successor to the first three Pecos Conferences appeared and quickly came to play much the same role of providing an occasion for professionals and some students, as well as a sprinkling of amateurs, to meet and learn of each other's recent field work, as well as discuss broader problems. The Chaco Anthropological Conferences, as they were called, began in 1937 at the Chaco Canyon field school, which was sponsored by the Anthropology Department of the University of New Mexico, founded and chaired by Hewett. Although their sponsorship was different from that of Kidder's Conferences, they continued the function so well that I have felt justified in considering them Pecos Conferences *de facto* even though perhaps everyone did not regard them so *de jure*.

FIRST CHACO ANTHROPOLOGICAL CONFERENCE, 1937 (FOURTH PECOS CONFERENCE)   The site of the Chaco field school was in many ways ideal for the Conferences, as the University of New Mexico had built facilities for up to one hundred students and a large teaching and support staff (Fig. 4.1). Following the close of the field school in the late summer these facilities could provide housing and meals for a conference larger than any field camp could accommodate.

Donald Brand, Florence Hawley, and Frank Hibben (1937) provided some details of the facilities of the 1937 season, which included "four blocks of tents which were disposed in a sinuous line along the foot of the cliffs on the south side of the Chaco arroyo, opposite Pueblo Bonito, and extending west for a furlong [one-eighth of a mile] from Casa Rinconada." The more permanent Chaco Canyon Research Station "provided a lecture hall (which was also used as a dining room), kitchen, storerooms, library, toilets, and showers." Although there

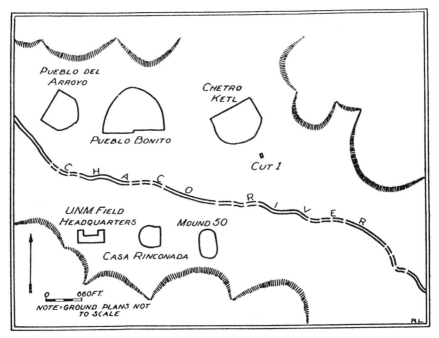

4.1 Map of part of Chaco Canyon, including University of New Mexico field headquarters, where the Chaco Anthropological Conferences were held, beginning in 1937. From "Tseh So . . ." by D. D. Brand and others, University of New Mexico Press, 1937.

were a well and windmill that supplied water from the edge of the arroyo, lack of wind often required closing down the indoor showers and toilets. Groceries came from Gallup, a hundred miles to the south; lighting was by Coleman lamps, kerosene lamps, and candles; the kitchen range was fueled with "soft coal from a nearby seam in the canyon wall, and juniper wood hauled from an area several miles to the north of the canyon." The sketch map in the 1937 report, showing the location of the field headquarters, is also reproduced in *American Antiquity* (Senter 1937: 70). Robert and Florence Lister (1981: 112) add their own impression of the field school's setting.

Brand, Hawley, and Hibben made no mention of the Conference that followed the close of the 1937 field school season, but they included a roster of the school's staff and students, and it can be assumed that many of those listed as "faculty" remained for the Anthropological Conference after the field school closed. The list of field school lecturers names Brand (anthropologist and geographer), Ernst Antevs (geologist), George P. Hammond (historian), Hawley and Hewett (archaeologists), Leslie Spier (ethnologist), Julio Tello (Peruvian archaeologist), and J. Eric Thompson (Mayanist). Excavation supervisors, who doubtless also remained for the Conference, were Wesley Bliss, Hibben, and Donovan Senter. Alden Hayes and Robert Lister appear on the list as "camp boys," and Robert Spier as "general utility boy." Among the students a few can be identified who went on to become professional archaeologists: John M. Corbett, John M. Goggin, Hulda Hobbs, Donald J. Lehmer, and Carolyn M. Miles (later Mrs. Douglas Osborne).

No report on the 1937 Conference was published, as far as is known, and the files of the Department of Anthropology, University of New Mexico, and those of the Museum of New Mexico lack any record of it. One additional glimpse, however, comes from Alden Hayes (letter to Woodbury, 23 September 1981), who recalls that he was there, but says "I remember little about it." He then adds:

> Meals were fed in the big hall of the old university field school
> near South Gap and meetings were held in the big lab tent east
> of the building. I remember trying to talk to Julio Tello about
> peyote use in the Southwest in my cow-camp Spanish and find-
> ing that I could ask directions, order drinks, or brand calves
> in Spanish better than discourse on metaphysics. Leslie Spier
> was there, and I think Kidder. George Peter Murdock was there
> with his family and on the next to last day had to leave for Seven

Lakes and beyond right after a gully-washing toad-choker and was afraid of the road. Nan [Cooke] Smith asked me to help him out so I drove his car out to a point ca. 6 miles south where the surface was firmer and hiked back.

SECOND CHACO ANTHROPOLOGICAL CONFERENCE, 1938 (FIFTH PECOS CONFERENCE)   In the *New Mexico Anthropologist* it was announced in 1938 that

> the University of New Mexico again will serve as host to Anthropologists interested in Southwestern problems at a conference in the Chaco Canyon, August 27–28–29, 1938. . . . immediately upon completion of the Chaco Field Session, so that the housing and feeding facilities of the Research Station will be available for participants in the conference. . . . Only bedding need be brought since the University will undertake to provide cots, shelter, and meals. A "registration fee" of $3.00 will be charged to help defray expenses. A note of intention to attend should be in the hands of Dr. Donald D. Brand by August 15, so that suitable accommodations can be provided.
>
> It will be remembered by those who attended last year's conference, that this is an informal meeting of individuals interested in Southwestern Anthropology. No papers or "speeches" are to be given; there will be merely a "pooling" of information concerning current activities and problems, and an opportunity to become personally acquainted with workers in a common field [Anonymous 1938a].

Several things about this announcement are interesting. It is an advance notice in a generally available publication rather than a set of individual notices to the preceding year's attendees. Emphasis is on anthropology as a whole, not just archaeology. There is a registration fee. Notice of expected attendance is requested. The Conference has now become annual. It is stressed that no formal presentations are to be made, but pooling information on current activities sounds much like the "field reports" of later Conferences. In a sense, this was an institutional invitation rather than a personal one, and the Conference would not be guided by one or two individuals. Responsibility for the Conferences had now shifted from Kidder and his colleagues at the

Laboratory of Anthropology and from eastern institutions to Hewett and his circle, especially at the University of New Mexico. Emphasis should be on "his circle," as by this time Hewett's personal role was declining.

In a report on the 1938 Conference, Brand wrote:

> The Chaco Conference opened Saturday evening, August 27, with a discussion of the proposed central shard laboratory for Southwestern pottery types. The plan in mind included a committee . . . for the purpose of standardizing terminology of these areal pottery types. Consensus of opinion on this subject pointed to the fact that such a laboratory or clearing house would be difficult to set up, because of the difficulty of getting cooperation among the various workers in the Southwest. The obvious stumbling block would be in setting up such a standard terminology to which everyone would agree. If, however, such an organization could be made, it would be of great value in unifying this disorganized side of Southwestern archaeology [Brand 1938: 14].

Some progress had certainly been made since the 1927 Pecos Conference had considered the problems of "nomenclature . . . of pottery types" and a "clearing-house" for considering "names for design-elements." A major advance was the publication in 1936 of Hawley's "Field Manual of Prehistoric Southwestern Pottery Types," followed the next year by the "Handbook of Northern Arizona Pottery Wares" by Colton and Hargrave. In spite of the hopes raised in the 1938 Chaco Conference, no cooperative clearinghouse or laboratory has ever been set up for the entire Southwest. Instead, several museums have expanded their collections of type sherds to include virtually the entire Southwest, and beginning in 1958 a series of "ceramic seminars" was held for several years at the Museum of Northern Arizona to reach agreement on particular groups of types.

The second topic discussed on the first evening of the 1938 Conference was "excavation and restoration." Brand reported:

> Dr. [Arthur H.?] Kelly of the National Park Service stated that he believes that there should be a more intimate relationship between archaeology and restoration—for the public. He pointed out that posterity deserves a right to the reproductions [sic] of the past, and, if archaeology cannot produce the whole past, it

has no right to restoration [excavation?]. The question was also brought up as to whether any individual or institution has the ethical right to leave an excavation unprotected. Better methods of stabilization were mentioned; these include dry barrelling—as a means of draining water—and cement as a cover for walls [Brand 1938: 14].

Sunday morning began with a presentation by Malcolm Farmer and Mera of new information on Navajo archaeology, particularly based on Farmer's work in the Cuba area of New Mexico. House types, chipped stone tools, and the origin of the conical-bottomed pot received particular attention. (See also Anonymous 1938b.)

The afternoon was devoted to reports of recent excavation, with several reports presented by others for those absent. Field work was reported from the following (an asterisk indicates those not present):

Ernst Antevs★	Paul S. Martin★
Donald Brand	Harry Mera
J. O Brew★	Earl H. Morris★
Harold S. Colton	Paul Nesbitt★
Byron Cummings★	Paul Reiter
Bertha Dutton	E. B. Sayles
Gordon Ekholm★	Watson Smith
Odd Halseth	Irene Vickery★
Emil Haury	Marie Wormington
Isabel Kelly	

Brand's report ends by listing fourteen colleges and universities represented at the Conference, seven museums and research centers, and three federal agencies (National Park Service, Office of Indian Affairs, and Soil Conservation Service). He estimated that about ninety individuals attended.

One recollection of this Conference comes from my chance meeting with James Spuhler on 11 June 1983, in the airport of Guangzhou (formerly Canton). Spuhler recalled that at the field school in 1938 and 1939 he had two jobs, librarian and truck driver, and that a few students stayed on as helpers for the Conference each year. In 1938 Roberts, James Ford, and E. H. Spicer were among those present, and the emphasis at the Conference, he recalled, was on archaeology, especially debating the merits of Kidder's Pecos Classification versus the

Gladwin scheme, and also the question of adapting McKern's taxonomic system to the Southwest. Fred Eggan "spoke out for ethnoarchaeology."

In a report in the *New Mexico Anthropologist* there are brief summaries of the research reports, a few words or a sentence for each. Fifty-five names are listed for "others who were present but did not give reports." These include, among many others, Bartlett, Anne M. Cooke, Loren Eiseley, Franklin Fenenga, Guthe, E. T. Hall, Hulda Hobbs, Dorothy and John Keur, Dale King, Scudder McKeel, William Mulloy, Erik Reed, Malcolm Rogers, Spuhler with ten students from the University of New Mexico, Walter Taylor, Joe Toulouse, Richard Van Valkenburg, Joe Ben Wheat, and A. A. Whiteford. The two lists probably include a majority of those who were active in Southwestern research at the time. Only six of those listed as present had been at previous Pecos Conferences, indicating a rapid dropping off of participation by many who were active earlier and the addition of a large number of new participants—a new scholarly generation that had emerged since the end of the 1920s. However, one kind of continuity, even more important than that of individual participants, is represented by the closing words of Hobbs's (1938: 52) short report in *El Palacio:* "The conference afforded a fine opportunity for people with kindred problems to exchange ideas for mutual benefit." This was the central purpose of the first Pecos Conference and has continued to be important through the Chaco years and right up to the present.

THIRD CHACO ANTHROPOLOGICAL CONFERENCE, 1939 (SIXTH PECOS CONFERENCE)   In the July 1939 issue of *American Antiquity* there was a short notice from Brand, similar to that of the previous year in the *New Mexican Anthropologist* but briefer: "The annual Chaco Conference will be held at the University of New Mexico's Chaco Headquarters August 26 to 28. All professionals are cordially invited to attend. Board and lodging will be provided free of charge to active professional anthropologists (be sure to bring your own bedding)" (Brand 1939: 71).

Although Brand emphasized "active" and "professional," a participant of that year recalls that students were not excluded from the Conference (Nathalie F. S. Woodbury, verbal communication, 20 March 1982). There is no list of those who attended in 1939, but Leslie Spier was in charge of the field school and presided over the Conference (Donald Brand, letter to Emil Haury, 24 February 1939), and

Frank Setzler of the U.S. National Museum codirected the excavations (McGregor 1939: 163). The field school at Jemez Canyon that summer was run by Homer G. Barnett. In addition, departmental faculty from the University of New Mexico would have been at the Conference.

In January 1940, *American Antiquity* carried a short report on the 1939 Conference, which is worth quoting in full:

> The third annual anthropological conference sponsored by the University of New Mexico was held at Chaco Canyon August 26th to 28th, with an attendance of ninety-nine, Dr. Leslie Spier reports. Although the majority were archaeologists there was a fair representation of ethnologists and others specializing in the Southwest. A running survey was made of the area from central Mexico to Colorado and Utah, and from Texas to southern California, with informal reports on current field investigations and discussions of their implications. By reason of the presence of a number of workers from each of the regions, special attention was given to cave and other cultures of the Big Bend, Texas, to early horizons of southern Arizona and west Texas, and to a new set of discoveries in Michoacan and neighboring states in central Mexico. (It is worth noting for other conferences that the survey approach was favored by participants as against that of discussing set problems.) [McGregor 1940: 247].

More information on this Conference comes from a letter from Haury to Brand (11 September 1939). Brand arrived at the Conference on Sunday afternoon, 27 August, too late to see Haury, who wrote:

> I am sorry that I did not get to see you at Chaco this summer to express my feeling of satisfaction over the outcome of the Chaco Conference this year. It was all in all a very good session, and I think everyone went away with new ideas, fresh vigor, and new contacts. . . . Our summer work [at the Bear Ruin, Forestdale Valley] was quite successful, although it did not add materially to the Mogollon problem on the side of origins. Paul Martin's work south of Reserve [at the SU site] made a big step in this direction. I am more convinced than ever in the reality of Mogollon, and I believe there are a number of others who are of the same opinion.

In his reply to Haury (15 September 1939) Brand said, "I am still hoping that we can have a junta at which all individuals interested and versed in the Mogollon question can 'have it out.' "

The growing interest in the Mogollon "problem" is also emphasized in "Notes and News, Southwestern Area," in *American Antiquity:* "One of the most interesting and pertinent problems now under examination in the Southwest is the Mogollon Culture" (McGregor 1939: 162). Four institutions were cooperating in its investigation: Martin for the Field Museum of Natural History, at the SU site near Reserve, New Mexico; Haury for the Arizona State Museum, at Forestdale, near Show Low, Arizona; Nesbitt for the Logan Museum, Beloit College, at the Starkweather Ruin, also near Reserve; and W. S. Fulton for the Amerind Foundation, on the extension of Mogollon culture to southeastern Arizona. Nevertheless, Brand's "junta" on the Mogollon was not to be at a Pecos Conference but at the next Southwestern Division meeting of the AAAS, held in Tucson in December 1939. There was a Mogollon symposium, where evidence was presented to link the latest stage of the Cochise culture with the beginning of the Mogollon. Also, discussion "helped to define the [Mogollon] problem in various regions. That it was a diffuse culture all agreed, but in defining derivations there was no real unanimity. Mogollon Culture still remains somewhat indefinite" (Malouf 1940: 85). In 1948, at the Pecos Conference held at Point of Pines, there would be another "junta" to "have it out," as Brand had urged.

Well before 1939 an important new source of financial support for American archaeology had reached significant proportions and should be mentioned. The role of "relief archaeology" in the Southwest is indicated by the following short report for "Notes and News" in *American Antiquity:*

> After an unusually active field season in the Southwest during the past year, present plans indicate less feverish times for archaeologists here. WPA [Work Projects Administration] and other projects have reached the point in many cases where it is now necessary to turn to laboratory evaluation of results and suspend field work until these are completed. . . . Erik K. Reed contributes the news that WPA work is being continued at Quarai, Kuaua (Coronado State Monument), and Pueblo Grande. The work at Pecos with NYA [National Youth Administration] and Forest Service CCC [Civilian Conservation Corps] labor has also continued. The National Park Service ruins stabilization

program with Navaho CCC labor has gone ahead under Gordon
Vivian at Chaco Canyon National Monument, and, under junior
archaeologist Steen assisted by Paul Ezell, at Tonto National
Monument. In the upper ruin at Tonto they have been finding
unusual textiles and other specimens. The only other National
Park Service CCC archaeological project at present is the excavation at the University Ruin in Tucson which is being carried
on for Haury by Julian Hayden [Malouf 1940: 84–85].

FOURTH CHACO ANTHROPOLOGICAL CONFERENCE, 1940 (SEVENTH
PECOS CONFERENCE)   The 1940 Conference was somewhat like the
1931 Conference, as it was held in conjunction with another major
event, in this case the U.S. Coronado Cuarto Centennial, marking the
400th anniversary of the arrival in New Mexico of the great Spanish
conquistador, Francisco Vásquez de Coronado. The U.S. Congress
appropriated $200,000 for the event, and in addition to New Mexico's
celebration there were observances in Arizona, Texas, and Kansas.

The Coronado Congress had five divisions: Hispanic Letters, History, Fine Arts, Southwestern Literature, and Anthropology (Anonymous 1940b: 150). The congress was to follow immediately after the
Bandelier Centennial Conference in Albuquerque (Lange and Riley
1966: 3).

The Anthropology Conference was under the chairmanship of
Brand, and Hewett chaired the Bandelier Centennial. Correspondence
in the files of the Arizona State Museum provides several glimpses of
Brand's work for both the congress and the Chaco Conference. On
13 January 1940 he wrote to Haury:

> As you have probably heard the Coronado Cuarto Centennial
> Commission is, this year, undertaking a varied program of re-
> search, publication, pageants, fiestas, and scientific conferences
> in those Southwestern states that were crossed by Coronado in
> his entrada of 1540–1542. . . . If possible, I should like to sched-
> ule the Annual Chaco Anthropological Conference so that it
> will tie in with the other Coronado Cuarto Centennial Confer-
> ences, i.e., about the 13th, 14th, and 15th of August, instead of
> August 31st to September 2nd at which time it would normally
> fall. If feasible, I should like to do this because of the greater
> possibility for getting Mexican and Eastern United States scien-
> tists interested in the anthropological sciences to attend. We

are already planning on devoting a considerable portion of the Chaco Conference to a discussion of anthropological problems mutual to Mexicanists and Southwesterners. We are inviting a number of the leading Mexican anthropologists. . . . Would you be able to attend this conference should it be held August 13th to 15th instead of the end of the month?

Haury replied on 16 January saying that the dates of 13–15 August "will suit me very well indeed since that will fall at the very end of our field season," and added, "I expect to be in Albuquerque this Saturday for an Executive Committee meeting of the A.A.A.S. and am looking forward to seeing you."

By July Brand's plans were advancing, and he wrote Haury (5 July), as he probably did other Southwestern anthropologists expected at the Conference:

> I hope nothing will prevent your being present for the Chaco Conference August 13th to 15th. Naturally, your family are quite welcome also, but just remember to bring plenty of blankets. We will provide board and lodging as usual, at no cost to those invited. In the near future can you let me know just who all will be coming to the Conference from your Department and the Arizona State Museum? All bona fide professional anthropologists are quite welcome.

He continued his letter with details that reflect the extent to which advance commitments were being secured, in contrast to earlier (and many later) less formal Conferences:

> Fred Eggan, of Chicago, was through here the other day on his way to Oraibi and at that time kindly consented to direct the Conference discussion of recent ethnologic work in the Southwest. Now I am looking for suggestions concerning individuals who are best informed as to current work in the Southwest and Mexico along the lines of archaeology, prehistory (earlier than Basket Maker), linguistics, physical anthropology, dendrochronology, primitive art, human geography, etc. Should Dr. Douglass be able to attend, of course he would be best for dendrochronology. If not, there would be present yourself, Florence Hawley, and [John] McGregor. I am not sure what physical anthropologists plan to attend. Neither [Wilton M.]

Krogman nor [T. Dale] Stewart will be present. You, [Norman] Gabel, and [Clyde] Kluckhohn are physical anthropologists of a sort. Frank Roberts or [Edgar] Howard can handle prehistory. [Ignacio] Marquina can take care of Mexican archaeology. [René] d'Harnoncourt, [Miguel] Covarrubias, Kenneth Chapman, or someone else may be able to handle primitive art. Ralph Beals won't be present, but [Morris] Swadesh or Jimenez Moreno can handle both linguistics and ethnology for Mexico. I don't know who would be best for Southwestern linguistic studies. I shall try to outline anthropological overlaps and connections between Mexico and the Southwest.

For the events of both the Albuquerque and the Chaco Conferences we are fortunate to have a detailed report in the *New Mexican Anthropologist* (Anonymous 1940a). It provides an excellent picture of anthropological research in the Southwest and Mexico at the time. Brand's planning was extremely successful, and "more than 150 delegates attended the Anthropology conference, including a group of eighteen Mexicans." The membership of the Mexican delegation is interesting for the light it throws on professional activities in Mexico and the relationships existing between Mexican and U.S. anthropologists at the time:

> Professor Diodoro Antúnez, Instituto Politécnico Nacional, and Señora Antúnez; Ing. Salvado Barcena; Dr. Daniel Rubín de la Borbolla, Instituto Politécnico Nacional; Mr. Jean B. Johnson, Departamento de Asuntos Indígenas, and Mrs. Jean B. Johnson; Dr. Isabel Kelly, Research Associate, University of California; Dr. Paul Kirchhoff, Instituto Politécnico Nacional; Dr. Norman A. McQuown, Instituto Politécnico Nacional and Departamento de Asuntos Indígenas; Ing. Ignacio Marquina, Instituto Nacional de Antropología, and Mrs. Susana Barcena de Marquina, and daughter; Professor Miguel Othón de Mendizábel, Instituto Politécnico Nacional; Eduardo Noguera, Instituto Nacional de Antropología, and Mrs. Margarita A. Noguera, and daughter; Dr. Jorge A. Vivó, Instituto Politécnico, and Instituto Panamericano de Geografía e Historia.

The first formal session of the Anthropology Conference was Monday afternoon, on the University of New Mexico campus. Ignacio Marquina, chief of the Mexican Department of Prehispanic Monuments, "summarized recent work in Mexico," and Frank Roberts of the Bureau of American Ethnology "presented a general summary of archaeologic work in the American Southwest." That evening at a banquet for the Mexican delegation they were welcomed by Dr. J. F. Zimmerman, president of the Coronado Congress, and Dr. Rubín de la Borbolla responded. After the banquet the anthropologists joined the Fine Arts Conference members in the Alvarado auditorium and heard René d'Harnoncourt, general manager of the Indian Arts and Crafts Board of the U.S. Department of the Interior, speak on "Primitive Arts and Crafts in Mexico and the Southwest." This was followed by a talk on "European Influence on Indian Design Styles" by F. H. (Eric) Douglas, director of the Denver Art Museum.

The next morning, Tuesday, 13 August, "the majority of the anthropologists participating in the Albuquerque Conference drove out to the Research Station of the University of New Mexico, in Chaco Canyon . . . [for] the fourth Chaco Conference."

The account of the Conference in the *New Mexico Anthropologist* is probably the most detailed Pecos Conference report ever published and provides a valuable picture of Southwestern (and Mexican) anthropology half a century ago. Rubín de la Borbolla described in detail the status of physical anthropology in Mexico (a dearth of research in spite of abundant material). Fred Eggan, chairing a session on ethnology, described the trend in the Southwest as "away from the Pueblos toward non-Pueblo groups," and current work was reported on by Paul Kirchhoff, Jean B. Johnson, Father Berard Haile, Leland C. Wyman, Clyde Kluckhohn, Florence Kluckhohn, Margaret E. Fries, Solon T. Kimball, Flora Bailey, Edward H. Spicer, Omer C. Stewart, Mischa Titiev, Edward Kennard, Wayne Dennis (the last three reported by Eggan), Hawley, Halseth, Ralph Linton, Donovan Senter, and J. C. Weckler. This is the most extensive presentation of ethnological research at any Pecos Conference up to this time and few, if any, since then have matched it. In general, the Chaco Conferences were more broadly anthropological, although not slighting archaeology, than most of the subsequent Conferences.

The archaeological session, chaired by Roberts, began with "an instructive discourse on architecture for central and southern Mexican cultures" by Ignacio Marquina. Eduardo Noguera then summarized the past thirty years of archaeological research in Mexico, followed by reports on recent work by Isabel Kelly, Stallings, Walter W. Taylor, Roberts, Hibben, Joe Ben Wheat, Ernst Antevs, Elmer Smith, and Colton. Roberts also spoke about the Mexican sherds found at Pueblo

Bonito, apparently never reported on. James Judge (letter to Wood-bury, 10 September 1981) said, "Tom Windes informs me that they are not lost, but are at the American Museum of Natural History."

Archaeology continued into an evening session, chaired by Haury, who reported on his own work and was followed by Carr Tuthill, Halseth, Dorothy Keur, Roy Malcolm, Malcolm Farmer, Richard Murphy, and Betty Murphy, the last six all describing research on Navajo sites. To open a discussion of Mexican-Southwestern relation-ships, Herbert J. Spinden described the evidence at Pueblo Bonito of influence from and trade with central Mexico. Roberts and Haury dis-cussed other lines of evidence. Mexican-Southwestern relationships would not be discussed again until the 1954 Conference, at Globe. At Fort Burgwin in 1959 the subject would receive further attention.

The final session combined linguistics, ethnobiology, and anthro-pogeography, with reports on the development in Mexico of techni-cal manuals in native languages, on Mexico versus the Andes as the place of origin of maize, and (by Linton) on the possibility that the Southwest's prehistoric population ceiling was set by the balance of starch (maize) and protein (beans) in the diet.

At the conclusion of the report in the *New Mexican Anthropologist,* it is stated that "the above paragraphs represent a digest and abstract from longhand notes taken by three students," a reportorial role that has reappeared at some subsequent Pecos Conferences, although filled more often by professional archaeologists or their wives than by stu-dents. The report ends with a list of delegates, totaling 144 names. It includes only a few "Founders," who had attended the 1927 Con-ference—Colton, Halseth, the Haurys, Nusbaum, the Robertses, and Spinden.

Looking at the 1940 Conference as a whole, it was by far the largest yet (although figures for 1937 are lacking) and had a well-planned and highly structured program. It confirmed the trend of the Chaco Con-ference of including a broad spectrum of anthropological subjects. Its unique aspect was the number of distinguished Mexican anthro-pologists attending, a result of the preceding (subsidized) meeting in Albuquerque, the Coronado Cuarto Centennial. It is impossible to estimate how far the detailed record that was published for the 1940 Conference (the only detailed report since 1927) may have influenced future Conferences, but even for those not present in 1940 it made clear the scope and direction that had been established.

In addition to the "official" published report there is another ac-count of the 1940 Conference, a student's view, in a long letter from

Clifford Evans, U.S. National Museum (who in subsequent years was an experienced meeting goer) to R. B. and N.F.S. Woodbury (11 September 1980), in which he responded to a request for his recollections of the 1940 Conference. The details are so illuminating that it is worth quoting at some length. After answering an unrelated inquiry, Evans continued:

> Now for the attendance of C. Evans and Kep [Ralph Kepler] Lewis at the Chaco Conference in August of 1940. . . . Kep Lewis was at USC [University of Southern California] getting a Masters and I had entered there as a Junior in Sept. 1939. . . . We had decided that we had better get some field training and Haury at U of Arizona offered the two of us assistance to pay part of the credit tuition at U of Arizona if we could come a week early and also do a certain amount of work around camp during the season to help earn our keep. . . . So poor boys Kep and Cliff came from LA in Kep's old 1935 or 1936 Ford car. . . . and were the whole summer of 1940 with Haury, et al., at Forestdale. . . . Well, it was a good summer and lots of big names came through. This meant a lot to both Kep and me, and especially to me, for I had wanted to be in archeology since 10 years of age. . . . That summer was my idea to test myself and see if this was what I wanted. Emil Haury had a great influence in encouraging me to continue. . . . In Haury's camp that summer [we had] the usual group of SWestern visitors, Odd Halseth, Ernst Antevs spent a month with us, Linton, Colton, Tuthill, Spicer, etc., came thru. Then Emil told us about the Chaco meeting and Kep and I pooled what little money we had and decided that if his car would hold together we would . . . attend the meeting. . . . So we left Forestdale by the back roads thru the Mogollon and White Mountains and came into Zuni Pueblo and then . . . made it to Chaco Canyon and camped there with our sleeping bags. . . .
>
> Well, you can imagine what it meant to meet all those names, which were known to Kep and me from the literature. My recollections are very, very strong that it was a truly Western spirit the way everyone mixed together. Now of course in those days the facilities at Chaco were not exactly what you would call super, but they tended to the easy mingling of everyone together. I would say that this was one of the things that impressed me most—no snobbery, no discounting that Kep and

I were students, and I was an undergraduate at that. Nobody asked, nobody cared. We had been with Emil at Forestdale and that was enough. We were interested in archeology and that gave us the "right card of introduction." We were camping, like a lot of others, and nobody held that against us. Persons I remember meeting there . . . and with whom we had more than a limp handshake were Isabel Kelly, Paul Kirchhoff, Ignacio Marquina, Erik Reed, Frank Roberts, Florence Hawley, Bertha P. Dutton . . . , Dorothy Keur . . . , and Frances Elmore.

Now others gave their talks and we were interested and I can say it was very impressive to see the calmness of these great names in handling discussion. Particularly I remember Herbert Spinden and Donald Brand, and Frank Roberts and Haury in that vein.

Now to answer your questions specifically and to offer a few comments. . . .

Interaction between junior and senior archeologists: already mentioned. I noticed no hierarchy. Total exchange. Again, I attribute this (after 40 years later and can look back on it) to the environmental situation under which we met in Chaco. In a hotel it is easier for age, sex, and interest grouping to occur in bars, restaurants, etc. . . .

Interaction between ethnologists and archeologists: at this meeting I did not see any real schism. Seemed like there was a good mixing of everyone. But again you have an environmental situation in the Southwest: you can't study the modern Indians without knowing the past, etc., and vice versa. Definitely not like today. Also the generation of ethnologists in that group were a lot broader and less narrowly specialized than you get today in many, many ethnologists.

Formal versus informal exchange of ideas, and presentations. I can definitely comment on this at Chaco meeting of 1940 and on up until about mid-1950s. There was free discussion and the chairmen of sessions encouraged it and if it was slow to develop they knew how to get it going. Not this pettiness you get in recent years, but honest-to-goodness exchange of ideas. Remember everybody was in the same session. No concurrent sessions. And since it wasn't a place [where] you just dashed out to the nearest bar, or went shopping, or dashed off to the local art gallery, *everybody* [emphasis in original] was there.

. . . In terms of scholarly and scientific [content] . . . this one was excellent. . . . If the flavor of the 1940 one was like the early ones and those meetings shortly after the war when the groups were still small, I think they would have been very important to bring together an exchange of ideas. . . .

Then Kep and I left, hoping our minuscule finances would allow us to get back to LA; luckily all we needed was gas and oil so we made it. Both of us were happy we had gone.

In closing his letter, Evans explains his decision, in spite of the stimulation of Forestdale and the Chaco Conference, to go into South American instead of Southwestern archaeology. "I began to think of all the archeologists behind [each] sagebrush in the SW and how it would be all the harder to get back in, for each one would want to prove himself right, and I had seen in 1940 interesting differences of opinions that sort of got swept under the rug unless they were Haury's, Colton's, or Roberts'."

FIFTH CHACO ANTHROPOLOGICAL CONFERENCE, 1941 (EIGHTH PECOS CONFERENCE) No published report of this Conference has been found, nor any correspondence or records referring to it. Since Roberts again directed the excavations by the Chaco Canyon field school that summer, it is possible that he presided over the Conference.

Brand probably again made whatever preconference plans were needed. Possible participants staying on from the field school are suggested in a monthly report (July 1941) by Lewis T. McKinney, custodian of Chaco Canyon National Monument. The school's staff consisted of Antevs, C. Keith Barnes, Florence Cline, Harry Hoijer, Elizabeth Bacon Hudson, Charles Lange, William Mulloy, Paul Reiter, Roberts, Spier, and Wyman, with Ed Dozier and Dave Skeet as interpreters. Special lecturers for the field school were Colton, Walter Cline, Wayne Dennis, Alfred E. Hudson, Martin, and Anne Cooke Smith. In addition, we have some personal recollections that help fill the gap in formal records and reassure us that a 1941 Conference really took place. Robert L. Stephenson, of the University of South Carolina, wrote (letter to Woodbury, 11 January 1982) that:

I was at the Chaco Conference in 1941. That is where I first met Dr. Roberts. Some of those others who were there as I remember were Dr. H. P. Mera, Dr. Alex Krieger, Sylvanus G. Morley, and Cyrus Ray. . . . Alex came up from Texas with me. . . .

I particularly remember Dr. Mera with his ice cream suit [white linen?]. It was very hot and every time Dr. Mera would get up to say something he would carefully stand, put on his coat, button it up, make his statement, take his coat off, fold it carefully and put it down to sit on until he had something else to say, at which time he would repeat the process.

This was the last Pecos Conference for several years. During World War II travel was drastically curtailed, anthropologists were dispersed in a great variety of military and civilian roles, and most scientific meetings were canceled. In many ways, the post-1945 world was very different, changed irreversibly, and it is not surprising that when the Pecos Conference was revived in 1946 it took a somewhat different pattern from what had gone before.

5
The Revival after World War II, 1946 and 1947

When World War II came to an end with the Japanese surrender in August 1945, Southwesternists, like other Americans in every walk of life, were eager to get back to normal as quickly as possible, picking up the threads of research, writing, field work, curating, teaching, and study.

The diversion of archaeologists to war-related activities took many forms, from combat duty to intelligence in both hemispheres to home-front responsibilities. Some archaeologists also found time to fit in a limited continuation of research and writing. At the Museum of Northern Arizona, Flagstaff, for example, Harold S. Colton, in addition to his local civic activities and his war-related research, continued his study of the Sinagua culture (Colton 1946). At the same time, at Gila Pueblo, 130 miles to the south, Harold S. Gladwin was analyzing his own data on the "Flagstaff culture" and the region's tree-ring dates. He reached drastically different conclusions from Colton (Gladwin 1943). Gila Pueblo was also preparing other reports at this time, such as "The San Simon Branch: Excavations at Cave Creek . . ." (Sayles 1945); "Tree-Ring Analysis: Problems of Dating, I . . ." (Gladwin 1944); and "The Chaco Branch: Excavations at White Mound and in the Red Mesa Valley" (Gladwin 1945).

Still farther south, Emil W. Haury was able to complete excavations at Ventana Cave, seventy-five miles west of Tucson on the Papago Reservation, assisted by Wilfred Bailey and Julian Hayden, with funds from the Indian Division of the Civilian Conservation Corps (Haury and others 1950).

During the summer of 1944 the Bluff Ruin, an early Mogollon site in the Forestdale Valley, was excavated by the Arizona State Museum,

Tucson, with semisubterranean houses dated at about A.D. 300 (Haury and Sayles 1947).

On the other side of the United States, an impressive backlog of reports was being prepared for publication at the Peabody Museum, Harvard University, under the stimulus of its director, Donald Scott (*Teocentli,* No. 37, June 1944). J. O. Brew's report on excavations at Alkali Ridge, southern Utah, in 1931–33, was nearly ready for the printer (it appeared in 1946). Mischa Titiev's "Old Oraibi" was published in 1944; Haury's monograph on the Hemenway Expedition's 1887–88 work at Los Muertos, southern Arizona, came out in 1945; and C. B. (Burt) Cosgrove's "Caves of the Upper Gila and Hueco Areas in New Mexico and Texas" was published in 1947, completed by his widow and longtime partner in research, Hattie Cosgrove. Also, work continued, at least briefly, on the preparation of the hundreds of drawings for Watson Smith's "Kiva Mural Decorations at Awatovi and Kawaika-a," which was published in 1952 (Smith 1952a). Also at Harvard, Walter W. Taylor was able to complete his dissertation and defend it in the winter of 1943, before entering military service. Later, after revision, it was published by the AAA (Taylor 1948). It immediately aroused strong reactions to his criticisms of the research and publication of some well-known archaeologists, including, from the Southwest, Kidder, Haury, and Frank H. H. Roberts. Later, the constructive side of his analysis began to be recognized as an important part of a gradual but profound change in archaeological thinking, culminating in the New Archaeology.

Elsewhere a few other major archaeological reports were appearing or in preparation during the war years and immediately thereafter, such as E. T. Hall's "Early Stockaded Settlements in the Governador" (1944) and George Carter's "Plant Geography and Culture History of the American Southwest" (1945), with its controversial views on the introduction of agriculture into the Southwest. But these were exceptions to the general curtailment of research and publication from 1942 through 1945, and in most cases represented the completion of work begun long before.

After the war, field work in the Southwest resumed slowly. In the summer of 1946 the Arizona State Museum began its long excavation program at Point of Pines in the Mogollon country, on the San Carlos Indian Reservation, successfully combining field school instruction with problem-directed research (Haury 1989). Also in the summer of 1946 the University of New Mexico revived its annual field school—

its sixteenth season, but not in Chaco Canyon this year. Students lived on the campus, working at two sites on the Rio Puerco of the East, a Pleistocene cave deposit and a small Pueblo III ruin. That same summer the Chicago Natural History Museum (now the Field Museum of Natural History) resumed excavation of the SU site in southwestern New Mexico, where Paul S. Martin had started work in 1931 but suspended it in 1941.

There was, therefore, a great deal of personal "catching up" to be done in 1946 among friends and colleagues whose contacts had been severely restricted for four years, and there was also considerable activity to report on and discuss since the preceding Conference at Chaco in the summer of 1941 (Reiter 1946).

SANTA FE, 1946 (NINTH PECOS CONFERENCE) The postwar revival of the Pecos Conference began in April 1946, when Haury wrote to Erik Reed (now back at the National Park Service in Santa Fe after his military service) suggesting the need for a conference in the coming summer. Haury began with the sort of jocular greeting with which people often mask more serious feelings: "Welcome back. It is good once again to see your familiar scrawl in correspondence. Jess[e L. Nusbaum] had written that you were back, fat but not too sassy." Then Haury came to the more important part of the letter, from our standpoint: "I had talked with a couple of people about the possibility of the Southwesternists getting together sometime this summer, and Santa Fe strikes me as the best spot. Keep your ear to the ground, and when occasion presents itself put in a plug for the idea" (Emil Haury, letter to Erik Reed, 9 April 1946).

The next letter in the material from the files of the Arizona State Museum is a reply by Reed dated 17 June, in which he says that he has

> written an identical letter, copy inclosed, to J. O. Brew, Don Lehmer, Earl Morris, Eric Douglas, Stallings, Malcolm Rogers, Malcolm Farmer, Art Woodward, Dr. Colton, Paul Martin (and Rinaldo), the University of New Mexico, and J. Charles Kelley at Texas. The N.P.S archaeologists will presumably include Jesse Nusbaum, Dale King, Charlie Steen, Gordon Baldwin from Boulder Dam, and myself. . . . The other five Santa Feans are Dr. Mera, Stanley Stubbs, Walt Taylor, and Hulda Hobbs and Marjorie Tichy from the Museum downtown.
>
> Personally, I hope to exclude inconspicuously anyone else

from the Museum, such as Reginald [Fisher], and I plan to forget Dr. Renaud. Do you agree? And whom have I forgotten that we should get . . . ?

Reed's proposed program suggests new interests and concerns among Southwesternists, including the Mogollon, archaeological methodology, and the administration of archaeological sites and their interpretation to the public. The geographical scope had broadened, as well. In his letter Reed stated that the meeting would be "an informal conference of active Southwestern archaeologists . . . [on] August 20–22 at Santa Fe, at the instance of Emil Haury . . . held at the Laboratory of Anthropology." He added that an attendance of about fifteen people from out of town was expected, ten resident in Santa Fe, and "five or six from the University of Albuquerque [sic]." Events would prove this prediction wrong. Reed continued:

> No formal program is envisioned; Haury and others feel that what is needed is a small get-together to discuss current concepts and recent developments, an informal exchange of ideas, since there has been no meeting of Southwestern archaeologists during the last few years. One full day, at least, should be devoted primarily to "Recent research and the Mogollon Culture" (Haury, Martin, Colton); if possible I should like a morning session on "General approaches to archaeological methodology" (Walter Taylor) and an afternoon on "Administrative and interpretative problems" (Laboratory of Anthropology and National Park Service officials); the third day can be concerned with any other subjects anyone wants to bring up—particularly, perhaps, northern Mexico (Brand, Taylor, Haury, Stallings) and Yuman-Patayan archaeology (Colton, Malcolm J. Rogers, if he can come, and Gordon C. Baldwin), and/or Navaho archaeology (Farmer and Ned Hall, if they can be here). Each session will be in the nature of a seminar [Erik Reed, letter to J. O. Brew, 17 June 1946 (the same letter going to the others listed above)].

Contrary to most Pecos Conferences, there was no specific time assigned to "recent field work reports," probably because Reed felt that too little had been done to merit a separate session, and also because the focus was to be on major problems, rather than on details. The selection of discussion or seminar leaders was a pattern that was to recur frequently in subsequent years, a compromise between the unfocused and rambling sessions that often resulted from the absence of a leader and the overly formal (and for many years rejected) presentation of prepared papers in a fully planned session. The range of important topics and the desire to give adequate attention to new problems with vigorous disagreement expected (Mogollon, for example, and to a lesser degree, Yuman-Patayan archaeology) necessitated this degree of planning.

Haury found Reed's proposals highly satisfactory, and he wrote Reed:

> I approve heartily of your plans for the conference. To avoid possible repercussions from H S Gladwin it might be well to send him a letter. He is pretty certain not to come anyway and even if he decides to come it should be interesting. Renaud is actually not much involved, it seems to me, in the sort of things we want to talk about [letter of Haury to Reed, 30 June 1946].

But plans for the Conference were not quite as acceptable to some others as to Haury, as hinted in a humorously phrased but doubtless seriously meant complaint by Paul Reiter of the University of New Mexico. In a letter to Haury, after commenting on the current field session of the university, he added:

> As you doubtless know E. Reed is taking your name in vain re some dam meeting in Santa Fe on August 22 or thereabout. It's "Dr. Haury thinks—" and "Dr. Haury says—" etc and since all the others are away except [Frank C.] Hibben why I suppose I outta go. . . . Will you Please drop me a note and tell me what Eric can't, to wit is the meeting you are having the kinda bull session where I can bring some graduate students or do you want to limit the attendance somewhat? Such information would be gratefully received by yrs paul [Paul Reiter, letter to Emil W. Haury, undated].

The student problem was taken up seriously by Reed in a letter to Haury (9 July 1946) in which he listed those "definitely planning to attend," including "Reiter and Cal Burrows [Carroll Burroughs] from U.N.M.—plus a group of youngsters which the latter is taking on tour, who he says are serious students and I hate to refuse, although I don't like the idea very much; maybe they can be there just part of the time." Reed listed in this letter as definitely unable to attend Brew,

Eric Douglas, Donald Brand, W. W. Hill, Leslie Spier, Art Woodward, and E. B. Sayles, and as "not yet heard from" Earl Morris, J. Charles Kelley, and Gladwin.

After all the invitations had been sent and an unknown number of volunteers accepted or rejected, the list had grown well beyond the thirty or so Reed had planned on back in June. So it was not quite the "small get-together" of Haury's original suggestion. Nevertheless, almost every individual at the Conference can be identified as making significant contributions to Southwestern studies, so in this sense it still remained very much a working conference rather than a program presented to an interested but nonparticipatory audience.

The detailed report on the Conference in *El Palacio* (Bartlett and Reed 1946) lists forty-eight names, and with the addition of Reiter's and Burroughs's fifteen unnamed students the total is sixty-three! The list that was published (Table 5.1) is an interesting indication of individuals and institutions then active in the Southwest. Ethnography, as was so often the case, is poorly represented. Only fifteen of these individuals were on Reed's original list of twenty-three (Erik Reed, letter to Emil W. Haury, 17 June 1946).

There were short reports on the Conference in *American Antiquity* (Reed 1947b) and in *American Anthropologist* (Bartlett 1946), both emphasizing that the Conference was "continuing the tradition of the Pecos Conferences and Chaco Conferences." In this spirit, and contrary to Reed's proposed agenda, "the first day was spent in renewing acquaintances, reviewing the accomplishments of the past few years, and considering problems for discussion" (Bartlett and Reed 1946: 269). Perhaps the Pecos tradition of informality was too strong to be abandoned quickly. But, getting down to business, Haury was elected chairman of the Conference and Katharine Bartlett its secretary.

Before the "seminar" sessions on the topics chosen by Reed there were reports of work in progress and wide-ranging suggestions on the needs of Southwestern anthropology. The suggestions included more joint archaeological-ethnological studies (Leslie White); attention to the areal extent of the Hohokam and to Navajo, Pima, and Papago archaeology (Haury); more work in northern Mexico (Taylor); less costly publication methods (Colton); and the need "to get cultural [anthropological] materials into the schools" (Ruth Underhill).

It is noteworthy that the term *Patayan,* which appeared in Reed's initial agenda, was used in at least two of the first day's reports. It was a relatively new addition to the roster of Southwestern prehistoric "cultures," first used in 1938 by Lyndon Hargrave in the Museum of

Table 5.1. Participants in the 1946 Pecos Conference, Santa Fe
(Bartlett and Reed 1946: 275–276)

Leslie W. White, University of Michigan
W. S. Stallings, Taylor Museum, Colorado Springs
Dorothy Luhrs, University of Southern California
Malcolm L. Farmer, San Diego Museum of Man
Ruth Underhill, U.S. Indian Service, Santa Fe
Mr. and Mrs. Arnold Withers, Columbia University
Paul Reiter, with Carroll A. Burroughs, Herbert Dick, Charles Lange, and
 fifteen other advanced students; Florence Hawley, and Mr. and
 Mrs. Robert H. Lister, University of New Mexico
John B. Rinaldo, Chicago Natural History Museum
Dr. and Mrs. Emil W. Haury, and Mr. and Mrs. Arthur Kent, University
 of Arizona
Theodore Stern, University of Pennsylvania
Mr. and Mrs. Carr Tuthill, Amerind Foundation, Dragoon, Arizona
H. Marie Wormington (Mrs. Peter Volk), Colorado Museum of Natural
 History
Dr. and Mrs. H. S. Colton, and Katharine Bartlett, Museum of Northern
 Arizona
Albert Schroeder, Grand Canyon National Park
Gordon Baldwin, Boulder Dam Recreational Area
John L. Cotter, Tuzigoot National Monument
Louis R. Caywood, Walnut Canyon National Monument
Mr. and Mrs. Odd S. Halseth, Phoenix
Dr. and Mrs. Walter W. Taylor, Santa Fe
Dr. H. P. Mera, Santa Fe
Jesse L. Nusbaum, Erik K. Reed, Charlie R. Steen, Dale S. King, U.S.
 National Park Service, Santa Fe
James W. Young, Kenneth M. Chapman, Stanley A. Stubbs, and Jean Cady,
 Laboratory of Anthropology, Santa Fe
Bertha P. Dutton, Edwin N. Ferdon, Marjorie F. Tichy, and Hulda Hobbs,
 Museum of New Mexico
Joseph Toulouse, Los Alamos
Francis Elmore, Santa Fe

Northern Arizona's *Museum Notes* (Hargrave 1938). *Patayan* was proposed as a substitute for Gladwin's *Yuman Root,* a term considered by most as unacceptable for an archaeological culture, since it was the name of a historic Native American group and implied a connection or relationship that was far from proved (see also Colton 1945).

The second and third days of the Santa Fe Conference were devoted to specific problems and topics, including all those originally proposed by Reed. In addition, the Conference approved the proposed reorganization of the AAA (as described by Leslie White). This was the first time that the Pecos Conference had considered the anthropological profession's structure, reflecting the widening interests and professional participation of Southwesternists.

Taylor chaired a discussion of concepts and methods of archaeology, beginning with a plea that "we must advance beyond chronicle into synthesis and interpretation, [with] bold hypotheses, inferences, and interpretation of ideas and behavior."

In the session on "early man" Bartlett demonstrated that there was no "gap" between Folsom and later cultures, contrary to the long-held view (see Roberts 1937: 25–26).

Reed presented a detailed discussion of relationships among prehistoric culture units, including the closeness of Chaco to Mesa Verde and their connection to modern Tanoan-speaking groups, and grouping Mogollon-Mimbres, Cibola-Sinagua, and Hopi-Zuni as distinct from the Anasazi of the San Juan and Rio Grande. These were ideas he was publishing in several significant articles derived from his first Ph.D. dissertation, said to have been rejected by Harvard University as not based on original field work.

The Hohokam, Mogollon, and Patayan were examined in terms of origins, distribution, and relationships to historic groups. Discussion of the northern and eastern peripheries, including the Panhandle culture of the Canadian River, reflects a relaxation of the narrow view of what was "Southwestern" that had frustrated Curry Holden at the 1929 Conference. Northern Mexico received attention from several participants, not as a "periphery" but as a major part of the "Southwest." It would be another three years, however, before Kelley would begin his research in northern Mexico, which was so significant in demonstrating the continuum that existed from the civilizations of the south to the farming villages of the Southwestern United States.

In the final session the interpretation of archaeology to the public was discussed by Dale King, Marie Wormington, and others. The latter would soon publish her important popular summary, *Prehistoric Indians of the Southwest* (1947), and her *Ancient Man in North America* had appeared in 1939 (expanded and republished in 1944, 1949, and 1957). Anthropological material for high school classrooms would be slower to appear, but between 1962 and 1969 a dozen books and instructional kits resulted from the AAA's Anthropology Curriculum Study Project (see the project's 1972 final report). For the primary grades it was agreed at the Conference that many museums were successfully presenting archaeological concepts and information.

Finally, Jesse Nusbaum advised the meeting that anyone planning to excavate on Indian lands should secure a permit from the appropriate tribal council, a reflection of the slowly increasing control over their lands that Native Americans were gaining. Nusbaum also reported that there was a move in Congress to repeal the Antiquities Act of 1906 and urged archaeologists to express their strong opposition to repeal. Perhaps partly because of the archaeologists' opposition, the act was not repealed, and new, more stringent laws were passed in future decades.

Before the Conference ended, Haury "invited the group, and Southwesternists not attending this meeting, to his camp [Point of Pines] for a similar conference next August." This invitation was to be the subject of some confusion and much correspondence between Haury and Reiter in the months ahead, and eventually it would be agreed to hold the 1947 Conference at Chaco Canyon and the 1948 Conference at Point of Pines.

Bartlett and Reed conclude their report on the 1946 Conference with the observation that

> throughout the discussions there was a tendency to synthesize the results of archaeological research to present broad pictures of the movements of prehistoric populations and their affinities with present Indian groups, etc., and an interest in popularizing the results of archaeological research. These are new trends in Southwestern archaeology that will be interesting to watch [Bartlett and Reed 1946: 275).

We cannot compare the 1946 Conference with earlier ones as confidently as we would like because of the incompleteness of the record for many of the years. But comparing 1946 with the well-recorded 1940 meeting, a striking difference can be seen, as implied by Bartlett and Reed. The 1940 Conference spent the greater part of its time on reports of specific, individual field work just completed, whereas in 1946 many major problems of wide interest were discussed at length. In the years ahead there would continue to be field reports as well as symposia and syntheses, with frequent disagreement as to the proper balance to be sought. But to an important degree 1946 set the Conferences on a new course, with increased attention to large problems and less time for details of each site dug or surveyed.

It offers an interesting insight into the reliability of individuals' recollections of past events in which they took part that I was told during the 1982 Pecos Conference (1) that the major topic of the 1946 Conference in Santa Fe was "Early Man"; (2) that Frederick W. Hodge was there (he appears in neither the roster of attendees nor the reports on the meeting); and (3) that Willard F. Libby was the last speaker on the program and caused great excitement with his report on the development of carbon-14 dating. However, Frederick Johnson has written (1951) that the possibility of dating archaeological material by this method was first announced in 1949.

SIXTH CHACO ANTHROPOLOGICAL CONFERENCE, 1947 (TENTH PECOS CONFERENCE)   By the time of the 1947 Conference, the last at Chaco, there had been a substantial increase in field work in the Southwest, accelerating from the slow postwar start in 1945–46. The summer of 1947 saw field work by the University of Arizona at Point of Pines; by the University of New Mexico at its field school in Chaco Canyon and reconnaissance in southeastern Chihuahua; by the University of Texas in central and west Texas; by the University of Utah in caves on Stansbury Island in the Great Salt Lake; by Gila Pueblo on Mesa Verde and at Springerville, Arizona; by the Chicago Natural History Museum at prepottery and later sites near Reserve, New Mexico; in Colorado by the Colorado Museum of Natural History in cooperation with Denver University; and by the National Park Service in the Davis Dam area on the Colorado River. Field work was clearly getting back to its prewar pace.

The increase in archaeological activity at this time is also reflected in the creation of two new anthropology departments with strong archaeological emphasis, one at the University of Colorado, with Robert Lister full time and Earl Morris part time, and the cooperation of Robert Burgh (Reiter 1948a: 271). The other was at the University of Utah, with Southwestern archaeology the responsibility of Elmer Smith (Reiter 1948b: 73). Archaeology now had a place in anthropology departments in all of the Four Corners states as well as in neighboring Texas and California.

During the next few summers there would also be field work in the Southwest by the Museum of Northern Arizona, the Peabody Museum, Texas Tech at Lubbock, and the Amerind Foundation, with projects ranging from early man and Cochise sites to the late prehistoric. Pipelines and dams began to require preconstruction archaeological investigation, such as Stanley A. Stubbs's work in the lower Chama Valley, preceding the flooding of the Chamita Reservoir. For the 415-mile natural gas pipeline built from New Mexico to the Colorado River, Nusbaum, as consulting archaeologist of the National Park Service, would perform a heroic task in arranging for complete survey and all appropriate excavation, on only a few weeks' notice (Nusbaum 1956). At Willow Beach on the Colorado Albert H. Schroeder excavated in advance of flooding by the Davis Dam Reservoir. Such projects as these would increase in size and number in the years ahead, involving virtually every institution with archaeological interests in the Southwest.

Haury, as noted earlier, had invited the Conference to come to Point of Pines in 1947, but Reiter had expected that the Conference would return again to Chaco Canyon. The friendly rivalry between the universities of Arizona and New Mexico can be read between the lines of the extensive correspondence between Haury and Reiter, through which the misunderstanding or disagreement was finally resolved. It is tempting to quote all of it, but selections will have to suffice.

On 29 November 1946 Reiter wrote Haury a long letter about departmental matters at New Mexico, including the possibilities of Arizona students enrolling at the Chaco Canyon field school for credit at Arizona, and future archaeological plans by the University of New Mexico for work in New Mexico, Chihuahua, and Baja California. He also wrote about the Conference for next summer, as follows:

> I've been meaning to write to you about the Chaco Conference. I believe you indicated in Santa Fe the need for such a thing, but I do not recall whether you feel we should have a meeting at any of several locations, or whether you would approve another Chaco Conference at Chaco. If the latter, I'd suggest the dates of July 28, 29 and 30. As usual we would be glad to furnish food for those days to all and sundry who would bring their own bedrolls and not be too choosy about their lodgings. If you approve of a Chaco Conference next summer, I'll include it in a published field session announcement, and in our summer session catalogue, in January.

Haury apparently did not reply to Reiter immediately, but on 27 January 1947, he wrote Martin at the Chicago Natural History Museum, thanking him for his hospitality during Haury's recent visit to Chicago. Haury added, "I had the devil of a time getting home since the plane was grounded in Oklahoma City. Finally made it by train after some 65 hours en route." Then he came to the matter of the 1947 Conference, which he felt should not be held in New Mexico, in spite of Reiter's letter of 29 November. Haury said:

> We are counting on you coming to Point of Pines next summer and you should know that we are tentatively planning a conference there sometime in August. This will have to be after the students have gone. Conference plans are tentative I must emphasize since Paul Reiter has raised the question of whether it should be at Chaco. My feeling is that most people have seen that country and should be given a chance to see a new part of the Southwest.

Finally, on 4 February 1947 Haury answered Reiter's letter:

> It has taken a long time to get around to your letter. . . . The chief reason for the delay being that I have not been able to see my way clear as yet to make any concrete suggestion. . . . at Santa Fe I extended an invitation to meet at Point of Pines in August about the 15th. I realize that the area is a little difficult to get to and that we don't have the facilities as yet that you have at Chaco but I would like to have our buddies see this new part of the Southwest. Don't get me wrong, I am not hipped on this and I made the overture chiefly to keep the conference idea alive. If the majority want Chaco that is where it should be.
>   Sorry to be so inexplicit but that is where the matter stands at present.
>
> Yours as always,
> Emil
> Emil W. Haury

Reiter replied to Haury's letter quickly (on 7 February) and in some distress:

> Dear Komrade Emil:
>   My Christ I've sure dropped a brick. No, I did *not* know that you planned a conference at Point of Pines. I understood that eventually [you] planned one or several there but that your buildings won't be completed in time for 1947. And I checked with [Carroll A.] Burroughs [who received his B.A. at New

Mexico and had a long career in the National Park Service]
and [Schofield] DeLong [an architect with the National Park
Service], both of whom were at Santa Fe, and this was their impression also. . . . I definitely did not know that a conference was
planned for the coming summer. . . .

I'm sorry I came off with the wrong idea, but I had somehow
envisioned the Point of Pines conference in the future at a more
distant date. . . . You write "If the majority want Chaco—"
How the hell do I know. Shall I try to find out?

I'm kinda upset about this but you big lug why didn't you
write me more sooner like; my field session is all set up down
to dates and truck-load lists and budget. . . . Honest, I didn't
know your plans included next summer, but I'll defer in any way
possible. Let me know as soon as you can whether I should get
a straw vote on localities or should drop it quietly like the brick
it is. . . .

Lemme know how things go, and I'm sorry about the mixup.

Sincerely,
Paul

Or, hey, big boy! Would you consider having a Chaco conference this summer with the understanding that next summer it
would be Point of Pines? Of course, I'd wanna bring a small
group of students and expect you will too.

Haury responded promptly, perhaps feeling some sense of relief at
the possibility of being able to wait a year before hosting the Conference at Point of Pines—the camp not yet complete and the logistics
of caring for such a large group posing substantial problems. He was
conciliatory about the misunderstanding and accepted Reiter's final
suggestion, but needled him for not knowing of the Arizona invitation.

The serious details of planning were taken care of in the next few
weeks, although the partly humorous tone of the letters continued.
Reiter said in a letter of 15 February:

Herr Komrad Emilski:
Thanks for yrs. Yes, I'll inform all northern comrades of the
conference. Matter of fact, we will get out a double postcard announcing the conference with an attached postcard for reply. . . .
The text will read:

The Sixth Annual Chaco Anthropological Conference will be held at the University Research Station, Chaco Canyon, New Mexico, on July 28th, 29th, and 30th. The first meeting will be held at 2 pm on July 28th. Visiting authorities will be asked to chairman [*sic*] the different meetings and all professional anthropologists are cordially invited to attend. The University will furnish board and all the available room, but guests are asked to bring their own bed rolls and sleeping bags. The program will be determined by the wishes of those attending [a contrast to 1946].

Please indicate your intentions regarding attendance on the attached card.

With the 1947 and 1948 Conference schedule settled satisfactorily, the correspondence between Reiter and Haury now turned to the question of what the Conference should be called. There had been no consistent terminology so far, with the 1927 and 1929 Pecos Conferences at Pecos, the "Third Biennial Pecos Conference" in 1931 at the Laboratory of Anthropology in Santa Fe, and five Chaco Anthropological Conferences from 1937 through 1941. There seems to have been no doubt in the minds of participants that all of these, despite their various names, served the same purpose—an informal meeting to exchange information and ideas. With a letter to Haury on 21 February 1947, Reiter not only raised the question of the appropriate name for the Conference but had serious questions about its essential nature and future locations.

Some of the lower elements around here and I have been muttering about conferences. Got a long letter from Jesse Nusbaum in the same mail with the enclosed [no enclosure with this letter in the Arizona State Museum files] and Jesse keeps talking about the "Pecos" conferences, those literally at Pecos and those at the Laboratory of Anthropology in Santa Fe. Then you mention that Kidder might totter out this way during the summer and two of our graduate students awakened with the pregnant suggestion that the term Pecos Conference might be continued. We'll give up our "Chaco Conference" and have a Pecos Conference at Chaco Canyon this year. The confab at the laboratory in Santa Fe last summer might have been called a Pecos Conference for the first conference of that kind at the Laboratory was called the Pecos Conference (1931).

In my mind (quiet!) there is a distinction between the conference held out in the field, at excavations during the summer, where open discussions occur rather than around a University or a mess of hotel rooms. Further, there is the more personalized (like Ivory Flakes) element of having a small staff serve as the host rather than a larger institution like the University of Arizona. Further, at Pecos and at Chaco itinerant guests usually got fed or something, and this, too, is different. Now you don't wanna have a Chaco Conference at Point of Pines do you? And maybe Texas or Utah or Colorado might sometimes get interested, so why not revert to the original idea of the Pecos Conference and hold it at different locations each year as the different institutions are willing to play the host.

These are useful observations on the nature of Pecos Conferences, but the suggestion of "Pecos" as a permanent name did not take hold immediately. Eventually, two years later, the name "Pecos Conference" was adopted on a permanent basis, regardless of each year's location. But in 1947 Haury's acquiescence was somewhat unenthusiastic, and the name for the Conference continued to be troublesome. On 8 October 1947, in regard to the following year's Conference, Haury wrote Reiter, "Do you agree that we should refer to this junta as the Southwestern Archaeological Conference? Change if needed [the notice going out in the mail] to anything but the Chaco Conference at Point of Pines!"

When the 1947 Conference was reported in *American Antiquity* the following year, it was referred to as "the Southwestern Archaeological Conference," although the announcement in the same journal in July 1947 called it "The Sixth Annual Chaco Conference of Southwestern Anthropologists."

To Kidder in 1947 it was still "the Southwestern Archaeological Conference" when he wrote of looking forward to attending it at Point of Pines the next year (*Teocentli,* No. 45, June 1948). This problem of a name was finally resolved at the 1949 Conference, when Bartlett proposed and it was agreed by vote that the name would henceforth be "the Pecos Conference," in honor of A. V. Kidder and the first Conference at Pecos in 1927. No more Conferences were named for their locations.

Turning at last to the 1947 Conference itself, under whatever name its participants may have thought of it, the record is more complete than for some of the earlier Conferences at Chaco, thanks to reports in *American Antiquity* (Reiter 1948a) and *El Palacio* (Reed 1947a), immediately followed by "Random Notes on the Chaco Conference" by Odd S. Halseth (1947), all of which are used in the following account.

We do not have a roster of attendees at the 1947 Conference, but Reed's report mentions thirty-three names (see Table 5.2). There were apparently some sixty-five others at the Conference, as indicated in the AAA *News Bulletin* item, which says that President Clyde Kluckhohn "discussed current activities of the Association with the approximately one hundred anthropologists present." From the names in Table 5.2 it appears that New Mexico, including the National Park Service, was strongly represented, and Arizona only slightly.

Reed's report states that there was the "usual 'news roundup,'" with active Southwesternists present reporting on their current research projects"; it then lists "topics receiving more extended discussion":

> the relationships between the archaeological and ethnological approaches, or field of investigation; archaeological classification and terminology in the Pueblo area; types of stone tools representing "early man" in several areas of North America; the need for counter-propaganda to defeat attempts to sabotage the Lacey Act of 1906 for the protection of American antiquities.

Reiter reported that the chairmen elected for various sessions were Taylor, Kluckhohn, Reed, and Kidder, and said that "the majority of the discussions were of a generalized nature and a considerable emphasis was placed upon ethnological as well as archaeological problems and progress. The mutual interdependence of the two related disciplines was more strongly brought into relief than at former meetings."

The last point can be illustrated by Fred Eggan's recollection of an informal conversation during a Chaco Conference, probably in 1947. He remembered (conversation with Woodbury, 6 October 1978) that at one of the Chaco Conferences, "when Clyde Kluckhohn and Paul Reiter were there," a group was sitting and talking one evening. Reiter said to Eggan, in more or less these words, "You're an ethnologist— tell us, what was the social organization of the Anasazi, the Hohokam, and the Mogollon?" Eggan recalled, "We'd had a couple of drinks and felt relaxed, so I free associated and came up with the social organization of all three, each different. Reiter didn't say anything for a couple of minutes, and then said, 'Well, I'll be God-damned!'" Thus was archaeology's and ethnology's interdependence demonstrated.

The "brief comments regarding field work" that Reiter listed also reflect the increased participation of nonarchaeologists in this Confer-

Table 5.2. Partial List of Attendees at the 1947 Pecos Conference, Chaco Canyon
(Reed 1947a; see *Note*)

John Adair, Ph.D. candidate in ethnology at the University of New Mexico

David Baerreis, University of Wisconsin

Carroll Burroughs, University of New Mexico

H. T. Cain, San Diego Museum of Man

Alfred Dittert, archaeology student at New Mexico

Herbert Dick, Harvard graduate student

Bertha Dutton, Museum of New Mexico

Fred Eggan, University of Chicago and Vice-President of the American Anthropological Association

Edwin H. Ferdon, Museum of New Mexico

Odd S. Halseth, Pueblo Grande Museum, Phoenix

Frank Hibben, University of New Mexico

Bert Kaplan, graduate student in psychology at Harvard

A. V. Kidder, Chairman of the Division of Historical Research, Carnegie Institution of Washington

Dale S. King, National Park Service, Santa Fe

Clyde Kluckhohn, Harvard University and President of the American Anthropological Association

Florence Kluckhohn, Cambridge, Massachusetts

Alex Krieger, University of Texas

H. P. Mera, Museum of New Mexico

Jesse L. Nusbaum, National Park Service, Santa Fe

Joaquin Ortega, University of New Mexico

Donald Pitkin, beginning graduate student at Harvard

Verne F. Ray, University of Washington

Erik K. Reed, National Park Service, Santa Fe

Paul Reiter, University of New Mexico

Robert G. Rose, Superintendent, Mesa Verde National Park

F. V. Scholes, historian, University of New Mexico

Albert H. Schroeder, National Park Service

James Spuhler, Ohio State University (he had just received his Ph.D. in physical anthropology at Harvard)

Charlie R. Steen, National Park Service, Santa Fe

Walter W. Taylor, Museum of New Mexico

Gordon Vivian, National Park Service

Evon Z. Vogt, a graduate student at the University of Chicago

Don Watson, National Park Service Naturalist at Mesa Verde National Park

---

Note: This list may represent those reporting field work. An estimated 65 others were present but no full roster has survived.

ence. There were eight archaeological reports—on Mesa Verde, Chaco Canyon, Salado and Pima population sources, the Southern Pueblo periphery, Southwest and Plains influences in Texas, Colorado River sites, and surveys of the San Agustin Plains and Cebolleta Mesa. In addition there were seven reports by students and colleagues of Kluckhohn, most of them on research on the Navajo of the Ramah area; they included Evon Vogt, John Adair, Bert Kaplan, Geza Roheim, Donald Pitkin, and James Spuhler. The only other nonarchaeological report listed by Reiter is "social organization and change in [the] Pueblos" by Eggan. This nearly even balance of subfields reflects the long-standing tradition at the Chaco Canyon field school of substantial attention to all branches of anthropology.

One event not reported in any official account, a reminder of the lighter side of the Conferences, is recalled by Edwin N. Ferdon, who was long associated with the School of American Research and the Museum of New Mexico, and attended many of the Conferences at Chaco. He wrote (letter to Woodbury, 6 April 1985), "The 1947 conference was the one when Paul Reiter in his welcoming address took off on Frank Hibben to the embarrassment of all since Frank was there in the audience." Ferdon also recalls that he and others "viewed the 1947 conference as a 'Pecos Conference' and not a Chaco Conference."

As with the 1946 Conference, a major part of the meeting was spent on selected topics, ranging from the particular, such as projectile point terminology, to the general—the "relationship of Archaeology to Ethnology; [of] social organization to ground-plan and architecture and of ethnological material culture to archaeological; the integration of the two; and the need of ethnological study of material culture as intensive as social organization studies" (Reiter 1948a: 273). It would be twenty-four years until the publication of *Navaho Material Culture* by Clyde Kluckhohn, W. W. Hill, and Lucy Wales Kluckhohn (1971), although work had already begun in 1944 on this landmark study.

Another broad topic explored was the question, "how far does one dare go in making ethnological conclusions from archaeological evidence?" (Reiter 1948b: 74). The discussions also included the relationship of Mogollon to Anasazi, Southwestern-Mexican relations, and "mutual influences of returning Indian veterans on their own native communities." Finally, attention was given to the National Park Service's problems of (1) presenting accurate but simplified archaeological information to the public, and (2) dealing with increasing needs of restoration with a "critically diminishing budget." In the years ahead, "restoration" would largely be replaced by "stabilization," preserving what had survived but not rebuilding what was gone.

At the closing business session two matters were acted on, the first of which probably had some useful results. These were (1) the formation of a committee to pass a resolution regarding the Antiquities Act, and (2) the formation of a committee to examine possibilities of clarification and the possibility of definition of the terminology of Southwestern archaeology. It would be interesting to know if Kidder had any comments on the success with which these "possibilities" had been examined at the first Pecos Conference, twenty years before.

A rather different picture of the 1947 Conference emerges from Halseth's typically individualistic "Random Notes" (Halseth 1947). He wrote that "new and factual contributions . . . were so few that impressions become highlighted in a reflective mood with a few reminiscent shadings. Although archaeology is ageless, archaeologists are not; at the Chaco meeting there seemed to be signs of qualms in the ranks." He also commented that "the printed page seems to have lost a lot of its former Mosaic finality in archaeology, both to the authors and to the younger students, more and more of whom seem to be 'from Missouri.'" The greater participation of ethnologists in this Conference led Halseth to say that

> there was a time, not long ago, when an ethnologist wandering into an archaeological seance was looked upon as a Mexican at a Zuni masked dance. Now the two are actually courting each other and a few are sleeping in the same bed, which—scientifically speaking—is a good token.

And he continued later on the same topic: "The growing tendency of even highly specialized dirt archaeologists at the Chaco Conference to consider their findings as components of anthropological disciplines is a hopeful sign of better integration of all approaches to historical research." In another vein Halseth said:

> It was heard, for the first time, I believe, from specialists that anthropology has a definite obligation to the public and should slant some of its reporting in this direction. . . . After all, every archaeologist is a student of anthropology, and who has a greater responsibility in the application of basic human principles to present and future living than the student of human affairs?

Halseth's "for the first time" was an exaggeration, of course. It was just the year before that he had heard Underhill urge the preparation of materials for high schools that would incorporate anthropological findings. But Halseth may have had in mind the wider, adult public that deserved good "popular" writing on anthropology's findings. It would be only two years until Kluckhohn's *Mirror for Man* would be published by McGraw-Hill, the winner of a $10,000 first prize in the Whittlesey House—Science Illustrated contest "for the best book on a scientific subject written for the layman" (AAA *News Bulletin*, No. 1, April 1947). It was chosen from 250 entries and the runner-up was by Gladwin (no doubt his *Men Out of Asia,* published in 1947 by Whittlesey House and McGraw-Hill, two years before *Mirror for Man*). Kluckhohn's book was a popular success and would be followed in the decades ahead by many more books by scholars who could write for, rather than down to, lay readers.

The year 1947 was probably the high-water mark for ethnological participation at a Pecos Conference, partly a result of a younger generation of archaeological and ethnological students trained in anthropology departments that expected their students to be familiar with all four subfields.

6
In Full Stride, 1948–51

From 1927 through 1947 the Pecos Conference did not move out of New Mexico, shifting only as far as Santa Fe for its third meeting and then to Chaco Canyon for the next six Conferences.

With the 1948 meeting at the University of Arizona's field school at Point of Pines, located on the San Carlos Indian Reservation in east-central Arizona, a new pattern began. The Conference would meet in a different location every summer, sometimes returning to a previous location, such as Santa Fe, but also moving to new areas with new sponsorship. This peripatetic tradition had a healthy influence on the Conference, as it was never in danger of "belonging" to any one institution or group. Also those attending the Conference constantly had opportunities to see new and less familiar parts of the Southwest, something favorably commented on in several of the responses to the questionnaires which I prepared for distribution to those attending the 1979 Pecos Conference. The burden of holding the Conference, as well as the visibility and its satisfactions, were more widely shared than before.

Point of Pines, 1948 (Eleventh Pecos Conference)   Archaeological field schools with academic credit developed out of the earlier practice, which began soon after 1900, of taking a few students into the field to assist a senior archaeologist and to learn through direct experience (see Gifford and Morris 1985, the source for details on the University of Arizona field schools, which follow). Byron Cummings, who came to the University of Arizona in 1915, had made summer archaeological field trips for many years while teaching at the University of Utah, and continued the practice at Arizona, adding academic credit for the summer's work in 1919. In 1934 he began digging at the site of Kinishba, a masonry ruin in east-central Arizona, and from 1934 through 1937 he had a permanent camp there for the summer field school. Emil Haury, who succeeded Cummings as head of the department of anthropology in 1937, set up a new field school at Forestdale, in the Mogollon Rim country, which operated in 1939, 1940, and 1941. In planning for postwar field work, Haury and E. B. Sayles of the Arizona State Museum, Tucson, surveyed the eastern San Carlos Indian Reservation in the summer of 1945 (Haury 1945a), particularly in the vicinity of Point of Pines, literally, a point of the pine forest reaching far out into the grasslands. It is about fifty-five miles east of Globe, but the distance by the rough and tortuous road is much more (Haury 1989: fig. 1.1).

Digging was under way at Point of Pines the next summer, with ten college students. Haury commented in *Teocentli* (No. 41, June 1946) that "on the strength of the number, size and time range of the ruins in this section a good many years of work lie ahead." His prediction proved correct—excavation in the Point of Pines area continued for the next fifteen summers. In 1947 the field school was in full swing, with students not only from the University of Arizona but from across the country, and construction was progressing well. It was probably fortunate, however, that preparations for the Pecos Conference could wait until the following year.

There was a mail announcement of the Conference, as was customary, sent to all who had registered the previous year and some others known to be interested. And the Conference was also announced in appropriate national journals. "By unanimous vote the participants of the Southwestern Archaeological Conference at the University of New Mexico's Field School in Chaco Canyon have agreed to hold the next conference at the University of Arizona's Point of Pines camp late in August, 1948" (Reiter 1948a: 270).

> The Southwestern Archaeological Conference dates . . . will be August 24, 25, 26, 1948. A cordial invitation is extended to anthropologists to attend the meeting. While the discussions will center about Southwestern archaeological problems, efforts will be made to keep the scope broad enough to hold the interest of those not primarily engaged in this field. . . .
> Through the courtesy of the Viking Fund, Inc. of New York [later the name was changed to Wenner-Gren Foundation for Anthropological Research], the University will furnish board and such lodging in tents (capacity about 65) as will be available. Participants are requested to bring small tents if possible and their own bed-rolls [Haury 1948].

On 10 September 1947 Haury wrote Paul Reiter seeking the benefit of Reiter's long experience in managing the Chaco Conferences:

I hope that the plans for the Conference next summer completely meet with your sanction and approval. This is not an attempt at piracy but rather carrying out the idea we discussed a year ago involving moving the Conference about to different places from year to year. I do think that there is something definite to be gained by this sort of an arrangement. . . .

I am sure that you will understand that organizing and running the Conference will be a new experience for me and I hope I can count on you to tip me off on the operating procedure. We have the list of those to whom you sent invitations. Perhaps you have some ideas that this should be expanded or cut. Also, past experience should have taught you what to do and what not to do, facts which should be useful to us, too.

Haury quickly followed this with a shorter inquiry on 15 September, as follows: "Dear Paulos—How much do you figure it cost you to put on the Conference at Chaco this last summer? Yourn, Emil W. Haury." Reiter replied at length, combining his usual humor and sarcasm with a good deal of solid information. This letter, dated 29 September 1947, is the first detailed account we have of the costs, management, and logistics of a Pecos Conference. We are fortunate that he wrote in such detail.

Dear Emil:

Well, well so you are gonna have a conference, huh? How much does it cost? I dunno. How do ya do it? I dunno. I'm really a help, huh?

Anyway, here's how it went. We bought enough food to feed 80 people for three days and a lot left over to take to Mexico [on a postconference research and reconnaissance trip]. We did not have a separate series of food orders because we had been feeding 80 people right along all summer. Had some left over before the conference, bought more, and more left over afterwards. The "cost of food alone" estimate was 1.22 per person per day [$293] so the food was good. We kept on our kitchen staff (and added some) but absorbed their extended salaries in our field session budget. I imagine our total "extra" expense for the conference, trucking, water and light service, a coupla Navahoes to clean hogans [the dormitory buildings] and rooms for two days, etc.

etc. was perhaps $125.00, excluding the food at 1.22 per day per person. . . .

You don't need—after running the Santa Fe meeting the way you did—any suggestions from me on operating procedure or agenda. My part was brief. I asked them, at the first session (1) to let us know if we could make them more comfortable (2) that for early risers there would be coffee steadily from 6:00 on through breakfast (a really popular idea) (3) suggested meal hours and asked for changes (none) (4) asked them to elect a chairman, which they did. This chairman ran—extemporaneously—the first meeting. Then he carried over and as soon as the second meeting convened he asked for nominations for a new chairman, etc. etc., and the big idea seemed to be to hear from everyone in much the same manner that you managed it in Santa Fe. Incidentally, if I were you, I'd ask as many people as possible to sleep out on their own, thus implying a limitation of room. Also, couples don't appear to mind being broken up if necessary. Chairmen were Erik Reed, Walt Taylor, AVK [A. V. Kidder] and Clyde [Kluckhohn].

Actually, I think the cost is largely determined by the number of student helpers you can acquire. I kept about 30 students in camp and furnished their board with the understanding that they could "listen in" but keep still and that they work. Divided them up into a highpowered "greeting" committee, car parkers, luggage toters, etc. Then I made a "sleeping list" which the greeters followed, and it all went off without a hitch. Even kept on our mechanic who spent full time (and then some) fixing a few tires, doing a retiming job, etc. Of course, this was an unnecessary frill, but we had the guy on the payroll all summer anyway. . . .

Well, I don't know anything about conferences, but I think we had a good one. Sorry you couldn't make it, but I understand the circumstances. . . .

Let me know if I can furnish more dope: I know this is far from satisfactory.

Best,
Paul

By the end of February Haury began receiving letters from Southwesternists who planned on coming to the Conference at Point of Pines or who wanted information about the Conference. Most of these letters need not be quoted here, but they are a good reminder—

from a file more complete than most—of how much paperwork was involved, even back in 1948, in setting up the arrangements for a Pecos Conference.

For example, Arnold Withers wrote to ask if he and Allison could bring their daughter, and Haury replied, "I expect that some people . . . will bring children and as long as such people stand ready to provide the personal requirements (bedding, etc.), also keep them in tow, I can't object, so will expect the three of you." As predicted, several parents did bring children—ten are listed in the Guest Register, belonging to six families. Theodore D. McCown wrote from Berkeley asking if "casual visitors" (meaning himself) could come, and Haury said yes. He wrote Erik Reed expressing concern that W. C. Holden and William Pierce were bringing their students, commenting, "I will have to clear most of mine out to make room, and I hate to kick them out and have another group of students come in. Hand-picked graduate students, of course, would be welcome." Reiter wrote that he would be unable to come to Point of Pines (just as Haury had been unable to go to Chaco in 1947). Earl Morris and Frank Roberts were urged to attend; the former did, and the latter did not.

To J. O. (Jo) Brew, at the Peabody Museum, Harvard University, Haury wrote (19 July), "I am still counting on your being here, and since you are now the big wheel [Brew had just succeeded Donald Scott as director] you should be able to lock the door and bid everybody good-bye." As we will see, Brew did come, and he played an important role in the Conference.

Haury wrote Watson Smith (14 July), who was at the Museum of Northern Arizona, Flagstaff, saying, "No one from Flagstaff has written yet that they will be here. Put pressure on Colton and the rest, will you? We are expecting a good attendance and should have a profitable time. Besides, I'd like to see you again." Smith replied (18 July):

> Your stupendous map [discussed below] leaves me practically no alternative to planning a trip to Point of Pines. I have been hoping that I could manage it, for the social and intellectual fare that I know it will offer—and now the geographical lure is added to the others. . . . I will try at once to seduce some others from Flagstaff to come.

Harold S. Colton (Fig. 6.1) wrote Haury the next day (19 July) that he, Mrs. Colton, and Katharine Bartlett would be there for the Conference. Smith's "pressure" had worked.

Smith wrote again (3 August) asking if he could bring two or three

6.1 *At the Point of Pines Conference in 1948* (left to right): *Paul S. Martin, Earl H. Morris, A. V. Kidder, Jesse L. Nusbaum, and Harold S. Colton. Arizona State Museum negative no. 3242vv.*

of the students who had been working with him at Wupatki National Monument, provided they had their own camping equipment for meals and sleeping. "I think the boys will get a great deal out of the meeting, and so does Dr. Colton."

Another prospect of student attendees came from Malcolm F. Farmer, of the San Diego Museum of Man, who wrote (6 August) "I am planning to be at the Point of Pines session and as far as I know now will bring along a couple of students from here. Both are working for us at present." Haury responded (10 August), a little less cordially than he had to Watson Smith, that "we are trying to discourage a lot of extras unless such groups are able to take care of all their wants, including food."

With Paul S. Martin (Fig. 6.1), Haury had a more extended and complicated preconference exchange of letters. They were, of course, old friends, and Martin's interest in the Mogollon had begun when he visited Gila Pueblo and talked with Gladwin, Sayles, and Haury in the 1930s (Longacre 1976). Since 1939 he had had a permanent field headquarters near Reserve, New Mexico, and although he had never had a field school, many students received training in archaeology there and elsewhere under his stern but kindly guidance. He wrote Haury on 12 July,

> Don Collier, John Rinaldo and I expect to attend the conference at your camp. We are bringing our own bedrolls. Do you want us to bring cots and mattresses also? We have no tents to bring. I think Don and John would be willing to sleep outdoors, but I would like to be tucked away in a tent if possible.
>
> The main purpose of this letter is to ask you if it would be possible for me to have some food each meal without any wheat in it. I cannot eat pies, cakes, pastry, gravies, or anything made with wheat flour. I never eat bread anyhow, and if I could avoid stews or other dishes prepared with flour I could get along very well. I hesitate to mention this matter because know that it is somewhat of a nuisance, but I do want to attend the conference very much.

Haury reassured Martin with a reply on 19 July:

> I am hoping that a few people will bring cots, because I suspect that there will be from 75 to 100 people here. We will have either tent space or a cabin spot for you, and I am sure that we can take

care of Don and John also under cover. First come, first served, so get here in good time.

I know our cook will be willing to take care of your dietary wants, and the best thing to do will be to work this out with him when you get here. He is an excellent cook and wants to oblige.

But on 26 July Martin wrote again, this time greatly concerned about the number of participants that Haury had predicted:

I note that there may be 75 or 100 people there. That is far too many. This will be like another Xmas meeting [of the AAA and the AAAS] where nothing is decided and informal talks will be impossible. I think all students and hangers on should be excluded. Several of my students wanted to come and I told them nix. I understand that [Herbert] Dick's whole party is coming. I hope not [it didn't] as this should be a very informal conference for full-grown [sic] professionals only. Can't you restrict this meeting to Southwesterners who hold full time jobs in anthropology?

Haury's reply on 5 August reflects the serious concern that he and others besides Martin were feeling about the increasing size of the Conferences and the inclusion of students in growing numbers. It was a problem that would be discussed further in the coming years, with gradual relaxation rather than tightening of rules on attendance.

In general I agree with you that we will have too many people; but I don't feel it is my place to say who can and can't come, since the tradition was started back in 1927. [Martin and Haury were both students when they attended that meeting.] Furthermore, one could hardly expect a man who is out in the Southwest with a wife to park her in some strange town while he is off gabbing. It is a problem I suppose faces all conferences, and while I think that more could be accomplished in a smaller group I don't know at the moment how the restrictions can be set up so that there won't be a lot of hurt feelings. This is a subject which might be profitably discussed during the session. We tried two years ago to hold such a restricted conference with the result that a great many people were peeved at Erik Reed and myself, who instigated the thing.

It is obvious that sessions will have to be broken down into special discussion groups, and those, I think, will be small enough so that something can be done.

I will end this selection from preconference correspondence with a letter from W. W. (Nibs) Hill (Fig. 6.2), an ethnologist at the University of New Mexico, and a colleague of Reiter, whose humor may have been contagious. Hill wrote on 9 August:

> This is to let you know that I am looking forward to occupying the bridal suite at the Point of Pines conference. I shall arrive sometime in the afternoon of the 24th, and bring Herb and Martha Dick with me. I want you to understand that the ethnologists of the world do not work short seasons, and this is cutting right in[to] the middle of my Santa Clara [Pueblo] field work. Therefore I expect to be royally entertained on arrival.

For the Conference itself we have an abundance of data from the files of the department of anthropology at the University of Arizona—as host institution it allowed little to escape its recordkeeping. In addition, there are published reports—in *American Antiquity* and *El Palacio,* and by the San Diego Museum of Man (*News and Views from the California Tower*). An important innovation at this Conference was an "official" record of the proceedings; Pat Wheat (Mrs. Joe Ben Wheat), an anthropology student at the University of Arizona, was the recorder. The transcription of her notes fills fifty double-spaced typed pages, with more and better details than exist for any previous, and many subsequent, Conferences. Finally, we have the original Guest Register, on which each arrival filled in his or her name, "complete mailing address" (some are much less than complete), and the date and hour of arrival. There are 136 entries, including the Point of Pines staff and several Apache tribal representatives who attended the opening session. How many of these 136 were housed by the field school and how many were camping on their own is not certain, but Haury has said that "in addition to our permanent facilities we put up 23 tents, hoping that everyone would find shelter" (Haury 1989: 51).

The map referred to enthusiastically by Smith states, "Globe to San Carlos—23 miles" and "San Carlos to Point of Pines—75 miles," adding "no gas en route, NO EATING PLACES, Carry WATER, also CHAINS (there may be too much water)." The map shows that after leaving the San Carlos Indian Reservation agency headquarters and passing Tiffany's store, the road crosses the railroad tracks twice in

6.2 W. W. (Nibs) Hill, Pecos Conference, Flagstaff, 1953. Museum of Northern Arizona negative no. 74.1344, photo by A. O. Brodie.

two miles, turns east and goes over a bridge. After about twenty miles it turns north and soon crosses a flowing stream in Warm Springs Canyon. A little farther north is a more difficult crossing, the Big Rocky (now Rocky Gulch), which Haury labeled "Dangerous crossing if running. Good bottom but deep"—a warning that in those days was well understood by all who ventured off the paved roads of the Southwest. After passing Dehorn Corral on the right and Chiricahua Butte rising high on the left, there was a steep, winding road marked "Slow going here." This took the traveler over the northeast end of Nantack Ridge, to the relatively level grasslands to its north. At Pole Corral the maps says "25 miles to go" and indicates a telephone, and just before the turnoff to the Black River Pumping Station there is another telephone, at Clover Well. These were not booths with a pay phone, but simply a phone mounted on a phone pole, usable by anyone in trouble, with one, two, or more rings for the desired location. The last turnoff was to Clifton, far to the east, and one mile farther the traveler came to the Point of Pines camp, tired, dusty (or muddy, if the luck was bad), and relieved to have arrived safely. There is no doubt that regardless of the hour there was someone to welcome each arrival.

The Conference opened after lunch on the afternoon of Tuesday, 24 August, with a welcome by Clarence Wesley, chairman of the San Carlos Apache Tribal Council, on whose land the Point of Pines field school stood. He was followed by a representative of the U.S. Indian Service and by the vice president of the University of Arizona. Haury was elected general chairman of the Conference, and a "program committee" was named, to plan the sessions ahead; it consisted of Brew, J. Charles Kelley, Martin, Theodore D. McCown, and Reed. Kidder was asked, and agreed, to talk about the course of the Pecos Conference, since the first one twenty-one years before.

The rest of the afternoon and the following morning were devoted to the traditional presentation of short, informal reports on recent field work (Fig. 6.3). There were thirty-eight reports, mostly on archaeological work but including Kluckhohn (Fig. 6.4) on the Ramah Project, a multidisciplinary study of a small Navajo community south of Gallup, New Mexico; Odd Halseth on recording Pima and Papago songs; Federico Vidal (a Harvard University graduate student) on his study of Indian Service administrative practices; and Ernest Hill (University of New Mexico) on his study of the Utes of northern Utah. But this is only four nonarchaeological reports versus thirty-four archaeological, in contrast to the nearly equal division at

Chaco Canyon the year before. On the first evening Kidder gave an illustrated lecture on the remarkable mural paintings of Bonampak, a Maya ruin in the Chiapas jungle, recently explored by the Carnegie Institution of Washington, under Kidder's supervision.

The second afternoon began a series of general discussions of specific topics, the first being the problem of *Yuma* as a term for projectile points. It was agreed to abandon it in favor of a binomial system for points previously called Yuma (Reiter 1949; P. Wheat 1948: 24–25). Next, connections between Texas and the Southwest at the preceramic level were considered, followed by an account of Basketmaker II material near Durango, Colorado, and finally, "the probability of the Cochise pattern underlying and contributing to the later Anasazi, Mogollon, and Hohokam developments" (Haury 1949).

On the evening of 25 August an organizational meeting was held to form a Western Branch of AAA, an example of an important but often overlooked role of the Pecos Conference (and, in fact, of many conferences) as a spawning ground for new organizations. The organizing committee members were Malcolm F. Farmer (chairman), McCown, Viola Garfield, and F. H. Douglas, the latter two not at the Point of Pines meeting.

The most important event of the Conference took place the next morning—a panel discussion on the Mogollon culture, cochaired by Sayles and Martin. As Haury (1949) reported in *American Antiquity*, "This discussion, lively and informative at times, obtuse at other times, did at least bring certain problems into the open and showed the great need for more energetic wielding of the shovel." There is an oral tradition, which has been confirmed by Haury (letter to Woodbury, 19 May 1986), that when the panel was seated Brew's place was marked by a basketball on which a large white "8" had been painted, reflecting his minority position, on the defensive as the skeptic who doubted the utility or justification of the Mogollon concept (Fig. 6.5). Other panelists were Haury, Reed, Kidder, Colton, Sayles, Donald Lehmer (a University of Chicago graduate student who was on the Point of Pines staff that summer), John Rinaldo (Martin's field director at Pinelawn), and Stanley Stubbs (Laboratory of Anthropology), a remarkably knowledgeable and experienced group. Martin began by reading from an article by Brew and Edward B. Danson (a University of Arizona student who was doing his graduate work with Brew at Harvard University), which said, in part: "Between the two [Anasazi and Hohokam] an enigmatic Mogollon culture is postulated, an intriguing prospect as yet not supported by a sufficient number of

6.3 Meeting under the pines at Point of Pines in 1948. Arizona State Museum negative no. 3242a.

6.4 Clyde K. M. Kluckhohn, Point of Pines, 1948. Arizona State Museum negative no. 7944.

distinct traits to give it acceptable validity as a useful concept in our historical reconstructions" (Brew and Danson 1948: 211–222).

Having thus thrown down Brew's gauntlet, so to speak, Martin yielded the floor to Brew, who elaborated his doubts about and objections to the Mogollon concept. As recorded by Pat Wheat, he said:

> we have the Pueblo people—not a linguistic classification, but we have the culture; Hohokam sites dug by Gila Pueblo produced a number of striking traits. It seemed reasonable to think that the archaeologists had discovered something for which there was enough evidence to substantiate defining a separate culture. We are in a stage where the cautious person winds up behind the 8-ball. Herbie Dick . . . [has] a considerable amount of perishable material with Alma Plain pottery [which] gives us a lot more to work with . . . to see if this manifestation down here is of the nature which people as a whole call [a] "culture." The difference between myself and the people here is that they may be using an archaeological definition which seems to be a confusing rather than a useful technique [P. Wheat 1948: 30].

Martin responded, in part (again quoting Pat Wheat's record): "There is in my estimation, a fallacy in Brew's approach. E. W. Haury is the father of the Mogollon, published first on it, and has some pertinent remarks to make." Haury then said:

> I am not the first man who had the idea. Mera recognized some separation ceramically from the northern materials. We came into this material through a survey for Gila Pueblo from Reserve, New Mexico, down into the Mimbres. During the course of a large survey you pick up differences in cultures of people. As a direct result of these original surveys we excavated the Harris site and Mogollon Village in New Mexico. Will take the blame for the name. Felt it would be better to bring something out rather than to leave it unpublished. . . . I can see the Mogollon as an entity occupying a large geographical area, as large as the Basketmakers and larger than the Hohokam [P. Wheat 1948: 31].

There was then a discussion of whether Apache sites could be identified as an "Apache culture," if it were not already known, and Kidder commented that he had moved from "opposed to Mogollon originally," to seeing it "as an extremely important problem." Lehmer and

6.5 J. O. (Jo) Brew, Point of Pines, 1948. Arizona State Museum negative no. 7879.

Reed added further comments, as did Albert H. Schroeder, Deric O'Bryan, Taylor, Sayles, and Colton. Brew repeated his doubts, and Martin remarked that "the Mogollon were a pretty low, simple development that can't be explained away—it did exist." In Pat Wheat's summary it is obvious that no consensus was reached. The eleven pages on this session in her notes make fascinating reading, reflecting the issues and biases of the time, and particularly the problems of deciding which and how many diagnostic criteria are needed to define a distinct "culture," and what "base" the gradually differentiating cultural traditions of the Southwest came from.

The record shows that Brew was in the minority but continued to be unpersuaded. For the moment Reed had the last word, saying:

> There is actually not as much divergence as there seems. Around 850 to 900 we find strong [sic] surface buildings as dwellings with a definite ceremonial chamber, a gray corrugated pottery, black-on-white [pottery], pebble axes, no cranial deformation. In the Mimbres we have red ware, plain ware, red-on-brown. How can you consider that these pit house redware groups are the same as Anasazi? [P. Wheat 1948: 40].

Like Reed, Martin considered the question of the distinctiveness of the Mogollon settled. The following April his report on his 1947 excavations was published, "Cochise and Mogollon Sites, Pine Lawn Valley, Western New Mexico" (Martin and others 1949). In an introductory section he traced the origin and development of the concept and its slow acceptance, but said, "It seems evident to all who have worked in the Mogollon area . . . that Mogollon culture is a valid concept and corresponds to a reality" (p. 40). A few years later Fred Wendorf ably summarized the continuing dispute, identifying the issues and disputants. He listed the archaeologists who were Pro-Mogollonists (further split into two disagreeing schools) and Anti-Mogollonists (Wendorf 1953: 4–5). He observed that "the controversy over the Mogollon remains even today a paramount issue among Southwestern archaeologists." His summary, like the 1948 symposium, brought into clearer view the basis of disagreements, the problems, and the need for more data. There have been other Pecos Conference symposia on contested issues, but probably none more important in defining the issues of a major controversy.

The Conference reconvened after lunch, and the final afternoon, before a short business meeting, was devoted to "The Transition to

History," chaired by Edward H. Spicer of the University of Arizona, an ethnologist, applied anthropologist, and student of social change particularly known for his work on the Yaqui of Sonora and Arizona. Four topics were proposed for discussion: "Archaeological inferences from ethnological data; ethnological identity of archaeological complexes; non-Pueblo peoples; acculturation"—a sufficient agenda for one afternoon.

The discussion was lively and ranged widely, but lacked a central issue, in contrast to the morning's session. Among the speakers were Spicer, McCown (a physical anthropologist at the University of California, Berkeley), Schroeder (National Park Service), Haury, Kelley (University of Texas, Austin), Terah L. Smiley (Tree-Ring Laboratory, University of Arizona), Brew, Kidder, John Adair (an ethnologist who had just received his Ph.D. at New Mexico and was joining the faculty of Cornell), Stephen Borhegyi (who had recently left Hungary and, with help from the Viking Fund, was beginning graduate study in the United States), and Halseth (archaeologist at Pueblo Grande Museum in Phoenix). Unfortunately the record suggests that most seem to have said more about their own interests and specialties than about the topics proposed. Kivas, witchcraft, possible Hohokam-Pima continuity, Spanish records of early native groups on the Texas coast, and many other matters were touched on at greater or lesser length.

As became traditional at Pecos Conferences, the last afternoon included a short business meeting, the most important action of which was to appoint an interim committee to arrange the place and time of the next summer's Conference: Colton (chairman), Stanley Stubbs (Fig. 6.6; Museum of New Mexico), and Martin. Haury responded to Halseth's suggestion that they return in 1949 to Point of Pines, saying, "This is something that should be passed around. Chaco Canyon had it for years. It seems to me it should go to Santa Fe, the Museum of Northern Arizona, and other places." He proved prophetic (or persuasive?), as the 1949 meeting was in Santa Fe and that of 1950 in Flagstaff.

The possibilities for establishing a ceramic repository were discussed, which would have permanent sherd collections more comprehensive geographically than those of the Museum of Northern Arizona and the Laboratory of Anthropology, each of which specialized in its own region. A letter of appreciation was voted to the Viking Fund, in thanks for its financial assistance to the Conference. The last official act of the Conference was a proposal by Spencer Rogers

6.6 Stanley A. Stubbs, Pecos Conference, Flagstaff, 1950. Museum of Northern Arizona negative no. 12.888, photo by A.O. Brodie.

for a vote of thanks to the cook. Appropriately, soon after, dinner was served. The cook deserved this expression of thanks. Haury has described his task: "The register showed 136 signatures, including our own small group. That number put a considerable strain on our kitchen crew, for they served three meals a day, each with three settings. Thanks to the skill of our cook, Don Swartz, and his helpers, the operation moved smoothly" (Haury 1989: 51).

Haury has also described an innovation at the 1948 Conference:

> Although one sees many old friends and makes new ones at these meetings, the gathering also provides an opportunity to discuss matters of mutual professional concern with colleagues. More often than not, a serious discussion is interrupted by a third person, thus bringing the exchange to naught. To discourage this sort of incident, we drew a north-south line through an area near the dining hall where the sessions were to take place under the trees. A large picture of a bull's head was posted on the east side of the line, carrying the implication that people in conversation, or having a "bull session," east of the line were not to be interrupted. Gatherings anywhere else were to be joined freely. The plan worked and was appreciated [Haury 1989: 51–52].

During the months following the Conference Haury received some enthusiastic and complimentary letters about it. He could feel great satisfaction not only in its general success and in the capability the staff of the new field school showed, but also in the large number of people who had seen for the first time an important and attractive part of the archaeological Southwest.

During the 1948 meeting Kidder noted that the Pecos Conference "had come of age" with the twenty-first anniversary of the 1927 Conference. But 1948 was notable in other ways, also. It was the first Pecos Conference held outside New Mexico and marked the beginning of a practice that was continued of moving annually to a different location, although some were repeated during the coming decades. It is by far the best recorded Conference up to that time, thanks to Pat Wheat's extraordinarily detailed recordkeeping. As Haury had expected, the Conference introduced many Southwesternists to the Point of Pines area, a section of the Mogollon country little known to most of them. Its broad grassy meadows and stands of huge ponderosa pine are in marked contrast to such areas as the Four Corners and Chaco Canyon, already familiar to most. The Mogollon symposium set a pattern followed in many subsequent Conferences, of a panel discussion among selected experts on a subject of broad importance; this had been done at Chaco Canyon from time to time, but those records are too sketchy to identify subjects covered. From now on a half-day symposium was planned for almost every Conference. The attendance at Point of Pines exceeded that of any previous Conference, except for the 1940 meeting, which had the special attraction of being held jointly with the 400th anniversary observations of Coronado's entrada.

SANTA FE, 1949 (TWELFTH PECOS CONFERENCE) The return to Santa Fe's Laboratory of Anthropology only three years after the Pecos Conference met there in 1946 came a year sooner than originally intended. Colton, chairman of the 1948–49 interim committee on arrangements, wrote on 7 January 1949 to Stubbs at the Laboratory that he was "unable to arrange satisfactory [meeting] quarters at Flagstaff" and urged that the meeting be held in Santa Fe, to "establish the custom of alternating between New Mexico and Arizona." He proposed to invite the Conference to the Museum of Northern Arizona for 1950. Meanwhile, a grant of $500 to assist the Conference had been received from the Viking Fund.

Although hosted by the Laboratory of Anthropology, the sessions were held at the Santa Fe Indian School of the U.S. Indian Service, which charged $2.75 per day per person (breakfast 50 cents, lunch 75 cents, dinner one dollar, and room 50 cents).

Although Stubbs took charge of arrangements in Santa Fe, Colton continued to be involved in the planning, writing Stubbs at length (18 April 1949) about his concerns as whether anthropologists of all subfields should be invited, whether graduate students should be included, and whether to include undergraduates at field schools (or ban them unless introduced by "an invited member").

Stubbs replied to Colton at length on 5 May 1949, saying that he had talked with Reed and several others. His suggestion on whom to invite was (1) archaeologists working in the Southwest or adjacent areas; (2) "cooperative scientists," such as Antevs, Helmut de Terra, and Volney Jones; (3) "ethnologists working actively in the Southwest and whose approach to the subject is sympathetic to archaeology, such as Fred Eggan [Fig. 6.7] and [W. W.] Hill"; and (4) a "limited number of students." Colton and Stubbs were thinking in terms of "invitations" rather than a general announcement and a completely open Conference. Stubbs suggested admitting graduate students "if they are working on advanced problems of Southwestern archaeology, such as

Don Lehmer, Fred Wendorf, several from Arizona and New Mexico Universities," but only "if introduced by [an] invited leader." He also commented that "we cannot very well ban undergraduates if they show up. When Reiter brought his student group to the 1946 Conference here in Santa Fe, he told them to look and listen, but keep their mouths shut. . . . This policy might [again] be applied."

The records from 1949 do not indicate any students "banned," and there is, unfortunately, no copy of Stubbs's reply to a letter he received from John C. McGregor, dated 9 August 1949. It said, "I plan to come and bring our entire group of 7 students with me [from Flagstaff]. Would you let me know if we must bring bedding, beds, or what? . . . Do not hesitate to say if I am bringing too large a group. It is our intention to sit quietly by and listen, but I feel, since this is a serious group of students, that it will be a well worthwhile experience for them." He listed the students at the end of his letter: "Miss Elaine Bluhm (U of Chgo), Jeremiah Epstein (U of Ill), William Walter (U of Ill) . . . , William [R.] Adams (U of Indiana), Douglas Schwartz (U of Kentucky), William Taylor and Donald Downey (U of Toronto)."

Stubbs added, in his letter to Colton of 5 May, that the Viking Fund gift might be used to reduce participants' costs at the Indian School, to "hire a good stenographer to take down a full record of [the] conference and make mimeographed copies to send to those who attended," and, if it was not contrary to Viking Fund policies, to provide a dinner or cocktail party for those attending the Conference. As it turned out, Stubbs's suggestions seem to have been followed, with the important exception of the stenographic record.

The Laboratory of Anthropology, hosting the Conference for the third time, was now eighteen years old. Its resources had dwindled seriously after the initial years of support by John D. Rockefeller, Jr., and it "carried on its work without endowments, without tax support from city, state or [federal] government, depending from year to year solely upon the loyal cooperation and contributions of its many friends . . . numbering in 1947, 1000" (Chapman 1949: 22). The Laboratory's research continued, nevertheless, and its Surface Survey of Archaeological Sites of the Southwest had recorded 2,400 sites, about two-thirds within New Mexico, with sherd collections from the sites available for study (Chapman 1949: 23). Its summer field training program had lapsed after eight years, but many of the ninety students who had had summer fellowships had gone on to anthropological careers and formed an impressive group of "graduates." Now, in 1949, a merger of the Laboratory, the School of American Research, and

6.7 Fred Eggan, Pecos Conference at Flagstaff, 1953. Museum of Northern Arizona negative no. 74.1343, photo by A. O. Brodie.

the Museum of New Mexico was being discussed—a merger that in the end was never fully achieved. The relationships of these organizations (and the role of the Indian Arts Fund) continued to be byzantine in their complexity. But it seems unlikely that these past and present administrative problems greatly concerned the conferees in August 1949. A more immediate and exciting matter was brought to their attention.

At the opening session, on the afternoon of Monday, 22 August, James Arnold of the Institute for Nuclear Studies, University of Chicago, spoke about the progress that had been made in the dating of archaeological materials by the newly developed carbon-14 method. No dates had yet been released, and dating of bone material did not appear possible, but it was expected that other organic material up to 25,000 years old could be dated. A committee had been formed to select samples for dating, and material from the Southwest was to be "channeled through" Roberts at the Smithsonian. Successful results in dating "known" specimens (from the Old Kingdom in Egypt, for example) would be announced in December 1949 and the first "authoritative list for general use was released by [W. F.] Libby in pamphlet form on September 1, 1950" (Johnson 1951: 3). Substantial support for the work that led to this successful point came from the Viking Fund, and eventually other foundations and several universities would provide funding for radiocarbon laboratories and the dating of archaeological samples. In August 1949, the effect of the method on archaeology in the future could not yet be seen, but its great promise was welcome news. Roberts, it should be noted, was not sitting back and waiting for samples to be submitted. On 30 June 1949 he wrote to Haury about the possibility of using teeth for dating ("Dr. Libby stated that it would take at least two to two and a half pounds of teeth to run the test") and also commented, "I trust that Sayles will be able to get out to some of the Cochise sites and collect some charcoal because that will certainly be very helpful in getting dates on cultures of that horizon."

After this exciting start, the Conference settled down the next morning to the traditional reports on recent archaeological work. The report in El Palacio (Bartlett and Reed 1949) lists twenty-one speakers, who described work ranging from central Florida (John Goggin) to Inyo County, California (F. W. Hodge reporting M. R. Harrington's work at a Pinto Basin site), and Wendover, Utah (Jesse D. Jennings). There were four reports on the Peabody Museum's work at Quemado, New Mexico, and two on the Point of Pines field school in

Arizona. The majority of reports were on work in Arizona (six) and New Mexico (nine), with one each from Colorado and Nevada. In chronological terms, the reports ranged from an estimated 3000 B.C. to late Pueblo III. Many of the archaeologists reporting, some of them near the start of their careers, continued to be active in the Southwest in the years ahead: William Y. Adams, Edward B. Danson, Herbert Dick, Jesse D. Jennings, Robert Lister, Robert McGimsey, McGregor, Reed, Reynold Ruppé, Raymond H. Thompson, Richard Shutler, Wendorf, and Joe Ben Wheat.

Tuesday afternoon began with a color film shown by Frank Hibben of several pueblo sites, including the towers of the Gallina District of northern New Mexico. Schroeder then discussed Salado-Sinagua relationships in the Salt River Valley. A short ethnological session followed, with reports by Florence Hawley on work with the Puerto-cito Navajo, by Ruth Underhill on her use of myths as a guide to Navajo history, by Karl Schmitt on work with the Wichita, and by Leland C. Wyman on his study of Navajo ethnozoology. The roster of registrants includes six others whose work then or subsequently was mainly ethnographic: Flora L. Bailey, Edward Dozier, W. W. Hill, Kate Peck Kent, Harvey C. Moore, and Elisabeth Tooker. So the small representation of ethnology continued as in the past, ten out of eighty-four registrants. A preliminary list of reservations, on Laboratory of Anthropology stationery, lists under "no" Harry T. Getty, E. Adamson Hoebel, Harry Tschopik, Robert H. Lowie, Leslie Spier, Leslie White, Kluckhohn, Omer C. Stewart, John Adair, Ralph Linton, Spicer, and Solon T. Kimball, suggesting that invitations or announcements had gone to them but that negative replies had been returned. If this is the case, more ethnologists declined than accepted (however, the "no" list also includes more than thirty archaeologists).

The report of the Conference by Bartlett and Reed makes no mention of social activities, but a letter from Withers to Haury (7 February 1950, mainly devoted to his work at the University of Denver), mentions what must have been one of the high points of the meeting, the cocktail party: "I remember vividly how deeply many of us missed you at the Santa Fe gathering last August. Despite your absence it was a successful meeting, although more on the social than the scientific side. The thing that really broke it up was holding the Viking Fund cocktail party on the second instead of the third day. You missed a really laughable—almost pitiful—session on the morning of the third day. Sometime I'll tell you about it if someone else hasn't."

On the morning to which Withers refers,

the subject of discussion was interpretation of anthropology, with Dr. Walter W. Taylor as chairman. Topics included . . . interpretation in museums . . . [and] anthropology as a subject for teaching in grade schools, high schools, and colleges. The consensus of opinion was that general anthropological material and ideas could be very successfully incorporated at the fourth grade level and up, in connection with history and geography courses, and should be taught to all children, and be a requirement for all college students [Bartlett and Reed 1949: 312].

The Conference closed with the usual short business meeting, which voted thanks to all who had contributed to the meeting's success and appointed an interim committee for the next meeting, scheduled in late August 1950 in Flagstaff: Reed (chairman), J. B. Wheat, and Malcolm Farmer. The published report does not mention one other event, which was described by Stubbs in a letter of 10 October to Paul Fejos, expressing thanks for the Viking Fund's assistance. He adds, "In honor of Dr. A. V. Kidder who inaugurated these annual Southwestern gatherings in 1927 at his excavation camp at the ruins of Pecos Pueblo, these meetings will henceforth be called the 'Pecos Conferences.'" Thus the two-decade-long uncertainty about "what to call the thing" was ended, and "Pecos Conference" was agreed on as the official name, wherever the meeting might take place. Stubbs does not mention that the suggestion of the permanent name was made by Katharine Bartlett.

The pattern of this 1949 meeting closely followed that of previous meetings: reports on field work, mostly archaeology but some ethnology; a general discussion of a previously chosen topic, this time the use of anthropology in museums and schools; and a few "special" presentations, James Arnold on carbon-14 dating, Schroeder on the Salado and Sinagua, and Hibben's movies. The "student question" was discussed once more, before the Conference, and the registration list shows that students did indeed come with several of the "invited" participants. Gradually this was ceasing to be an issue as the role of advanced students as junior colleagues seemed to be recognized at least tacitly.

FLAGSTAFF, 1950 (THIRTEENTH PECOS CONFERENCE)   As Colton had hoped, it was possible for the Museum of Northern Arizona to host the 1950 Conference, although a pattern of alternating between New Mexico and Arizona, as he had suggested, never developed. The location did shift every year from now on, with many new locations coming into the cycle.

The museum to which the Pecos Conference came had grown significantly since its modest beginnings only a little over two decades before (Smith 1969). Across Fort Valley Road from the museum a research center was growing, and not only was there space for work in archaeology, geology, and botany, but also seven small houses, converted from farm buildings, provided living quarters for visiting couples and a dormitory for six single men. Besides expanding its research, the museum was attracting increasing numbers of visitors— 18,580 in 1950, nearly three times the population of Flagstaff. Many of the visitors were tourists en route to or from the Grand Canyon, only eighty miles up the road beside which the museum stood. The museum was host in 1950 to more than the Pecos Conference; in May, jointly with Arizona State College, Lowell Observatory, and Grand Canyon National Park it hosted the Southwestern Division of the AAAS, and in September the Meteoritical Society met at the museum.

It would, however, be another three years before additional anthropological staff joined Colton and Bartlett. A substantial part of the archaeological research was done by associates (one-year appointments) and research associates (continuing appointments), such as Wesley Bliss, James Brewer, Robert Euler, Paul Ezell, Schroeder (Fig. 6.8), Dick Shutler, and Wendorf (Fig. 7.2) in the first category, and Flora Bailey, McGregor, Gladys A. Reichard, and Wyman in the second. The museum had established itself as a major center for Southwestern research and for the dissemination to the public and to scholars of information on all scientific aspects of the Colorado Plateau.

Archaeology at the museum had a busy year in 1950, with the site survey continued, as time permitted, by Bartlett and Colton (forty-four additional sites), excavation at the Twin Buttes site in Petrified Forest National Monument directed by Wendorf, and work at a small site near Snowflake by George Ennis. The museum also took part in the archaeological survey along the right-of-way for a new pipeline crossing northern Arizona, as described below (Colton 1951: 65–66).

On 25 July an announcement was mailed to "those who plan to attend the Pecos Conference," presumably using the mailing list provided by Stubbs from the year before. Colton began by saying, "The meeting will be held on the camp ground of the Museum of Northern Arizona, August 23, 24, and 25. The camp ground of the Museum, called the 'Hill,' lies three miles north of Flagstaff on the right side

6.8 Albert H. Schroeder arriving at the Pecos Conference, Flagstaff, 1950.
Museum of Northern Arizona negative no. 12895, photo by A. O. Brodie.

6.9 *Carroll Burroughs and Bertha P. Dutton, Pecos Conference, Flagstaff, 1950. Museum of Northern Arizona negative no. 12906, photo by A. O. Brodie.*

of Fort Valley Road opposite the Museum entrance. Accommodations on cots will be available for a limited number of men who bring bedrolls and apply in advance for space. There will be ample space for those prepared to camp." For "better accommodations" Colton suggested the Monte Vista Hotel and the Park Plaza and El Rancho motor courts, and for meals Vandevier's Lodge, the Monte Vista, and Andrews' Cafe. He also announced: "A picnic lunch will be served each day on the Museum grounds. As the Conference received no grant this year to cover expenses, it will be necessary to charge $1.00 each for the three luncheons."

A list titled "Acceptances for Pecos Conference—1950" has 71 names, with 1, 2, 3, 4, or 5 after each for the number in the party, for a total of 118 (the registration list has 82 names, with no spouses or children). Eleven of the acceptances are marked "student." The list also indicates that accommodations with the Coltons were arranged for some (Harriet Cosgrove, Kidder, Bartlett), and Tent #1 was assigned to Elaine Bluhm and Bertha Dutton (Fig. 6.9).

The Conference began Wednesday morning (Fig. 6.10), 23 August, with a welcome to those attending and the announcement that next year the Conference would return to Point of Pines. Following tradition, the afternoon was devoted to field reports on current archaeological work. The session was presided over by Kidder, who mentioned his pleasure with the decision to make permanent the name "Pecos Conference." He also reported the recent death, at Cody, Wyoming, of the Harvard geologist Kirk Bryan, who had worked closely with archaeologists at Pueblo Bonito, Awatovi, and many older sites.

Elaine Bluhm, who was on Martin's field staff that summer, kept a detailed record of each speaker and his or her report (Bluhm 1950), similar to the record Pat Wheat had provided in 1948. As Colton later reported, "The sessions were held in the pines on the 'Hill' under a canvas shelter to keep off the sun and the rain" (Colton 1951: 64). In Flagstaff heavy afternoon rains are not uncommon in August.

The archaeological reports continued through Thursday morning, with Haury (Fig. 6.11) presiding, and totaled twenty-seven, ranging chronologically from the Horner Site, near Cody, Wyoming; Bat Cave, New Mexico; and the Concho area of Arizona, to the Pueblo IV site of Paako, New Mexico, and "documentation work for the Navajo tribal claims" by Malcolm Farmer, who was working as staff archaeologist for the Navajo Tribal Council.

The Navajo claim was for about $8 million, and "the opposition

6.10 Registering at the Pecos Conference, Flagstaff, 1950 (left to right): James C. Gifford, Wilma Kaemlein, Betty Tooker, and Katharine Bartlett. Museum of Northern Arizona negative no. 12893, photo by A. O. Brodie.

6.11 *Emil W. Haury and Paul Ezell, Pecos Conference, Flagstaff, 1950. Museum of Northern Arizona negative no. 12871, photo by A. O. Brodie.*

expert, the witness for the defense [the U.S. Government]" would be Hill (Bartlett 1951b: 362). The role of expert witness represented a new direction for Southwestern archaeology and ethnology, carrying out research designed to collect evidence for a legal hearing, in this case the claims of the Navajo for recompense for land taken from them in the nineteenth century. The Indian Claims Commission had been created by Congress in 1946, to permit tribes to bring suit to collect claims for alleged treaty violations (an act of 1863 had barred Indians from suing the government, reflecting northern resentment over the fact that some tribes had sided with the Confederacy in the Civil War). In the next few decades an enormous amount of archaeological and ethnohistorical research would be accomplished to support or oppose the flood of Indian tribal claims brought to the Indian Claims Commission. By 1964, 588 claims had been filed and 50 already settled for payment by the government of $94,915,000 (Brophy and Aberle 1966: 24).

The field reports at this Conference had another innovation—reports on salvage archaeology, as it was then called. Stubbs surveyed for sites that would be flooded along the Chama River, where a new dam was planned, and partially excavated two of them. This was not on the scale of the immense archaeological salvage work along the Missouri, but it marked the beginning of the impact that public works projects would have in the Southwest. Another, larger salvage project was reported by Jesse Nusbaum (Fig. 6.12); it consisted of survey and excavation along the 451-mile, 40-inch pipeline from Farmington, New Mexico, to the Colorado River at Topoc, Arizona. The pipeline was being built by El Paso Natural Gas Company. Nusbaum, as consulting archaeologist to the Department of the Interior, had learned on 14 July 1950 of the proposed pipeline and immediately began discussions with the National Park Service, the Navajo Tribe, the El Paso Natural Gas Company, the Museum of Northern Arizona, and the Laboratory of Anthropology to sponsor and finance archaeological research along its route. His amazing energy and persuasiveness were rewarded, for by 19 August he had secured agreements among all those concerned and field work was under way in both Arizona and New Mexico!

Wendorf directed the field research, assisted by Ezell (Fig. 6.11), Bliss, William Bullard, and Francis E. Cassidy. It was a "crash program," developed to meet an emergency, and was planned, financed, staffed, and carried out in record time. In the next few years, pipelines, electric transmission lines, and more dams, highways, and other

6.12 Arnold (Arny) Withers, Jesse Nusbaum, and John Corbett, Pecos Conference, 1950. Museum of Northern Arizona negative no. 12878, photo by A. O. Brodie.

massive activities that threatened archaeological resources would challenge Southwestern and other archaeologists to divert attention from their internally generated "problem" research to the externally imposed demands of "salvage" research. Eventually the attitude that salvage work was second-class archaeology would disappear, and it would be recognized that "problems" could be attacked even as sites were being found and tested in advance of large-scale construction.

The Thursday afternoon session was listed on the program as "sociological, ethnological, and applied anthropological field work" with Kluckhohn presiding. There were fifteen reports, a substantial increase over the previous year. Those reporting were Hill (for himself and Stanley Newman), Karl Schmidt, Underhill, Charles E. Dibble, Reichard, William Y. Adams (Fig. 9.2), Halseth, Bartlett, Haury (for Muriel Thayer Painter, Spicer, and Harry Getty), Dutton, Taylor (Fig. 6.14), Bruce Inverarity, Verne Ray, Kluckhohn (for himself and Evon Z. Vogt), and Monroe Edmonson. Their reports ranged from the Northwest Coast to the Spanish-Americans of Ramah, New Mexico, and included the Arapaho, Wichita, Utes, Navajos (religion, grammar, and economics), and the Pueblos of New Mexico.

The final day of the Conference began with a session announced as "Interpretation of human history," chaired by Martin. It was a free-ranging series of comments not easy to summarize (Bluhm 1950: 17–21). Underhill spoke about the need to introduce the concept of culture early in college courses, while Halseth urged that students (in elementary school, apparently) be given "what we know are facts before starting on anything that is opinion." Malcolm Farmer described starting school children with material culture, making "arrowheads, pottery, etc." and then being introduced to "a culture other than their own," making Indian costumes and learning dances. Kidder commented on the importance of teaching that human beings live by cultural, rather than instinctive, patterns. Hamilton Warren, who had been invited to discuss his Verde Valley School in Sedona, a few miles south of Flagstaff, stated that the "school was started with the idea of teaching students to take their place in society" and appreciate cultures different from their own. Several weeks each year were spent in the field on the Hopi and Navajo reservations and in a village in Mexico. He commented that "we have to learn to live together and this should be done when the child is very young." Taylor, Verne Ray, Reed (Fig. 6.13), and a few others added descriptions from their own experience in communicating with students or the general public concerning the viewpoints of anthropology. The second invited speaker

6.13 Erik K. Reed at Awatovi, 1939. Museum of Northern
Arizona negative no. 72.578, photo by Marc Gaede.

6.14 A. V. Kidder, Walter W. Taylor, and Emil W. Haury, Pecos Conference, Flagstaff, 1950. Museum of Northern Arizona negative no. 12908, photo by A. O. Brodie.

was Dean O. Meredith Wilson of the University of Utah, who said in his closing remarks that "it is clear that no facts have any meaning until they can be collected into generalizations. Every teacher tries to convey the meaning of facts through generalizations."

For the second half of the afternoon, with a rapid change of focus, the Conference turned to a "Seminar on pottery types and associated traits in West Central New Mexico and East Central Arizona," chaired by Haury. Discussion centered on brown wares and their typological subdivisions, particularly on the basis of temper, and on dating and areal relationships.

As was customary, a short business meeting ended the Conference, with the resolutions including the following: "It was also moved and seconded that the chairman should write to the Pipe Line Co. [El Paso Natural Gas Co.] and express our approval of their cooperation, and hope that it will continue when the pipe line is extended to California."

There was a report on the Conference in the "Notes and News" section of *American Antiquity* (Bartlett 1951a), summarized from the "minutes" by Bluhm. George W. Brainerd reported on the Conference quite briefly in *Masterkey* and included the comment that "to one absent from the Southwest for twelve years, the return was surprisingly easy, as well as pleasant. General problems were not snowed under by archeological minutiae, and the reports ranged over considerable time and space" (Brainerd 1950: 202). Bluhm's detailed record was not published, although Reed, Colton, and Haury corresponded about the possibility. Reed suggested that the Mexican *Boletín Bibliográfico* might publish the full report. However, in the end nothing came of this, so this Conference, like others, was reported in print relatively briefly, and only north of the international border. In spite of suggestions made from time to time, no transcript of an entire Pecos Conference has ever been published or distributed. By contrast, the Plains Conference and Great Basin Conference have published proceedings of some their meetings (see Woodbury 1985a).

Point of Pines, 1951 (Fourteenth Pecos Conference) Planning for the 1951 Conference began with a letter from Haury to Withers and Stubbs, dated 16 February 1951, which began:

> The time is approaching when we should be thinking about the Pecos Conference at Point of Pines. In case you had forgotten,

6.15 A. V. Kidder and Erik K. Reed, Pecos Conference, Flagstaff, 1950. Museum of Northern Arizona negative no. 12874, photo by A. O. Brodie.

the two of you and I were appointed the Committee to arrange for the session this summer.

Our Field School will be over about August 10th, so I would like to suggest either August 15, 16, and 17 or August 16, 17, and 18 as most suitable dates from our point of view. This would also fit in pretty well with the [Hopi] Snake Dance and Gallup Ceremonial.

I have not applied to the Viking Fund for a grant this year. I have swung around to the opinion that each person attending the Conference should be asked to pay a flat fee to cover food costs. . . . $8 per head should carry the freight. How do you feel about this?

Withers replied on 23 February, approving the $8 fee. As to the program, he said,

My personal feeling is that we should not eliminate the participation of our ethnological friends, and should have one session devoted to their work and problems. I have wondered if we might prevail upon Ned Spicer to chair such a session. If we had a session on the "enemy peoples" or on the intrusions and movements of many groups in all parts of the Southwest it would be something that both groups could kick around. But I don't know which or how many ethnologists may attend the Conference.

Stubbs, replying on 26 February, also approved of the $8 fee and raised some questions about details for the mail announcement.

Haury replied (letter of 13 March) with information for Stubbs's announcement: "I see no reason why people should not cook on camp fires if they wish to do so but the announcement should state that meals will be supplied. . . . Cooking one's own meals will not obviate the fee." He agreed that a statement on liquor should be made, and said he was sending 100 mimeographed maps. He also agreed that "students should not be excluded altogether" but that "faculties who have students in the field . . . should be instructed to make selections of the better ones." From Haury's comments it is clear that field reports were still a problem, too often too much said about too little: "Progress reports on archaeology should be broken down by areal divisions and those reporting should be warned to make their summaries, summaries in fact and not reports on the post holes." He also suggested a session on "the north versus the south pueblos problem . . . in the light of Erik Reed's ideas in the S.J.A. [*Southwestern Journal of Anthropology*]" (Reed 1946, 1950). In both of these suggestions Haury was trying to shift the Conference away from excessive detail and toward looking more carefully at the larger questions of interpreting evidence for significant, large-scale relationships.

On the problem of which ethnologists might be participating, Haury wrote Withers on 19 July with three names (and wonderfully simple addresses where they could be reached in the field): Dave Aberle (c/o Walter Olson, Navaho Service, Window Rock, Ariz.); Evon Vogt (Box 33, Fence Lake, New Mexico); Julian Steward (Kanab, Utah). Haury added, "There should be about 100 people on hand, maybe more if there are a lot of ringers. I think we'll have the mechanics in hand by the 15th, that is unless I have trouble with the cook."

Finally on 24 July Withers wrote Haury that Aberle had agreed to help with the ethnological part of the program, Schroeder had "replied that he will take the 'enemy peoples' discussion," and Reed would "run the northern and southern pueblos discussion."

Martin wrote on 30 July in his customarily serious, even anxious tone, regretting that he could not attend the Conference and continuing:

I should like to ask you if I may permit Elizabeth Morris, daughter of Earl Morris, to come in my place. She can and would be glad to sleep out and will come equipped with proper duffle so that she will put no strain on your sleeping accommodations. She has been helping at the [Chicago Natural History] Museum two quarters [her Antioch College off-campus session] and is one of the ablest people I have in camp. The Conference would do her much good and I promise that she will in no way interfere with the proceedings. Would you be willing to let her come?

Martin added that Bluhm, John Rinaldo, and Arnold Besser, all of the Chicago Natural History Museum Expedition staff, would also be coming, and that Besser, like Morris, could sleep out and cook his own meals.

Haury replied (7 August): "Certainly will be glad to have Elizabeth Morris. Both she and Arnold Besser can count on taking their meals with us, since we are planning to feed 150. I cannot promise tent space, but we'll do our best." Martin had also asked about the condition of the road through Morenci, as the shortest way for Rinaldo and the others to get from Glendale, New Mexico, to Point of Pines. Haury's reply is a reminder of how travel has changed since then:

> As far as I know the road through Morenci is open, although the [San Carlos Apache] Reservation gate is usually kept locked, and the key is under a rock near a little stump to the south of the gate. That is, if somebody hasn't put it someplace else. If there have been heavy rains, the Eagle Creek ford might stop John. He should inquire in Morenci before proceeding. In short, if I were John, I would try to come in that way if the weather has not been bad the day or two before. It would save him many miles [a trip of about 35 miles versus 170].

As she had at the 1948 Pecos Conference at Point of Pines, Pat Wheat kept a record of the speakers and sessions, which in its typed form runs to twenty-seven pages (Wheat 1951). Most of what follows comes from Wheat's record, although specific citations are not given in the text.

The first afternoon had twenty progress reports on current archaeological field work, chaired by Jesse D. Jennings. Besides reports on more traditional summer projects, salvage work was described by Wendorf, Ezell, and Nusbaum (the El Paso Natural Gas pipeline), by Stubbs (the Chama), by Charlie Steen (White and Red rivers of Arkansas), and by Schroeder (Lower Colorado River). The emergency nature of the pipeline work is emphasized by Wendorf's statement that "the crew had to move an average of 10 miles per day in order to stay ahead of the bull-dozer crew." National Park Service work was taking place at Mesa Verde (a search for earlier sites on the Mesa top, to disperse the growing flood of tourists inundating the "cliff" ruins), at Montezuma Castle, in Chaco Canyon, and at Gran Quivira mission. Taylor and Adams reported on an ambitious project, "concerned with the correlation of cultural change with environmental change . . . in the Hopi area (Tsegi, Navaho Mountain, San Juan, Tuba City, Kayenta) during the great drought period, 1276–1299, with analysis based on mammal bones, flora, etc." Other reports ranged from Fremont and earlier materials in the vicinity of Grand Junction, Colorado (Lister, Marie Wormington, and Dick), to Quiburi mission village in southern Arizona (Charles C. Di Peso). Jennings closed the afternoon session "by reemphasizing the importance of synthesizing" (probably feeling that it had been notably absent), and urging the combination, for interpretation of data, of archaeology, history, and ethnology. Perhaps he can also be credited with having the archaeological reports completed in a single afternoon.

The next morning Haury took the conferees on a tour of sites being excavated in the Point of Pines area (Fig. 6.16). The afternoon began with reports on ethnology and applied anthropology, the session chaired by Vogt, who began by describing the work that Spicer and John Adair were doing under the sponsorship of Cornell University—a program to teach Navajos to raise sheep and goats more successfully, and an effort "to bring about a greater degree of understanding and cooperation between the Indians and the Indian Service." He also reported on Aberle and Harvey Moore's study of peyote among the Navajo, and John Roberts's research at Zuni Pueblo. In addition, Verne Ray described the research potential of the Human Relations Area Files, Florence Hawley Ellis discussed pueblo "magic" in kiva ceremonies, Bruce Ellis reported on a study of San Ildefonso pottery making, Wyman presented his Navajo ethnobiological research, Adams discussed Navajo response to wage work opportunities, and Robert McNair spoke on the effects of Christian missionary work among the Navajo. There were also short reports on studies of farming success in Oregon, a wealthy California "colony" of Bohemian farmers, and clan organization of the Apaches.

The 1951 Conference had three problem-oriented sessions, a high point in the slowly growing acceptance of symposia and roundtable sessions. The first, continuing the Thursday afternoon session, was on "The Enemy Peoples," chaired by Schroeder. The central concern was "when and why did the abandonment of prehistoric population centers in the Southwest occur." The scarcity of evidence of violence or invasion was noted, as well as the number of sites in "defensible positions, and many others . . . actually fortified." There is no hint in the record of ethnological participation in this session, and the discussion seems to have been entirely archaeological, contrary to Withers's original hopes.

The conferees were entertained in the evening by a group of Apache "Devil Dancers," five dancers and six musicians (which Haury noted in his penciled records cost $150). These were probably Crown (or *gaan*) Dancers, with dark buckskin or cloth masks topped by elaborate wooden ornaments. As Haury has noted (1989: 65), this was "the first time that many conferees had seen these impressive masked dancers."

The last day of the Conference, Friday 17 August, began with the second roundtable, "Northern and Southern (or Eastern and West-

6.16 Joe Ben Wheat at the Crooked Ridge Site, Point of Pines, with a group of 1951 Conference participants. Courtesy of David A. Breternetz.

ern) Pueblos," chaired by Reed. He summarized the evidence for a significant cultural distinction between the "northern" area (circular kivas, black-on-white or gray pottery, lambdoidal cranial deformation, full-grooved stone axes, and domestication of the turkey) and the "southern" area (rectangular kivas, brown pottery, occipital deformation, and the three-quarter grooved axe). These ideas were what Haury had in mind in his suggestion to Withers, and they had been published by Reed in the articles mentioned above, as well as in articles in *El Palacio* in 1948 and 1949. Thus the speakers in this roundtable were already familiar with Reed's position, and they tended to discuss either local variations and exceptions, or additional distinctions of possible importance.

Florence Hawley Ellis "bridged the gap between archaeology and ethnology by noting the different kinship systems and social organizations of the northern and southern groups," classification "on the vertical system" in the north and a "lineal system" in the south. She, unlike the other archaeologists present, had added substantial ethnological research to the archaeology she had done since the late 1920s. The record does not indicate that any consensus was reached, but the session demonstrated that focus on a specific proposition could elicit a great deal of informed comment and information.

A short business meeting was held after lunch. An interim committee for the next meeting was appointed, consisting of Reed, chairman, with Jennings and Brew. Stubbs issued an invitation by the Museum of New Mexico to meet in Santa Fe the next year, and it was unanimously accepted. Haury proposed that a telegram greeting be sent to Kidder, who was unable to attend because of illness. This concluded the business meeting.

The remainder of the afternoon began with a discussion of the implications of carbon-14 dating. Jennings then outlined the idea of what he later named the Desert culture (see Jennings 1953: 208), "a substratum of culture, similar to the Basketmaker . . . extending over a wide area of the Southwest." He suggested that "the Cochise culture arose from this basic culture." That there was no further discussion may have been due to the concern of Conference members to start their homeward trips as soon as possible over the long, rough road to San Carlos. After two brief announcements by Nusbaum, on the development by the National Bureau of Standards of a new, "liquid" dating technique, and on "recent actions taken by the government in enforcing the Antiquities Act," the meeting ended at 3 p.m.

Haury's penciled notes on the logistic side of the Conference contain an interesting record of the dining hall's activity. Tuesday evening before the Conference, 60 dinners were served; on Wednesday 93 lunches and 102 dinners. Thursday's lunch through Friday's breakfast ran at 110 for each meal. By dinner on Friday the number dropped to 73 and the same at breakfast the next morning. The final entry is 16 lunches on Saturday. Altogether 1,014 meals were served at a cost estimated by Haury at $975. Most of this was covered by $832 paid at registration.

7
GLOBE TROTTING IN THE FIFTIES, 1952–57

When the Pecos Conference returned to Santa Fe in 1952, it was continuing the established tradition of museums, field schools, and research centers as hosts. But in 1954, a federal organization, the National Park Service, would be added to the still very small circle of host institutions. This was due in no small part to the increasingly professional research orientation of Park Service archaeology. Interpreting archaeology to the American public was as important as ever, but it had become clear that interpretation needed up-to-date scientific data, from the research of archaeologists both within and beyond the National Park Service. The Pecos Conference met in Globe twice in the 1950s under National Park Service auspices, and in the decades ahead it would be invited to several of the Southwest's major archaeological parks and monuments, including Mesa Verde, Pecos, Salinas, and Bandelier.

SANTA FE, 1952 (FIFTEENTH PECOS CONFERENCE) As chairman of the interim committee, Erik Reed began making plans in March 1952. In a letter to Emil Haury (27 March), he asked what dates Haury preferred. In his reply on 2 April Haury suggested the latter part of August, "between the Snake Dance and [the Gallup Ceremonial]," and eventually 11–13 August was selected.

The next question to be discussed was attendance by ethnologists and students (archaeologists were expected to come, anyway). On 30 June W. W. Hill wrote to Stanley Stubbs, saying,

> There have been a whole flock of visiting ethnologists that have come through and many of them will be here [Albuquerque] the whole summer. I do not know what the ethics of the situation

are but I am quite sure some of the following might wish to attend the Pecos Conference. They are all professionals of more or less extent. I will leave it up to you whether they should be issued invitations or not.

Dr. David Aberle
Dr. Harvey Moore
Dr. Robert Young
(all of whom will be at Window Rock, Arizona)
Father Berard Haile, St. Michaels, Arizona
Stanley Rosenberg, Kayenta, Arizona
Tom Sasaki, Fruitland
John Connolly, 2nd Mesa School, Keams Canyon, Arizona.

It is surprising, in view of the professed desire to have ethnological participation and the fact that some of the ethnologists listed by Hill had attended one or more previous Conferences, that there still seemed to be uncertainty about being "welcome" or qualifying for "invitations." Evon Z. Vogt wrote to Reed (14 July): "In accordance with your earlier request, I have been attempting to discover which ethnologists are in the SW this summer who are likely to show up at the Pecos Conference." Vogt then listed his own and twenty-one other names under "Will Attend": John M. Roberts, Watson Smith (Zuni law), Tom Sasaki, Clifford Barnett, Hill, Florence Hawley Ellis, Stanley Newman, George Parkman, Lee Wyman, Flora Bailey, Bertha Dutton, Bruce Inverarity, Dale King, Leslie White, Frederick Slight, Karl and Iva Schmitt, A. H. Leighton, C. H. Lange, Robert Euler, and Malcolm Farmer. A second list was headed "Will Possibly Attend," and consisted of Ralph Patrick, Gladys Reichard, Dave Aberle, Harvey Moore, Clara Bilik, George Rossel, Fred and Dorothy Eggan, Stanley Rosenburg, John Connolly, Father Berard Haile, and Robert Young.

Finally, the "student problem" was not yet entirely settled. Vogt wrote to Edward Dozier (at Polacca Day School, Polacca, Arizona) on 31 July, as follows:

> I see no intrinsic reason why it would not be all right for you to bring your students with you to the Pecos Conference. . . . I would personally very much welcome their presence at the Conference and would like to hear field reports from each of them. We ordinarily urge all of the advanced students we have work-

ing on the Values Study to attend the Conference and to give reports.

As this would be the twenty-fifth anniversary of the first Pecos Conference, Haury and Reed had urged A. V. Kidder to come, and sometime in July in an undated memo Reed wrote to Haury that "Jo Brew, now en route to Capetown, has written that Dr. Kidder *will* be out this summer, at P. of P. with you, presumably to Pecos Conf here. Yes?"

Reed wrote Haury on 15 July saying,

> I finally realized the other day that *the* topics requiring discussion this year are (1) the articles by Daifuku and by Martin and Rinaldo on attempted general reclassification of Southwestern archeology, and (2) changes in the Southwestern picture resulting from radiocarbon dates on Cochise and Mogollon and particularly on early corn.

Reed was referring to "A New Conceptual Scheme for Prehistoric Cultures in the Southwestern United States" by Hiroshi Daifuku (1952), who received his doctorate from Harvard University in 1952, taught at the University of Wisconsin and Beloit College, and then went on to the Museums and Monuments Division of UNESCO. Reed was also referring to "The Southwestern Co-tradition" (Martin and Rinaldo 1951).

The registration total was 152, the largest Pecos Conference up to that time (in 1940 in Albuquerque and Chaco Canyon there were 144 participants). Not until 1966, in Flagstaff, is it certain that this 1952 figure was exceeded, although J. O. Brew estimated that about 200 may have been at Fort Burgwin in 1959.

During the 1952 Conference J. Lee Correll, then at the International Museum of Folk Art, Santa Fe (and later an archaeologist for the Navajo Tribe), kept detailed notes, later typed up as "Proceedings" (Correll 1952). Most of what follows comes from this record, which is not cited for each detail.

The Conference opened on Monday, 11 August, at the Laboratory of Anthropology; in introducing Boaz Long, director of the Museum of New Mexico, Santa Fe, Reed remarked that "the Pecos Conference is not an organization; it is under way when two people from different institutions get together." Reed nominated Kidder as chairman of the Conference. Katharine Bartlett invited the Pecos Conference to come to Flagstaff the next year, which would be the twenty-fifth anniversary of the Museum of Northern Arizona. The invitation was accepted, and an interim committee was named: Harold S. Colton (chairman), Walter W. Taylor, and Verne Ray. Stubbs urged everyone to sign up for the Pecos picnic, and Long pointed out that Pecos Pueblo, with eighty acres of land, had been given to the State of New Mexico by the Gross-Kelley Company of Santa Fe; members of both the Gross and Kelley families would be there, "and since Pecos badly needs many things, it might be a good idea to keep this in mind." Actually, Long oversimplified the change in ownership, as Pecos Ruin went from the Gross-Kelley Company to the archbishop of Santa Fe, who then transferred it to the School of American Research, from which it later went to the State of New Mexico (Kelly 1972: 205–208). The Pecos National Monument would not be established until 1965.

Archaeological field reports occupied the afternoon session; the summaries fill fifteen double-spaced pages of Correll's report. At Kidder's suggestion, they were presented in geographical order, starting with Utah and continuing through Colorado and Arizona to California, then back to New Mexico and Texas. Correll's notes indicate that Kidder commented briefly on many of the reports. For example, after Hugo G. Rodeck's description of his progress in collecting photographs of all known Mimbres pottery, Kidder "told of [a] Mimbres collection given to the crown prince of Sweden to further the Cosgrove dig financially." This probably refers to the excavation of the Swarts Ruin, by Burton and Harriet Cosgrove, and seems to be a bit of otherwise unknown archaeological history (or folklore). Occasionally a report contained an element of humor, as in Frank C. Hibben's report that he had received a telephone call about a human skeleton found embedded in the clay near Clovis; two dentists had examined the skeleton and pronounced it human, but it turned out to be a dire wolf with a projectile point embedded in the chest cavity. A report by Florence Ellis is summarized as "Doing archaeology on the place [Pojoaque] as a mask for ethnology. Not supposed to do ethnology with students, however, has 13 students. . . . Some of students carried on archaeology at all times while others did ethnology."

Tuesday 12 August began in the Museum of International Folk Art with reports on ethnology and applied anthropology, Fred Eggan presiding. Hill reported on the effort to raise money for the publication of Haile's "The Blessing Way." (Haile died in 1960 and so did not live to see the work published, but under the skilled editorship of Leland C.

Wyman, the volume finally appeared years later; see Wyman 1970). Besides research in the Southwest—Navajo, Zuni, and Hopi—there were reports on the Point Four Program, in which technical assistance was being provided to what are now called "developing" countries by Gordon MacGregor and Edward T. Hall.

For many participants in the 1952 Conference the high point was the lunch at the ruins of Pecos Pueblo, for which 129 signed up. Correll writes that "after a lunch of ham, potato salad, all the trimmings, beer, and ice cream, the conference went to the ruins where Dr. Kidder gave a short history of the excavations." Haury "on behalf of the whole group" then presented Kidder with a miniature silver trowel, engraved "Pecos Conference, 1927–1952," to commemorate this silver anniversary and to honor Kidder for founding the Conference (Lewis 1952).

The Conference reconvened at 3 p.m. for the completion of the ethnological reports, including one by Fred Sleight (Rollins College, Florida) on his efforts "to define the Navajo terrain and domain as of 1846," in support of the Navajo Claims Case, and one by Robert McNair (University of Tennessee) on his study of missionary work among the Navajo and their attitudes toward churches and Christianity. Additional archaeological reports were then heard, with J. Charles Kelley (University of Southern Illinois) reporting on his work in Durango and Chihuahua, one of the first substantial programs by North Americans in the vast portion of the "Southwest" that lies in northwestern Mexico. Reed said that the National Park Service had taken over the areas of the River Basin Archeological Salvage Program that lay outside the Missouri River valley, and that it was currently working in Arkansas. The Park Service was also continuing its research at Chaco Canyon (Gordon Vivian) and Grand Canyon (Joe Ben Wheat). In an echo from the past, Albert Schroeder reported that he was writing up the 1934 WPA—National Park Service work of Ben Wetherill in Zion Canyon.

To end the afternoon program Fred Wendorf showed a movie of the excavation of Cuyamungue Pueblo, fifteen miles north of Santa Fe and occupied from the 1200s to soon after 1700. "Intended for the layman, this educational film represents an attempt by a scientific organization to present to the non-professional the purposes and values of archaeological exploration and excavation" (Lewis 1952: 10).

Wednesday, the last day of the Conference, began with a talk by Haury, illustrated by slides, of the excavation at Naco, a mammoth kill site in southern Arizona. The rest of the morning was devoted to an open discussion of recent classifications proposed for the South-west. James B. Griffin (University of Michigan) chaired the session and first called on Kidder, who described the lack of names or identifi-cations for cultures or periods in the Southwest in the 1920s. As Cor-rell reported, "[The] second day at 1927 Pecos Conference, Kroeber, Waterman and Kidder decided to straighten out the problem. Water-man, according to Kidder, was actually the progenitor of the [Pecos] classification."

Haury then described the origin of Harold S. Gladwin's root-stem-branch scheme for "ordering knowledge." Next John Rinaldo spoke about his growing concern that too little attention was paid to "what was held in common but more to distinctions between regions." He felt that Wendell Bennett's work in Peru was a good example to fol-low (see Bennett 1948) and that Southwestern cotraditions could be defined, each with common elements. He described the Southwest since 2000 B.C. in terms of "Pre-ceramic, Early agricultural, Forma-tive, Classic, and Renaissance." Colton described the genesis of his classification for northern Arizona, growing out of the difficulty of using Gladwin's system and the realization that the Kayenta was not the only "branch" in northern Arizona. Next on the program was Reed, who pointed out that "interest shifted from taxonomic to nar-rative or historical approach some twelve years ago. . . . Rather than argue over classification—one must first decide what differentiates culture[s]." He then commented on the problem of Pueblo-Mogollon distinctions.

Since Daifuku was not at the Conference, Wendorf presented the "new conceptual scheme" of his 1952 article, which was conceived independently of the Martin-Rinaldo system. A general discussion followed, with many reactions and viewpoints expressed. Schroeder spoke up for the Patayan. Colton observed that "classification and taxonomic systems deal with analysis; therefore must go into de-tails. The broad general terms deal with synthesis. Thus both must be considered according to their use. First one must analyze, then syn-thesize." F. H. (Eric) Douglas (Denver Art Museum) commented that thinking in the Southwest was too limited, and that relations to the rest of North America and to Mexico should be considered. William Wasley (University of Arizona) spoke in strong support of the value of the cotradition for finding unity across the entire Southwest and for broad comparisons with other areas, especially Mexico. Finally, Grif-fin observed that "the Southwest" had different boundaries at different time periods, and "proposed that a series of charts be drawn up showing southwest limits in time and space for the next meeting." Kidder asked Colton to chair a committee to do this, and he also suggested that mimeographed summaries of the field reports be sent in advance, to be available at registration. They could be read before the session began, and the time devoted to questions. Although this suggestion of Kidder's fell on barren ground, a "temporal-spatial synthesis" was prepared by Colton, Edward Danson, and Wendorf and presented at the next year's Conference. A series of maps, showing the extent of "the Southwest" at different time periods, would be part of a report at the 1955 Pecos Conference (Jennings 1956).

After lunch, Kidder surveyed progress in understanding the development of corn. Griffin then described the recent information from Earl Morris's Durango Basketmaker sites, from Bat Cave, and from Tularosa Cave. He proposed that corn reached the Southwest about 2,000 years ago, but noted that the problem was still far from being fully settled. Herbert Dick and Reynold Ruppé briefly reported their recent corn finds. Then, with directions from Wendorf for reaching Cuyamungue, Kidder announced that the conferees would move to the site. After a tour of the excavation, the Conference was officially adjourned at 4:10 p.m.

There is little doubt that all those fortunate enough to have attended this twenty-fifth anniversary Conference considered it to have been a great success. Years later Marjorie Lambert (conversation with Woodbury, 4 March 1980) told me that of the many Conferences she had attended, the 1952 one was the best of all, and its highlight was the picnic at Pecos and the presentation of the silver trowel to Kidder.

FLAGSTAFF, 1953 (SIXTEENTH PECOS CONFERENCE) Only three years after the Pecos Conference was held in Flagstaff in 1950 it returned there, meeting from 17 through 19 August, just before the Museum of Northern Arizona's twenty-fifth anniversary celebration (Bartlett 1953; Colton 1953).

The museum marked the anniversary with the announcement of staff additions and changes. Malcolm Farmer came as assistant director, to succeed E. D. McKee, who became director of research; Bartlett became anthropologist and curator of books and records, succeeded as curator of anthropology by Robert C. Euler. Finally, there was the announcement of the addition of a new 12,000-square-foot building at the Research Center to house all the biological and anthropological collections, the library, laboratories, and offices, freeing the museum building's galleries for new exhibitions.

Southwestern anthropology as a whole had also grown rapidly during this quarter century. For example, by the 1940s and 1950s many new names appear in the pages of *American Antiquity* and other journals, representing a generation that had begun the study of anthropology some years after the first Pecos Conference.

A broad review of the scope and status of Southwestern anthropology would take place a few months later in 1953, in Tucson at the December meeting of the AAA. Edward H. Spicer, Haury, and others arranged a symposium, which was so well received that it was published as a special Southwest issue of *American Anthropologist* (Haury 1954), the only regional special issue that journal has ever had. The symposium provides an excellent view of the state of Southwestern anthropology in 1953.

The early 1950s seem to have been a time of stock taking by anthropologists in general. In 1950, under the leadership of Griffin, a conference on archaeological field and laboratory techniques was held (Griffin 1951). Among the papers was Waldo R. Wedel's "The Use of Earth-Moving Machinery in Archaeological Excavations," describing the usefulness of heavy equipment—a radical innovation then, which later became a standard and well-accepted technique. Another sign of changing times is the paper, "The Use of IBM Machines in Analyzing Anthropological Data," by Frederick P. Thieme; this was before the day of electronic computers, but archaeologists were beginning to borrow from sociologists and physical anthropologists better ways to record and analyze large quantities of data.

The 1953 Conference was well attended, with slightly fewer than the year before, but more than most previous Conferences. The museum's "Pecos Conference Attendance List" has the names of 108 registrants, and under "No. in Party" it has a good many 2s, for a total of 134 (many of these wives were active participants, of course). Their institutions range widely, from the American Museum of Natural History, and Johns Hopkins, Yale, and Cornell universities in the east, to museums and universities across the country to the West Coast, and including the Second Mesa, Arizona, Indian Service School, the El Paso Natural Gas Company, and the Navajo Tribal Council.

The Conference began Monday 17 August, with registration on the Museum patio in the morning, and reports on current archaeological research in the afternoon (the program stating clearly, "Limited to 10 minutes each"). Notes made available by Florence Ellis (Fig. 7.1) mention the following:

Erik Reed on the late prehistoric period in the Southwest;

Albert Schroeder, reporting that "New patterns of Sho-shonean-like culture replaced P II in Ariz. strip and Nev. and Utah. Perhaps these people are early Mojaves and other Yumans responsible for problems of San Juan in late 1200s";

E. B. Danson, reasons for permanent abandonment of West Central New Mexico after 12th C.;

Paul Martin, Tularosa Phase site, Pine Lawn Valley;

Robert Lister, Chihuahua cliff dwellings;

Paul Ezell, arch[aeological] delineation of a culture boundary [in extreme western Arizona].

The official program for Tuesday 18 August lists:

9–12 A.M. Reports of current ethnological research (limited to 10 minutes each);

12:30 P.M. Picnic lunch, courtesy of the Museum, at the Research Center;

2–5 P.M. Symposium: "The Origins and Dispersals of Agri-culture in the Southwest."

Florence Ellis's notes include fourteen speakers on ethnology or ap-plied anthropology: Ruth Underhill, W. W. Hill, Esther Goldfrank, Edward Dozier, Clyde Kluckhohn, David Aberle, William H. Kelly, John Adair, Adamson Hoebel, Clara Lee Tanner, George Fathauer, Harry Getty, William Smith, Charles Lange, and John Connelly. In addition there was a report on Southwestern linguistics by Stanley Newman with comments by Harry Hoijer and a paper by Kimball Romney, of which Ellis notes, "Zuni and Keres arrived in area *after* Tanoans and took over their pattern of culture, according to linguistic evidence," to which she adds, "Sounds wrong." James Spuhler re-ported on the nature of physical anthropological data on Southwestern Indians.

Wednesday morning there was a symposium, "A Proposed Temporal-Spatial Synthesis of Southwestern Cultural Horizons." Back in July the museum had sent to expected attendees a four-page statement prepared by Colton, Wendorf (Fig. 7.2), and Danson, pref-aced by a reminder that this had been requested by the 1952 Conference and was being sent for study before the Flagstaff Conference so that "interested persons have this opportunity to familiarize themselves

7.1 *Florence Hawley Ellis, Pecos Conference, Flagstaff, 1953. Museum of Northern Arizona negative no. 74.1325, photo by A. O. Brodie.*

with the proposal." The synthesis was ambitious, comprehensive, and innovative. It defined the Southwest as including both banks of the Colorado River, parts of Sonora, Sinaloa, and Chihuahua, east to the Pecos and Canadian rivers, north to the Arkansas River at Pueblo, and west to the Virgin River drainage (not quite Reed's famous definition of the Southwest—"Las Vegas to Las Vegas and Durango to Durango"—but close). Six main cultural periods were proposed:

1. Pre-10,000 B.C. . . . hunting of now extinct animals.
2. 10,000–1500 B.C. . . . approximately equal gathering and hunting. . . .
3. Early Agricultural Period—2500 B.C.—A.D. 500 . . . Basket Maker II, Chiricahua, San Pedro, Concho—San Jose. . . .
4. Formative Period 500–900, Anasazi
   1–500, Hohokam
   1–900, Mogollon
   ?–1800, Patayan
5. Florescent Period 900–1300, Anasazi
   500–1100, Hohokam
   1000–1300, Mogollon
6. Fusion Period 1300–1600, Mogollon-Anasazi
   1100?–1600, Hohokam

Appendixes listed suggestions received by Danson in a seminar at the University of Arizona and by Wendorf at a meeting at the Laboratory of Anthropology.

This is probably the most original, carefully formulated, and clearly presented scheme for Southwestern prehistory prepared specifically for any Pecos Conference since the first one in 1927. However, it did not receive the careful and extended discussion that the original Pecos Classification did. There were comments by only a few people, and the session ended early. This apathy, if that is not too strong a word, may be due to a declining interest in broad cultural classifications in Southwestern (and other) archaeology, in favor of examining the processes of culture change and inferring social structure from prehistoric data. In any case, this commissioned cultural classification was not generally adopted by archaeologists in the years ahead. Codifying past knowledge can be useful but excites less interest than opening up new lines of investigation.

At the business meeting later the same morning, an invitation was accepted from the Southwestern National Monuments to meet in

7.2 *Harold S. Colton and Denver Fred Wendorf, Pecos Conference, Flagstaff, 1953. Museum of Northern Arizona negative no. 74.1341, photo by A. O. Brodie.*

1954 at Gila Pueblo, Globe. An interim committee was appointed, with Dale King (chairman), Thomas Onstott, and Richard Woodbury. There were resolutions noting the deaths of Paul Reiter and Tully H. Thomas, and appreciating the excellent cooperation in archaeological salvage by the El Paso Natural Gas Company along the rights-of-way of its pipelines.

The final session on Wednesday afternoon was a third symposium, on Salado, Hohokam, and Sinagua.

This somewhat sparse record hardly does justice to what was one of the best planned and best attended of Pecos Conferences. One additional item in the correspondence files of the Arizona State Museum, Tucson, indicates how a conference can lead to later exchanges of information with significant results. On 20 November Haury wrote Martin, at the Chicago Natural History Museum: "The other day Ned Danson handed me a memo dating from the Pecos Conference at Flagstaff to the effect that you wanted to see Joe Wheat's thesis. I have just sent this to Sol Tax [University of Chicago] and you might arrange with him to have a look at it." This was Wheat's Ph.D. dissertation at the University of Arizona. Tax's and Martin's reading of it helped lead to its publication—in two parts, *Crooked Ridge Village* (1954) and *Mogollon Culture Prior to* A.D. *1000* (1955), a major synthesis ordering much hitherto disparate material.

COMMENT ON NATIONAL PARK SERVICE ARCHAEOLOGY The 1954 Pecos Conference was the first of many hosted by the National Park Service (NPS). It was in Globe again in 1957 and 1962, partly in Santa Fe and partly at Pecos National Monument in 1970, at Mesa Verde National Park in 1974 and 1980, at Pecos National Monument in 1977, 1982, and 1987, at Salinas National Monument in 1985, and at Bandelier National Monument in 1989. No other organization has hosted so many of the Conferences. In Globe, the NPS occupied Gila Pueblo, where Gladwin and his staff had worked for many years. After Gladwin formally dissolved the Gila Pueblo Archaeological Foundation in 1951, the building was purchased by the federal government and became the headquarters for Southwestern National Monuments in 1952 (Haury 1988).

NPS archaeologists had been active in Pecos Conferences from the beginning, and in the previous two decades the archaeological activities and staff of the Park Service had expanded substantially. The earlier period of NPS archaeology in the Southwest has been described by Schroeder (Albert H. Schroeder, letter to Woodbury, 2 November

1986), as "practically nil until the early 1930s when Civil Works Administration funds and projects were set up . . . primarily for stabilization and surveys," but also involving some excavation. This included work by Charlie Steen in the Citadel area and by Dale King at Nalakihu, both in Wupatki National Monument; Earl Jackson and Sallie Pierce at Montezuma Castle; and Ben Wetherill in Zion National Park. The National Historic Sites Act of 1935 "mandated structural preservation," which "led to a formal ruins stabilization program under Steen and [Gordon] Vivian, and later Roland Richert."

After World War II archaeology resumed in the national parks and monuments, some of it funded by outside grants and private funds, such as Wendorf's 1947 work at Petrified Forest National Monument and Watson Smith's at Big Hawk Valley at Wupatki National Monument. Schroeder observed that "it was the success of these projects that led the NPS to begin budgeting for the area excavations, the budget cycle then taking about three years to come through with the funds." Survey and excavation at Mesa Verde were done by James A. (Al) Lancaster, Jean Pinkley, Phil Van Cleave, and Don Watson. Schroeder was assigned in 1950 to the Bureau of Reclamation to excavate at Willow Beach on the lower Colorado. Vivian excavated at Gran Quivira in 1951, and later Schroeder was "put on loan to the Museum of New Mexico for a salvage project (Bureau of Public Roads) in the Apache Creek—Reserve area of western New Mexico."

Then in 1956 the NPS Mission 66 program was established, with small archaeological projects "by area personnel, and large projects by the Regional Office [in Santa Fe]" and other large projects by contract. By 1962 the NPS had five archaeologists in Washington, fifteen in regional offices, including seven at the Southwest Archeological Center (which had succeeded the "coordinating superintendency" in Globe), and thirty-five in field areas, the many national parks and monuments. From maintaining federally protected archaeological sites and supervising visitation by the public, the NPS had grown to include a large, active, professional archaeological research staff. In 1954 the process was already well under way.

GLOBE, 1954 (SEVENTEENTH PECOS CONFERENCE)   In a letter of 30 April King, interim Conference chairman, said that there would be two or three symposia and added for reassurance to those who might be skeptical of "planned" sessions, "There will, of course, be the usual opportunities to meet old friends and catch up on what is happening and what is planned." In this same letter King announced, "In addition, the group of folks interested in the proposed Great Basin Archeological Conference have been invited to hold their organizational meeting jointly with our group. Their attendance should provide much of mutual interest."

On 30 July King sent out a general announcement from the Southwestern Monuments Association in Globe, a private group dedicated to support of the Southwestern monuments and able to provide modest funds for activities not within the Park Service budget. Its headquarters was in Gila Pueblo, and the two organizations worked closely together. The Pecos Conference was announced for 30 August–1 September.

The announcement provided a detailed program, beginning Monday with registration in the Council Hall of Gila Pueblo, the room where Gladwin had held his many famous discussion-and-argument sessions with Southwestern archaeologists invited to Gila Pueblo when it was a private research center. At 10 a.m. there would be "Words of welcome" by John M. Davis, General Superintendent of Southwestern National Monuments, followed by archaeological field reports, with Haury as chairman. The afternoon was to be devoted to "social anthropology field reports," chaired by William H. Kelly, who had founded the Bureau of Ethnic Research at the University of Arizona in 1952. On Tuesday morning any remaining field reports would be completed, and then the first of four discussion sessions would be held, "The federal government's future role in the field of anthropology." At "6:30-ish" there would be a "Free Beef Barbecue at back of Gila Pueblo near pool," followed at dusk by Indian dances.

Wednesday, the final day, had morning and afternoon special sessions: "Current developments in Geochronology," moderated by Terah L. (Ted) Smiley of the University of Arizona Tree-Ring Laboratory, and "Problems in Archeology of Aboriginal-Spanish Contact Times in the Southwest," moderated by Brew, of Peabody Museum, Harvard University.

In spite of these careful plans, one aspect of the Conference did not go as expected—the organizational meeting for the Great Basin Archeological Conference (GBAC). In response to a request for his recollections of the 1954 Pecos Conference, Jesse D. Jennings wrote (letter to Woodbury, 13 June 1980) in some detail:

> Such an opportunity delights me because it might be possible
> through your history to clear the record of a series of unfor-
> tunate events that have plagued me for many years, or at least

have led to misunderstandings and unnecessary antagonisms
by some southwesterners against both the GBAC and me. The
story is green in my memory and goes essentially like this. . . .
As you may know, I had been instrumental in helping establish the Southeastern Archeological Conference [in 1938]. . . .
Similarly I have been deeply involved in the resuscitation of
the Plains Archeology Conference in 1948 (I think [correctly])
and was subsequently able to publish those proceedings as a
UUAP [University of Utah Anthropology Paper]. The advantages which flow from any informal regional conference are so
obvious that I thought I should attempt to develop a similar
conference in the Great Basin after I had arrived in Utah.

To that end I wrote to a number of people and determined
there was some interest in such an organization. With a very
modest grant from Wenner-Gren I did limited travelling to
arouse interest during the spring and summer of 1954. During
the summer I learned that Dale King was appointed chairman
of the Pecos Conference. . . . I wrote him saying it would be
nice for the organizational session of the GBAC to be held in
conjunction but *one day earlier* [emphasis in original] than the
Pecos Conference, asking at the same time whether he would
distribute to both my list and his the details, date, etc. of the up-
coming Pecos Conference session. To this he cheerfully agreed
and I sent him my list of interested people, a kind of rough
agenda, and $50 to offset expenses of mailing and preparation of
a program. . . .

So what happened? Total, complete misfire. King diverted the
money to the barbecue (as explained to me at the barbecue) and
cheerfully, without thought, arranged the organizational program for the GBAC to occur on the same day and in complete
competition with the first day of the Pecos Conference meetings.
I was furious but helpless, so I stood there and watched what
I feared was both the beginning and end of the GBAC tran-
spire. The GBAC weathered the incident handily, but I think the
Great Basin Conference still suffers from the misunderstanding
that occurred at that first session. Many people have confided to
me that they were annoyed, thinking that I had personally arranged the overlap and confusion in an effort to cripple the Pecos
Conference in order to strengthen the GBAC!

Although the Great Basin Archeological Conference did indeed
come into formal existence, there is no mention of it in the unpub-

lished report on the Pecos Conference prepared by Danson (1954). On the other hand *American Antiquity* (Meighan 1955) carried a four-and-a-half-page report on the Great Basin Archeological Conference, prepared by Clement W. Meighan, University of California, Los Angeles.

Besides providing a list of reports, Danson (1954) includes an aspect of the Pecos Conferences often unrecorded—the important assistance from local organizations and people. A public address system was loaned by the Elks Club and chairs by the Globe High School. Other kinds of help came from the Globe Chamber of Commerce, the All-American Distributing Company, Purity Brands Ltd., the Two Lanes and Sunset clubs, and half a dozen residents of Globe, including Ernst Antevs, who donated the cost of the tortillas and buns for the barbecue. King thanked Antevs in a letter of 13 September and mentioned that the Southwestern National Monuments' costs were just over one hundred dollars, thanks to all the assistance received.

About 120 people participated in the Conference, but unfortunately no list of registrants survives. At the start of the Conference greetings were telegraphed to Kidder and to Frederick Webb Hodge, the oldest surviving "Founders."

The archaeological field reports, chaired by Haury, included twenty-five speakers and ranged in time from Clovis and "Yuma" points in the high passes of the Colorado Rockies, reported by Wheat, to eighteenth-century Spanish and seventeenth-century Tewa remains beneath Santa Fe, reported by Bruce T. Ellis. Other speakers included Bryant Bannister, William Bullard, Danson, Dick, Bertha Dutton, Florence Hawley Ellis, Euler, Hibben, Jane Holden, Robert Lister, Alan Olson, Rinaldo, Schroeder, Charlie R. Steen, Stubbs, Raymond Thompson, Vivian, Wasley, Wendorf, Arnold Withers, Woodbury, and Barton A. Wright. Archaeological reports continued in the early afternoon, and "ended with a summary of the Southwestern National Monuments' activities, past and proposed, by Dale King" (Danson 1954: 6).

The remainder of the afternoon included ethnological reports by Charles Cobb, Henry F. Dobyns, Euler, Gordon Hewes, Schroeder, Elisabeth Tooker, and Vogt. Particular attention was given to Indian claims cases, including Walapai, Papago, Pima, Yavapai, and Acoma. A related report, by Gordon Hewes, dealt with the way the Utes of Colorado used the $6 million they received as recompense for 1,000 acres of land. Monday ended with an illustrated talk by Ruth Simpson and George Carter on their putative "Early Man" finds in southern California.

The Tuesday morning symposium chaired by Reed surveyed the

federal government's future relations to anthropology. Filling NPS archaeological positions was said to be difficult. This was a time of rapidly expanding archaeological activity all across the country, and too few beginning archaeologists were emerging from the graduate schools. The River Basin Surveys were described, emphasizing the extent and value of interagency cooperation, particularly the Smithsonian Institution, the National Park Service, and the Federal Bureau of Public Roads. W. J. Kellar, district engineer of the New Mexico Bureau of Public Roads, and Wendorf, of the Museum of New Mexico, described the cooperative arrangement they had worked out for archaeological salvage along highway rights-of-way, a model that was eventually copied in several other states.

Tuesday afternoon discussion was on southern Arizona–northern Mexico connections, beginning with an illustrated report by Charles Di Peso (Amerind Foundation) of the archaeology of the Paloparado site, near Tumacacori, south of Tucson, a site documented in the journals of Father Francisco Kino and Juan Mateo Manje in the late 1600s. Discussants were Paul H. Ezell, Schroeder, and Dobyns.

Tuesday evening both conferences were guests of the Southwestern Monuments Association at the barbecue supper, which was followed by performances by a group of Zuni dancers.

The symposium Wednesday morning on "Current developments in geochronology" was chaired by Smiley and included eleven reports on a great variety of chronological methods and problems, including stratigraphy, paleontology, palynology, and carbon-14 dating. That afternoon Brew led a discussion of aboriginal-Spanish contacts. Speakers were Di Peso, Dobyns, Schroeder, Ezell, Rex Gerald, [Gwyneth?] Harrington, Thomas B. Hinton, Raymond H. Thompson, Watson Smith, and Bruce Ellis.

The Conference concluded with a short business meeting that included the appropriate votes of thanks, the acceptance of an invitation from the Museum of New Mexico to meet in Santa Fe in 1955, and the appointment of Wheat, Steen, and Stubbs as an interim committee for that Conference.

The 1954 Conference was notable in several respects. It added the National Park Service to the circle of organizations hosting Pecos Conferences. It held *four* planned sessions, all apparently successful. Perhaps most significantly, it saw the founding of the Great Basin Archeological Conference, reflecting a widening awareness of the value of regional conferences. This started a successful and continuing GBAC, which in 1961 became the Great Basin Anthropological

Conference. In some respects it has surpassed the Pecos Conference in effectiveness, to judge by an innovation at its 1964 meeting—an "All-Conference Symposium" as a regular, continuing means for assessing the current status of anthropological research in the Great Basin. The 1964 symposium was published, with eight papers and nearly 100 pages of comments (Madsen and O'Connell 1982).

SANTA FE, 1955 (EIGHTEENTH PECOS CONFERENCE) The Eighteenth Pecos Conference opened at the Laboratory of Anthropology on Monday morning, 15 August. Following registration (115 individuals are on an alphabetical list) the Conference's first session was held that afternoon and, as tradition dictated, was devoted to archaeological field reports.

The opening session was chaired by Lister with twenty-four speakers, most of whose reports were summarized later in *American Antiquity* (Danson 1956). The list of those reporting field work probably includes a majority of those active in Southwestern archaeology at the time, although there are a few glaring exceptions, such as Martin and Haury, neither of whom was at the Conference. Subject matter ranged widely in time, from association of Clovis points with extinct megafauna (Estancia Valley) to seventeenth- and eighteenth-century church foundations in Santa Fe. The Four Corners states were well represented, plus Texas and northern Mexico. Jesse Nusbaum reported that six separate pipeline surveys were currently under way, covering large parts of the Southwest. He also said that two Ute Indians had found the mummified bodies of two American soldiers in a cave, still wearing U.S. Army uniforms, and had reported their find to the Department of the Interior and the U.S. Army.

Tuesday morning the Conference heard ethnological reports in a session chaired by Euler. Reports "ranged from central California to [the] Central Valley of Mexico." Of the 115 names on the Conference registration list, at least 17 can be identified as having ethnological interests.

On Tuesday afternoon Stubbs presented "a factual summary of upper Rio Grande archaeology . . . [covering] present day archaeological knowledge from the early man finds up to the historical period." He was followed by Wendorf, who "indicated problems still to be solved and periods and areas needing work" (Danson 1956: 339). Such summaries of the area in which a Conference took place became fairly frequent in the years to come, although not as strong a tradition as field reports.

The presentation at the Pecos Conference of interim results of the Society for American Archaeology (SAA) Seminar on the American Southwest was a unique event in Southwestern archaeology, and part of a larger event, unique for American archaeology as a whole. Robert Wauchope, president of SAA in 1954–55, conceived the idea of a series of seminars on major archaeological problems. With the approval of the society's executive board, he requested and received substantial financial support from the Carnegie Corporation of New York (see Wauchope 1956). Four seminars took place during the summer of 1955: "An Archaeological Classification of Culture Contact Situations" (Gordon R. Willey, chairman); "An Archaeological Approach to Cultural Stability" (Haury, chairman); "The American Southwest: A Problem in Cultural Isolation" (Jennings and Reed, cochairmen); and "Functional and Evolutionary Implications of Community Patterning" (Richard K. Beardsley, chairman).

The seminars each had six to eight members, who prepared and shared papers in advance. Each group then met for about three weeks. For the Southwestern seminar, the group consisted of the cochairmen, and Griffin, Kelley, Meighan, Stubbs, and Wheat, with Dee C. Taylor as recorder. The Conference was fortunate to hear the interim results of this intensive reexamination of the Southwest. As the group reported,

> The very existence of a seminar, its purpose to isolate the origins of traits seen in the Southwest and considered to be of external derivation, is in itself a matter of great significance in anthropological theory. As recently as fifteen, even ten, years ago the dedicated Southwestern specialist (with notable exceptions) devoted his analytic skills to discovering and describing the cultures of a drainage system or a series of contiguous sites, or at best the relationships of one culture variant to some other found outside our area of definition. Southwestern relationships to cultures lying north, south, east, or west, either early or late in time, have been for many years ignored, blandly dismissed, or categorically denied. When they have been recognized, these relationships have not been explained or studied [Jennings 1956: 67].

The reports of the seminar were published promptly, with the reports of the other three, as SAA Memoir No. 11. The seminar offered many new, sometimes iconoclastic ideas, too many and too complex to summarize here. The Southwest was examined in terms of four sequential stages: the Base, Emergence, Specialization and Divergence, and Crystallization and Resistance. A series of maps showed the boundaries of the Southwest and the extent of Anasazi, Hohokam, and Mogollon at six time periods from A.D. 900–1900. After Jennings presented a summary of the findings, the members of the seminar answered questions from the floor.

At the brief business meeting an invitation was accepted to meet at the Museum of Northern Arizona in 1956, and an interim committee was appointed composed of Malcolm Farmer (chairman), Thomas Cain, and Fred Peck.

FLAGSTAFF, 1956 (NINETEENTH PECOS CONFERENCE)   When the Pecos Conference met in Flagstaff 16–18 August 1956, it was the third time that the Museum of Northern Arizona had been host in seven years—remarkably generous support for a relatively small and far from affluent institution. There was a professional anthropological staff of only five: Colton, Danson, Bartlett, Barton, Wright, and David A. Breternitz. This repeated hospitality reflects the dedication of the Coltons to the Conference and its purposes, and to the support of Southwestern archaeology as a whole. As has happened frequently, there was confusion as to *which* Conference this was. The registration forms said "29th Annual Pecos Conference"; actually it was the twenty-ninth anniversary of the first Conference, but only the nineteenth Conference to take place, as it was not until 1946 that the Pecos Conference became an annual event.

The registration list has 100 names on it, many familiar from previous Conferences. Under "Profession" most list themselves as archaeologists, but a few are "anthropologists" or "ethnologists," and there are a "paper shuffler" (King), "museologist" (Wright), several park rangers, a naturalist, a dendrochronologist, a linguist, and 27 who list themselves as "student." The fears of the past about permitting students to attend were pretty well over, although perhaps some were still inclined to listen more than they spoke. Nevertheless, at least five "students" gave field reports—William Beeson, Rex Gerald, Michael Harner, Elizabeth Morris, and William Roosa. More and more archaeological projects were depending heavily on the participation of those who were technically "students," but who in terms of experience and skills were the equal of many of their seniors.

At the opening session Danson, who had been appointed assistant director of the museum earlier that summer, announced the death on

24 June of Earl Morris, one of the Southwest's most respected archaeologists and one of the "Founders" at the first Pecos Conference. Later,
Danson said that he would arrange an appointment for anyone who
would like to visit Colton at his home. Colton did not want to undergo
the strain of meeting and greeting scores of friends and strangers during the Conference sessions. He was recovering from recent surgery
(Jimmy H. Miller, letter to Woodbury, 10 February 1987).

There is an excellently detailed record of most of the sessions, made
by Elaine A. Bluhm (Bluhm 1956), who for several years had been in
the field with Martin in the Reserve area. However, the record of who
reported during the Friday morning session is confusing: in the report
by Danson for *American Antiquity* (Danson 1957) there are six reports
that do not appear in Bluhm's record, and she includes four people not
mentioned by Danson (so much for the dependability of contemporary documentation). The session, chaired by Raymond H. Thompson, probably included about fifteen reports, which, as in most years,
ranged from "early man" to late prehistoric and early historic. Several reports were on extensive survey programs, on "salvage" work
in connection with highway building, or on Indian land claims cases.

The last part of the morning session was devoted to ethnological reports, chaired by Vogt. There were only three, a sharp drop from the
preceding years: Florence Ellis (pottery making at Sia Pueblo), Euler
(the similarity of Cochise milling stones to those of some present-day
groups, such as the Walapai), and Dobyns (early Walapai farming, as
described by an elderly informant for Dobyns's land claims research).
Each of these "ethnographic" reports obviously had significant implications for archaeology.

Friday afternoon had concurrent sessions, one on "Early Man" and
one on linguistics (Fig. 7.3). Bluhm's report includes only the former.
It was chaired by E. B. (Ted) Sayles of the Arizona State Museum,
and seven reports were presented:

> David Breternitz,   Museum of Northern Arizona—a Cochise
> site upstream from the proposed Glen Canyon dam site
> William Wasley,   Arizona State Museum—the Lehner site,
> southern Arizona, with Clovis points and butchering tools
> associated with the bones of nine young mammoths
> William B. Roosa,   University of New Mexico—the Lucy
> site, east of Albuquerque, surface finds suggesting a long
> occupation, with Clovis, Sandia, Folsom, and Pinto points

Raymond H. Thompson, University of Arizona—crema-
tions at the Cienega site, Point of Pines, with C-14 dates of 3000
and 4200 B.P.

Douglas W. Schwartz, University of Kentucky—caches of
split-twig figurines from Grand Canyon caves

Richard Shutler, Jr., National Park Service—Stewart Rock
Shelter, Nevada, preliminary tests producing material from
2000 B.C. through Pueblo to Paiute

Terah L. Smiley, University of Arizona—work of the Laboratory of Tree-Ring Research on the physical and climatic history
of the Southwest for the past 10,000 years.

In closing, Sayles pointed out the change in "early man" research
from the singlehanded approach of the past to the current productive
collaboration of specialists in many disciplines.

At the business meeting on Saturday morning the NPS invitation
extended by King to meet in Globe in 1957 was accepted. Schroeder
was elected chairman, with Thompson and Breternitz the other committee members. There was disagreement on the best date, Stubbs
favoring an earlier date, to avoid conflict with the Santa Fe Fiesta,
but the majority preferring later in August. It was agreed that with
this in mind the date would be set by the committee. They chose
26–28 August. Bluhm's record includes the recurring hope for distribution to participants of a report on the Conference: "Dr. Danson
asked that those interested in receiving a mimeographed copy of the
notes of this year's Conference signify their interest. The members as
a whole said that they would like to have such a copy if it becomes
available. It will be free" (Bluhm 1956: 5). As far as is known, no such
notes were ever distributed.

"Response was slight" to Breternitz's offer of a field trip to the
Mt. Elden pit house, as well as the one behind the Research Center. Finally, Euler "asked the Conference to pass a resolution on the
preservation of historic documents, to be sent to public officials." A
resolution was passed, and Dobyns was asked to send the resolution
"to the proper officials" (Bluhm 1956: 5). The usual motions of appreciation were also passed, and an expression of hope for Colton's
continued recovery.

The remainder of the morning was devoted to a symposium,
chaired by Schwartz, "on the 1100–1300 period in the Southwest, each
speaker reporting on his own particular geographical field for that

7.3 *The linguistic session at the Pecos Conference, Flagstaff, 1956. Carl and Florence Voegelin at left rear corner of table. Museum of Northern Arizona negative no. 12924, photo by Christy G. Turner II.*

time period. This was a new approach, and it was hoped that it would stimulate some interesting discussions" (Bluhm 1956: 5). The session began with Smiley describing the climatic conditions of these centuries. He was followed by regional reports by Rex E. Gerald, Wheat, Michael Harner, Ezell, Di Peso, Stubbs, Wheat again, Danson, King, Stewart Peckham, and Thompson. After a break for lunch the session continued, with Schroeder, Breternitz, Shutler, Euler, Dobyns, and Douglas Schwartz, as well as Euler reporting for Edward Dittert, who was not at the Conference.

The report on the Conference in *American Antiquity* (Danson 1957: 326) summarizes this final session as follows:

> The discussion was divided into the major river drainages, and archaeologists familiar with particular drainages spoke of the over-all picture of those areas. The period discussed was one of crowding together of the Puebloans into large and often defensively located pueblos, of large-scale movements of people, and of the abandonment of large sections of the Southwest previously occupied by pueblo builders.

An aspect of the Pecos Conferences that has always been important but rarely recorded is the many meetings of two or more individuals with specialized common interests, who find the Conference an opportunity to compare notes, make plans, argue, and sometimes initiate important scholarly work. Euler recorded one of these occasions in his "Ceramic Patterns of the Hakataya Tradition," saying, "To those archaeologists who have worked in the area it is probably well known that the framework for the Hakataya concept was developed by a small group during the 1956 Pecos Conference in Flagstaff" (Euler 1982: 53). At this same Conference the ideas for "Ceramic Variety, Type Cluster, and Ceramic System in Southwestern Pottery Analysis" were first formulated on the porch of the Museum's Gate House in discussion among David Breternitz, James Gifford, Joe Ben Wheat, and William Wasley (Wheat, Gifford, and Wasley 1958). The ideas were presented for consideration by the next year's Pecos Conference and published soon after. How many other ideas, concepts, or plans were conceived at Pecos Conferences we will never know, but year in and year out there has been no other meeting at which so many Southwesternists were brought together in an informal setting with time for "private" sessions of the kind mentioned by Euler.

GLOBE, 1957 (TWENTIETH PECOS CONFERENCE)   It is difficult to determine whether some Pecos Conferences actually had much more extensive planning than others, or whether that impression is simply because more records survive from some years than others. As time went on, the Pecos Conferences had more planned sessions, which required more letter writing, although the informal "reporting" sessions continued, mainly consisting of archaeological field reports.

The start of 1957 planning was a letter from Wheat, of the University of Colorado Museum, sent out in March 1957. It begins, "Dear Colleague," and summarizes the ceramic variety and type cluster concepts that he and his colleagues had discussed the previous year at the Pecos Conference. He observes that new pottery type definitions are appearing with increasing frequency and that

> this proliferation of named types has alarmed many archaeologists. However, there can be no legitimate doubt that if we are ever to understand the complex ceramic history of the Southwest we must be free to analyze to as fine a point as necessary to localize in time and space the infinitesimal variants of pottery which constitute history.

He urges the need for "a more formal recognition of the broad general [ceramic] groups" and proposes that it be discussed at a session at the next Pecos Conference. He concludes,

> The proposal is simply that a general term be given to each major cluster of specific types. There would be perhaps 50 (or less) of these inclusive names. Specific types would, at least for certain problems, simply be termed variants of the general type.

Kidder, just back in Cambridge after two months in Guatemala, responded enthusiastically to Wheat's ideas (A. V. Kidder, letter to Joe Ben Wheat, 22 April 1957):

> I have read with great interest and much satisfaction your recent discussion of pottery nomenclature, with which I entirely agree. As a matter of fact, I sometimes feel like an elderly rabbit returning to his home brier patch to find that he has left ten thousand descendants, as I believe I was one of the first if not the first person who gave a name to any type of Southwestern pot-

tery, namely Biscuit! Anyhow, you are perfectly right in feeling that the thing has got now so complicated that there should be a grouping.

As will be seen later, Wheat's idea was the basis for an important session at the Pecos Conference that summer, but it was not included in the preliminary program that Schroeder, chairman of the interim committee, sent out on 6 May. The date was set for 26–28 August, with regrets that it conflicted with the Great Basin Conference of 26–27 August at San Francisco State College. Monday 26 August was to be devoted to field reports. Tuesday morning would have five concurrent "small discussion group sessions," with the following possibilities suggested: (1) problems relating to the earliest ceramic sites in the Southwest; (2) historical documents relating to the Southwest, their collection and preservation; (3) the proposed Hakataya (continued from 1956); (4) problems concerned with land claims archaeology, the availability and use of data involved; (5) archaeological societies and the amateur. Numbers 2, 3, and 5 survived in the final program, with "early ceramics" proving so popular that a separate, nonconcurrent session was set up for this. Topic 4 was replaced with "Biological materials from excavations." Later, another topic was added, "The student and opportunities for summer research."

In Schroeder's preliminary program Tuesday afternoon was to be the "Status of Southwestern prehistory (Facts, Hypotheses and Blanks). A 'stock-taking' session'." Following a short business meeting, Wednesday morning would be for "Critical periods in Southwestern prehistory and history as related to ecology and/or cultural change," and the afternoon was "open for suggestions."

Why Wheat's suggestion was not included on the preliminary program is not clear. It may have simply been a matter of timing, people depending more on mail than telephone in the 1950s. However, the omission was rectified, apparently as a result of a letter to Schroeder, dated 31 May 1957, and signed by Breternitz, Wasley, Gifford, and Gerald. No response has come to light, but in the final (undated) announcement that Schroeder sent out, the Wednesday afternoon program was to be:

Ceramic problems and terminology. Chairman: Joe Ben Wheat.
   To date the following subjects have been suggested for consideration:

(1) Types and variants;
(2) Ceramic influences from the south to north;
(3) Development and meaning of the Jeddito style;
(4) Ceramic repositories and their function.

This is not quite what Wheat had proposed, but "the Jeddito style" was one of the examples in his original letter, and "types and variants" was a topic easily expanded into consideration of "groups."

The original "stock-taking session" was better defined as "Discussion on present status of archaeological and ethnological research in the Southwest and other problems led by a panel consisting of [Ignacio] Bernal, Danson, [Florence] Ellis, Haury, Stubbs, and [Walter W.] Taylor." Schroeder had invited ten Mexican archaeologists to this Pecos Conference, but unfortunately only Bernal was able to attend. He was asked to chair this session. In a letter to Florence Ellis and Danson (24 July 1957), Schroeder explained in detail what he had in mind:

> Several problems such as the following are the type of thing we will deal with in this session: . . . What constitutes a pattern? Must it be specific basic traits or a percentage of traits? What kind of traits are needed to postulate a population shift? Is the Southwest a culture area in prehistoric times or a meeting place of several distinct cultures? Co-tradition, etc. How far south into Mexico do Southwestern cultures extend? Do such extensions vary or oscillate with time? What are the tie-ins between preceramic and ceramic cultures? Can we demonstrate culture growth in any one culture of the Southwest as resulting from indigenous development, or is extra-local influence (diffusion to migration) the prime factor? Where does ecology enter into it? Are population shifts the result of ecological changes, internecine strife, intrusions of other groups? What evidence do we have of nomadic groups in the prehistoric Southwest?

Although some of these questions may seem naive thirty years later, they represent the significant efforts being made in the Southwest at the time to move beyond additional refinements of chronology and fuller descriptions of ceramic, architectural, and other remains toward a better understanding of the processes and relationships that shaped the long sequence of cultural changes that had already been defined. "Critical periods in the Southwest" had four suggested subjects: (1) early ceramic sites in the Southwest; (2) Basket Maker III in the Rio Grande; (3) 1100–1250 west of the Continental Divide; and (4) 1540–1600 in the Rio Grande.

Thus the Pecos Conference was becoming much more "structured" than in previous years. The strong emphasis on archaeology reflected a problem Schroeder mentioned in his final announcement: "As yet we have not received any suggestions from ethnologists, linguists or others for individual sessions on Tuesday morning." He also took an unequivocal position on the long-standing question of student participation:

> For several years we have noted a drop in the attendance of students at our conferences. We hope that the summer field schools that close down before the conference will have a good representation of students at the meeting. Before long they will be the professionals in the field and there is no better way for them to become acquainted with the people or problems involved than to attend an informal gathering such as the Pecos Conference. Out of such contacts interesting and needed summer research projects or employment possibilities could well develop.

This is the clearest statement yet in the surviving records of the Conferences, firmly extending an invitation to students to come, without any of the qualifications of the past (such as "listen but keep quiet," or "advanced" students only). Lister expressed his agreement in a letter to Schroeder from Escalante, Utah, dated 30 July 1957:

> Dear Al—
>   Looks like you and your committee have done a good job in lining up the PC program. Sorry I haven't been of any aid to you [due to being in the field]. . . . Your remark . . . about student participation is just the opposite from those made by Paul Martin when he declined to participate in the "stock-taking" session. He believes students should not be allowed to attend! Says it clutters up the place—they take all the chairs, make the group so large he can't chat with his friends—etc—etc—I agree with you! Pardon the scribble. Just in from the field & dead tired. For the next couple of weeks we are going to work the areas down close to the [Glen Canyon] dam site.
>
> Sincerely,
> Bob

Another comment on the changes taking place in the Conference occurs in a long letter from Haury to Kidder, dated 3 July 1957. It covered a variety of other matters, and included this paragraph:

> The Pecos Conference coming up this summer in Globe in August will mark the thirtieth year and it would be wonderful if you could join in on that occasion. My own feeling about the Conference at this point is that it needs the guiding hand of the tried and true persons like yourself, Colton, and maybe I can count myself in with the younger Old Guard. The tenor of the Conference has changed, not that it shouldn't, but I am a little apprehensive about the direction in which it seems to be going.

Haury's misgivings were probably related to the increasing number of planned sessions, with speakers selected in advance and topics specifically defined, rather than to the increased attendance by students.

After all the careful planning, the letter writing, the selection of chairmen for sessions, the Conference finally convened. The report in *American Antiquity* (Lister 1958) says that "over 100" attended, but the registration list has only 80 names. This is about the same as the year before but much less than the 1952 and 1953 Conferences at Santa Fe and Flagstaff. The location of the Conference in Globe may account for the fact that thirty-six participants listed an Arizona address, compared to only sixteen from New Mexico, eleven from Colorado, and three from Utah. Others came from as far away as Mexico, Illinois, Florida, Virginia, New York, and Massachusetts. Although membership in the SAA is only a rough clue to the number of practicing archaeologists in the Southwest at that time, figures in *American Antiquity* (Meighan 1958) show that Arizona had forty-two members, New Mexico thirty-eight, Colorado twenty, and Utah ten. California leads the list with 129 members. The overwhelmingly Southwestern representation at the 1957 Pecos Conference does reflect the strong growth of local research institutions, in contrast to the 1920s and 1930s, when a larger proportion of Southwestern research was done by archaeologists from eastern and middle western institutions.

The most detailed record of the 1957 Conference is by James C. Gifford and Carol A. Gifford, who kept notes on the discussions of ceramic terminology and on some of the other sessions as well (Gifford and Gifford 1957). The briefer report by Lister (1958) comments that "field reports for the 1957 season emphasized the large amount of salvage archaeology underway in the Southwest," including the

Upper Colorado Basin project, a natural gas pipeline in northeastern Arizona, and highway salvage in New Mexico and Arizona.

The notes by the Giffords list the archaeologists in charge of various parts of the Colorado River Storage Project: Steen, Edward Dittert, Jr., Jennings, Lister, Breternitz, and William Y. Adams. They add, "They are all eagerly searching for assistants, $4200 for anyone with an M. A.; $4800 for Ph.D." Schroeder was right, the Pecos Conference was a good place to learn about jobs.

For the stock-taking session Tuesday afternoon there are notes by Haury (Arizona State Museum Library Archives) that provide one expert's informed judgment of the state of Southwestern archaeology in 1957. He observes that the first Pecos Conference "considered what to us now seems a simple picture of SW Cult[ure] History (seemed complex then)," and points out that since then the Hohokam, the Mogollon, and the Desert culture have been added, and "*the end not in sight*" (his emphasis). He also notes that "obviously new ideas, new names will emerge, and problem is partly *taxonomic.*" His notes indicate topics for the stock-taking session, "Areas of Study needing attention": (1) Basketmaker open sites ("Mogollon far better known, stands out by contrast"); (2) Hohokam ("recent changes in concepts require that these be argued with shovel—need fresh data" [which he did seven years later]); (3) settlement studies ("Hope this will be more than a fad—an especially worthwhile area"); and (4) "correl[ated] with above is need for detailed environmental studies." Finally he comments on the "tendency to explain all new traits as product of a *migration*" (his emphasis) and mentions criteria needed to justify such an explanation. We "ought to guard against the kind of 'fatalism' that [the] word migration seems to evoke."

The Giffords' record complements Haury's notes, summarizing comments by the other participants (Gifford and Gifford 1957). Bernal urged more investigation in the area between Mesoamerica and the Southwest, and the better definition of the southern limit of the Southwest. "And with all due respect says Bernal to Taylor, 'we must come out of the caves' and dig the big sites, the cities, the mounds, and temples in northern Mexico so as to see the relationship of the southwest to central Mexico."

Di Peso described the advantages of a long-term project with a specific orientation, in his case continuity in the Pimeria Alta, working back from the historic, combining history, ethnology, and archaeology.

"Colton said that 30 years ago there was also a stock-taking session.

Everyone had an area then. The Anasazi were all finished, there was no need to work on that anymore. . . . It is now known that our knowledge of the Anasazi is almost non-existent."

Prompt preliminary reports and small site reports were urged by Florence Ellis, rather than waiting for big, final reports. She also spoke of the need for "more integration between ethnology and archaeology."

Speaking of the Rio Grande, Stubbs reviewed all the problems needing further study in that Rio Grande area. Finally,

> Dittert rose to give a very good defense of salvage archaeology that seemed to refute very nicely some derogatory remarks against salvage archaeology made by Taylor. Bernal felt that the only real danger posed by salvage archaeology is that it might be considered an end in itself, and . . . the ultimate goals and objectives of archaeological work might be obscured or ignored.

To judge from this detailed summary by the Giffords, the stock-taking session brought out a healthy diversity of views, pointed out many areas or problems needing better attention, and fulfilled quite well the intentions of the program planners.

The Wednesday morning business meeting brought out sharp disagreement on where the next Pecos Conference should be held, according to the Giffords' notes. "An invitation from J. Charles Kelley to come to Durango was ruled out on account of distance," although many felt that since northern Mexico "was in a real sense part of the Southwest it was in our best interests to try to schedule a conference there." Bernal offered to help with arrangements to meet at the University of Chihuahua, with one day spent at the Amerind excavations at Casas Grandes. "Dr. Haury rose to announce his opposition to this. His position . . . [was] that the Pecos Conference was founded in the Southwest heartland of Arizona and New Mexico and ought to stay that way" (Gifford and Gifford 1957). In Schroeder's minutes of the business meeting he states that Haury felt that meeting so far to the south "might deprive students from attending the conference." He urged acceptance of an invitation to go to Albuquerque, and this proposal was approved, with the suggestion that "Chihuahua might be considered the next year." Hibben, who had extended the invitation to Albuquerque, was appointed chairman of the 1958 program committee, with Marjorie Lambert and Wheat as the other members. Schroeder raised the question of a registration fee for the Conference, and Haury spoke in favor of this, proposing a one dollar charge. Alan Olson suggested increasing it to two dollars, and this was put to a vote and approved. It would pay for registration, name tags, and one luncheon. The remainder of the morning was devoted to the critical periods discussion with Thompson as chairman.

Finally there came the session on pottery taxonomy, chaired by Wheat. "There was a favorable expression of opinion in general . . . and there was a . . . willingness to see the entities formulated as outlined and an encouraging number of persons seemed willing to try it with respect to their own material" (Gifford and Gifford 1957: 5). It opened with Wheat's review of the sequence of thinking that led to his "Dear Colleague" letter. Gifford then read a series of definitions of the proposed terms, "using Kiet Siel Polychrome as an example," and Colton expressed his approval of the concept. Breternitz "commented on the varieties of Jeddito as an example of this concept." Wheat pointed out that the scheme permitted greater splitting and "also for synthesizing for teaching purposes . . . trying to please both the splitters and the lumpers." Less than a year later "Ceramic Variety, Type Cluster, and Ceramic System in Southwestern Pottery Analysis" by Wheat, Gifford, and Wasley (1958) was published (see also Gifford 1960; Smith and others 1960).

This concluded the final day of the Conference, one of the most carefully planned yet, with extensive examination of problems, new ideas, and neglected areas, in the spirit of the first Conference thirty years before. Field reports occupied one day, but panel discussions and planned sessions with invited participants filled the second and third day, with what appear to have been excellent results. In *Teocentli* (No. 61, November 1957) Haury commented that "at the end of the summer a better than usual Pecos Conference at Gila Pueblo in Globe was stimulating."

A further comment on the 1957 Conference occurs in a letter from Haury to Kidder (6 September 1957):

> Although the Conference was attended by fewer people than in recent years, it was generally agreed that the junta came off well and the time invested brought appropriate returns. There were almost no ethnologists there and almost all discussions centered on archaeological problems. I think Colton and I were the oldest "dogs" present and the crowd as a whole was characterized by its youthfulness. We were all sorry you could not make it.

8
The Wild Years, 1958 and 1959

As recent Conferences had demonstrated, archaeological (indeed, all anthropological) activity in the Southwest was expanding rapidly in the mid 1950s. A quick look through the "Notes and News" section of *American Antiquity* makes this clear. For example, in 1956 there were three major pipeline projects under way, one from the San Juan Basin to Washington and Oregon, another from Bloomfield, New Mexico, to Phoenix, and one from the Green River to Denver and Laramie. The Museum of Northern Arizona, Flagstaff, was completing additional surveys in Glen Canyon. In New Mexico the Shiprock Irrigation Project and the Navajo Dam Project involved extensive salvage archaeology. In 1957 Paul S. Martin and John B. Rinaldo completed the first season at the Chicago Museum of Natural History's new Southwestern headquarters at Vernon, Arizona. Charles Di Peso was starting his major excavation program at Casas Grandes, Chihuahua, for the Amerind Foundation. A new series of ceramic taxonomy conferences began at the Museum of Northern Arizona, under the leadership of Martin, examining the classification of Cibola White Wares. Joe Ben Wheat, of the University of Colorado Museum, Boulder, continued excavation at Yellow Jacket in Colorado. In addition, in the "Notes and News" reports for 1956–58, more than one hundred other Southwestern archaeological excavations, surveys, and field projects are reported.

Publications on the Southwest or of importance to the area were also plentiful at this time. In 1958 there appeared *Method and Theory in American Archaeology* by Gordon R. Willey and Philip Phillips, the first hemisphere-wide framework attempting to order the chaos of myriad cultures, complexes, foci, phases, and other taxonomic units. More clearly than ever before, archaeologists could see the Southwestern

United States in relation to the entire hemisphere. The previous year a monograph of a very different kind had appeared, a landmark of great significance to the Southwest, "The Cultivation and Weaving of Cotton in the Prehistoric Southwestern United States," by Kate Peck Kent (1957). This synthesis and interpretation has stood the test of time so well that it was reprinted in 1983 by the School of American Research. The growing awareness in the 1950s of the interrelationship between past cultures and their environmental settings is exemplified in "Climate Change and Culture History in the Grand Canyon Region," by Douglas W. Schwartz (1957) and in "Ecological Interpretation in Archaeology: Part I" by Clement W. Meighan and others (1958). In the same issue of *American Antiquity* there appeared "Ceramic Variety, Type Cluster, and Ceramic System in Southwestern Pottery Analysis," by Joe Ben Wheat, James C. Gifford, and William W. Wasley, the final result of their session at the 1957 Pecos Conference. At all levels—theory, acquisition of data, interpretation, analysis, synthesis, and new perspectives—changes, advances, and innovations had become more numerous than ever before.

ALBUQUERQUE, 1958 (TWENTY-FIRST PECOS CONFERENCE) The twenty-first Pecos Conference was held in Albuquerque on 15–17 August 1958, at the University of New Mexico, the first time it had met on a campus. This setting reflects the growing logistical problems of the Conference; the traditional "field" location was becoming more and more difficult for those responsible for providing meals, housing, and meeting space. It may also be that archaeologists were growing fonder of urban comforts than of roughing it out of doors. However, the Conference would not again be held on a campus until 1965, at Trinidad State Junior College, Colorado, and then in 1967 at the University of Arizona, Tucson. The invitation by Frank C. Hibben, of the university's anthropology department, to meet on the New Mexico campus had been accepted the previous year, and Albert H. Schroeder wrote to Hibben (9 September 1957) to inform him of this. He also said:

> You probably can guess what followed [acceptance of the Albuquerque invitation]. You were elected interim chairman! Marge Lambert and Joe Ben Wheat were nominated to the committee to assist you. Incidentally, I gave Marge the complete mailing list we used for this last conference for your reference. . . . One thing was brought up which you should know. A resolution was

passed to charge a registration fee of two dollars to take care of mailings, name [tags] and holders, and a free luncheon. If no luncheon is planned, the fee can be reduced to one dollar.

The preliminary announcement for the 1958 Conference included a few innovations:

Accommodations will be available in the new air-conditioned dormitory [a Conference first] of the University of New Mexico. Singles will be about $3.00; doubles and married couples about $2.00 each. . . . Suggestions for the improvement of the Conference are invited. The emphasis will be on informality and conviviality [and so it turned out].

The tentative program was traditional in coverage: the first day for registration and field reports, followed by cocktails and dinner; the second day for two sessions, one on early man and the other on Indian claims archaeology and salvage archaeology. The third morning would have a short business meeting, followed by a field trip to Pottery Mound, the large Pueblo IV site a few miles south of Albuquerque, where Hibben had recently found numerous impressive kiva murals (see Hibben 1975). For the afternoon there was proposed a session on "Archaeological Progress in the Southwest."

The list of registrants for the Conference has 140 names, of which about a dozen can be identified as ethnologists. The weakness of ethnological participation in the Pecos Conference was continuing, even though the University of New Mexico was an active center of ethnological research. Geographically the Conference participants were extremely diverse, with every part of the country represented. From nearby the numbers were the largest—twenty from the University of New Mexico; twelve from the Museum of New Mexico, Santa Fe; sixteen from the National Park Service (Southwestern parks, monuments, and administration); twelve from the University of Utah; nine from the Museum of Northern Arizona; nine from the University of Colorado; and six from the University of Arizona. In addition, more distant institutions were represented: the universities of Harvard, Cornell, Columbia, Princeton, Chicago, Oklahoma, Illinois, Washington, Mississippi, Denver, Indiana, and Southern Illinois; Dartmouth and Beloit colleges; and from abroad, the University of Oslo, Norway, and the State University of Belgian Congo, Elisabethville. Many smaller museums and other institutions were also represented, constituting a far more cosmopolitan and varied group than at the earliest Conferences.

We have no details concerning the field reports or the speakers in the several symposia, but—perhaps reflecting a clear sense of priorities—the Pecos Conference Archives in the Laboratory of Anthropology include a sheet of instructions with map for the Saturday evening "informal Southwestern Barbecue garden party" at the home of Mr. and Mrs. John S. Barnes on Rio Grande Boulevard, about five miles north of Central Avenue (then Route 66).

One detail of the field reports has survived in oral history, as related by William Y. Adams (conversation with Woodbury, 20 April 1984). Jesse D. Jennings, for the report on the University of Utah's Glen Canyon Project, made a point of calling on one participant after another to stand and report on his part of the work. "He was like an orchestra leader, giving the signal to one after another to add their bit," Adams recalled. This continued for some time, and the audience grew restive. Adams went up to the chairman of the session and asked if he could be called on next. When Jennings was finished, Adams was called, and he "asked all those who had worked on the Museum of Northern Arizona Project" to stand. Nettie, his wife, the only other person on the project, rose. Adams's jest brought down the house, and Jennings never forgot and perhaps never forgave him. Later that day, Emil W. Haury, who had missed the morning session, said he had heard that there was some sort of contest that morning, and would "all those who had been at the Point of Pines Field School please stand up." About half the audience rose.

The business meeting was chaired by Marjorie Lambert and opened with Fred Wendorf of the resolutions committee proposing thanks to the Conference's hosts and to the Barneses for the barbecue, and greetings to "Founders" Hattie Cosgrove, Jesse Nusbaum, and Harold Colton, who had been unable to attend. Recognition was given to Edmund Schulman for his important contributions to tree-ring research.

Another resolution was not so easily approved. It committed future Conferences to sessions on "Interpretation and the Museum." Objections to the form of the resolution were made by Haury, Jennings, Lambert, Bertha Dutton, and Stanley Stubbs. Raymond Thompson and Adams proposed, as a compromise, that it be a recommendation to the interim (program) committee and that "sessions be scheduled as needed." In this form the resolution was passed. To judge from subsequent programs the need has hardly ever arisen.

Stubbs reminded the Conference that "photographs, notes, or any other materials pertinent to the conference" were welcome for the Pecos Conference Archives at the Laboratory of Anthropology.

An invitation by Di Peso for the 1959 Conference to come to Casas Grandes, Chihuahua, was withdrawn. An invitation was offered by Wendorf, on behalf of the Wichita Foundation, to meet at the Fort Burgwin Research Center near Taos, and another invitation was made to meet at the Museum of Northern Arizona. After a short discussion the Fort Burgwin invitation was accepted. The final business was the appointment of Wendorf (chairman), Richard Woodbury, and Robert Lister to the interim committee. The meeting adjourned, and a group gathered for the Pottery Mound field trip. The final session of the Conference was "Archaeological Progress in the Southwest" on Sunday afternoon, chaired by Bruce Ellis.

A comment by Hibben in *Teocentli* (November 1958) hints at the informal side of the Conference. He noted that "many of the discussions centered around the Pottery Mound mural paintings. A great many valuable suggestions were made by various conference members." He added, "The conviviality of the Conference was also an outstanding feature." Responses to my 1979 questionnaire are more explicit. One says, "The night we 'destroyed' the women's dorm at UNM in Albq will remain a high water mark in some sort of historical sense." Another is more detailed, although names of individuals are deleted here for obvious reasons:

> 1958—Party at ? house, with —— putting a toad into a hollowed out hamburger bun & offering it to ——, who accepted. Later, the party at the girls' dorm, with —— (I think it was he) pouring rum on his chest & lighting it, while a gaggle of admiring girls watched. —— and —— playing football with full beer cans, then opening them. —— strolling along the parapet of the 3rd floor balcony playing his guitar & falling off, to save himself by one hand, etc., etc.

In subsequent years the Albuquerque Conference was remembered with embarrassment or disgust by some conferees, who used such terms as "a drunken brawl" and "disgraceful."

FORT BURGWIN, 1959 (TWENTY-SECOND PECOS CONFERENCE) This meeting was a first in two ways: it was the first held at the Fort Burgwin Research Center, ten miles south of Taos, New Mexico, and the first at which the proceedings were taped (although this had been urged several times in the past). There were to be two more Fort

Burgwin meetings, in 1963 and 1981, but unfortunately only once more (1960) would the record of a Conference be preserved on tape, although it was urged from time to time that "someone" do so. This record of the 1959 Conference was the work of John L. Champe, who at the age of forty-two had left a successful business career in Nebraska for a new career in archaeology, partly through the influence of his close friend, W. Duncan Strong of Columbia University. He became active in the Plains Conference and in the 1950s began recording the meetings on tape (Henning 1980; Lambert 1961). So it was natural that when Champe attended his first Pecos Conference he continued this practice. The 1959 tapes run to about twelve hours; a transcription (partly verbatim, partly paraphrased) fills seventy single-spaced typed pages. A few short sections are garbled or missing, and the identity of some speakers is uncertain, but a great deal of the Conference is preserved in full—brief reports, symposium presentations, comments, questions, arguments, even jokes. The tapes are a unique and invaluable part of the Pecos Conference Archives. They were copied onto cassettes in 1987 for listening and transcribing for use in this history, as the original large reels had become too fragile for frequent starting and stopping. (The copying was expertly done by Jaap van Heerden of the University of Massachusetts Audio-visual Media Center. The transcribing was done by myself and by Sue Ruiz, Arizona State Museum, Tucson.)

Besides possessing the technical skill to record a conference, Champe had an assertive and delightful personality. This is well illustrated in a message that Lambert sent to Wendorf on 7 August:

> The inclosed should either alleviate or increase your concern
> as to whether J. Champe is coming to the Pecos Conference. I
> knew J. Champe was musical and witty, but hadn't realized until
> the receipt of this, that he was also a poet. The inclosed, I would
> say, compares favorably with "What's a-Brewin' at the Ruin,"
> and the "Athapascan B.'s." Keep this, if you see fit, with this
> year's collection of Pecos Conference archives.

Wendorf saw fit and the following was preserved for posterity:

GYROPANIC

The other night I dreamed a dream,
As clear and plain as day.

I dreamed about a Conference,
Up north of Santa Fe,
A table green—and at the head,
Sat Chairman Charlie Steen.
Stern was his physiognomy—
Judicial was his mien.

At length, Dave Baerreis rose and said,
"You really need no brains,
To see that when it's not Southwest,
It really must be Plains."
But I replied, "Down—David Boy—
One major point you've missed.
Your thesis cannot be maintained,
Those Plains do not exist."
With eloquence I plead my cause,
Dave's hip and thigh I smote.
Until, at last, came Marjorie,
To bring me Baerreis' goat.

O! Call my friends to rally round,
And bid my foes decamp.
For sure as taxes, death, or rent—
Lo! I am coming—

—Champe

The record made by Champe provides the names of most speakers and topics for the entire two days. Some of the informal yet serious atmosphere can be sensed from the tapes and, I hope, from this greatly abbreviated version of them.

The Fort Burgwin Research Center occupied a partially reconstructed pre–Civil War U.S. Army fort. In 1957 excavation was begun by the Texas Tech University field school, directed by Wendorf. The nearby Pot Creek Ruin was tested and in later seasons extensively excavated. The research center had financial support from the Wichita Foundation. By 1959 the restoration of the fort was well advanced, and it provided an attractive and comfortable setting for the Conference.

During the meeting Wendorf reported that the total registration was 160. J. O. Brew estimated the audience at "approximately 200."

On Friday morning, 28 August, Wendorf introduced Ralph M.

Brown, president of the board of trustees of the Fort Burgwin Research Center, with the comment that if it were not for Brown "we wouldn't be here." Wendorf then made several announcements about the schedule of sessions, and issued invitations for Friday night to beer and supper at the Millicent Rogers Museum in Taos and to a Mexican dinner and beer Saturday night at Fort Burgwin, catered from town ("I won't try to cook it," he promised). When he asked for other announcements, the Southwestern Monuments Association said it was selling books at a 20 percent discount, including Kate Peck Kent on Tonto textiles, Julian Hayden on the University Indian Ruin, and Earl Jackson and Sallie Van Valkenburg on Montezuma Castle archaeology. This may be the first time a table of books for sale had been set up at a Pecos Conference, a practice that was eventually to grow to substantial proportions.

Lister chaired the morning session of field reports, asking that each be no more than ten or fifteen minutes, with "no measurements of arrow points."

The reports were numerous and detailed, with summaries of their recent work by the following: Wendorf (Pot Creek Pueblo, at Fort Burgwin); Stubbs (at Pecos and Quarai); Stewart Peckham (highway salvage work in New Mexico); Alfred E. Dittert (sites on the Pine and Piedra rivers that would be flooded by the Navajo Dam on the San Juan); Herbert Dick ("Old El Rito" near Abiquiu, New Mexico); Marie Wormington (Folsom and Eden material near Las Vegas, Nevada); Rex E. Gerald (salvage work near El Paso); Douglas Osborne (Wetherill Mesa Project, with an NPS budget of $795,000 and a National Geographic Society contribution of $250,000—amounts previously undreamed of in Southwestern archaeology); Alden C. Hayes (the Wetherill Mesa survey); Richard Wheeler (Wetherill Mesa laboratory work); Wheat (sites near the Yellow Jacket Ruin); Arthur H. Rohn (Chapin Mesa survey); Cynthia Irwin-Williams (the Magic Mountain site near Denver); Joel Shiner (NPS work in Chaco Canyon); Paul Long (salvage work by the Museum of Northern Arizona); Alfred E. Johnson (Turkey Creek Ruin at Point of Pines); Alan P. Olson (Dry Prong great kiva at Point of Pines); Wasley (University of Arizona highway salvage); Adams (the Museum of Northern Arizona's part of the Glen Canyon Project); Christy G. Turner (study of prehistoric Southwestern teeth); Robert C. Euler (archaeological survey of the Havasupai Reservation with Henry Dobyns); Lister (University of Utah's part of the Glen Canyon Project and continued work at the Coombs site in Utah);

Lyndon L. Hargrave (ecological clues from identification of archaeo-logical bird feathers); Woodbury (farming terraces at Point of Pines and a reappraisal of Hohokam canals); Paul Schultz Martin (no rela-tion to archaeologist Paul Sidney Martin) (postglacial environment of the Southwest).

Because the reports were taped, there is a record of comments and asides as well as of archaeological information. For example, Osborne said the Wetherill Mesa crew of thirty included both Navajos and stu-dents, and "they worked well together, the Navajos setting a good stiff pace and it makes the students work hard to keep up." Wasley commented that highway salvage work in Arizona had come to a halt for a year and a half and "then sprung to life up on Highway 66. The Navajo Tribe held up realignment until they were assured there was to be archaeological salvage. This shook up the Highway Department a good bit," and money was provided. Lister said that at the Coombs site they hired local farm hands rather than have students and a field school. "In about five weeks we have gotten twice the amount of work done as last year." He also made a plea for anyone with archaeological experience to apply for jobs on the Glen Canyon Project—there were still more jobs than people. When Olson was asked how he knew the kiva at the Dry Prong site was a great kiva, he said, "I was told it was a great kiva when I was sent to excavate it."

When the afternoon's field reports were concluded, Brew turned the microphone over to Wendorf, who said, "Don't forget, tonight at 6 o'clock at the Millicent Rogers Museum, you're all invited for a sandwich and beer, also the Kit Carson Museum in town." He ex-plained how to get to the Pot Creek Ruin, and with somewhat more difficulty, how to find the Millicent Rogers Museum in Taos. He added, "You might like to know the registration—as of right now there's 160."

The next day began with a session on Southwest-Plains relation-ships. Charlie Steen said it was suggested for this meeting

> because the Taos-Picuris area has long been noted for its large
> number of Plains characteristics, Plains traits . . . in the local
> culture. And everyone talks very glibly of the relationship of
> the Pueblo Indians of the northern Rio Grande here with the
> Plains, particularly in late prehistoric and early historic times.
> The panel we have seems to be loaded [laughter] pretty much
> with Plains people, rather than Southwesterners. . . . The panel
> which I've seen consists of John Champe, Alex Krieger [River-

side Municipal Museum, California], Al Whiting [Dartmouth College Museum], Herb Dick [Trinidad State Junior College, Colorado], and Bob Bell [University of Oklahoma]. Why don't you gentlemen come on up and sit at the table here, face your tormentors, talk into this thing, and we'll get started.

Steen was right that Plains-Southwest relationships had often been talked about, but he might have added that a few people had made substantial contributions to the subject. Foremost of these was Krieger, who in 1946 had published a major study, "Culture Complexes and Chronology in Northern Texas, with Extension of Puebloan Datings to the Mississippi Valley." He had also presented these new ideas in an address to the SAA at its Indianapolis meeting in May 1946. He drew on a vast knowledge of archaeology from Arizona and New Mexico through Texas to the Mississippi and provided the basis for all future studies of the subject. A decade later a further examination of the problem of Plains-Southwest connections was made in the 1955 seminars held by the SAA. One of them was on the Southwest (described earlier; see Jennings 1956), and it examined, among other things, the appearance in Basketmaker III and Pueblo I of new ceramic forms, with striking parallels in the Arkansas-Missouri area, as well as other traits that seemed to link the Southwest with the Plains. But with a few minor exceptions many Southwesternists had remained little concerned with these external relationships, as Curry Holden had observed at the 1929 Pecos Conference. Now the time seemed right for a serious examination of the whole subject.

Champe began the session, commenting on the traditional distinctions made between "the quiet, cooperative, studious, ceremonious Pueblo Indians as against the hell-raising Indians of the Plains. Compare, if you will, one of those . . . cooperative Santo Domingo traders . . . in the Hall of Ethnology [with] a tall, handsome, Dionysian hero, looking for all the world like John Corbett with feathers in his hair [laughter], tearing around the High Plains, stampeding buffalo over a cutbank." He explained that these stereotypes might be useful for the introductory course but would not be "very helpful for what we want to talk about today." He did not, however, make any specific reference to Ruth Benedict's *Patterns of Culture* (1934), which had popularized these stereotypes.

Champe proposed that the direct historical approach be used "to find out which group of Indians met what other group of Indians, where they were and when they did it."

Krieger then pointed out that intermarriage may have often occurred as a result of trading trips, thus accounting for traits of material culture appearing far from their origins. As an example he cited Pueblo-like architecture in the Antelope Creek focus, the economy and material culture of which were otherwise typical of the Plains. Finally, Krieger suggested that migration could be the cause of some similarities, such as those between Caddoan and Southwestern vessel forms, or cordmarked pottery coming from the Plains to the Southwest.

Steen then called on Bell, who said:

> In Oklahoma we do get some Southwestern trade. . . . Basically our trade objects . . . from the Southwest are found in the western parts of the state. And as you go out [west] through the Panhandle we get more and more contact items, predominantly potsherds, late Pueblo III—Pueblo IV material, predominantly glazes from the Rio Grande area or from the Taos district. We occasionally get . . . turquoise beads or raw turquoise matrix.

Whiting was called on next. Best known as an ethnobotanist, he had degrees in both anthropology and botany, but in this instance he turned his attention to ceramics. He spoke at some length on the problem of where Taos "fitted" between the Pueblo and Plains cultures. He found that Taos pottery contained chlorite and that Picuris pottery did not, and that at Taos pottery was often coated with piñon gum, but Picuris pottery was not. Whiting spoke of the problem of "Taos being un-Hopi-like," and argued that the Hopi and Zuni are atypical Pueblos, greatly influenced from Mexico, whereas "Taos and Picuris are probably as early a Pueblo group as we know . . . a survival of, shall we say, Pueblo III or Pueblo II."

Krieger commented briefly on Whiting's paper and then at length on the abandonment of Pueblo sites in eastern New Mexico about 1400–1450. He suggested that the hundreds of campsites in the Texas Panhandle represent "some of those people who were leaving the Southwest proper, went over here [pointing to a map] and established settlements, where they managed to survive, for . . . perhaps one or two hundred years."

Dick described the Purgatoire River as a boundary, north and east of which Pueblo settlement scarcely extended. Instead there are rock circles, probably brush roofed, with cordmarked pottery of an Upper Republican appearance. He proposed that the local cultural tradition about 2000 B.C. to A.D. 1300 was only lightly modified by Plains influence from one side and Pueblo from the other.

Champe asked if he could make some comments and referred to "the curious break at about 1300 between the Aksarben and the Central Plains, the Antelope Creek in the Panhandle, and Pueblo influences of any kind." He continued, "The people you are calling Plains, with whom the Rio Grande people were in touch, were apparently Caddoan peoples of say 1000 or 1100 or 1200 A.D."

George Trager (University of Buffalo) spoke last:

> I've been working on Taos and other Southwestern linguistics for some time, and I would like to explain . . . that you're going to have to do something about the linguistic relations . . . to bring them into keeping with the kind of theories you set up. . . . Only the Keresan speakers have any possibility of really having been here a long, long time. . . . The Tanoans . . . have to be late. [It is] showable now that Kiowa is rather closely related linguistically to Tanoan and the separation cannot be more than 1500 years. The separation of Tanoan from Uto-Aztecan, in my opinion, does not go back more than another 1000. . . . The Tanoans moved into the Southwest . . . let's say sometime between 500 and 1000.

At the end of Trager's remarks Steen closed the session. Before the business meeting, for which no information survives, Brew, with elaborate remarks and compliments, presented a scroll to James A. (Al) Lancaster bearing eighty signatures, in appreciation of his accomplishments as "loyal friend and valued colleague; discoverer, excavator, preserver." Thus the Pecos Conference was three years ahead of the Department of the Interior, which honored Lancaster in 1962 with its Distinguished Service Award (Brew 1963).

The Saturday afternoon session was on relationships between Mexico and the Southwest. This was a topic not wholly new to the Pecos Conference. The archaeology of Mexico was discussed by several speakers at the 1940 Conference (Albuquerque and Chaco Canyon) but without focusing on Southwest connections. A session on Southwestern-Mexican relationships was suggested in 1947 for that year's Conference at Chaco, but it is not known whether or not the session took place. In Globe in 1954 Di Peso spoke on southern Arizona—northern Mexico connections, with comments added by Paul Ezell. Slowly the isolationist attitude evaporated. Archaeologists came to see the Southwest's farming as deriving from Mexico or Central America and came to accept the fact that pottery was earlier in Mexico than the Southwest, making the once discussed independent invention highly improbable. But it was not until 1945 that a comprehensive survey of the evidence for Southwestern-Mexican contacts was published, Haury's "Problem of Contacts between the Southwestern United States and Mexico," in the first issue of the new *Southwestern Journal of Anthropology* (1945c). The conservatism of archaeologists is reflected in the fact that in *Indians before Columbus* (1947) by Paul S. Martin, George Quimby, and Donald Collier there is virtually nothing about the dependence of the Southwest on Mexico for basic cultural elements, such as maize and ceramics. Similarly, Marie Wormington's *Prehistoric Indians of the Southwest* (1947) touched only briefly on Mexican sources for farming, pottery, figurines, or ball courts (comparing the last only with the Maya and suggesting a possible Southwest source for Mesoamerican ball courts!). Even Harold S. Gladwin, who could argue in 1947 that most of New World civilization came well developed from the Old World (see *Men Out of Asia*), had only the sketchiest of references to Mexican sources for Southwestern corn and pottery in *A History of the Ancient Southwest* (1957). Southwestern isolationism died hard.

A vigorous blow against it came in 1955, when the School of American Research published Edwin Ferdon's "Trial Survey of Mexican-Southwestern Architectural Parallels," which identified certain building details, particularly in Chaco Canyon, that seemed to have Mexican prototypes, such as core masonry, square columns, platform mounds, column-fronted galleries, and circular masonry towers. This was greeted with both skepticism (Lister 1957) and cautious partial agreement (Schroeder 1956).

After Haury's 1945 beginning, the most thorough examination of Southwestern-Mexican relationships was by J. Charles Kelley, one of the speakers in this Conference. At the Fifth International Congress of Anthropological and Ethnological Sciences, held in Philadelphia in 1956, Kelley had presented "North Mexico and the Correlation of Mesoamerican and Southwestern Cultural Sequences" (Kelley 1960). This summarized his work in Durango in 1952, 1954, and 1956, sponsored by Southern Illinois University. He effectively bridged the long presumed "gap" between southern Arizona and the northern Mexican cultures, providing not only trait comparisons but also chronological sequences to link the areas. Others had worked productively in northern Mexico—J. Alden Mason, Donald D. Brand, Lister, Gordon

Ekholm, and Isabel Kelly, for example—but Kelley made the most successful attempt to link his Durango sequence and its traits, on the northern periphery of Mesoamerica, with cultures far to the south and to the north. His presentation at Fort Burgwin summarized persuasively the connections he had identified.

Turning back now to the afternoon of 29 August, the session, chaired by Woodbury, began with a discussion of the Amerind Foundation's excavations at Casas Grandes. Di Peso, its director, could not be present, but Wendorf, Lister, and Kelley, who had recently visited the site, described the work there.

Wasley then discussed his work at the Gila Bend site in southern Arizona, particularly the pyramidal structure with six building phases, dating late in the Sacaton Phase, probably 1100 to 1150. In spite of its apparent Mesoamerican inspiration, there were no intrusive ceramics from the south.

Following this, Schroeder, Wasley, and Lister spoke of several ambiguous sites, suggestive of platforms or pyramids. Kelley urged "the assembled card-carrying Southwesterners, if there are any more of these sites hidden out there that you're afraid to talk about, the time is here to come out in the open now. It's safe!" This was welcomed with general laughter. Then Kelley described the impression he had had on a recent visit to Snaketown of the "regularity of the mound construction . . . [and] the axes of the mounds surround[ing] a central plaza." He concluded, "I have a very strong feeling that Snaketown, as the very heart of the Hohokam set-up, is going to turn out to be a good, neatly oriented, Mesoamerican site, and that the refuse mounds are a little bit more than that. This is in the realm of fantasy, but somebody's got to find out about it."

The major presentation of the afternoon session was by Kelley, describing the work in Durango that he had reported on in Philadelphia. Kelley began by observing that when he first heard of Wasley's work at Gila Bend, it was mentioned "sort of timorously that there was a truncated mound," which was then called a "platform mound." Then at the Salt Lake City meeting of the SAA, Wasley spoke about a "truncated mound" and then a "pyramidal mound," and finally a "pyramid." This, Kelley said, "has really broken the log jam." He also commented, "Southwesterners from now on—and, I trust, Mesoamericanists as well, are going to have to be *both* Southwesterners and Mesoamericanists."

Kelley discussed in detail the problems of determining relationships between "the Chalchihuites Culture of Durango, a peripheral

Mesoamerican culture itself, and the Hohokam," first in terms of chronology and second on the basis of numerous specific parallels of pottery decoration. He concluded:

> This is the basic picture of Mesoamerica and Southwest relations as we are seeing them at this time, with very strong evidence of Chalchihuites influence in the Hohokam, very strong evidence for the Guasave influence on the Late Hohokam and probably on the Anasazi. Very weak and only suggestive evidence for the earliest materials in the Pioneer and equivalent Mogollon horizons.

Among the comments that followed was Erik Reed's observation that "the Gadsden Purchase was a very unfortunate historical event . . . [a few unintelligible words]. The Hohokam would still be in Mexico, where they obviously belong." Prolonged laughter greeted this remark.

Kelley went on to discuss the pyramid and ball court at the earliest period of the Schroeder site in Durango (no relation to Albert H.), the "roadways radiating out from" La Quemada site, "just plain good Maya roads," and the apparent contemporaneity of metal in late Chalchihuites and the late Sedentary of the Hohokam.

Woodbury asked Lister to bring the session to a close, with "the last word" on Southwestern-Mexican relationships. Lister pointed out that "J. Charles [Kelley] . . . said . . . most of the last words. I can see by some of the nodding heads here that it's time to cut it, and Fred [Wendorf] said just two minutes." He then spoke of the recent decreasing skepticism of these cultural relationships, and the general use of "the term Sierra Madre Corridor," in contrast to the earlier expectation that the West Coast must be the main route of contacts. Now, the Sierra Madre was no longer seen as a barrier but "more favorable to colonization, to occupation, than either the West Coast or the Central Plateau." He also described his own work in Chihuahua, looking for links with early Mogollon, and closed by emphasizing that "many elements, over a long period of time spread northward along" the Sierra Madre Corridor.

The Conference adjourned after this final session, a session that was more far-reaching in its presentations and discussions than was usual at Pecos Conferences. It placed on a firmer footing than ever before the great debt that Southwestern cultures owed to Mesoamerica and highlighted the remarkable progress in clarifying these connections made by the Southern Illinois University work of Kelley from 1952 to 1956. Kelley had closed the long presumed gap between the Southwest and Mesoamerica.

The Pecos Conference Archives, as might be expected, have no information on Saturday evening's social events, but Anne Woosley (letter to Woodbury, 4 October 1982) was told by a friend, speaking of the Conference at Fort Burgwin, "how terrible all of those awful archeologists were!"

> I [Woosley] was told in some detail how guests of the Sagebrush Inn complained about noise continuing into the early morning hours and that the Inn's owner went to calm the merriment himself. As the story goes, he was pulled into a particular room and separated from all his clothes, whereupon he was released into the Taos night air.

9
RETURN ENGAGEMENTS AND THE
FARTHEST SOUTH, 1960–63

After the shenanigans of the 1958 and 1959 meetings the Conference returned to its normal tranquility in Flagstaff. The extended discussion of Southwestern-Mexican connections in 1959 at Ft. Burgwin may have been influential in overcoming in 1960 the long-standing reluctance to hold a meeting south of the border. Northern Mexico is, after all, an important part of the archaeological "Southwest." In addition, Nuevas Casas Grandes, Chihuahua, at which a meeting was planned, is not as far south as Durango, for which the Conference had earlier declined an invitation.

FLAGSTAFF, 1960 (TWENTY-THIRD PECOS CONFERENCE)   For a second and unfortunately last time, John Champe recorded a Pecos Conference on tape (Fig. 9.1) as he had done in 1959, and therefore we again have a wealth of detail absent from other records. As with the 1959 tape it is tempting to quote at length, but the approximately eight hours of tape fills 185 pages (double spaced) in transcription, and therefore selection is obviously essential. In addition, there is a one-page report on the 1960 Conference by Charles Rozaire in the *Newsletter of the Archaeological Survey Association of Southern California* (Rozaire 1960) and one paragraph in *American Antiquity* (Wasley 1961). The many details recorded for this Conference illustrate both its informality and the great amount of information reported and discussed.

No copy of the registration sheets has been found, but Wasley (1961) reported a registration of 203, the largest yet and not exceeded until the 1966 Conference, again in Flagstaff.

The Conference began with Friday morning, 27 August, devoted to registration (Fig. 9.2) and an opportunity for renewing friendships and catching up on news and gossip, always important aspects of these

9.1 The 1960 Conference at Flagstaff. John Champe (plaid shirt) and his recording equipment are at the table in the foreground. Museum of Northern Arizona negative no. 3154, photo by Christy G. Turner, II.

(or any) conferences. Archaeological field reports began after lunch, chaired by Raymond H. Thompson. He introduced Harold S. Colton, director of the Museum of Northern Arizona, which was hosting the meeting. Colton welcomed the group and reminded them of the "terrific downpour" that had driven them indoors at a previous Conference at the museum. Danson announced the Saturday luncheon, the Sunday trip to Page and Glen Canyon, and a Hopi Snake Dance on Sunday.

The first three field reports concerned the Museum of Northern Arizona's pipeline and highway salvage by Alan P. Olson and Wesley Bliss and Glen Canyon work by A. J. Lindsay. Although full of descriptive detail as well as preliminary interpretations, the three reports run to only seventeen minutes on Champe's tape—a demonstration of the incorrectness of the frequent complaint that "no one can really say anything with a ten-minute limit." David Pendergast next described the University of Utah's Glen Canyon program, including mention of delays caused by an outbreak of coccidioidomycosis ("valley fever" or "desert fever") among the work crew. Pendergast also described the surprise request by the Utah State Parks Commission for suggestions of areas that might be made into state archaeological parks. Other reports concerned NPS research at Natural Bridges (Philip Hobler), Montezuma Well (Edmund J. Ladd), and Walnut Creek (Michael Moll), and the trip to Finland by Charlie Steen to study the Nordenskiöld collection from Mesa Verde and try (without success) to arrange for some of it to be returned to the United States.

Douglas Osborne introduced the Wetherill Mesa staff to report on Long House excavations (George Cattanach), the start of work at Mug House (Arthur Rohn), the Wetherill Mesa survey (Alden Hayes, who described using low-powered radio transmitters and a radio direction finder for quickly triangulating sites in heavy tree growth), and water control systems (J. Anthony Pomeroy). The Olson-Chubbock bison kill site of eastern Colorado was reported on by Joe Ben Wheat, who also read for Marie Wormington a disclaimer of views attributed to her in a *New York Times* report on Juan Camacho's proboscidian excavations near Puebla, Mexico. Continuing work at the Fort Burgwin Research Center was described by Fred Wendorf, including a six-week experimental course in salvage archaeology involving selection of sites on a hypothetical right-of-way, three weeks for digging and three weeks for report writing. The Museum of New Mexico's excavation of dry caves in the Alamo Hueco Mountains of southwestern New Mexico was described by Marjorie Lambert and Richard

9.2 Registration at the Flagstaff Pecos Conference, 1960. William Y. Adams and unidentified volunteer workers. Museum of Northern Arizona negative no. 13969, photo by Christy G. Turner II.

Ambler and the museum's highway salvage work by Stewart Peckham, who reported his success in locating pit houses with a proton magnetometer.

Salvage work was reported on some of the 400 sites to be flooded by the Navajo Reservoir Project, ranging from Basketmaker II to the eighteenth century (Alfred E. Dittert and Frank Eddy). Arthur Jelinek described the University of Chicago's work in the Pecos Valley, and Robert Euler reported on survey work along the Little Colorado River.

After the Friday field reports Christy Turner gave a slide talk on Glen Canyon pictographs (see Turner 1963).

The Saturday sessions began at 10 a.m. with Paul S. Martin describing the Chicago Natural History Museum's work in the Vernon, Arizona area—palynological research, continued site survey, and excavation of the Hooper Ranch, where a crypt in a kiva contained a painted stone "proto-kachina." David Breternitz described his work at Cameron, "the garden spot of northern Arizona." Bryant Bannister reviewed the current projects of the Laboratory of Tree-Ring Research, including dating old hogans for Navajo land claims, restudy of Museum of Northern Arizona specimens transferred to the Laboratory, analysis of Wetherill Mesa material and specimens from forty-six Chaco Canyon sites, the 400-year floating chronology from Casas Grandes, Chihuahua, and Wesley Ferguson's progress in dating sagebrush. He also mentioned that A. E. Douglass, at ninety-three, still occasionally came in to work in his office.

Additional reports included the Arizona State Museum's excavation of the ball court at the Gatlin site near Gila Bend and the Gila Bend stage station of the 1860s (Wasley); water control devices, such as walls, terraces, and grids, found widely in the Southwest (Richard B. Woodbury); the fifteenth and final season at Point of Pines, including Turkey Creek Pueblo and two pit house sites (Alfred E. Johnson); identification of plant materials at the Missouri Botanical Garden (Hugh Cutler); the University of Illinois excavations at the Pollock and Pershing sites near Flagstaff (E. B. Danson for John C. McGregor); and identification of Hopi traditional sites for the tribe's land claims case (Danson).

The morning ended with four ethnological reports: Paul Ezell of San Diego State College on work in Baja California with the Kamia, Euler on his and Henry F. Dobyns's study of self-identification among three Pai groups, Jerrold Levy's study for the U.S. Public Health Service defining who were the leaders of local Navajo communities, and

9.3 Conversations after a session, Pecos Conference, Flagstaff, 1960. Museum of Northern Arizona negative no. 64.277, photo by Christy G. Turner II.

Carl Voegelin on several linguistic projects by his Indiana University group based at the Museum of Northern Arizona, including trader Navajo, Apache songs, and linguistic domains.

The session closed with a comment by Rozaire on the Southwest Museum's program of transferring to tape the recordings made many years ago on cylinders by Frances Densmore, Charles F. Lummis, and George Wharton James. The Museum of Northern Arizona then hosted a luncheon for the Conference participants and their families (Fig. 9.4).

The business meeting had been shifted to Saturday afternoon, on the reasonable assumption that Sunday morning would see many people making early departures. Danson gave details of the Sunday morning Glen Canyon tour offered by the Bureau of Reclamation. The first order of business was selecting a location for the next year's meeting, and Emil Haury described his discussions with Ignacio Bernal concerning a joint meeting in Ciudad Chihuahua with the Mesa Redonda of the Sociedad Mexicana de Antropología. He suggested starting the day before the Mesa Redonda sessions with field reports, and then continuing in joint sessions focusing on Mexican-Southwestern relationships. There would also be an opportunity to visit Di Peso's work at Casas Grandes. Lengthy discussion followed. Finally Danson asked for a show of hands: "All who cannot be there raise their hands." The dissenters were apparently in the minority.

An unusually large number of resolutions was proposed and passed, beginning with the customary expressions of grief at the deaths of two "valued friends and colleagues," Stanley H. Stubbs and Clyde K. M. Kluckhohn. Albert H. Schroeder presented the next resolution: "Be it resolved that the 1960 Pecos Conference commend the Navajo Tribe and in particular the Navajo Rangers for their active protection of the archaeological sites on the Reservation and their proposals to excavate, develop, and interpret many of these sites within proposed Navajo parks."

The next resolution was from Thompson: "Resolved: that the 1960 Pecos Conference expresses its sincere gratitude to John Champe . . . for recording the sessions of the conference."

Haury spoke next with a resolution to encourage the National Science Foundation (NSF) to proceed with its efforts to issue the new "International Directory of Anthropologists" as soon as possible. The NSF-sponsored directory was never completed, however.

Lambert then spoke of the death of Karl Ruppert, who had worked

9.4 Lined up for lunch, Pecos Conference, Flagstaff, 1960. Museum of Northern Arizona negative no. 64.275, photo by Christy G. Turner II.

with Neil Judd at Pueblo Bonito and then turned to Maya research. An appropriate resolution was approved.

An unidentified speaker suggested a resolution based on Pendergast's statement on "the Utah State Parks Commission . . . complimenting them on their efforts or activities to establish archaeological areas in Utah." Danson asked Pendergast to write the resolution. From the audience a voice said, "I would suggest we send a copy to the Arizona Parks Board" (laughter).

Danson announced that a telegram had been sent to A. V. Kidder, where he was vacationing in Maine, saying, "The old guard fondly remembers the first Pecos Conference under your inspired leadership; new blood evident in present conference insures future of a noble tradition."

Immediately on the conclusion of the business meeting Danson turned the chair over to Haury, who presided at the afternoon symposium, entitled "Land Use and Settlement in Arid Environments." He described the growing worldwide realization of the importance of arid lands as increasing population made ever greater demands on the resources of the better watered parts of the world. He mentioned UNESCO's concern with the problem, recent attention to it by the AAAS, and the University of Arizona's Arid Land Utilization Program.

Then, to begin the symposium, he introduced William Y. Adams, who described the program of archaeological research he was directing in the Sudan in areas along the Nile that would be flooded by the new Aswan Dam, areas that constituted most of the land occupied in the past.

Following this expansion of the Pecos Conference's horizon to northeast Africa, Haury proposed a hypothesis as a basis for discussion. He suggested that corn arrived in the Southwest via the Cordilleran chain but had "not much of a cultural ripple" among recipients who "were already heavily dependent upon gathering natural foods, plant foods in particular," so that "for two thousand years there was no perceptible impact by corn on society." Haury went on to discuss the nature of the first "villages" in the Southwest and their characteristics, as well as the possible importance of new varieties of corn arriving in the Southwest two millennia after the first introduction. He added that when corn became important, water control systems began to develop, although it was not yet possible to date them or quantify their contribution.

Woodbury was then called on to discuss his research on arid lands utilization, including estimates of the extent of Hohokam irrigation and other smaller scale water control techniques.

Wheat pointed out the importance that effective storage arrangements might have in making settled village life and the production of a corn crop worthwhile.

In response to a question by Danson, Cutler said that the early pod corn did not have each kernel tightly covered and would probably "produce as much food as the Navajo fields you see along Highway 89 near the Gap, between Flagstaff and Page," about twelve bushels an acre. "I think you could get a surplus from the early hard corn," but more with the first hybrids, "about the time we have our first Bat Cave corn."

Schroeder spoke of the need for quantified studies, to include, among other things, hunting tools, gathering tools, and storage facilities. The next speaker in the symposium was Lindsay, who reported in detail on the water diversion system on Beaver Creek, a small tributary of the San Juan in southern Utah.

Haury raised the problem of how prehistoric population estimates could be made and called on Odd Halseth to discuss the matter for the Salt-Gila area. Halseth recalled that years ago there had been a "chamber of commerce estimate" of a prehistoric population of 250,000 in the Salt-Gila valley. So Senator Carl Hayden asked Halseth to consider the question, and Halseth concluded that, judging by the size and distribution of historic Pima villages, "the Salt River never had more than 12,000 population."

Haury closed the session with comments on the variety of problems that been touched on and the fact that each one needed more attention. Danson then invited the Conference to attend the open house at the museum that evening to see the recently completed wing with its new ethnology exhibits.

NUEVO CASAS GRANDES, 1961 (TWENTY-FOURTH PECOS CONFERENCE) The growing maturity that characterized Southwestern archaeology by the end of the 1950s can be appreciated from Robert H. Lister's paper for the symposium, "Twenty-five Years of American Archaeology," at the twenty-fifth annual meeting of the SAA, held in New Haven, Connecticut, in May 1960 (Lister 1961). Particularly relevant here is his comment on the relationships of the greater Southwest in all directions, especially the south:

> It is to the south, however, that Paul Bunyan-size strides have been made. A gap, this time one between the Southwest and

Middle or Nuclear America, has been closed. No longer do we have to state that "it is *believed* that the Southwest was influenced by developments from nuclear America," for we can now demonstrate that the two areas were linked. It is apparent that initially maize spread from south to north, followed by pottery making, and then by such elements as certain architectural forms, clay figurines, pottery forms and decorative styles, shell ornaments, copper bells, mosaic disks and so forth [Lister 1961: 43, emphasis in original].

A Four Corners view had been succeeded in the 1930s and 1940s by a Southwestern view, and now a continental view had become acceptable. Appropriately, a meeting of the Pecos Conference in Mexico would finally take place.

Although there were complaints from time to time that the Pecos Conference "just wasn't the way it used to be," it is an indication of its vitality that it *did* change as the years went by, rather than settling into mere empty ritual. For example, 1961 saw a significant advance, the first Pecos Conference held outside the United States. Northern Mexico was a logical choice for a Conference site, considering the close archaeological ties it was now acknowledged to have with the part of the "Southwest" situated above the border. There would be another Mexican Pecos Conference in 1968, its first day in El Paso and its second in Ciudad Juárez, across the Rio Grande. The next meeting in Mexico would be in 1976 at Kino Bay, Sonora, on the gulf of Baja California. In 1991 the Pecos Conference met again at Casas Grandes, this second time headquartered at Viejo Casas Grandes.

Planning for the 1961 Conference at Casas Grandes began immediately in August 1960 with letters among Bernal, Haury, Di Peso, Wasley, Schroeder, Walter Taylor, and others on dates, programs, individual speakers for the chosen topics, local arrangements, and other details of planning. Dates of 23–25 August were agreed on, and Nuevo Casas Grandes was chosen for the location, in preference to Ciudad Chihuahua. In the end, contrary to the original expectations, it proved impractical to meet jointly with the Mesa Redonda of the Sociedad Mexicana de Antropología, whose theme for its 1961 meeting was appropriately "El Noroeste de Mexico." Extensive instructions for crossing the international border in a car were sent out for Pecos conferees driving to Nuevo Casas Grandes, as well as road directions. The accompanying maps are the most elaborate for a Pecos Conference since the meeting at Point of Pines in 1948!

Thanks to a letter from Di Peso to Haury (14 November 1978) we have a full list of the fifty registrants. Since this was the first meeting to be held in Mexico, the names are of interest (Table 9.1). Di Peso mentioned that there were also ten spouses in attendance, and that "the barbecue included an additional 47 local folk," so the total for the festivities was over 100. He commented that "the conference resulted in a better understanding between Mexican and United States archaeologists. It led to William B. Griffen's Ph.D. dissertation in historical archives of [the] area, and perhaps was the last of the informal 'campfire' conferences." The program as summarized by Di Peso was:

Wednesday
    General field reports
    Talk by Ignacio Bernal
    Evening barbecue
Thursday a.m.
    Casas Grandes ruin visit
Thursday p.m.
    Arid land symposium
    Convento ruin visit
    Study lecture—Casas Grandes
Friday a.m.
    Northwest Chihuahua pottery analysis
Friday p.m.
    Southern Athabascans
    Evening party (poolside)

David Brugge's notes on the speakers in the various sessions are a valuable record of current findings and ideas, but they can only be summarized here. In the field report session some fifty projects were described by twenty-two speakers. The projects ranged from salvage work at damsites, along highways, and on powerline rights-of-way to the survey by the Arizona State Museum, Tucson, for a location for the field school that would succeed Point of Pines, the Glen Canyon Project's excavations on Cummings Mesa and Lost Mesa, and the Wetherill Mesa Project's work at Long House and Mud House. Survey and excavation in northern Mexico were reported by Rex Gerald, J. Charles Kelley, Taylor, and Di Peso. It is noteworthy that Henry A. Carey, of Lexington, Kentucky, attended the 1961 Conference; he had published in *American Anthropologist* "An Analysis of the Northwestern Chihuahua Culture" (Carey 1931). This was based on his doctoral dissertation at Columbia University and reported his field work in

Table 9.1. Registrants at the 1961 Pecos Conference, Nuevo Casas Grandes

George Agogino	Rex Gerald	Stuart D. Scott
Bruce A. Babbitt	S. Gilbert	Walter Sims
Paul Babbitt	James Hester	O. T. Snodgrass
Ignacio Bernal	Nancy Johnston	Edward H. Spicer
Roland B. Brassburger	J. C. Kelley	Walter Taylor
David Breternitz	Harlan Kinsey	Raymond H. Thompson
S. Brooks	Alexander J. Lindsay	Wheezer Veasey
David M. Brugge	W. A. Longacre	Julie Vihel
H. Thomas Cain	Ralph A. Leubben	R. Gordon Vivian
Carlos Caraveo	Paul S. Martin	William W. Wasley
Henry A. Carey	Rosemary Mudd	Oswald Werner
Beth Colvin	Jane Nettle	Joe Ben Wheat
Hugh Cutler	George K. Neumann	Ralph E. Wheeler
Charles C. Di Peso	Alan P. Olson	Arnold Withers
Frances Di Peso	Richard Pailes	Malcolm Withers
Bertha Dutton	Jean M. Pinkley	Leland C. Wyman
Robert E. Euler	Albert H. Schroeder	

1928 and 1929. It may also be noted that Kidder had written on Casas Grandes pottery in 1916.

The principal speaker in the session on the occupation and utilization of arid lands was Cutler, of the Missouri Botanical Garden. He described the advantages of arid regions for incipient farmers, the potential for cultivation of various wild plants of arid regions, and the varieties of maize occurring prehistorically and recently in northwest Mexico and the adjacent United States.

The panel on ceramic relationships of northern Mexico and the Southwest had many details presented by Di Peso and Kelley, who pointed out similarities between earlier Chihuahua and Durango wares and those of the Mogollon. Later pottery tended to be not only more varied but often identifiable with limited areas.

The Friday afternoon symposium on the southern Athabascans began with Schroeder's presentation of historical details on the first mention by Spanish explorers of Athabascan groups and the problem of identifying them in terms of current linguistic and ethnic terms. James Hester (Museum of New Mexico) then reported on the archaeological evidence for Athabascans in the Southwest, beginning around

1500 in the upper San Juan area, arriving via the High Plains rather than an intermontane route. Ralph Luebben (Arizona State College, Flagstaff) then pointed out that as early as A.D. 1200 there was crude gray ware in the Southwest that somewhat resembled later Navajo pottery. Euler described the Navajo at the time of their arrival in the Southwest as having a camp-residence pattern, patrilocal bands, and an individualistic shamanistic religion. Andree F. Sjoberg, a linguist at the University of Texas, presented extensive ethnohistoric information on the Lipan and Jicarilla Apache in the eighteenth century and their contacts with the Comanche and French on the Plains, including hunting and trading trips to the Gulf of Mexico and Louisiana and as far south as Durango. The final speaker of the Conference was E. H. Spicer. He described the profound changes in Apache social organization, settlement pattern, subsistence, material culture, and religion that had occurred in only about a century. He characterized as a failure the effort by John Collier to train the Apaches in democratic processes in the 1930s with the creation of a tribal council: the council became essentially an arm of the Bureau of Indian Affairs rather than of the Apache Tribe.

An appropriate last word on the 1961 Conference comes from its chairman, Di Peso, who said (letter to Woodbury, 3 November 1981) that this was a landmark, "in that it was the first to be held in a cantina [at the El Rancho Motel]. Kept everyone in attendance, if nothing else. It was a red-letter day for Hugh Cutler when he discovered that the Mormons were still growing Chapalote in Chuchuichupa."

GLOBE, 1962 (TWENTY-FIFTH PECOS CONFERENCE)   Except for correspondence about the difficulties of agreeing on a location for the 1962 Conference, there is a singular lack of information on this meeting. As we have noted before, the traditional and continuing informality of the Pecos Conference often resulted in no one feeling responsible for preserving details of the registration, the program, and the associated events.

Olson, of the Museum of Northern Arizona, wrote on 4 June 1962 to Bertha Dutton of the Museum of New Mexico expressing concern over the lack of a location for a Conference later that summer, adding, "Some of us here in Flagstaff feel that the continuance of these meetings is very vital to Southwestern Anthropology. . . . We are working on a plan to hold the meetings near Cortez, or failing that, at the Museum of Northern Arizona." At about the same time (6 June) Erik K. Reed, regional chief of interpretation, National Park

Service, Santa Fe, wrote to Danson at the Museum of Northern Arizona about having a shortened Conference at Globe, two days of field reports only, because the SAA meeting in Tucson in May would be strongly Southwestern and the International Congress of Americanists in Mexico City in late August would reduce Pecos Conference attendance anyway. He also suggested a small meeting, with students and "outsiders" not notified.

Danson responded (13 June) offering the Museum of Northern Arizona's facilities but disagreeing that the Tucson and Mexico City meetings justified a briefer Pecos Conference. He also emphasized the importance of continuing the Conference: "I realize what a great benefit they were to me when I was teaching, for they enabled me to keep up with the latest finds and important information. . . . The experience of getting up and talking in front of a group was invaluable to me and, I know, to others. I think the Pecos Conference has a place in the archaeological picture of the Southwest that is important and therefore I am pleading for its continuation."

The outcome of this flurry of correspondence is reflected in Reed's official memorandum of 22 June to "Supervisory Archeologist, SWAC" (Gordon Vivian, Southwestern Archaeological Center). Reed refers to a memo of 9 April suggesting that the Pecos Conference be held by the Park Service at Gila Pueblo (so in June the outlook was not as bleak as Olson had supposed). Reed gives the dates for the Conference as 13–15 August and says, "The idea has been approved by the Regional Director." He continues:

> For the 1962 conference, you [Vivian] and I and Bert Dutton are functioning as the interim committee. Automatically, you will be the local arrangements chairman, with assistance of your colleagues at Gila Pueblo. I hereby volunteer, and appoint myself, as program chairman. Bertha will then, if agreeable (she is away until next week), handle notification business. She can obtain the current or 1961 list or card-file from Charley Di Peso, and hold onto it for use again in 1963 for the Fort Burgwin conference.

With this the archival records on the 1962 Pecos Conference come to an end. The report in *American Antiquity* (Johnson 1963) is unusually brief. Besides the dates and location we learn only that "field reports summarizing current research in the Southwest were presented and, in addition, discussions centering around problems of ceremonial architecture and the Pueblo I period were held." Perhaps the lack of information on who reported on what in 1962 is less important than the existing correspondence, which reflects the ongoing commitment of many Southwestern archaeologists to the Conference as an essential contribution to their work.

FORT BURGWIN, 1963 (TWENTY-SIXTH PECOS CONFERENCE) In contrast to 1962, there was no problem deciding where the 1963 Pecos Conference would meet. It would return on 6–8 September to the Fort Burgwin Research Center, where it had met four years before. It was to be a joint Plains-Pecos Conference. On 5 August 1963 Halseth wrote to Herbert Dick at the Fort Burgwin Research Center:

> I want to be present for whatever memorial part of the program your committee has planned for Ted Kidder. There are still a few of us around who attended the first Pecos conference, and I am sure that we, as well as a younger generation, would like to pay tribute to Kidder on this occasion.

Halseth was referring to the death of A. V. Kidder on 11 June 1963, at the age of seventy-eight—a man not only respected for his major contributions to both Southwestern and Maya archaeology and to archaeological research methods, but also greatly loved and admired by three generations of archaeologists who had been trained, helped, and inspired by him through the years (see Wauchope 1965). He was not only the founder of the Pecos Conference but also an archaeological pioneer and leader for more than four decades. Gordon R. Willey (1967: 293) wrote of Kidder, "The span of his life saw the transformation of archaeology in the Americas from antiquarianism to a systematic discipline. More than any other single person he was responsible for this change. He was the outstanding American archaeologist of his time." As it turned out, the "memorial" to Kidder was a long reminiscence and commentary by Halseth, most of it quoted in earlier chapters.

During the summer an announcement was mailed, headed "1963 Joint Plains-Pecos Conference, Ft. Burgwin Research Center, Taos, New Mexico." The program was described as follows:

> The first day of the conference is to be devoted to current research reports with concurrent sessions, one for the South-

western reports, the other for Plains reports. The second day of the conference is to be devoted to an analysis of Plains-Southwestern contacts during the Historic Period. This session will feature a series of introductory papers on the problem to be followed by a general discussion, led by selected discussants. The third day of the conference is reserved for any remaining field reports or other subjects which may be of general interest.

A Saturday evening barbecue with entertainment was also announced, and as usual prompt motel reservations were urged, "as September is still within the tourist season." Ample facilities for camping were also available at Fort Burgwin.

The final program for the Saturday symposium identified two topics and several speakers:

1. "The Entradas and Other Problems," chaired by Preston Holder (University of Nebraska), with four speakers: John L. Champe (University of Nebraska), "Location of El Cuartelejo"; James H. Gunnerson (completing a doctorate at Harvard University), "Problems in Plains Apache Archaeology"; E. Boyd (Museum of New Mexico), "Historic Artifacts from SW Sites"; Waldo R. Wedel (U.S. National Museum), "Problems for Future Research."

2. "The Athabascans & Nearby Pueblos," chaired by Charlie Steen (National Park Service, Santa Fe), also with four speakers: Galen Baker (Trinidad Junior College), "Archaeology of SE Colorado"; Roy L. Carlson (University of Colorado Museum), "Navajo Sites of the Gobernador Locality"; Harold Huscher (River Basin Surveys, Smithsonian Institution), "Plains Influences Directly Recorded in Navajo and Western Apache Culture"; Herbert W. Dick (Fort Burgwin Research Center), "Archaeology of the Taos-Picuris Region."

In addition, there were four discussants listed: "Dave Brugge, Waldo Wedel, Al Schroeder, and Jim Hester." The content of the program has survived, thanks to the extensive notes that Brugge took and later recorded on a cassette. Some twenty people gave field reports on more than twice that number of research projects.

The 7 September session on Plains-Southwest relations followed the announced sequence of topics and speakers. Some of the same ground was covered as in the 1959 symposium on Plains-Southwest relations, also at Fort Burgwin. In addition, Gunnerson spoke at length on the identification of Dismal River as Apache and on related western Plains sites. Brugge's notes indicate for Boyd only that slides were presented; Wedel discussed the dating problem for the entry into the Plains of such traits as the serrate flesher and the epiphysial hide scraper. Baker described the archaeological materials from the Cimarron Ranch of the Boy Scouts of America. James Hester spoke of the cultural contacts of the Navajo in the 1550–1600 period. The session concluded with George Trager (State University of New York at Buffalo) reporting that the separation of Kiowa from Tanoan was at about A.D. 500–700.

Although these papers individually made useful contributions to the study of Southwestern-Plains relations, collectively and more importantly they demonstrate that understanding the Southwest was increasingly seen as requiring an examination of vast areas beyond its boundaries, in this case the Plains, but in others the Great Basin, California, or Mesoamerica. The isolationist attitude of earlier Southwestern studies was now replaced by a far broader perspective.

It is probable that a bare summary of speakers and topics misses the most important aspect of a session such as the one on Plains-Southwest relations—the opportunity for scholars to become better acquainted and learn more about each other's work. Informal discussions outside of scheduled sessions are important at any scholarly meeting, and the Pecos Conferences' relatively isolated settings improved such opportunities. Every motel room, bar, restaurant table, and campfire could become the scene of exchanges as important as those scheduled on the program.

Lambert described the informal aspects of the Conference in appropriate terms in her November 1963 letter in *Teocentli:* "It was great fun seeing so many of you during the Pecos-Plains Conference at Fort Burgwin in Taos. . . . The parties and social gatherings were as much fun as the sessions, and all of us are agreed that the Plains friends should meet more often with the Southwestern gang."

A business meeting was held on the final day, sending messages to absent members, thanking those responsible for the meeting arrangements and program, and selecting a location for the next year's Conference and an interim committee to plan it. The result of the last is reported in a letter (12 September 1963) from Hester to Danson:

At the recent Pecos Conference held at Ft. Burgwin, an invitation from the Navajo tribe to host the 1964 Pecos Conference at Window Rock was accepted. In addition, an interim committee was appointed to arrange details of this conference consisting of yourself as Chairman, and Martin Link and Dave Brugge representing the Navajo tribe.

10
From the Mountains to the Desert, 1964–67

Following the return in 1962 and 1963 to Globe and Ft. Burgwin, the following years saw not only the innovation of meeting at a Native American "capitol" but also the addition of two new campuses to the meeting locations, in Trinidad, Colorado, the farthest north yet, and in Tucson, an oasis in the Arizona desert.

Window Rock, 1964 (Twenty-seventh Pecos Conference)   On 27 August 1964, the *Gallup Daily Independent* reported, under the headline "135 ANTHROPOLOGISTS ATTEND CONFERENCE":

The 28th [*sic*] Annual Pecos Conference recently held at the Navajo Tribal Museum in Window Rock proved to be one of the most successful ever held. The sessions were attended by 135 Anthropologists from Japan, Nigeria, and colleges and museums throughout the United States. . . . Friday . . . evening [21 August] the Museum held an Open House with members of the Plateau Sciences Society providing the refreshments and hosting the visitors. . . . Lorenzo Yazzie and his Blue Eagles performed Indian dances several times during the evening. . . .
    Saturday evening the conferees and their guests, totaling 230 were treated to a Navajo-style barbeque of roast mutton, fried bread, beans, roasted corn and drinks. After supper, as the full moon rose over the pinyons, the group assembled around the bonfire for the evening program. The program of traditional Navajo songs and dances were presented by Judge William Yazzie and his group. As a finale a round dance was started in which everybody participated.

The 1964 Pecos Conference was unique, or perhaps one should say "even more unique" than most. It was the first time that the Conference was hosted by Native American organizations, the Navajo Tribal Museum, the Navajo Land Claims Department, and the Navajo Tribal Parks Commission. The Navajo Tribe had become a large, complex enterprise. Its operations included the Tribal Museum at Window Rock, where the meeting was held; its own newspaper, the *Navajo Times;* a police force; a park system; and its own tribal rangers.

An event of some importance to the Navajo Tribe should be mentioned here, as reported by Charlie R. Steen (1964)—the start of hiring archaeologists in staff positions in tribal organizations and federal agencies:

> The Bureau of Indian Affairs' Gallup Office has on its staff an archaeologist, Mr. George Cattanach, who is on assignment from the National Park Service. His duties deal principally with the problems of survey and salvage in advance of construction on Indian lands. He is also concerned with planning for conservation of prehistoric remains. . . . Working closely with Mr. Cattanach are Miss Shirley Sells, anthropologist in the employ of the Navajo Tribe, and Mr. Martin Link of the Navajo Tribal Museum.

In addition, Steen reported that

> the largest government landholding agency, the Bureau of Land Management, in December, also has put an archaeologist on its staff. He is stationed at the Salt Lake City office of the BLM and will work in that state, but will be available to other state offices of the Bureau.

As the Pecos Conference committee members wrote back and forth in the spring of 1964, several suggestions were made for the scientific sessions. David M. Brugge proposed to Edward B. Danson (28 March 1964) that there be a "symposium . . . covering both the Puebloan withdrawal and the expansion of the rancheria settlement pattern. . . . If possible it would be well to get people who would represent the various prevailing theories."

When the program was mailed out, it was accompanied by a page of information on travel and accommodations, which explained that "the only public transportation [to Window Rock] is from Gallup by mail bus (not recommended)." Besides information on program, travel, and accommodations, the participants received a handsome brochure in color, "Visit Navajoland U.S.A.," and three informative handouts—"Something about Navajo History," "General Information," and "Something about Window Rock." The Pecos Conference was now coming to the attention of chambers of commerce.

The Conference began on Friday, 21 August. Registration, in the lobby of the Tribal Museum, was followed by a welcoming address by Sam Day III, chairman of the Navajo Parks Commission and cohost of the Conference. Archaeological field reports then began, chaired by Lee Correll (an archaeologist and historian who worked for the Navajo Tribe), continuing after lunch with Alan P. Olson (curator of anthropology and coordinator of research at the Museum of Northern Arizona, Flagstaff) presiding. That evening the Tribal Museum held an open house. The program stated that "the field reports and symposium will be held under the ramada in the zoo, weather permitting." Brugge recalls that the weather was excellent for the entire Conference.

A few highlights of the Friday morning archaeological reports can be mentioned. Galen Baker of Trinidad State Junior College (Colorado) described work on Upper Republican sites found in salvage work for the Raton Pass Highway, and also his excavation at Fort Massachusetts near Fort Garland. From the Museum of New Mexico, Santa Fe, palynologist James Schoenwetter described the shift about A.D. 800 from winter rains to summer rains, with resulting increased erosion but improved moisture for growing corn. Stewart Peckham and Alan Brew (J. O. Brew's elder son) described progress on the museum's salvage work in the Navajo Irrigation area, where more than 1,700 sites had been located. Vernon Brook of the El Paso Archaeological Society described the society's recent work at both Puebloan and early man sites. This is probably the first time an amateur society reported its work at a Pecos Conference. The University of Colorado's second year in Dinosaur National Park was reported by David Breternitz, with a "terminal archaic" Fremont site and Plains influence from the northeast. For the Museum of Northern Arizona Olson described finding a small mound near Polacca Wash with a secondary burial of some thirty individuals. It would be several years before Christy G. Turner II identified these as evidence of cannibalism. Gwinn Vivian of the Arizona State Museum, Tucson, reported on its recent work on the Lower Gila Channel Clearing project from Painted Rocks Dam to the Colorado, with many historic Yuma sites;

as well as "Lower Colorado buff ware" sites, and at the Ranch Creek site with a possible Salado occupation overlying Hohokam.

Recent research at Mesa Verde National Park was described by Jean Pinkley, particularly the approaching completion of the Wetherill Mesa program. Finally, Erik Reed described work by the Fort Burgwin Research Center, including archaeological monitoring of the construction of the Picuris sewer and water system by Herbert Dick and architectural drawings of Picuris Pueblo.

At the Friday evening open house, Conference participants saw the impressive progress made in developing the new Tribal Museum—three exhibit rooms, library, zoo, and laboratory, as well as the astronomical observatory built by the Plateau Sciences Society.

Saturday began with ethnological reports, chaired by Jerrold E. Levy, who had been studying Navajo drinking patterns for the Division of Indian Health of the U.S. Public Health Service, and who was about to join the faculty of Portland State University.

Brugge's notes include one-to-one "conferences," such as a discussion with Lee Wyman about the "master file" on ethnobotany that Wyman was establishing at the Museum of Northern Arizona, to which Brugge later sent data he had accumulated during his land claims work. This, of course, is an example of how research is planned and advanced through innumerable impromptu discussions whenever the opportunity occurs—which it does, annually, at the Pecos Conferences and many other meetings.

The symposium on the Puebloan decline and the Rancheria expansion presented a wealth of information and interpretation. For example, the historic evidence for Athabascan arrival and expansion in the Southwest was reviewed by Albert H. Schroeder; he suggested that by 1400 Apaches might have reached the Texas Panhandle, resulting in the disappearance or displacement of the Antelope Creek Focus. He proposed that Navajo and Apache had separate histories until about 1750. Brugge spoke on recent advances in Navajo archaeology, citing tree-ring dates in the 1300s, which Alfred Dittert found unconvincing. Reed recounted the gradual withdrawal of the Puebloans from their maximum expansion, from Pueblo II onwards, accelerating in the 1300s, and resulting in only four areas of significant occupation by the sixteenth century. Omer Stewart spoke on the Shoshoneans. The symposium closed with a summary by Danson, as chairman, who emphasized the need for much more archaeological research on the Navajo, Yumans, and other Rancheria peoples.

Brugge (letter to Woodbury, 10 September 1988) reported on the business meeting:

Galen Baker asked that the [1965] meeting be held at Trinidad State Junior College in Trinidad, Colorado. The vote was to accept the offer and to meet there. Then Erik [Reed] appointed an interim program committee consisting of Baker, Dittert, and Olson; Dittert caught the chairman's job.

A field trip to Kinlichee Tribal Park was the last event of the 1964 Conference.

This year's meeting provided an impressive reminder to anthropologists that the Navajo had moved from being passive "objects" of research to being managers and supporters of research and communicators of its results.

TRINIDAD, 1965 (TWENTY-EIGHTH PECOS CONFERENCE)   As agreed the year before, the 1965 Conference was held at Trinidad State Junior College, Trinidad, Colorado. Located a few miles north of Raton Pass but about 1,800 feet lower, Trinidad is on the Purgatoire River (locally sometimes the "Picket Wire"), just east of the Front Range at the edge of the High Plains and only 130 miles from the Nebraska state line. The archaeological significance of this location suggested the subject for the Conference's half-day symposium. Galen Baker sent out a notice announcing the dates as 27–29 August. He continued:

> A symposium is planned to center around the archaeological materials of southeastern Colorado, dealing with Woodlands, Upper Republican (Aksarben), Pueblo and Historic Indian materials of this and adjacent regions. . . . A barbecue is planned for Friday evening. Campgrounds, not too far from the college, will be available. Those desiring camp space should write ahead of time so we can plan camping space accordingly.
>
> Let us hope that participants from all parts of the Southwest, the Great Basin and the Great Plains will be on hand to take part.

The list of those attending had 109 names on it, of which 10 are identified as "student"; there was no more controversy as to whether students could attend, and if so, whether they could do more than listen. More than ever, students were indispensable partners in most archaeological field research, often directing substantial parts of a project.

As would be expected for the first Pecos Conference in Colorado (hence, the farthest north yet) the state was well represented among the participants, with thirty-six attending. New Mexico (twenty-seven) and Arizona (eighteen) followed, with six from Texas and one to three each from Illinois, Indiana, Iowa, Maryland, Michigan, Montana, New Jersey, Oklahoma, Pennsylvania, Virginia, Washington, D.C., Wisconsin, and Utah. Surprisingly, next-door Nebraska was not represented. For Friday evening the program announced an "Open House—Laboratory and Museum—Trinidad Junior College campus (Lab located on basement floor of Scott Gymnasium; Museum on top floor of Berg Building)."

According to notes by Brugge there were at least thirty-seven archaeology field reports, starting Friday morning after the opening formalities. They included a report on Jemez Cave material extending from San Pedro Cochise to Pueblo IV (Richard Ford); a palynological record from A.D. 200–1825 (Schoenwetter); expansion of research at Mesa Verde by the University of Colorado; the correlation of European documentary records with climatic changes in the Southwest and Plains in the thirteenth century (Reid Bryson); pre- and postcontact sites in the Cochiti Dam area (Dittert); a boat survey of Marble and Grand Canyons, finding fourteen new sites (Walter Taylor, reported by Robert Euler); further work at Casas Grandes, including 1,700 macaw burials and evidence for a shift in trade from the Southwest to Mexico and Guatemala by the tenth and eleventh centuries (Charles Di Peso); the Picuris Pueblo Sewer Salvage Program, including twenty-five kivas (Dan Wolfman); and Arizona State University's survey of the Salt River Valley, with three hundred sites found.

Ethnological reports on Saturday morning began with Ford describing inter-pueblo trade in plant materials, followed by a report on Indian urbanization in Flagstaff and Winslow (Roger Kelley); the Hopi Indian Painting Research Project, securing explanations of each painting done over a five-year period by five artists (Bryan Harvey); Navajo relocation (Omer C. Stewart); and a comparison of Yavapai adaptation in Prescott and Clarkdale (speaker unidentified).

The Saturday afternoon symposium, "Archaeological Materials of Southeastern Colorado and Adjacent Regions," had ten speakers and was chaired by James B. Griffin. The papers were long and detailed and will only be summarized very briefly here. As far as is known the papers were not published, a shortcoming of nearly all symposia at Pecos Conferences, although most of the data and many of the ideas in the papers probably appeared in print in one place or another.

Breternitz (University of Colorado) began with an outline of the Northeast Colorado sequence, from Signal Butte II to historic tipi rings. Mike Glassow (Philmont Scout Ranch, Cimarron) described the archaeology of the Vermejo and Ponil drainages of northeast New Mexico, beginning about A.D. 1000 with rock circles, then pit houses with a few Pueblo sherds, and by the 1700s round-bottomed micaceous pottery in rock shelters. For eastern Colorado Arnold Withers (University of Denver) reported a sequence of generalized Archaic, Middle Woodland, and by about 1300 intrusive Southwestern pottery. Jack C. Hughes (Panhandle-Plains Historical Museum, Canyon, Texas) reported on the Antelope Creek Focus of the Texas Panhandle.

A survey of the lava mesas and river bottoms of southeastern Colorado was reported on by Robert G. Campbell (University of Colorado), including Archaic to Woodland campsites, rock shelters with "Yuma" points at the base of their refuse and corn agriculture at the top, "stone enclosure" sites with three-foot slab walls, small triangular corner-notched points, and cordmarked pottery. A few tipi rings had Apache pottery, probably of the late eighteenth century. Baker discussed the archaeological contact zone of the Purgatoire River, with Woodland and Upper Republican to the north and east and Pueblo influence from the southwest. By 1300 occupation ended, perhaps due to the arrival of Athabascans.

William G. Buckles (Southern Colorado State College, Pueblo) described a sequence of Ute occupation back to about A.D. 700, essentially a continuation of the Archaic pattern, but with occasional intrusive sherds from Fremont, Woodland, Upper Republican, Anasazi, and finally wickiups with white trade goods. The historic Indians of southeastern Colorado were discussed by Morris F. Taylor (historian, Trinidad State Junior College), using the extensive records of military campaigns from the mid-1800s onwards, involving Utes, Jicarillas, and Moache Utes, and a little later Cheyennes, Arapahos, Kiowas, Comanches, and others. This was followed by a historic overview of the area by Schroeder, and the view from the Kansas Plains by Waldo R. Wedel (Smithsonian Institution).

The symposium ended with a summary by Griffin, who pointed out that from 500 B.C. to the first century A.D. the projectile points of sites on the eastern flanks of the Rockies could be correlated with the Southwest, but that the westward expansion of Woodland and Upper Republican resulted in strong eastern influences in Colorado from the fifth to the tenth century.

At the business meeting Flagstaff was chosen for 1966, with the 1967 meeting to be in Tucson. Looking at the topics and areas covered during the Trinidad Conference, it is clear that it considerably expanded the traditional horizons of the Conference, particularly into distant parts of Colorado and eastward to the neighboring Central Plains. The Conference concluded with a Saturday evening barbecue and a Sunday field trip to sites in the Trinidad area that showed both Plains and Pueblo relationships.

FLAGSTAFF, 1966 (TWENTY-NINTH PECOS CONFERENCE) The largest Pecos Conference up to that time, with 227 names on the registration list, took place at the Museum of Northern Arizona from 26 through 28 August 1966. It was the fifth time the Conference had been held at the Museum (1950, 1953, 1956, and 1960), more times than at any other location except Chaco Canyon. The Conference would return to Flagstaff in 1972, 1978, and 1984. As was customary, an interim committee had been appointed, consisting of Euler (chairman), with Alexander J. Lindsay, Jr., and George J. Gumerman, all on the Museum's staff. On 7 June Danson, director of the Museum, sent out an announcement that the Conference would begin Friday morning, 26 August, and that "a luncheon is planned for Saturday noon and a bar-be-cue and beer dinner . . . for Saturday evening at the Museum. You will be interested to know that we plan to celebrate Dr. Colton's 50th Anniversary in archaeological work at this conference. His first site was dug in 1916" (Fig. 10.1).

The Conference began on Friday morning with registration, for the remarkably modest fee of $2, which included dinner Friday evening and lunch on Saturday. At 1 p.m. the Conference was welcomed by Danson, who began as follows: "It is a pleasure to welcome you all to the Pecos Conference . . . started 39 years ago, in 1927, by the late Dr. A. V. Kidder, and held under the junipers at Pecos Pueblo." He also said:

> For those of you in the Camp Ground, please be careful of fires. We have one large fire-pit area where a campfire can be built. The woods are dry; in case of an accidental fire, we have parked the pumper and pickup in the camp area. Please be careful. Also remember that some of those people camping are with their families and would like some sleep. Our night policemen have been told to break up any noisy or wild parties after midnight— and they mean business. I'll have no Taos or University of New Mexico fracases here.

Archaeological field reports, chaired by Walter W. Taylor, occupied Friday afternoon (Fig. 10.2). Twenty-eight are listed in the records,

10.1 Harry King, E. B. Danson, Harold S. Colton, Lyndon L. Hargrave, and David Arana, at the Pecos Conference, Flagstaff, 1966. Museum of Northern Arizona negative no. 66.1844, photo by Watson Smith.

10.2 Richard Ambler giving a field report at the Pecos Conference, Flagstaff, 1966, Raymond H. Thompson chairing. Museum of Northern Arizona negative no. 66.1961, photo by Parker Hamilton.

beginning with Al Hayes, Pinkley, Louis Caywood, and Lyndon Hargrave of the National Park Service, reporting on work at Gran Quivira, Pecos, and Zuni and on the ecological data to be derived from archaeological bird bones. From the University of Arizona there were reports by Laurens Hammack on Forestdale, Vivian on highway salvage, William Barrera on trincheras research, Jeff Brown on early man, Bryant (Bear) Bannister on the work of the Tree-Ring Laboratory, William Wasley on the identification in Magdalena, Sonora, of the grave of Father Eusebio Kino, James E. Ayres on the ongoing research at Grasshopper Ruin, and Emil W. Haury on his extensive 1964–65 excavation program at Snaketown.

The Museum of Northern Arizona was also well represented, with its recent research reported by Gumerman, S. Alan Skinner, William Wade, Danson, and Harold S. Colton, who described his research on dog skeletons from Southwestern archaeological sites (Colton 1970). Research at Yellow Jacket in southwestern Colorado was reported by Joe Ben Wheat, University of Colorado, and Cheryl White, University of Illinois.

Others who reported include Frank Smith and Owen Weir (San Diego State College), Baker (Trinidad State College), Euler (Prescott College, a new liberal arts college that held its first classes in the fall of 1966), Don Fowler (University of Nevada), John Fritz (Field Museum), and Breternitz (University of Colorado).

A second, shorter session of archaeological field reports, chaired by Florence Ellis (University of New Mexico), was held Saturday morning, concurrently with the ethnological reports—presumably reflecting an unfortunate idea that no one could be interested in both. The Museum of New Mexico's work was reported on by Dittert (salvage archaeology in the Gila Cliff dwellings), Jack Wilson (digging at Fort Fillmore), David Snow (the Cochiti Dam site), and Stan Bussey (the Navajo irrigation project). Larry Hammack of the Arizona State Museum reported on a Salado site on the Gila River, and Norman Ritchie reported on NPS work at Walnut Canyon. Brook, of the El Paso Archaeological Society, described its recent work, and the session closed with Ellis speaking about the archaeology of the Rio Grande Pueblos.

One surprising absence in the field reports is the work of Paul S. Martin and his students at Vernon; he attended the Conference with several students, but of them only John Fritz spoke. Martin had been at odds with Pecos Conference program planning in the past, urging prepared papers instead of extempore reports, as well as complaining that the Conference attendance was not restricted enough, and he may again have been so dissatisfied as to refrain from reporting.

The most exciting event at the Conference was unscheduled. It occurred early Saturday morning, as reported by Jim Garner in the Flagstaff *Arizona Daily Sun* (29 August):

> Somewhere this morning in the Great Southwest there is an unidentified woman driving a Volkswagen and probably spreading the word that Flagstaff has been buried under lava.
>
> It all began about 5:30 a.m. Saturday. Visiting archaeologists to the Pecos Conference at the Museum of Northern Arizona were camped out in tents behind the museum. It had been a long night.
>
> El Paso Gas has been rebuilding its main line through Coconino County. Part of it involves the releasing of pressure in the line. When this is done, the sound it makes is not unlike that of the firing of about 15 Atlas rockets—all at the same time. No one thought to inform the archaeologists that one such "pressure release" would be made Saturday morning.
>
> The dawn's early light was shattered, and we do mean shattered.
>
> Baroooooom!
>
> Archaeologists ran from their tents.
>
> Cries of "Dr. Colton was right; the Peaks are erupting" were heard. The Peaks being the San Francisco Peaks which, according to some experts, are dormant volcanoes; others contend they are extinct, etc.
>
> Anyway, it was "panicsville."
>
> The unidentified lady didn't wait around for the proper explanation. She tossed all her belongings in the car and headed out. Convinced that she had beaten the flow of lava by scant minutes. And undoubtedly scanning newspapers (wherever she may be) to find out how many were killed when the volcano erupted.

A good example of how folk history develops is the recollection in one of my 1979 questionnaires that the woman ran from her tent naked and drove off without her clothes.

Saturday morning, in spite of this early awakening, the Conference went on as scheduled, with six ethnological reports: Levy, the Tri-University field school; Mischa Titiev, Hopi ethnology and archaeology; Edward Dozier, flower paintings of Tesuque Pueblo; Robert

Black, Hopi ethnomusicology; Stephen Kunitz of the U.S. Public Health Service, Tuba City, measles among the Navajo; an unidentified speaker, archaeological and ethnological pollen correlations.

The Saturday morning business meeting, chaired by Euler, began with formal resolutions of condolence on the deaths of Odd Halseth, Frank H. H. Roberts, Jr., Gordon Vivian, and Jimmy Kewanwytewa. The last named, "Jimmy K," was the museum's best-known Hopi staff member, with thirty-two years of service. He was known to thousands not only for carving fine kachina figures but also for welcoming an audience while he worked. A telegram was sent to Madeleine Kidder in Cambridge, Massachusetts, recalling "with affection and admiration the man who originated [the] field conference tradition in [the] Southwest."

The Conference program does not indicate whether recognition of Colton's fifty years of archaeology was made at the business meeting or at the Friday night dinner in his honor, or both. In the summer of 1916, while the Coltons were vacationing in the Flagstaff area, their small son, Ferrell, picked up some potsherds and thus brought to his parents' attention a one-room malpais boulder site. It became Colton's first excavation, and the first of the nearly 10,000 sites in the region that he had recorded by 1966. He was, of course, an administrator as well, helping to build the museum into a large, effective research and training center with broad interdisciplinary interests and accomplishments.

The business meeting ended with the choice of the next year's meeting place. There were telegrams of invitation from both the president of the chamber of commerce and the mayor of El Paso, and a letter of invitation from Raymond H. Thompson of the University of Arizona. The invitation from Arizona was accepted, by a vote of seventy-two to sixty. El Paso was selected as the site for the 1968 meeting, a one-year postponement similar to the one made in 1965 when Flagstaff was selected over Tucson. Gradually and informally the Conference was moving to two-year planning, a recognition of the increasing complexity of arranging and running a meeting that had grown so large.

The final session, Saturday afternoon, was "Sinagua and Their Neighbors," chaired by Thompson. Its speakers and topics are listed in the program as:

1. David Breternitz: The Sinagua
2. Robert Euler: Prescott Branch
*3. Ray Ruppé: Bloody Basin (*Absent without leave)

4. Al H. Schroeder: Verde Valley
5. Jack Wilson: Eastern Sinagua
6. George Gumerman: Holbrook Chambers—x Winslow Branch
7. Lex Lindsay: Kayenta
8. Bill Wade: Virgin Branch (*sick*)
9. Dick Ambler: Fremont Branch
10. Raymond Thompson: Summary

As a final note on the seminar and the Conference, it is worth observing that information from Conference reports was beginning to be referred to in publications. Breternitz, for example, cites the 1966 symposium on the Sinagua as the source for new viewpoints on the effect of the Sunset Crater cinder and ash fall between 1065 and 1067 (Breternitz 1967: 74). Contrary to the long-held view of the beneficial effects of the ash and cinders, it was now argued that the ash fall might have been detrimental—an important question in understanding the rapid population changes in the area at the time. A thorough search of Southwestern literature would doubtless produce more references to Conference reports as a source of important new information and ideas, available before publication.

Tucson, 1967 (Thirtieth Pecos Conference) From the University of Arizona's department of anthropology and Arizona State Museum we have an overwhelming wealth of detailed information on the 1967 Pecos Conference. Other Conferences may have generated as many memos, drafts, letters, and lists, but this time copies exist of virtually all of them.

On 19 April an announcement was sent out by Edwin N. Ferdon, Jr., interim chairman, and William J. Robinson, program chairman. It specified the dates, 25 and 26 August, and the hosts, the Arizona State Museum, the department of anthropology, and the Laboratory of Tree-Ring Research. Besides the customary field reports there would be a half-day symposium on the Mogollon culture: "It will appraise the position of the Mogollon today after 30 years within the framework of Southwestern culture units. Particular emphasis will be placed on recent work and the tree-ring chronology." It was in 1948 that J. O. Brew as skeptic had confronted such Mogollon supporters as Haury, Martin, and E. B. (Ted) Sayles at a panel discussion at the Pecos Conference at Point of Pines. It was thirty years since Haury had offered the first definition of the Mogollon culture. This symposium, on Haury's home ground, was the right place for a new consideration of the Mogollon and its well-accepted position in Southwestern cultural frameworks. A symposium on the Hohokam would, of course, have been equally appropriate, as the pattern was evolving of focusing the Conference's half-day symposium on the immediate area of that year's location and archaeological issues related to it.

A final notice went to prospective attendees on 21 July:

> Dear Friend:
>
> We are all set for the PECOS CONFERENCE so clean up that last pit house, jacket that mammoth rib with the Clovis point in it, wind up that Jaguar XKE (did I write that?), and be sure to get down here by August 25. Registration will take place . . . [in] the Anthropology Building. And please do register. It will cost you $2.50 each, but for that price you not only can present your own words of wisdom at the meetings, but enjoy the Saturday evening soiree at the Lodge on the Desert, where swimming, beer, and good food will be enjoyed, while Mariachis play your favorite Mexican tunes.

With 248 registrations, this was the largest Pecos Conference yet. As was to be expected, the greatest number were from Arizona (104). New Mexico had 28, California 10, Colorado and Illinois each 7, Texas 6, Massachusetts 4, and thirteen other states plus the District of Columbia were represented. As usual, few ethnologists can be identified among those registered, perhaps 10 to 15.

The Conference opened Friday morning with a brief welcome from Thompson and a "40th Anniversary Recognition" by Haury, who recalled, as he had on previous occasions, the 1927 Conference in which he had taken part as a student, and which he now looked back on with some nostalgia as a small meeting where nearly everyone knew everyone else and a few trees provided a shady meeting space. Even now, forty years later, there were eight of the "Founders" present at this Conference (Fig. 10.3).

Field reports followed, chaired by Wasley (Arizona State Museum), and again we have Brugge's detailed notes on what many of the speakers reported, supplemented by the "Current Reports" section of *American Antiquity* (Lindsay 1968a, 1968b). Comparing the reports at the Pecos Conference and those in "Current Reports," it appears that a substantial part of all recent Southwestern field work was reported at the Conference. The reports continued in the afternoon, chaired

10.3 "Founders" at the Tucson Conference, 1967 (left to right): *Harold S. Colton, Alfred (Alfie) Kidder II, Hulda Haury, Paul S. Martin, Madeleine A. Kidder, Faith Kidder Fuller, Neil M. Judd, Emil W. Haury, Harriet S. Cosgrove, and Clara Lee Tanner. Arizona State Museum negative no. 15261.*

by Robert H. Lister (University of Colorado), and were completed Saturday morning, with Euler (Prescott College) chairing.

The business meeting, at 11:30 Saturday morning, began with a resolution thanking those responsible for the Conference, and then an "anniversary" resolution: "Resolved: That the 1967 Pecos Conference express appreciation to the original members of the first conference held at Pecos, New Mexico in 1927—and especially to those in attendance at this 40th meeting: H. S. Colton, Neil M. Judd, Madeleine A. Kidder [Fig. 10.4], Emil W. Haury, Clara Lee Fraps Tanner, Harriet Cosgrove, Paul S. Martin, and A. V. Kidder II—for their inspiration and contributions to the conference and to Southwestern archaeology." It was also voted to send telegrams of greeting to three of the 1927 participants who were not at this Conference—Kenneth Chapman, Jesse L. Nusbaum, and Erna Gunther (Spier).

An invitation was received and accepted from El Paso for the 1968 Conference. Rex Gerald and J. A. Griffen of the Centennial Museum, University of Texas at El Paso, were appointed interim chairman and program chairman, respectively. Invitations were also received from Prescott College for 1969, from Mesa Verde National Park for 1970, and from the Museum of Northern Arizona for 1971. As it turned out, only the first of these Conferences took place at the location proposed.

There is no detailed record of what was said at the Saturday afternoon symposium, "The Mogollon Today," chaired by Reed. However, a good idea of its contents is provided by the list of speakers and topics, and by a letter written by the program chairman (William J. Robinson, letter to Emil W. Haury, 29 April 1967):

> I hope . . . to stress the position of the Mogollon today . . .
> rather than a straight rehash of descriptive material. How does
> the Mogollon stand the test of time as a culture unit within the
> Southwestern framework? A great deal of recent excavation and
> a new tree-ring chronology may shed light on both the inter-
> nal chronology and the external relationships of the Mogollon,
> and I hope that they will be presented. The tree-ring chronology
> will be presented at the symposium and will also be furnished to
> participants far enough in advance that they may make use of it.

The topics and speakers, as listed in the final program, were:

> The Mogollon Pattern: Joe Ben Wheat
> The Mogollon Tree-Ring Chronology: William J. Robinson

10.4 Madeleine Kidder acknowledging applause during the 1967 Conference in Tucson. Behind Mrs. Kidder at left, Clara Lee Tanner and Hulda Haury, at far right Paul S. Martin. In foreground Harriet S. Cosgrove. Arizona State Museum negative no. 15266.

Northern Mogollon: John B. Rinaldo
Hohokam-Mogollon Relationships: Emil W. Haury
Early Horizons in the Navajo Reservoir: A. E. Dittert, Jr.
Southern Mogollon: Charles C. Di Peso
Early Horizons in the Puerco—Hopi Buttes Area: George J.
Gumerman
Mogollon Agriculture: Mark P. Leone
Summary: Erik K. Reed

The success of this symposium is indicated in a letter from Euler dated 28 August 1967, immediately on his return to Prescott, to Ferdon and Robinson:

> Many thanks for a fine Pecos Conference, climaxed by one of the best symposiums I have ever heard. I wonder if anyone made a tape recording of that symposium? If so, I should think it would be very worthwhile if it could be transcribed and distributed to those interested.
>
> As a matter of fact, I heard several comments during the Conference to the effect that it might be worthwhile if the entire proceedings were recorded and similarly distributed.

Such a suggestion had been made in previous years to no avail. The first and last complete tapings of Pecos Conferences were by John Champe at Fort Burgwin in 1959 and Flagstaff in 1960, and these remained in the Laboratory of Anthropology Pecos Conference Archives, untranscribed, until they were used for this history.

The 1967 Conference ended with the gala evening at the Lodge on the Desert, announced in the program as consisting of swimming (6–8 p.m.), mariachis (7–10 p.m.), and dinner (8 p.m.), with the notice that "beer will be served; booze may be purchased."

Undoubtedly the most personal published comment on the 1967 Conference appeared in a Tucson newspaper as an advertisement by the Hayden Excavation Service of Julian Hayden, an archaeologist of many years' experience who in 1988 would receive the SAA Crabtree Award for Avocational Archaeology:

> HAYDEN SAYS: IT'S WORTH NOTING THAT THE 40TH PECOS CONFERENCE IS AGAIN ON RIGHT NOW IN TUCSON. Yessir, 40 years ago a bunch of pot-busters and bone diggers got together at Pecos ruin to swap lies and work

out some sense to all the different kinds of pottery the Indians made in the Southwest. Such joreejawings have been goin on ever since, with the prime work of the conference being done over a jug of Adam's ale (branchwater to you) to lubricate the think glands in the evenings (the man said so, must be so). Well, as a maverick, we'll put our stick in and say that we'll bet a busted point these Clovis Mammoth Hunters, you been reading about in the papers, of 11,000 years ago or so, were a might snooty people. We bet they came down here following mammoth sign right down amongst some worm grubbers known to some of us as the San Dieguito people and to others as the Cochise, and looked down their noses at em and moved on, just like a bunch of Green Berets stalking thru a crowd of dough-foots. It's quite a conference, anyhow, and we're enjoying listening and not thinking much about HAYDEN'S PLANTING SOIL at the moment!

Hayden often discussed archaeological matters in his weekly newspaper advertisements. Fortunately, a complete file of these wonderful brief essays is in the archives of the Arizona State Museum.

II
THE TOUCH-AND-GO YEARS, 1968–71

By 1968 the New Archaeology reached the Pecos Conference, producing some distress among traditionalists and much satisfaction among its enthusiasts. In addition, as revealed by Robert Euler's inquiry after the 1969 Conference, there was substantial disagreement about and dissatisfaction with much of the format of the conferences. However, these small tempests eventually blew themselves out and by 1971 tranquility was restored.

EL PASO—JUÁREZ, 1968 (THIRTY-FIRST PECOS CONFERENCE) The Pecos Conference had met in Mexico before this, at Nuevo Casas Grandes in 1961, but the 1968 Conference site was not related to local field work. This Conference was marked by an important innovation in the program, a symposium on archaeological theory and application, rather than on the prehistory of the meeting area—a departure from tradition that was not quite a revolt of the "Young Turks" but was seen that way by some.

In July Rex E. Gerald of the El Paso Centennial Museum, interim chairman, and Vernon Brook, president of the El Paso Archaeological Society, sent out a lengthy letter with details of the approaching Conference, set for 23–24 August. The first day would be held at the University of Texas, El Paso, a cohost with the Museo de Arte e Historia Ciudad Juárez and the two organizations just mentioned. The Saturday sessions would take place in Ciudad Juárez.

The list of registrants totals 188, down sharply from the year before, but a sizable group compared to a decade earlier. El Paso itself was strongly represented with fifty-eight participants, reflecting the vigor of the local archaeological society. From the rest of Texas there only three names on the list! New Mexico had forty-four, Arizona twenty-four, Illinois thirteen, California twelve, and Colorado seven; the balance were from widely scattered localities, including New Hampshire, Massachusetts, Connecticut, South Carolina, Montana, Washington, Hawaii, Chihuahua, and Peru.

The Conference opened Friday morning, 23 August, in the Union Building, University of Texas, El Paso ("#2 on your map") with registration at $4 ("includes barbecue and beer Friday night"). Milton Leech, president of the university, welcomed the conferees, and at 10:30 field reports began, chaired by Stewart Peckham, of the Museum of New Mexico, Santa Fe. Although there is no complete list of speakers and topics, some details are contained in a report on the Conference in the newsletter of the Midland [Texas] Archeological Society (Stickney 1968).

The first eight field reports were given Friday morning by graduate students who were working under Paul S. Martin. These studies covered work done in the northeastern and east-central sections of Arizona. Among the topics discussed were "Upper Colorado Projectile Point Design Difference," "Net Population Flow in the Hopi Country of N.E. Arizona between A.D. 1250 and 1375," an explanation of random settlement, and computer archaeology.

At noon the Conference moved to a luncheon at the Sheraton—El Paso Motor Inn ("#1 on your map; appetites motivated by a light panel-discussion"). Field reports, chaired by George Gumerman, continued in the afternoon. In the evening the Conference migrated again, for "Barbecue and Beer at McKelligan Canyon Park, northeast El Paso (#8 on your map)."

Saturday the Conference met at the "I.S.S.S.T.E. Auditorium, ProNaF Area, Ciudad Juárez (Southeast of the Camino Real Hotel, #7 on your map)." The morning session was the symposium "Archeological Theory and Application—1968." This was the first time the half-day symposium, now a regular feature of Pecos Conferences, had been devoted to theory. It was chaired by Joe Ben Wheat of the University of Colorado, who was also the discussant at the close. The symposium papers provide an excellent view of the ideas of some of the most innovative younger archaeologists of a quarter century ago. A symposium program, with abstracts, was distributed, emphasizing still more the formality of the session, not much different from sessions at the national meetings of the SAA or other national organizations.

There were six speakers, and for each a portion of the abstract is quoted here:

Robert G. Chenhall, Arizona State University, "The Impact of Computers on Archaeological Theory": A brief framework of archaeological theory is created as a backdrop for the description of three recent archaeological studies that involved the use of electronic computers. Each . . . is then placed in the perspective of this theoretical structure, so as to highlight what has been done.

Fred Plog, University of Chicago, "Why a New Archaeology?": This movement should not be viewed as an attempt to abandon traditional archeology but rather as an attempt to add new elements of method and theory to a growing archeology. . . . We view archeology as a scientific-experimental rather than a purely historical-reconstructing discipline. . . . We accept the criterion of verifiability as the common denominator of scientific research. Research should be designed to test hypotheses and explanations, not just to collect data. . . . We hold a systemic rather than a normative view of culture. . . . Archeologists must . . . formulate their research problems in such a way that they are relevant to current anthropological, sociological, and economic problems.

Michael A. Glassow, University of California, Los Angeles, "General Systems Theory and Its Application to a Problem of Archaeological Explanation: Early Settlement Distributions in the Northern Southwest": General Systems Theory . . . may be [used] . . . to generate models for the explanation of cultural change from the Early to Late Basketmaker periods in the northern Southwest, roughly around A.D. 400. The testable propositions . . . would generally be subsumed under the first two Laws of Thermodynamics.

Arthur A. Saxe, Ohio University, "The Relevance of Role Theory for Archeological Interpretation of Burial Data": When archeologists excavate a set of burials they are not merely excavating individuals, but a coherent social personality who not only engaged in relationships with other social personalities but did so according to conventional rules of the larger social system.

Mark P. Leone, University of Arizona, "Environmental Control of Randomness": As the environment is more closely controlled, a culture's settlement pattern tends to become more random. This hypothesis has been tested in an area of the Southwest where dependence on agriculture is growing, and hence where the environment is held increasingly constant. . . . To discover the effects that social and ideological factors have on settlement pattern, nearest neighbor analyses were done on two archaeological field school camps.

Lyndon L. Hargrave and R. Roy Johnson, Prescott College, and Arthur H. Harris, University of Texas at El Paso, "The Economics of Prehistoric Peoples": Treatment of . . . biological materials [from sites] has progressed from merely listing species present . . . to sophisticated interpretation of the importance of these remains. . . . Attempts are being made to quantify amounts of plants and animals utilized and the consequential effect on the peoples involved.

An additional paper in the program was shifted to field reports, Paul Grebinger's examination of settlement patterns in the upper Santa Cruz drainage.

Much of this was far removed from the traditional content of Pecos Conferences but could hardly have come as a surprise, since the New Archaeology had been greatly influencing the field for at least the last five years and had its origins far earlier. Its foreshadowings can be found in Strong's "Anthropological Theory and Archaeological Fact" (Strong 1936), which shows a willingness, new at the time, to question archaeology's traditional goals, to examine the possibility of "the formulation of laws" (but with a negative verdict by Strong), and to view the testing of hypotheses as essential to progress in archaeology. In the next two years, "Ecological Aspects of Southwestern Society" (Steward 1937) and "Function and Configuration in Archaeology" (Steward and Setzler 1938) stated clearly a new way of looking at and using archaeological data. A further step, larger and more controversial, was taken by Walter W. Taylor in his "Study of Archaeology," published by the AAA in 1948. Ten years later, in their landmark volume, *Method and Theory in American Archaeology* (1958), Gordon R. Willey and Phillip Philips recognized the emergence and importance of "explanatory" archaeology and "processual interpretation." In a largely ignored essay, "Conjectures Concerning the Social Organization of the Mogollon Indians," Paul Martin and John Rinaldo (1950) anticipated some of the emerging ways of examining archaeological data.

Many archaeologists became acquainted with the New Archaeology in its full formulation with the publication of Lewis R. Binford's "Archaeology as Anthropology" in *American Antiquity* in 1962 (see also Binford 1964). He followed this with a symposium of like-thinking colleagues at the Boulder meeting of the SAA in 1963, which he has said was "poorly attended" (Binford 1972: 10). Binford organized a more ambitious, full-day symposium for the 1965 meeting of the AAA in Denver, "The Social Organization of Primitive Peoples." The audience, filling the auditorium to capacity, was highly enthusiastic, a great change from the year before (Binford 1972: 12–13). (Were "anthropologists" more receptive to new ideas than "archaeologists"?) The symposium papers were published in 1968 as *New Perspectives in Archeology* (Binford and Binford 1968).

The enthusiasm with which Paul Martin became a convert to the New Archaeology, an enthusiasm shared by his students at Vernon Field Station, is well described in his "Revolution in Archaeology" (Martin 1971; see also Martin 1975).

Nevertheless, not all archaeologists accepted the New Archaeology as a step forward, and some saw it as a threat that would replace their long established focus on culture-historical reconstruction of the past with dubious attempts to formulate laws and test complex nonarchaeological hypotheses. It is true, as Binford acknowledged in print, that he and his colleagues were sometimes impatient, scornful, or too singleminded, but he and others (Plog at this Conference, for example) also insisted that explanatory, scientific, deductive archaeology was meant to be an addition to and not a replacement of other archaeological methods.

One negative point of view, from an eminent traditional archaeologist, is given in a response to my inquiry, which Florence Hawley Ellis generously provided (11 April 1981). In her frankly expressed opinion, 1968 saw a marked change in the nature of the Conference, with some of the recent converts to the New Archaeology not yet outgrowing their arrogant views:

> My impression of the first very strong switch to emphasis on methodology rather than on new finds came out the year we met in Juarez, with some of the young fry, especially from [the] Chicago area, not even knowing pottery types or various things [which] Schroeder attacked them for being vague about—but they spent their entire time in giving papers which went into techniques of survey, etc.—forever. The main offenders (!) were Paul Martin's contingent. They—the louts—made a point of

leaving the room when the old conservatives got up to do their papers. For shame!

Ellis was saying here, more bluntly and openly, what a good many others felt at the time. Yet this generational and ideological split soon healed and eventually "louts" became well regarded senior members of the profession.

Following the archaeological theory symposium, there was a luncheon at the Museo de Arte e Historia de Ciudad Juárez ("#5 on map"; Fig. 11.1), arranged by Director Arq. Felipe Lacouture.

The business meeting in the afternoon received and unanimously accepted an invitation from Prescott College for the 1969 Pecos Conference. Gumerman, of Prescott College, was appointed interim chairman. "Invitations to hold the 1970 and 1971 Conference at Mesa Verde and Flagstaff, respectively, were not renewed, probably due to the absence of representatives from these areas." An invitation to return to Santa Fe at the "next available date" was extended by the directors of four institutions: the Museum of Navajo Ceremonial Art, the Museum of New Mexico, the School of American Research, and the U.S. National Park Service, Southwest Region. Although no formal action was taken, it was Santa Fe and Pecos that the Conference went to in 1970. The business meeting ended with resolutions thanking the host institutions in El Paso and Juárez, and expressing regret at the death of Kenneth Chapman of Santa Fe.

The remaining field reports came next, with Albert H. Schroeder as chairman. The final item on the program for Saturday is "3:00 pm— Tea Party (various bars, clubs, cafes, etc., Ciudad Juárez)."

The Sunday morning field trip went to the Fort Bliss Military Reservation, to see a small El Paso Phase site of the Jornada Branch of the Mogollon, dating between 1200 and 1400. The site was being excavated by members of the El Paso Archaeological Society, under permits from both the National Park Service and the U.S. Army Air Defense Center, which required renewal every month for the work to continue. The field trip was arranged by John A. Hedrick, the society's site survey director, and John W. Green, the site director.

Prescott, 1969 (Thirty-second Pecos Conference) The Pecos Conference of 1969, held at Prescott College, is unusual for what happened afterward rather than during the meeting. Following the Conference Robert C. Euler, chairman of the college's Center for Archaeological Studies, wrote to a number of participants, as will

11.1 Prelunch socializing at Ciudad Juárez, 1968 (left to right): Albert H. Schroeder, Robert C. Euler, George J. Gumerman, David M. Brugge, and Stewart L. Peckham. Photo courtesy of Brugge.

be described below, expressing his dissatisfactions and asking for comments and suggestions. This resulted in the first systematic examination of the Pecos Conference, its strengths and weaknesses, and considerably influenced future Conferences. Criticisms, however, tended to be of the Conference format in general rather than the Prescott Conference in particular.

The "invitation" letter to prospective 1969 attendees was sent out by Gumerman on 14 May. It specified the Conference dates as 22 and 23 August and provided a sketch map of the Prescott area to show the location of the college.

The efforts of Gumerman and Euler to improve field reports show in a handout headed "10 MINUTES PER PROJECT!" and indicating that the time should be used to give (1) the speaker's name and institution; (2) the research locale, problem, and justification; (3) high points of the work; (4) "tentative pre-analysis conclusions"; (5) relation to previous nearby research; (6) recommendations, if any, for additional research; and (7) probable outlet for publication. The handout closed with "ASK FOR QUESTIONS or ASK A QUESTION." We have no record of how well this good advice was heeded—probably least by those who needed it most.

There were 185 registrants at the Conference, nearly the same as the year before, but well over half were from Arizona, making this a less cosmopolitan Conference than some. There were thirty from New Mexico, Colorado, and California; twenty-one from the Middle West and East; and four from Oregon, Washington, and Calgary. The fact that Prescott College was a new institution, still small, hardly seems an explanation for the reduced attendance from distant places. Instead, its newness and experimental programs might have attracted more attendees. It is possible that the smaller attendance may reflect the discomfort of some "old" archaeologists with the growing role being played by "new" archaeologists, as well as the smoldering dispute over extempore versus written and read reports, a dispute that would soon erupt.

We have no official list of who gave field reports, but Ellis jotted down notes and again made them available to me. Her notes sometimes lack names and are occasionally ambiguous, but they give an excellent general view of the reports, which included the following:

Raymond H. Thompson,   the University of Arizona's continuing work at Grasshopper ruin
Euler,   Stanton Cave in the Grand Canyon

Gumerman, the Black Mesa field school, and plans to add an ethnological field school

Donald E. Dove, the Calderwood site near Phoenix

Stephen E. Plog, movements of culture vs. movements of people

Ezra Zubrow, energy and population in Hay Hollow

Frank Midvale, Hohokam canals twenty-five miles west of Phoenix

Laurens (Larry) Hammack, highway salvage in Arizona

William W. Wasley, the Charleston Dam survey (upper San Pedro River)

Richard J. Ambler, burials weathering out in the Long House Valley, Kayenta

Alan Brew, northwestern New Mexico archaeological survey

Michael A. Glassow, ecological studies on Ponil Creek, northeastern New Mexico

David Breternitz, Chimney Rock Ruin, Colorado, and the Mummy Lake study at Mesa Verde

Arthur Rohn, the Yellow Jacket area, northwest of Mesa Verde

Joe Ben Wheat, the upper Yellow Jacket area

William D. Lipe, Grand Gulch, Utah

Walter W. Taylor, the "master maximum method" of analyzing material culture

Don Fowler, Meadow Valley Wash, Utah

David Madsen, Fremont pictographs

Harvey M. Shields, rock circles in southern California

In spite of the fact that the New Archaeology had arrived at the Pecos Conference the year before, there is little evidence here that descriptive field reports were being supplanted by reports on explanatory archaeology, normative approaches, or deductive reasoning. Martin's students and colleagues at Vernon would be an exception—Fred Plog, Zubrow, and Leone—as would Taylor; the first three were converts to the New Archaeology and the last was one of its creators. During 1966–69 articles on the New Archaeology in the Southwest did not appear in *American Antiquity,* and books and monographs published in the late 1960s show the same continuation of traditional archaeological approaches.

The 1968 symposium in Prescott, "Human Ecology in the Southwest," was chaired by Taylor, of Southern Illinois University, and consisted of six papers, for which the program lists speakers but no titles. The subject matter, however, is mentioned in Ellis's notes: Taylor, ecological problems; Maurice (Spade) Cooley, U.S. Geological Survey (Ellis does not indicate the topic); Jerrold Levy, Portland State College, interaction of culture and environment; Paul Schultz Martin, department of geochronology, University of Arizona (not Paul Sidney Martin, the archaeologist), the first migrants to the New World as a cause of major environmental changes; William J. Robinson, Laboratory of Tree-Ring Research, University of Arizona, reconstruction of the climate of the prehistoric Southwest; William D. Wade, University of Colorado (in his absence the paper was read by Christy G. Turner), life tables as an important basis for reconstructing paleodemography, using data from Houck, Arizona.

The symposium was not very well received, as will be apparent in some of the comments to be quoted shortly in response to Euler's post-conference letter. A report on the Conference in *Masterkey* (Anonymous 1969) states: "The many discussions and definitions emerging from the group and its attending audience never clearly defined nor completely explained the topic presented; however, several interesting concepts developed from the day's proceedings."

The brief business meeting on Saturday afternoon voted a number of resolutions prepared by Ellis and Thompson: expressions of thanks and appreciation to the hosts and organizers of the Conference, including "the Prescott Branch of the Arizona Archaeological Society for the coffee, home-made cookies, and friendly atmosphere of the Hospitality Room." Greetings were sent to two 1927 Conference "Founders," Madeleine Kidder and Harold S. Colton, and felicitations to Colton on the occasion of his approaching eighty-eighth birthday. Regret was expressed on the death of Theodore D. McCown, University of California, Berkeley. Finally, in a departure from the customary resolutions, it was voted to "support the current efforts of colleagues in another region [not specified, but probably the Lower Mississippi] to expand federal archaeological authority with specific reference to the land-clearing activities in alluvial zones."

We turn now to Euler's postconference request for suggestions on how the Pecos Conferences could be improved. He wrote (4 September 1969) to some of those who had been in Prescott:

Dear Pecos Conferee:
As a follow-up to my remarks at the conclusion of the 1969
Pecos Conference when I indicated mild displeasure with the

typical field report-symposium organization of the Conference,
I thought I'd jot down some more specific yet still random
thoughts. . . . I'd appreciate it if you'd give me your ideas at your
convenience and I can then pass them along to Doug Schwartz
for whatever use he wishes to make of them for the 1970 Conference in Santa Fe.

First of all . . . in the 1st mailing to conferees in the spring,
include a return postcard asking each person to report the area
and topic of his field report. . . . These, then, could be organized
by the interim chairman in terms of related topics. For example,
if there are to be three reports on the archaeology of the Mesa
Verde area, have all three speakers at a table in a sort of informal
symposium; ask them to discuss the state of affairs in the Mesa
Verde, drawing upon their current field work for examples.
In this way, more synthesis and perhaps more theory could be
presented rather than the usual "I dug two more PIII sites."

Secondly, as for the formal afternoon symposium itself, . . .
those papers should speak directly to the selected topic rather
than tangentially as many of them did this year.

Euler received twenty-two replies to his letter, nearly all of them
long and full of detailed comments and suggestions. Most of the responses expressed agreement with Euler's suggestions, and many of
them complimented him on the excellence of the meeting, its arrangements, and setting. Many made specific comments about the
purposes of the Pecos Conference and suggested how they might be
accomplished. The 1970 Conference planners followed some of these
suggestions and received strenuous criticisms from a few archaeologists for their efforts. It is worthwhile to quote parts of the replies
that Euler received. What he accomplished was nothing less than the
first comprehensive appraisal of the Conference ever attempted. It was
taken seriously by the planners of the next Conference, and a new
format emerged, the first restructuring of the Conference in its forty-
three years on more than an ad hoc basis. Excerpts from the replies
follow:

At every Conference I have attended the low light of the Conference has been the formal afternoon symposium.

It would be desirable to have mini-symposia on certain areas
instead of the usual uninspiring field reports. . . . To me a symposium is more than just a bunch of people getting up and deliv-

ering papers about the same (or specific) subject—there should be a lot of give and take.

More structure is needed in the field report sessions. Please make greater effort to bring out problems rather than "what I dug."

I agree, the chairman of the field report sessions should know who they are going to be . . . so we can at least hear the reports in a logical manner. . . . I agree with Doc Haury, it should be informal (if this doesn't mean disorganized).

To me one of the important factors of the Pecos Conference is the personal contact with people who are working in the field and are in similar or adjacent areas with comparable problems to my own. Often at the larger national meetings there is not the opportunity for this personal contact and discussion, which has always seemed to me a function of the Pecos Conference.

I was greatly surprised and dismayed to learn, long after the conference was over, that some of the papers prepared by the Field Museum students were not allowed in the Field Report section. [This was a misimpression.] It is my opinion that the preparation required assures that papers by students will have greater content than 90% of the off-the-cuff reports given by more experienced field men . . . I got the distinct impression . . . that the expressions of dissatisfaction with formal reports were aimed more at suppressing new theoretical and methodological approaches in archaeological field work than anything else.

We all want to maintain the informal nature of this Conference. However, the minimum organization of field reports as suggested in . . . your letter appears to be an absolute necessity. . . . I would suggest that you not be too critical of the 1969 sessions. The opportunity to sit around a campfire amid the junipers and piñons and to talk on into the night with other southwestern archeologists—isn't this really the spirit of the Pecos Conference?

Several people have said that they felt that the "I dug two more PIII sites" talks were boring. . . . I do think it is valuable experience for the kids to be able to talk about their "sites." A final thought . . . I have always felt that the most successful Pecos Conferences were those that were held out-of-doors, where people could not show slides, and where the wind could blow away the cobwebs of one's mind.

I am all for more informality and [for] controlled field reports grouped together.

Salvage archaeology obviously dictates where one digs but there is no question but that the material found should be seen in the context of problems relating to that area or period.

Your idea of receiving advance notice of who wants to give field reports is a good one. . . . The main benefit, of course, is the chance that advance knowledge gives the organizer to arrange the reports intelligently. . . . Participants in a seminar should, I believe, have agreed among themselves what the focal point is and how each can bring his specialized knowledge to bear on that point. . . . I don't think the Pecos Conference should become a proving ground for term papers. . . . The health of the Pecos Conference has been due to its informality.

To me the need filled by the Pecos Conference is for a résumé of the status of current field research in the Southwest. . . . I was one who grumbled a bit about the use of the conference for the reading of term papers. We can't, and shouldn't, bar anyone from using the forum, but I wish we could discourage the use of the platform just for the earning of credit. Paul's boys are involved in methodology—not research. . . . The SAA and AAAS are good outlets for theory and synthesis. The Pecos Conference is the only thing of its kind that we have.

I too feel that more, rather than less, informality is needed. Nonetheless, time still needs to be allotted to the presentation of descriptive material in some sort of organized fashion. . . . but would personally like to see those papers which do not present new raw data excluded from the Pecos Conference.

I have seen the Conference progress steadily toward a more formal atmosphere and meager circumstances for individual participation. . . . Whatever is done, there is a need to bring the individual into more active participation, and this will be difficult to do.

Some sort of symposium or synthesis of the archeology of the general area in which the Pecos Conference is being held is always in order. This helps some of us government types in that it brings us up to date. . . . I would hope that any symposium would involve much floor discussion and audience participation.

Clearly, it is not possible to legislate or force interesting, concise and relevant field reports. The Haury-Martin exchange on prepared vs. non-prepared reports did not really get at the issues which are causing concern for many of us. . . . The report sessions must become a forum for exchanging ideas, not an excuse for exchanging anecdotes; discussions must focus on what was learned, not what was observed. . . . Symposia on the definition of some particular culture are too narrow, in my mind, to provoke real discussion. Symposia such as your Human Ecology one are too broad. . . . I sometimes get the feeling that my senior colleagues feel that debate, heated discussion, and strong disagreement have no place in intellectual affairs. . . . The most interesting aspect of [archaeology's] intellectual life is disagreement—disagreement between individuals and between groups of individuals or "schools." The issues that lie at the core of such disagreements are the ones which will provide exciting topics for symposia. . . . The desire for change, because almost everyone recognizes some problems, seems fairly general. We will be most likely to resolve these problems, I think, if we expect that it will probably take a period of years. The changes at a single Pecos Conference probably won't do [it].

Thank you for an interesting conference. . . . It fulfilled all the basic purposes of these meetings. One gets a chance to meet old friends and acquaintances, to hear . . . what they have been doing, and their plans for the future, then possibly catch up a little on current interests in the field. Isn't that enough?

Yes, I agree that the Pecos Conference this year sounded too much like "Well, we dug a PII site with PII pottery" with the addition of several terrible term papers and what appeared to be a poorly organized symposium on a currently "in" subject. . . . Future symposia . . . might . . . review the prominent holes or gaps in our knowledge. . . . We might also try to discuss terminology, preservation of sites from vandalism, professional-amateur relations, maintenance of study collections, etc.

I agree thoroughly with your recommendation of coordinating the talks on a given area. . . . And I also agree that any symposium ought to be more coherent or integrated than was the one last summer.

I was somewhat unhappy with parts of the Pecos Conference. It may be that I am just getting old and should bow to the newer way of doing things. However, it has been traditional that the Pecos Conference be an informal meeting where the active field workers get together at the end of the season and report on their findings. . . . Injection of the formal paper has no place in the Pecos Conference in my opinion. This is particularly true when the papers are sophomoric term papers. . . . The Pecos Conference conducted on the old concept fills a real need in Southwest archeology and is unique among scientific endeavors. I should like it to remain pretty much as it was.

Without presuming to encapsulate all the views expressed in these letters in a few sentences, it can at least be said that there seemed to be general agreement on several things. The field reports should be better grouped, and they should give more attention to the meaning of what was done than to the descriptive details. Specific recommendations for those reporting were suggested by several people. Students' "term papers" as well as the reading of any prepared papers were strongly objected to. Almost everyone valued the traditional informality of the Pecos Conference, a chance to meet one's colleagues and keep up to date on Southwestern research. The growing size of the Conference and the increased number of field reports were recognized, requiring more planning and "formality." But several saw this as being in conflict with the desire for "audience participation." The half-day symposium was examined in several letters, but no clear solution was proposed to either the problem of speakers talking about their own research instead of the subject of the session, or the difficulty of selecting a topic that was neither too narrow nor too broad. There was considerable agreement that the role of the chairman, whether of field reports or a symposium, was crucial to controlling long-winded talk on insignificant matters and to eliciting more comments and questions from the audience. Perhaps the use of the term *audience* is a clue to the central problem—the change from a conference in which everyone present had something to speak up about, to one at which the few spoke to the many. One of the few examinations of the conference phenomenon of which I know states, "To confer is to converse with; perhaps we should do that at conferences" (MacDonald 1962). This opinion was expressed in one form or another by many who responded to Euler's letter of 4 September 1969.

Even if no single formula for the "perfect conference" emerged from the replies to Euler's letter, there was a comprehensive view of many things that people wanted and didn't want, sometimes contradictory but often approaching a consensus, to be used as far as it might prove practical by the planners of next year's Conference. And as we shall see, much of it was used to good effect. Gumerman has commented (George Gumerman, letter to Woodbury, 2 August 1989) that, after a good many years of disagreement,

> I think the conflict between formal papers and field reports has sorted itself out in an interesting way. The Pecos Conference is still the Pecos Conference with all its informality and camping out. The regular and irregular meetings held on the Hohokam, Mogollon, and the Anasazi seemed to fill the gap for more synthetic prepared papers. It seems a good compromise and one that was selected almost subconsciously.

SANTA FE, 1970 (THIRTY-THIRD PECOS CONFERENCE) The planning committee for 1970 faced a daunting task: to arrange a Pecos Conference that would combine the best from traditional Conferences with at least some of the innovations urged in Euler's survey. The committee was chaired by Douglas W. Schwartz, School of American Research, with George H. Ewing and Stewart Peckham, both of the Museum of New Mexico, Bertha Dutton, Museum of Navajo Ceremonial Art, and Albert H. Schroeder, National Park Service. They were assisted by a local arrangements committee of ten people, a program development group of six, four people in charge of "Memorabilia," and for "Other Considerations" two Park Service stalwarts, Charlie Steen and Erik Reed. What roles all these people actually played is unknown.

On 18 February a memorandum was sent by Schwartz to "All Southwestern Anthropologists" stating that the meeting would be 21 and 22 August, at Santa Fe and Pecos, with at least part of it held outdoors, as at the first Conference. "The Planning Committee [here their names were listed] has carefully considered the comments arising from the Conference over the past few years, and have decided to make changes which we hope will relieve some of the problems of our growing size and diversity. These mainly relate to program policy." The memorandum went on to say,

> Except for the traditional business meeting, three half-day field sessions will be reserved for field reports. These are expected to be extemporaneous, no longer than ten minutes in length with no prepared papers read. Mimeographed abstracts and whole papers, of course, may be distributed and will be welcomed.

Reports will be grouped by area or topic. . . . We would like to encourage as many ethnologists, linguists, physical anthropologists, et al. as possible, working in the Southwest, to join us. . . . We are requesting that only one person on a specific project present a report. . . . Since the meeting will be held outdoors, it will not be possible to present slides, although a blackboard will be available.

The planning committee memorandum continued, "With the heterogeneity of our group and the dissatisfactions expressed recently, we have decided to hold no formal symposium." As it turned out, however, there was a symposium, of which details will be given below. "As a replacement for the formal symposium, on Saturday night individual meetings will be arranged for those groups who wish to meet together to discuss specific problems." Saturday morning would be left free to permit enjoyment of Santa Fe's annual Indian Market, "an excellent opportunity to see in one place what is going on in contemporary Southwestern Indian arts." The memorandum promised details on motels soon, mentioning the importance of reservations with deposits, as this was the height of the tourist season. And in closing it invited suggestions on the program, either by mail to Schwartz, or at the business meeting.

It was not long before "suggestions" were received, one of them addressed to the Pecos Conference Planning Committee by Mark P. Leone, who had recently joined the program in anthropology at Princeton University after receiving his Ph.D. from the University of Arizona in 1968. His letter (9 March 1970) is much too long to quote fully, but a few excerpts will indicate his views:

Gentlemen:
I feel I must protest some of the points in your recent memorandum on the 1970 Pecos Conference. . . . The ten-minute extemporaneous field report is not an effective medium of communication for complex research and was long ago abandoned by major scientific meetings. . . . Dictating mode of presentation seems outrageous, and coupling it with an expectation of ten minutes is a gratuitous affront. Few people can say anything extemporaneous that is simultaneously intellectually interesting to a diverse audience in ten minutes. . . . Perhaps the most exasperating point in your memo is the bland and buried phrase about liking to encourage other kinds of anthropologists working in

the Southwest to join in the Conference. This specious plea is part of the eternal litany of Southwestern archaeologists. They in fact provide neither the intellectually catholic atmosphere nor the concerted round of invitations and pressures needed to get ethnologists . . . [and others] to show up in any number. . . . The only item on your memorandum preeminently needing clarification is that concerning "one person on a project" presenting a report. Does project mean an institution? . . . Some institutions . . . offer aegis to as many as half a dozen separate research efforts at any one time. . . . How many reports does that mean might be offered?

Meanwhile Martin, of the Field Museum of Natural History in Chicago, had drafted a letter objecting to the planning committee's statement. He sent copies, dated 27 February, to several of his former students and to Thompson. Thompson (on 5 March 1970) replied with comments including, "I think you have made some good statements. In fact, I wondered why Doug had produced such an explicit document. I urge you to send it to him, but recommend that you tone down the end of your statement a little, perhaps by deleting the last paragraph altogether. . . . I disagree with you somewhat on the matter of 'field reports,' at the same time that I agree that we need more problems and interpretation."

Martin's letter, which he sent to Schwartz on 9 March 1970, first objected to meeting outdoors, even as "a well meant effort to recreate the atmosphere of our first Pecos Conference." He then described the synthesis achieved in 1927 and doubted that the 1970 Conference would "bring forth anything like the synthesis of present knowledge or the stimulus for new research which resulted from the first Conference." Martin then continued,

I regret that you say nothing about the quality of reports that might be expected. The usual field reports are a boring repetition of minute archaeological details. More importantly, most do not add to our understanding of Southwestern prehistory and do little to awaken interest in the potential of new directions for future research. Your decision that prepared papers may not be read is a real disappointment. This subject was taken up last year at the Pecos Conference by me, and I thought that general approval was given for reading papers. You have made no effort to upgrade the conference by requesting papers concerned with analysis [and] synthesizing.

Martin concluded: "I believe that the decisions you have made about the program policy are dangerous and ought to be seriously reconsidered. These decisions undermine even the minimum standards which we expect of ourselves (hopefully) and of our students both in the field and the classroom." He did not include the paragraph that Thompson had suggested omitting. In the 27 February draft it reads, "You state that comments received by the committee over the past few years were carefully considered. Pardon me, if I say bluntly that I cannot see that they were considered at all."

The background of Martin's views can be found in his two statements already cited, "The Revolution in Archaeology" and "Philosophy of Education at Vernon Field Station," in which he enthusiastically describes his conversion to the new goals of "advancing a hypothesis (. . . a statement of relationship between two or more variables)" and the testing of the hypothesis "with independent but relevant data. . . . to formulate probabilistic laws of cultural change." Impatience with those who differed with them is seen in both Leone's and Martin's letters, as well as eagerness to change the form and purposes of the Conference as rapidly as possible. By contrast, the writer of one letter to Euler quoted above, tempered his criticisms with the comment that the changes needed "will probably take a period of years."

In late June the Santa Fe planning committee sent out another memorandum, which dealt with both the general philosophy of Pecos Conferences and the specific plans for this one. It included some changes from the earlier memorandum, showing the effect of Martin's and Leone's letters, and perhaps other complaints no longer on record. But the tone was neither apologetic nor overly defensive:

> After a great deal of discussion concerning our initial announcement, the planning committee has come up with a schedule which not only maintains the informal aspects of past Pecos Conferences, but also takes cognizance of the diversity of interests and attitudes of all Southwesternists as their numbers continue to grow. *The philosophy of the Pecos Conference remains the same:* to provide a forum for those studying the culture of man in the Southwest, so as to pool knowledge and air differences

of opinion, to coordinate work with other fields of study and institutional representatives, and to consider the current status of archaeological research and related areas of interest [emphasis in original].

Friday morning and afternoon sessions would be for field reports, with these instructions:

For those who have not participated before, field reports should include the following basic data: Name of speaker, Name of institution represented, Locale of work, Research problem and its justification, High points of the project, Time-space aspects and relationship to areas studied nearby, Tentative conclusions [and] Plans or recommendations for future research.

Finally, it was emphasized that "field reports should be limited to ten minutes, plus another five minutes for discussion. We hope that most of these papers [*sic*] can be extemporaneous."

The dissatisfactions expressed in the letters to Euler, and doubtless in many informal discussions, suggested the following comments by the planning committee on the business meeting:

An important business session will be held on Friday afternoon, following the conclusion of the field reports. The place of next year's meeting will be discussed. Perhaps of greater concern this year, however, is just what direction the Pecos Conference is going to take: whether or not the pattern of this meeting in Santa Fe should be followed or modified at future Pecos Conferences. We hope that any of you who have definite feelings about the structure of the conference will discuss them at the meeting, and that we may come to conclusions which will give future conference hosts a definite base on which to make their plans [emphasis in original].

This announcement also said that the Pecos National Monument staff would conduct tours of the ruins after the business meeting and that a Friday evening "dinner with entertainment was planned," and warned that evenings in August could be cool and rainy.

A symposium was "being developed by Fred Plog" and would be on "Prehistoric Water-Control Systems in the American Southwest," with speakers on six areas ranging from northern Mexico to Mesa Verde. A session of prepared, formal papers was also announced:

> This is a departure from conferences of the past, but it is obviously a direction in which some people would like to go. Any formal paper which in previous years had been integrated into the field reports would now be presented in this session . . . [and] should focus on research conducted during the current year. This session will be chaired by Ezra Zubrow, and all correspondence relating to it should be sent directly to him c/o Field Museum Southwest Expedition, Vernon, Arizona 85940. These papers should be no more than 15 minutes long, with an additional five minutes for general discussion.

Return of an enclosed postcard was requested, to inform the planning committee of who would give reports and papers. Including Plog and Zubrow, both of whom had been at Martin's field research center in Vernon, was a tactful gesture toward Martin as well as a practical way to enlist the assistance of two of "his" most capable younger archaeologists.

Finally, to conclude this account of the unusually complex process of planning the Conference, another mailing should be mentioned. A memorandum of 30 March asked for an indication (on an enclosed postcard) of the topic and area of any field report that would be given. It also asked "if you plan to assemble a group for a mini-symposium on a specific subject (please specify) on the evening of August 22." The subjects and meeting places for these ad hoc sessions would be posted at registration. A list of twenty-four possible topics ranges from ceramic identification and trait distributions to economic archaeology, systems analysis, and health, education, and traditional history in the boarding school. With this the planning was completed for what was in many ways a new kind of Pecos Conference. Its innovations at least partly met the great variety of criticisms that had been expressed since the Prescott Conference.

With all the difficult decisions made, for better or worse, and myriad details worked out by those in charge of local arrangements, the Conference began on Friday morning, 21 August, with registration at the Laboratory of Anthropology. The first field report session was held at the Museum of International Folk Art, a few hundred feet away on Camino Lejo. The second session for field reports was at Pecos

11.2 The big tent and the conferees, Pecos National Monument, 1970. Arizona State Museum negative no. 27881. Photo by Helga Teiwes.

National Monument in the afternoon (Fig. 11.2). The business meeting was scheduled for 4:30, followed by a tour of the ruins, and at 6:30 "Dinner and Entertainment." This was generously hosted by Colonel E. E. Fogelson and his wife, the former Greer Garson (Douglas W. Schwartz, letter to the Fogelsons, 3 April 1970). They were enthusiastic supporters of Pecos National Monument, as well as many of the artistic and cultural organizations in Santa Fe. Their interest had been invaluable in protecting the Pecos Ruins from encroachment. "In 1964 they had donated 279 acres from their Forked Lightning Ranch to form a buffer zone around the . . . ruins" (Bezy and Sanchez 1988: 8).

The typed list of registrants, drawn up after the Conference, had 251 names, a record number for a Pecos Conference. The barbecue was attended by 350, which included people from the town of Pecos, with which the Monument staff had very cordial relationships. A special welcome was extended to Madeleine Kidder, who came out from Cambridge, Massachusetts. The other "Founders" at the 1970 Conference were Martin, Jesse Nusbaum, Hulda and Emil Haury, and Clara Lee Tanner (Fig. 11.3).

Once again Ellis's personal notes on the thirty-two field reports are our best source of information, although there is also a two-page list of speakers, apparently prepared for whoever chaired the sessions. But it has no topics for most of the speakers, except for being geographically subdivided—eight (!) areas for New Mexico (west-central, north-central, east-central, central, and so on), four for Arizona, and the remaining three areas listed as southwestern Utah, southeastern Nevada, and Colorado.

Ellis's list begins with a report on Grand Gulch, Utah, and continues with Mesa Verde; Black Mesa; early man near Greeley, Colorado; the Casamiro site, Prewitt, New Mexico; the North Rim of the Grand Canyon; Canyon de Chelly (two reports); the Joint Site, near Snowflake, Arizona; the carrying capacity of ecological systems; continuing work at Grasshopper Ruin; a Clovis site in the San Pedro Valley of southern Arizona; ecology of the Folsom type site; Las Colinas in Phoenix; Hohokam irrigation in the Buckeye Valley; salvage from historic buildings in Tucson's zone of destruction by urban renewal; the Cuervo-Puerco area; Mimbres sites; Spanish sites in the Chama Valley; a seventeenth-century Spanish site at Coronado State Monument, New Mexico; research at Arroyo Hondo, Santa Fe; Apache sites at Pecos and Las Vegas; and the early churches at Pecos. Three ethnological reports were given in the field report session: on Yavapai drinking, by Stephen J. Kunitz, University of Rochester;

*11.3 The "Founders" at the 1970 Conference (*left to right*): Hulda Haury, Paul S. Martin, Madeleine A. Kidder, Emil W. Haury, and Clara Lee Tanner. Arizona State Museum negative no. 27872. Photo by Helga Teiwes.*

on the ethnographic field school among the Black Mesa Navajo, by Jerrold E. Levy, Portland State University; and on Arizona Mormon ethnography, by Leone, of Princeton University.

There is a detailed list for the Saturday afternoon session of fifteen prepared papers, precisely listed for 1:30, 1:45, and so on. Seven of the papers were on studies of the Mormons, and others dealt with the University of New Mexico's field school in the Chama Valley, "prehistoric resource stress and models of field distribution," socio-political aspects of modern irrigation, disease variability in the White Mountain area of Arizona, economic development and growth, and the economy of the modern community of Pecos, New Mexico. The variety of topics, the preponderance of nonarchaeological topics, and the acceptance of prepared papers made this session very different from those of past Conferences, and presumably just what its organizers hoped for. In this sense it was a successful outcome of the disagreements that preceded the Conference, but it did not set a pattern that was consistently followed in the future. The gap between traditionalists and innovators remained, but the New Archaeology declined in importance as an issue, its tenets ever more widely accepted and its followers gradually less intolerant of other viewpoints. Its proponents changed, one might say, from crusaders to tolerated family members.

The Saturday morning symposium was unusually well organized, meeting excellently the challenge of past criticisms of sessions that lacked focus and permitted each speaker to go in his or her own direction. On 30 July Fred Plog had written with clear guidance for those who had agreed to give papers on aboriginal water-control systems in the Southwest. He wrote:

> Topic of papers. I intend to cover the following topics in my own paper: spatial variability in water control systems in the Upper Little Colorado, temporal variability . . . , natural environmental variables . . . [for] explaining variability . . . , social environmental variables . . . , impact of water control systems on their natural environment . . . and on their social environment. . . . Participants are most certainly not bound to a consideration of these areas.

Plog suggested a five- to ten-page paper and said that copies would be distributed at the first field report session, urging that each speaker bring about 150 copies. It was understood that papers would not be read, but only summarized by the speaker and discussed. The final program was as follows:

A descriptive summary of soil and water conservation practices and settlement patterns in the Kayenta Anasazi region, by Alexander J. Lindsay, Jr.

Social implications of Pueblo water management in the Northern San Juan, by Arthur H. Rohn

Irrigation and water works in the Rio Grande, by Florence Hawley Ellis

Water control in the Zuni area, by Richard B. Woodbury

Water control in the Upper Little Colorado, by Fred Plog

Prehistoric agricultural systems in the Vosberg locality, Arizona, by James B. Rodgers

Prehistoric "canal-irrigation" in the Buckeye Valley and Gila Bend areas in western Maricopa Country, Arizona, by Frank Midvale

The Casas Grandes area, by Charles C. Di Peso

Every paper was duplicated and available to the audience, as requested by Plog, another novelty for a Pecos Conference. This greatly increased audience participation. There was an audience of about sixty-five, in spite of the competition of the Indian Market and Indian dances.

As the planning committee had said in its announcement, the business meeting would be of unusual importance this year. It took place at 4:30 p.m. on Friday under the temporary conference tent at Pecos National Monument. A scribbled memorandum in Schwartz's handwriting outlines its general content. It began with the usual resolutions of appreciation to all those who had helped make the Conference a success. Next came the presentation by Schwartz of an award to Daniel T. Kelly. This award recognized the fortunate long-standing friendship between Kelly and A. V. Kidder and Kelly's role in deeding the site of Pecos, part of the Kelly lands, to the Archdiocese of Santa Fe, which in turn deeded it jointly to the School of American Research and the Museum of New Mexico. Subsequently, in 1963, Kelly was instrumental in seeing that the land was transferred to the National Park Service for development as a national monument. More of the background of these events can be found in *The Buffalo Head: A Century of Mercantile Pioneering in the Southwest* (Kelly 1972), the story of

Dan Kelly and his family, and of Gross, Kelly & Company, founded in 1867 (see also Anonymous 1970).

The next business to be taken up was choice of a meeting place for 1971. Schwartz recorded the vote as Tucson, twenty-nine; Fort Burgwin, forty-one; and Window Rock, sixty-nine. The meeting then took up what Schwartz's notes listed as "Program Philosophy for Next Year." Under this heading he notes the agenda that, as presiding officer, he had planned.

> This yrs. planning group [had] seen a developing split
> —reflected in past conferences
> —important that this be discussed
> —try to come up with a solution that is mutually satisfactory to all so we can get on with the objective shared by us all: trying to understand the nature of the SW option[s]
> —traditional—successful
> —formal—larger & changed nature of work
> —combination. chose this path this yr. reflected the needs of both groups.

As was often the case, no minutes of the business meeting were kept, and beyond this brief and informal agenda the only indication of how the business meeting went is contained in a letter from Haury to Schwartz (25 August 1970):

> Just a line to pay my respects and compliment you on the efficient handling of the Pecos Conference.
>
> I think the total effort deserves a high grade, but it is a matter of some concern that the gathering is getting so big that sheer mass will dictate where and how the meetings can be held. The business meeting could have developed into a cult orgy, but happily your skillful management prevented that "happening."
>
> Anyway please pass on to all of the people who helped you my thanks for a job well done.

The program at Window Rock in 1971 would continue this "combination" approach. Thus the 1970 Pecos Conference is an important watershed. Formal papers were finally accepted as a legitimate component of the Conference. The extemporaneous field reports continued as before, but with greater efforts to arrange them more meaningfully.

Since September 1947, when Paul Reiter responded to Haury's request for information on the logistics and costs of a Conference, there had been little information on the cost of a Pecos Conference. By 1970 the Conference had become much more complicated than the one in 1947, but most of the essential activities remained. A memo dated 9 September 1970 is headed "Pecos Conference—Unbalance Sheet." Its major entries are summarized in Table 11.1.

All in all $8.70 is a small discrepancy for an operation of this size, with so many details and so many people assisting. These figures do not include, of course, the contribution in staff time made by the Pecos National Monument and its considerable added expense in providing the tent under which sessions were held. Inevitably, future Conferences would become even more complex and costly.

But the final word should not be the balance sheet of receipts and expenses. Far more significant is the extent to which this Conference, after strong expressions of disagreement on the purposes and the appropriate form of the program, succeeded in accommodating these different views and in meeting so many of the demands made on it by all who were interested. Disagreements as strong as those of 1969–70 would not surface again until 1981, and in retrospect the 1971 innovations gradually appeared less extreme than they seemed at first.

WINDOW ROCK, 1971 (THIRTY-FOURTH PECOS CONFERENCE) The program for the 1971 Conference reflected changes in format that had been urged the year before but did not duplicate the 1970 program. It had a place for formal papers and one for the traditional field reports, and instead of a symposium there was a panel discussion on a topic of wide interest and with many divergent opinions.

Martin Link, curator of the Navajo Tribal Museum, the host institution, was 1971 chairman. Early that year Schwartz had written Link (11 January 1971) with "a few notes on last year's Pecos Conference which might save you a little of the time that I spent trying to consider what was important. I'll comment briefly on the items that I had on my work sheet." There follows a full three pages, with twenty-two numbered headings—announcements, accommodations, meeting rooms, and so on—an excellent set of guidelines for conference planning. Schwartz commented that although the sessions might all be in a single room, "last year we found that we were actually using three main areas; one for meeting, one for the display of publications, and one for coffee and general chitchat." Of registration he said, "This seems like a simple process, but it is amazing how many people we

Table 11.1. Costs of the 1970 Pecos Conference

Receipts

Fogelson gift	$250.00	
Registration and dinner fees deposited	1250.00	
Unaccounted for small change deposited	0.76	
Registration and dinner fees to Steen	200.00	
Total		$1700.76

Disbursements

Announcements: envelopes, printing, and mailing	96.09	
Registration supplies (tags, etc.)	40.88	
Plaque [the award for Kelly?]	6.20	
Refreshments [coffee $72.35, beer $180.00, ice $20.00]	272.35	
Dinner, W. C. Harvey Enterprises $750.00		
Balance due?	750.00	
Miscellaneous	15.65	
Total		1181.17
Supposed surplus		519.59
Cash in the bank		510.89
Unaccounted for shortage		8.70

needed to keep the flow going: cashiers, people signing receipts, individuals there to sign up people who had not determined before hand what paper they would give, somebody to answer questions on local arrangements, etc."

An equally demanding logistical element was the dinner:

> We arranged ahead of time with a caterer and went through a
> process of telling him over a five-month period, first, general
> estimation of cost, how many people would come, and then, as
> we received actual pre-registration, refining until the day before
> the meeting or the morning of the dinner when we told him the
> exact number based on ticket sales.

Schwartz's statement on program philosophy is a fine piece of understatement: "We spent quite a bit of time in the early [planning committee] meetings which we had in the fall and winter on what approach we would take. This was incorporated into the initial announcement and was modified right up to the end." On resolutions he observed:

"I found it useful to appoint somebody to this job far ahead of time. They still do it the night before, but know they have to do it and they can begin to think about what should be covered and said." He also commented on the problem of a symposium, saying, "If you want to have one I suggest that you include people in it who are really going to work at it."

Topic 19 is headed "Formal Paper Session." Here Schwartz distilled the experience of the past few Conferences and the diverging views expressed in 1970.

> I believe that on the basis of the experience we had, it is almost necessary to have one formal paper session for those people who do not feel that they can give off-hand field reports or individuals who want to do something besides field reports.

There is a five-part outline for the business meeting, the last item being "a discussion on program philosophy for next year. I am not sure it will make any difference in what is discussed, but I think people have to feel that they have had their say." This is not as cynical as it may sound—the angry outbursts from Martin and Leone the previous year probably derived partly from their feelings that plans were made and rules set down without an opportunity the previous year to discuss the pros and cons of the changes.

Link's arrangements at Window Rock indicate that he heeded many of these suggestions, but modified them to the circumstances of a very different setting for the Conference. His preliminary mailing mentioned that "this is the rainy season, so come prepared," and said that space would be available "to any institution wishing to display books and publications." At some earlier Conferences there had been announcements that certain publications were available, such as those of the Southwest Monuments Association, but by 1970 a full-scale book exhibit and sale had become an important part of the Conference. Link's tentative program included a "discussion centered on the theme, 'Should We Abolish the Antiquities Act?' "

A useful comment on this wording of the proposed discussion topic was sent to Link by Douglas H. Scovill, acting chief of archaeological research, NPS Southwest Archeological Center, Gila Pueblo, Globe. He wrote (2 June 1971):

> The question posed of "Should We Abolish the Antiquities Act?" will tend to force participants to one side or the other of a

strawman issue. . . . We suggest the question might be more appropriately framed as follows: How can we strengthen Federal, State, and Tribal laws relating to the preservation and conservation of archeological resources?

A final mailing headed "Welcome to the 35th [sic] Annual Pecos Conference," said, "Your host is the Navajo Tribal Museum and the Plateau Sciences Society." For the session of "formal papers" Link stated: "The Friday morning session will . . . include papers from field schools, other institutions, and individuals, and should focus on research in both archaeology and ethnology during the current year."

The Friday afternoon and Saturday morning sessions for field reports (27 and 28 August) would be "held under the Ramada at the Indian Camp just north of the Museum, and will be devoted to traditional field reports, [which] should be limited to ten minutes, plus another five minutes for discussion, and should be extemporaneous."

The "symposium" was an innovation, a discussion rather than a set of prepared papers, reflecting suggestions made to Euler and with the wording Scovill had suggested:

> The symposium this year will be more in the way of a panel discussion which in turn, should stimulate general discussion from the audience. The topic is a fairly controversial one, but one that should be aired and brought out into the open. The subject will be "How can we strengthen Federal, State, and Tribal laws relating to the preservation and conservation of archaeological and paleontological resources?"

Window Rock was described in the final mailing—its location, local shopping center, Arts and Crafts Guild, motor inn, and three available camping areas (Fig. 11.4).

At the Navajo Tribal Museum a reception and open house to celebrate its tenth anniversary would begin at 7 p.m. on Friday. A barbecue would be held Saturday evening near St. Michaels, followed by Indian dances.

Schwartz, in his letter to Link, commented that in 1970 the field trips didn't turn out as well as he had hoped. Link announced two field trips following the 1971 Conference:

> A choice of field trips will be offered to the conferees. If weather permits canyon travel, a tour will be given up into Canyon del

*11.4 The social hour at the Pecos Conference campground at Summit, near Window Rock, 1971.
Museum of Northern Arizona negative no. 71.346, photo by Marc Gaede.*

Muerto, but this will be restricted to 4-wheel drive vehicles. Another trip will be offered into the Manuelito area, a region rich in archaeological sites and a potential National and/or Navajo Tribal Park. If the Snake Dances are being performed on Sunday, individuals may wish to go to the Hopi villages and witness this event.

Although a resolution was passed at the business meeting, quoted below, there is no record of who spoke at the discussion of the antiquity laws or what views were expressed. Likewise, there is no record of who gave field reports or what they reported on, or of what "formal papers" were presented. This makes 1971 one of the most unsatisfactory Conferences in terms of recorded details of what took place. However, an attendance list was preserved, with 178 names and an organizational affiliation for nearly all of them. As would be expected, the Four Corners states are strongly represented, with a few also from California, Washington, British Columbia, Idaho, Nevada, and Texas. Farther east there are registrants from Kansas, Wisconsin, Illinois, Ohio, and Florida. To generalize, the Conference was increasingly a pan-Southwestern meeting with a far smaller proportion of attendance from elsewhere than in earlier years. Although academic institutions and museums are in the majority, federal agencies are quite strongly represented: two registrants from the U.S. Forest Service, two from the BLM, and twenty-four from NPS. In addition five people list Navajo Tribe affiliations, including the Ramah Navajo High School, the Navajo Tribal Museum, and the Navajo Tribe.

The final act of the Conference was a resolution deriving from the panel discussion. It was unanimously approved and sent to Rogers B. Morton, secretary of the interior, signed by Link, as chairman of the Pecos Conference, and by Schroeder, as chairman of the symposium. It stated:

Whereas: The rules and regulations accompanying the Antiquities Act of 1906 have not been revised since the year of its enactment, and,

Whereas: There are new landholding agencies such as NASA and the Department of the Navy which did not participate in the drafting of the original regulations, Now Therefore be it Resolved:

That the 1971 Pecos Conference hereby unanimously requests that the Secretary of the Interior convene a meeting, at the earliest possible date, to include himself, the Secretary of Agriculture, the Secretary of Defense, and the Heads of all other Federal Agencies whose land holdings include items of historical or archaeological significance, for the purpose of taking steps, with the aid of appropriate professionals, to review and (where appropriate) revise the regulations by means of which the Act of 1906 is implemented.

It would take us far from the Pecos Conference to survey the federal legislation and regulations that in the years ahead did greatly strengthen the intent of the 1906 act and further supplement it. An interesting sidelight on the efforts that were under way toward these ends comes from a letter to Link from Haury (3 November 1971), thanking him for the information on the Pecos Conference, and continuing,

> I think the proposal is proper and that the Uniform Rules and Regulations need to be reviewed. The idea of getting various Secretaries into the act is important also. Another suggestion I have is that we need a coordinator perhaps at the Assistant Secretary level to coordinate all the archaeological activities that are now taking place in the government. I am sorry I couldn't make the conference but as you may have learned, some of us were working in Denver at the time preparing for our session with Secretary Morton on September 3 [regarding NPS Advisory Board business].

12
Approaching Maturity, 1972–76

Although the conferences chronicled in this chapter saw continued tinkering with the formats of field reports and symposia, there were neither major changes nor substantial expressions of dissatisfaction with conference programs. The Conference was, in its late forties, achieving a considerable degree of maturity.

FLAGSTAFF, 1972 (THIRTY-FIFTH PECOS CONFERENCE) It is uncertain whether the 1972 Conference was the biggest yet, since the previous largest attendance, the 1970 Conference at Santa Fe and Pecos, is estimated as both 251 and 290 for participants, with 350 at the barbecue. For 1972 there are reports of "nearly 300" in the Museum of Northern Arizona's annual report for 1972, and "300+" in the newsletter of the Archaeological Society of New Mexico for 1 September 1972. Yet on the carefully prepared list of attendees (alphabetical, with mailing addresses) there are only 176 names. Even with the addition of a possible 100 or so spouses who did not register, and some participants who do not appear on the roster, the total would be short of 300. But we are not compiling a Pecos Conference Book of Records, so it is sufficient to say that there was a very large attendance—in the view of some old-timers, too large.

If a new record—or at the least a tie—were to be sought it would be for hosting the Conference for the *sixth* time, the Museum of Northern Arizona thus surpassing at this time all but the Chaco Canyon field school, where the Conference had met for the sixth and final time in 1947. However, the Conference already had met three times in Globe at the National Park Service center and would also be hosted by NPS at Mesa Verde in 1974 and 1980; at Salinas National Monument in 1985; at Pecos National Monument in 1977, 1982, 1987, and 1992; and at Bandelier National Monument in 1989. In addition the Park Service, at Pecos National Monument, shared responsibility with Santa Fe institutions for the 1970 and 1982 meetings.

The 1972 Conference was announced in May by postcard, giving the dates as 18 and 19 August. The interim chairman was Alexander J. Lindsay, Jr., and the cochairmen were William D. Lipe and R. Gwinn Vivian. On 2 August the full program was announced, as well as such details as a registration fee of $2 and a charge of $2 for each of the luncheons to be served Friday and Saturday. It gave information on camping, parking, pay phones, toilets, water taps for campers, messages, and emergency phone numbers for fire, sheriff, and hospital. The institutional host of a large meeting, such as the Pecos Conference had become, was faced with a wide spectrum of responsibilities and possible emergencies.

The program showed a return to tradition, with no formal papers, perhaps reflecting the views of the museum director, Edward (Ned) B. Danson (Fig. 12.1), who favored extemporaneous field reports as the heart of the Pecos Conference. On Friday morning, 18 August, registration would begin, and the day would be devoted to archaeological field reports. Saturday morning would have concurrent sessions, one to continue archaeological field reports, the other for ethnographic field reports. The half-hour business meeting would be followed by lunch, and the afternoon would be devoted to a symposium, "Yuman Research Problems," chaired by William H. Kelly, an ethnographer recently retired at the University of Arizona, where he had founded and directed the Bureau of Ethnic Research. Seven participants are listed: George Roth, Albert Schroeder, Henry Dobyns, Paul Ezell, Dorothy Hall, Marsha Kelly, and Robert Bell. Curiously, of all these, only two appear in the registration list, Schroeder and Hall. This may help explain the gap between "nearly 300" and 177. The AAA *Guide to Departments of Anthropology, 1972–1973* and the invaluable recollections of Schroeder (letter to Woodbury, 16 November 1988) provide identification for most of these participants. Roth was a psychological anthropologist at California State College, San Bernardino; Dobyns, an ethnographer and ethnohistorian on the faculty of Prescott College; Ezell, an archaeologist and ethnohistorian at San Diego State University; Schroeder, an archaeologist and historian on the NPS staff in Santa Fe; and Kelly, a student at the University of Arizona. Hall was working with the Colorado Indian Tribes near Parker and later was Arizona state preservation officer in Phoenix;

12.1 E. B. Danson and Paul S. Martin at the Pecos Conference in Flagstaff, 1972. Museum of Northern Arizona negative no. 72.2340, photo by Marc Gaede.

12.2 Robert Lister and Joe Ben Wheat, Pecos Conference, Flagstaff, 1972. Museum of Northern Arizona negative no. 72.2201, photo by Marc Gaede.

then, joining the U.S. Forest Service, he was stationed in California at Cleveland National Forest.

A field trip was planned for Sunday morning to visit several Sinagua sites being excavated by the museum, with Bruce Hudgens as guide for the trip.

One detail of this announcement echoes Danson's response to Robert Euler's 1969 inquiry, his preference for outdoor meetings "where the wind could blow away the cobwebs of one's mind." For the Flagstaff meeting, Danson said, "The meeting will be held under the pines [and] slide presentation will not be possible."

Just as for the 1971 meeting, there is a complete absence of information in the Pecos Conference Archives on who gave field reports, archaeological or ethnographic, or what was said at the symposium. The only existing report is the one published in the newsletter of the Archaeological Society of New Mexico, cited previously.

> The 36th [*sic*] Annual Pecos Conference on Southwestern Archaeology was held under the cool pines at the Museum of Northern Arizona in Flagstaff. The total attendance was 300+ and, as usual, more work was accomplished in informal discussions over lunch or beer.
>
> The 10-minute limitation on papers kept the sessions on schedule. The Symposium on Yuman Research Problems highlighted Saturday afternoon. Participants were . . . [as already listed].
>
> The Museum staff is to be congratulated on its attending to the small details which contributed to the success of the Conference, and the beautiful accommodations set up under the pines, complete with chemical toilets. (EDITOR'S NOTE: Thanks for the plentiful toilet paper and daily cleaning!).
>
> The 1973 Pecos Conference is to be held in Tucson, Arizona.

Fortunately Schroeder and Hall (letter from Schroeder to Woodbury, 16 November 1988) have recalled a few details of the Yuman symposium. Hall discussed the Mohaves; Roth, the Chemehuevi; and Dobyns, the Walapai. Ezell "reported on the excavations at the ghost town of La Paz on the Colorado River." Schroeder adds that:

> Discussions dealt with prehistory and history, noting the usual gaps spanning the two periods. Rogers' thesis of Yuman speakers moving into Arizona ca. 1400 vs. continuity across the gap,

Walapai-Havasupai ties, Hopi-Havasupai relations are a few aspects I can recall.

For the business meeting the official record is better. There are the texts of two resolutions, the first thanking those responsible for the Conference's "hospitality, facilities, and arrangements." The second was less routine. It was addressed to the Board of Geographic Names and Places and to Luna Leopold, chief research hydrologist, U.S. Geological Survey (USGS), Washington D.C. It pointed out that the USGS practice of identifying archaeological sites on its maps "often leads to increased pothunting and increased vandalism," particularly as there is very little protection of sites on public lands. The resolution urged a study leading to changes that would eliminate archaeological sites on these maps. My telephone inquiry in 1988 to the USGS Earth Sciences Information Center in Reston, Virginia, brought the response from Harry Zohn that significant archaeological sites, particularly those in national monuments or parks, "might be noted on a map," just as in the past, and as far as he knew there had been "no changes of policy."

As for the previous year, no report on the 1972 Conference was published in *American Antiquity* or in the journals of specifically Southwestern focus, except for the report just quoted from the New Mexico Archaeological Society's newsletter. Although the Conference grew in size, it is possible that the lack of published reports reflects the declining role that Southwestern archaeology was playing in the continent as a whole, while research expanded in many parts of the New World that had hitherto been relatively neglected and underreported.

Tucson, 1973 (Thirty-sixth Pecos Conference)   For only the fifth time in thirty-six meetings the Pecos Conference returned to a campus—a reminder of how strong the field conference tradition was and also of the frequent hospitality of the Chaco Canyon field school, the Museum of Northern Arizona, institutions in Santa Fe, and the National Park Service. A few decades earlier Tucson's summer heat would have made the Conference an ordeal, but air conditioning had virtually eliminated that problem by the 1970s. In July Vivian, as interim chairman, sent out a comprehensive notice of the meeting, to be held on the University of Arizona campus 17 and 18 August—no longer at "the end of the field season," as in earlier years. Cochairmen were Laurens C. Hammack and J. Jefferson Reid, with Sharon F.

Urban (known as "Shurban") in charge of local arrangements and Bruce B. Huckell managing registration.

This announcement describes an interesting innovation in field reports, which had been criticized in responses to Euler in 1969 for the lack of systematic organization or coherence at many past Conferences. In Tucson,

> we plan to organize the field reports on a topical and regional basis this year rather than a strictly regional approach. In doing so we hope to achieve more unity in the sessions. The report sessions will include, I. Field Schools, II. Sponsored and Private Research, and III. Contract Research.

The program would include "a session for prepared papers . . . scheduled for Saturday morning," a recognition of the dissatisfaction expressed in 1969. For all reports and papers a ten-minute limit was set and the use of slides discouraged.

Besides the new way of grouping field reports there was an innovation for the Saturday afternoon symposium, " 'Provenience Concepts: Room-fill and Floor.' This symposium, chaired by J. Jefferson Reid, will be organized by David R. Wilcox, Michael B. Schiffer, and J. Jefferson Reid. Questions to be considered by the organizers are appended." This would be a "method and theory" session rather than a consideration of an area or of regional relationships. The symposium questions that would be considered were:

1. What is the potential information in room fill?
2. How can relevant analytic provenience categories be identified in the field?
3. Can we define and objectively identify provenience concepts for regional comparison?
4. How can considerations of provenience concepts assist in the solution of information storage and retrieval problems?

The list of registrants for the Conference has 238 names on it, and appended to it is a list of 159 names of individuals, titled "additional mailing list," those not attending but who would be on the next year's mailing list. The combined total of nearly 400 can be taken as a minimum indication of how many people were known to be actively interested in Southwestern anthropological research in 1973. As would be expected, they were spread across the country from coast to coast, with the largest numbers in Arizona and New Mexico.

The program began Friday morning on the university campus, with opening remarks by Gwinn Vivian, Raymond H. Thompson, and Emil W. Haury. Surviving notes for Haury's remarks begin with a quotation from Paul S. Martin and Fred Plog's new (1973) book, *The Archaeology of Arizona: A Study of the Southwest Region:* "The Pecos Conference . . . [was] the first conference of Southwestern workers to discuss the new ideas that were rocking our world. It is still held annually although nowadays it is spiritless and given to mouthing old incantations; it needs a rebirth." Haury had circled *new* and written "to codify ideas that had accumulated up to 1927! The first time SW arch[aeologists] were talking *with each other!* & I think that's what the Conf should be today" (emphasis in original).

Marginal notes on this memorandum suggest the trend of Haury's further remarks: "What *are* the goals and aims of the conf? Intell[ectual] env[ironment] *has* changed since 1927—it is *not* the same today. What we need is for *us* to decide. . . . The value of the PC has been debated for years, the latest published statement of which I am aware is Martin & Plog." The published condemnation by Martin and Plog and Haury's response make it clear that the schism that surfaced in 1970, with criticism of the initial plans for the Conference in Santa Fe, had not fully healed. But the large attendance year after year indicates that dissatisfaction was not widely and strongly enough felt to discourage participation. Regardless of ongoing discussion of the "ideal" format for the Pecos Conference, it continued to be enthusiastically supported.

With William Robinson chairing, reports began at 9:30 Friday morning, with field schools. The reports listed were: New Mexico (Jim Judge, Stan Bussey); Colorado (Charles Adams, Dave Breternitz, Carmie Lynn Toulouse); Arizona (Izumi Shamada, Stephanie Whittlesey, David Wilcox); California (Ezell or Barbara Loughlin). Before the luncheon break, private research was presented, with reports by Florence Hawley Ellis, Ted Frisbie, and Timothy Kearns.

The afternoon session, with Keith Anderson chairing, was devoted to sponsored projects, presumably those of institutions rather than "private" individuals. The reports listed were: New Mexico (Doug Schwartz, Cynthia Irwin-Williams [2], Randy Morrison, John Thrift, Tom Windes, Donald Phibbs, Patty Jo Watson or Steve LeBlanc); Arizona (Lex Lindsay, Don Morris, Jim Schoenwetter, Fred Gorman); Utah (Bill Lipe); California (Ezell or Loughlin). That evening the

Mexican dinner was held at 8:30 for the fortunate sixty who had secured tickets.

Saturday began with field reports on contract archaeology, chaired by J. Jefferson Reid. The July announcement of the Conference had said:

> A Contract Research session will, we hope, elicit reports from persons preparing studies for Environmental Impact Statements, etc. If the response for this session is great enough, we will begin it with a summary of current legislation, its impact on cultural resources, and some thoughts on the future of archaeology.

The list, which included Friday's reports by category and state, merely has an alphabetical list for contract archaeology, without any indication of whether the suggested "summary of current legislation" was presented, but the number of reports, nearly two-thirds as many as on Friday, reflects the great expansion that was occurring in contract research. Those reporting were: Bruce A. Anderson, Breternitz, David E. Doyel, Ezell, Loughlin, Rex E. Gerald, Mark Grady, Alexander J. Lindsay, Ronald V. May, Lloyd M. Pierson, Schroeder, Douglas Scovill, Ric Windmiller, Don Wood, Kearns, Keith Anderson, and Mark Raab.

The program does not indicate any session for ethnological reports, and none of the ethnologists and linguists who had reported at recent Pecos Conferences appears on the registration list. The Conference had once more reverted to its traditional archaeological exclusiveness.

Saturday morning ended with the business meeting, for which Urban, of the Arizona State Museum, has provided notes. There was no "old business." New business began with a telegram to Mrs. A. V. Kidder, in Cambridge, Massachusetts. Then the problem of the next year's meeting place was discussed, and Ronald R. Switzer, superintendent of Mesa Verde National Park, said that new facilities had become available there, making a Pecos Conference possible there for the first time. Meeting places further into the future were also discussed, as Urban's notes conclude:

1974—Mesa Verde;
1975—Salmon Ruin;
1976—Hermosillo [Kino Bay];
1977—Pecos (50th Anniversary) & every 5 years;
1978—Flagstaff (50th Anniversary for MNA).

It is remarkable, in view of the informality of the Pecos Conference and its lack of permanent officers, headquarters, dues, and other customary organizational paraphernalia, that the next five meetings all took place as scheduled at the 1973 business meeting! The Conference was achieving a stability and continuity often lacking in the past.

The Saturday afternoon session was the symposium, "Provenience Concepts, Room-fill and Floor," chaired by one of its organizers, Reid. Not only was the symposium taped, but a transcript was available for use in this history.

The presentations and discussions at the symposium were long and complex, and here I can only quote parts of them and briefly describe the rest. Part of the information on a mimeographed sheet that was distributed is given in Figure 12.3.

The handout illustrated a few of "a large set of acceptable provenience designations that can be generated, depending on the specific content assigned to the terms by an investigator." One of the examples is: "B(1)(c)C. In this statement, a nonportable object has been culturally deposited when a behavioral space was abandoned. A firepit falling into disuse at the same time as the plaza in which it functioned was abandoned could be symbolized by this expression."

In spite of gaps in the transcript it is apparent that there was lively discussion following the initial statements, and that skepticism and disagreement were sometimes expressed. It is probably Wilcox who spoke first:

> Are you bothered by cultural irregularity? At this time I'll give a definition of a [concept of?] provenience that I use and will attempt to illustrate it as I go through this discussion in the hopes of eliciting further discussion (laughter). You've got the bag and you've got something to put in the bag. . . . there is the problem of how you decide up here [?] which of these you put in the bag and which you don't. . . . The problem of that inclusion applies to that object or any collection of objects to the set and what goes into a set or what doesn't go into a set. The problem of provenience is deciding which rules to use or what to use as a rule and what we are suggesting here is that you have to select inclusion rules [?] that are going to help us to talk about past human behavior and in general how to find a provenience concept.

The next speaker was Schiffer, who discussed first the problem of the comparability of data and then the distinction between archaeolo-

This handout represents a trial formulation of a systematic lexicon and grammar for designating behavioral proveniences.

Basic concepts and definitions

A. *Portable object.* A cultural artifact which in normal use is not fixed at one location.

Examples: most pottery, chipped stone, bone tools.

B. *Nonportable object.* A cultural artifact which in normal use is fixed at one location.

Examples: mealing bin, firepit, doorway, wall, ventilator.

C. *Behavioral space.* A unit of space within which activities were carried out.

Examples: roof, floor, plaza, corridor, courtyard.

A grammar is presented "by which the depositional processes relating portable objects to nonportable objects (A to B), portable objects to behavioral spaces (A to C), and nonportable objects to behavioral spaces (B to C) can be designated."

			at the construction of (a)
	culturally (1)		during the use of (b)
A or B is		deposited	B or C
	nonculturally (2)		at the abandonment of (c)
			after the abandonment of (d)

12.3 Information from a handout for the symposium on "Provenience Concepts: Room-fill and Floor" in Tucson, 1973.

gists' "unit of recovery space," by which they record an excavation, and the "systemic context units for behaviorally significant proveniences. . . . Systemic context provenience answers the question, 'How are these materials culturally deposited?' The identification of materials resulting from the same process will go a long way toward solving the comparability problem."

Reid then returned the discussion to the "grammar" of the handout, saying, "We must devise an exclusive grammar with which we can express to others, to ourselves first, but to others, the systemic relationships between the material objects and behavioral spaces that we have observed in the field." He concluded, "Now is the time to consider how to store information for efficient and behaviorally meaningful manipulation of [unintelligible] the future. I think we have prepared statements by Patty Jo Watson and Steve LeBlanc." Much of the ensuing exchange is difficult to follow satisfactorily, due to gaps (probably some of the speakers were not at the microphone).

Irwin-Williams commented, "Now when we got to the Salmon site it was quite evident that we had to set up a totally computerized system and this had a couple of extra benefits in addition to the fact that we can record and [unintelligible] rather quickly. One of them is that it has made us think consistently . . . because the computer format doesn't have any room for [haziness?]."

It is not clear in the transcript when Watson followed Irwin-Williams, but the answer to a question was, "Yes, I certainly do. Yea, absolutely, both Mr. [?] and myself do this two or three times every day just to make sure no one is goofing up. I was born a field archaeologist and I haven't changed a bit; the idea of being tied up in a lab—I couldn't take it." From the audience came the comment, "Yea, Patty!" Later she repeated that "we are constantly running morning and afternoon checks on what's going on in the site, so I think there is a good bit of control, though it is a little bit like a zoo sometimes."

Another exchange related to digging in quadrants and the technique of recording in order to have a "three-dimensional diagram" of the fill. "You asked about quads and we do quads but the quads aren't done for behavioral reasons largely, except in a very gross way, they are done for stratigraphic reasons. Now the grids are done for behavioral reasons."

It is clear, in spite of the gaps in the record, that the informal, colloquial exchanges reflect a serious concern with difficult problems. Discussion often veered from the lexicon and grammar presented at the start to problems of recording data in the field and the relationship of "recovery spaces" to "behavioral spaces." But since the purpose of a symposium is to exchange ideas rather than reach consensus on a conclusion, the full and sometimes skeptical participation by the audience as well as the symposium planners is a measure of its substantial success.

This unique and lively symposium was the final scheduled event of the 1973 Conference. The rapid give-and-take, the questions and doubts, the explanations, and the search for areas of agreement might, with little stretching of the imagination, be thought of as echoing the vigorous and exploratory nature of the first Pecos Conference.

Mesa Verde, 1974 (Thirty-seventh Pecos Conference)   The National Park Service wisely made careful plans for hosting the Pecos Conference at Mesa Verde National Park on 19 and 20 August 1974. Even though no registration list has survived (unless buried deep in some NPS warehouse containing old records) and admitting the possibility of exaggeration, the estimate of more than 400 in attendance makes it the largest Conference yet, by a good margin. The staff at Mesa Verde was, fortunately, used to handling overflow crowds every summer, closing camp grounds when they were full, holding tours to a manageable size, and directing visitors to less crowded areas (if there were any in August).

The interim chairman of the 1974 Conference was Breternitz (University of Colorado); the chairman of local arrangements was Switzer, general superintendent of the park; and the program chairman was Euler (Fort Lewis College). Details of the arrangements appear in the July 1974 *Mesa Verde Black on White* (11, No. 7), a mimeographed newsletter for the park staff (it also announces "The First Annual Mesa Verde Bed Race" for 16 August, with complex and fascinating rules, and "Jesse Walter Fewkes Day" for 24 August). The Pecos Conference was to be preceded on 18 August by a meeting of the Southwestern Anthropological Research Group (SARG, founded in 1971), chaired by Lipe, of the Museum of Northern Arizona, Flagstaff. Although the SARG meeting was independent of the Pecos Conference, most or all of its group were also Conference participants.

The first day of the Pecos Conference would be devoted to the customary field reports, all morning and afternoon, followed by a barbecue at 6:30. Field reports would continue on the morning of 20 August; the business meeting would take place from 1:30 to 2 P.M.; and then a four-hour symposium would be held, "Cultural and Environmental Change in the Mesa Verde Area."

In the information for conferees, an "important notice to those planning to present field reports" said that "in order to stimulate informal discussion and to provide adequate time for each report, all presentations of field work must be oriented either to some aspect of cultural process (for example, sociopolitical structure, economics, environmental adaptation, etc.) or to the dynamics of culture history." This was a positive way of saying what had often been said negatively— don't just report the size and location of fireplaces or list the pottery types found. Instructions to speakers continued with a worthwhile innovation: "If you wish merely to *describe* your summer survey or excavations, please send a one-page, typed abstract, not later than August 10th, to Ronald R. Switzer. . . . It will then be xeroxed for distribution at the conference." Eleven of these have survived (perhaps all there were) in the Pecos Conference Archives and will be described later.

It was also urged that each institution select one speaker to report on each major project and one to summarize several minor projects. This was a relaxing of the earlier limit of one report per institution. These instructions ended, "We hope, in this way, to make the Pecos Conference a more valuable contribution to contemporary archaeological thought."

The Park Service set up a preregistration system; a fee of $7.50 included registration "plus coffee, donuts and one adult barbecue ticket," and a Pecos Conference sticker also provided free admission to the park for those registering before 15 July.

Those who came to the Conference received the most impressive handout of any Conference thus far: the official NPS pocket guide to the park; a brochure, "Welcome to Colorado's Mesa Verde Country," from the Mesa Verde Country Innkeepers Association, describing other national monuments and scenic areas; a twenty-four-page "Pictorial Guide to Mesa Verde National Park" by Ansel F. Adams; a mimeographed sheet for park visitors with details of self-guided and ranger-guided tours, and the evening campfire program; and a notice, "Trail Information—Hiking in Mesa Verde N.P. is RESTRICTED"—all this in a two-pocket folder decorated with a Mesa Verde black-on-white mug on the cover.

Unfortunately, after this good start our information on the Conference becomes much less complete. There is no registration list or field report program. Fortunately William A. Perret, president of the Albuquerque Archaeological Society, reported on the Conference in the society's newsletter (Perret 1974), including these comments:

The Conference . . . was in an ideal setting. For this occasion
the National Park Service had opened the old campground—
presently the picnic area—for tent and camper use so that we . . .
were able to stay on the rim of Chapin Mesa overlooking Spruce
Canyon. All sessions of the Conference, except the barbecue
were held at the old campfire amphitheater, also on the rim
overlooking Spruce Canyon. Some estimate of the caliber of
the papers presented may be made from the fact that those hard
stone seats . . . were filled most of the time.

Ellis's 1974 Pecos Conference notebook provides a good idea of the
scope of the field reports:

Dan Wittard, high density of Archaic sites
Dick Chagman, tool manufacture and use as man-environ-
ment interaction
Al Hayes, what happened A.D. 500–1000?
David Kirkpatrick, Cimarron area
Stan Bussey, Winston, a big Mimbres-Salado site
Cynthia Irwin-Williams, settlement patterns south of Cabe-
zon [New Mexico]
Perre Moran, Chaco road systems
Peter Pillis, study of modern Grand Canyon trail systems
A. E. Dittert, north side of Gila, sites and dams
Donald Weaver, Agua Fria area
John Clonts, training Indians for salvage on their own reser-
vations
"Grasshopper man [Reid], wants recollections of old timers,
collecting tapes on devel of SW archeol."
David Wilcox, Hay Hollow
Howard Davidson, Kaiparowitz Plateau
Ted Frisbie, ethnoarchaeology, Pueblo trade networks

In addition, the eleven handouts, a rarity at Pecos Conferences, provide more details of some of these reports.

1. "University of Colorado Archaeological Research Cen-
    ter, Mesa Verde National Park," describing four separate
    programs.
2. "Gu Achi Site, Papago Indian Reservation, Arizona," by
    John P. Clonts, NPS.

3. "Seri Indian Food Plants," by Richard Felger, Arizona-Sonora Desert Museum, and Mary Beck Moser, Summer Institute of Linguistics, University of North Dakota.

4. "The Colorado State University Archaeological Field Program in Northwestern Colorado," by Calvin H. Jennings.

5. "Johnson Canyon [southwestern Colorado] Project," by Bruce G. Harrill, Laboratory of Tree-Ring Research, University of Arizona.

6. "Archaeological Research at Nambe Falls, New Mexico," by Mark Henderson, Southern Methodist University.

7. "Excavations at Milk Ranch Point, San Juan County, Utah," by Bruce D. Louthan, Brigham Young University.

8. "Photographic Reconnaissance of Canyon del Muerto and Black Rock Canyon, Canyon de Chelly National Monument," by James T. Rock, NPS.

9. "Archaeological Survey of Los Alamos County," by Charlie R. Steen, NPS.

10. "Survey of the Santa Cruz River and Arroyo Seco Drainage Systems, New Mexico," by Alston Thoms, Texas Tech University.

11. "Archaeological Investigations in the Two Forks Reservoir Area, Colorado," by Ric Windmiller, University of Colorado.

Robert Lister, Chaco Center, NPS, chaired the symposium, "Cultural and Environmental Change in the Mesa Verde Area." It is summarized in considerable detail by Perret in the newsletter report cited above and by William R. Sundt in two subsequent issues of the same newsletter (9, Nos. 11 and 12). More details are provided by Jack E. Smith, chief archaeologist, Mesa Verde National Park (letter to Woodbury, 8 December 1982). Alden Hayes began by outlining the cultural sequence of the Mesa Verde area, specifying the major features characterizing Basketmaker III through Pueblo III and then describing the environmental history of the region. Breternitz then pointed out the ways in which Mancos Canyon differed from the Mesa Verde proper, including mention of cannibalism in the 1200s. Arthur Rohn, Wichita State University, whose work was in the Montezuma Valley, northwest of Mesa Verde, suggested that *it* was the heartland of the cultural region and Mesa Verde was peripheral—smaller sites, fewer kivas per site, fewer tower structures, and no stockaded villages. The Cedar Mesa area was described by Lipe, who said that after Basketmaker II it was a western periphery of the Mesa Verde district, its pottery similar to Mesa Verde but "a different dialect." Irwin-Williams, of Eastern New Mexico University, discussed the San Juan area, and Thor N. V. Karlstrom, Center for Astrogeology, USGS, reported on the "correlation of geological, dendrochronological and pottery stratigraphy" on Black Mesa.

The business meeting was limited to the customary matters, beginning with notice of the deaths of Paul S. Martin, Anna O. Shepard, Ernst Antevs, and Frank Midvale.

SALMON RUIN, 1975 (THIRTY-EIGHTH PECOS CONFERENCE)   Until the 1970s the Salmon Ruin, a large Chacoan outlier, was relatively unknown to most Southwestern archaeologists. It is on the San Juan River, a few miles south of Aztec Ruin National Monument, about three miles east of Bloomfield, and about fifty miles north of Chaco Canyon. Then in 1971 Irwin-Williams began investigations there, which were expanded to a full-scale research program from 1972 to 1978. The work is described (Lindsay 1974) as having 100 students and specialists "investigating the large-scale Chacoan intrusion into the area as it typifies the peripheral Chacoan manifestations and as a key to improved understanding of the Chaco phenomenon itself." The Salmon site, most of it built in the eleventh century, was the second largest of all Chacoan outliers, surpassed only by the Aztec West Ruin, and was among the largest of all Chacoan buildings (Vivian 1990: 74). A field laboratory had been set up at the new San Juan County Archaeological Research Center and excavation was continuing in 1975, when the Pecos Conference met there. So this meeting represented a return to a scene of active field work, as had been the case at Pecos, Chaco Canyon, Point of Pines, Fort Burgwin, Nuevo Casas Grandes, and Mesa Verde.

For the Salmon Ruin Conference, Irwin-Williams was program chairman, Jo Smith of the San Juan County Museum Association was local arrangements chairman, and Karol Klager, of the same museum association, was coordinator. The Conference took place on 15 and 16 August, with a meeting of SARG on 14 August and an optional field trip to Chaco Canyon on 17 August, as well as the possibility of attending the rodeo and Indian games and dances and seeing exhibits of Indian crafts and arts at the Inter-Tribal Indian Ceremonial in Gallup, about 125 miles away to the south.

Conference participants received nine pages of program and information, including the following:

To Those Planning to Present Field Reports. Presentations
which simply describe field work will be limited to five minutes. Presentations which deal with the larger implications of
the field research (in terms of culture dynamics, culture history,
culture/environmental interaction, etc.) will be limited to 10–
15 minutes. . . . Institutions should select one speaker to report
on each major project and/or one speaker to summarize several
minor projects.

Registration, at $7.50, included "conference costs, coffee, soft drinks,
doughnuts, and one Barbecue/Beer ticket." There were also additional barbecue tickets as well as optional lunch tickets: $1.50 first day
(Navajo tacos), and $1.25 second day (picnic lunch). Further, "because
excavations are still going on at the Salmon Site, and because many of
the high masonry walls have not yet been stabilized and are extremely
dangerous, we request that Conference participants visit the ruins *only*
on the regularly scheduled tours (Friday 1–2 P.M. and Saturday 8–10
A.M). . . . We also request that you sign up for the tour time which
you prefer."

We have no record of the attendance—once again the list of registrants has disappeared—but the unfamiliar location and an active
excavation program promised a large crowd.

The meeting of SARG the day before the start of the Pecos Conference was reported on later during the Conference by Lipe, who
explained that SARG had held a closed meeting, a small working session focused on its data bank and cross tabulation of variables from
the bank and on analysis of patterning in the data.

From the standpoint of sources for this history, 1975 is important as
the beginning of detailed notes on the Conferences by Urban, which
she has generously made available. For 1975 her notes fill more than
twenty-six pages of a large notebook and include nearly all the reports,
with a paragraph for each.

The first day began with registration and announcements, followed
by field reports. There was an announcement that the 1976 Conference would be at Hermosillo, Sonora, as planned the previous year.
And Urban (1975) noted that "Cynthia [Irwin-Williams] will not hold
another meeting!"

The field reports provide an excellent panorama of archaeological
research going on in the Southwest in 1975. They began with New
Mexico, and speakers included (affiliation is given when known):
Stewart L. Peckham (Museum of New Mexico), Albert E. Ward

(Museum of Albuquerque), (?) Hacker, and Paul Grigg, all describing work at historic sites; Joseph Gallagher (Southern Methodist University), Brantley Dam on the Pecos River; Jack Bartram (University of New Mexico), Tijeras Pueblo; Mark Kinsey (Southern Methodist University), Nambe Falls; Stanley D. Bussey (New Mexico State University, Las Cruces), work at a bulldozed forty-room pueblo between Luna and Springerville; Steven A. LeBlanc (Mimbres Archaeological Center), Mattocks and other Mimbres sites; David M. Brugge (National Park Service Chaco Center), eighteenth-century Navajo sites in the Chaco area; Pierre E. Morenon (Eastern New Mexico University and Southern Methodist University), survey in Carson National Forest, northern New Mexico; Frank J. Broilo (Office of Contract Archeology, University of New Mexico), survey in northwest New Mexico, on Navajo Reservation; David Stuart and William Allen (also Office of Contract Archeology), one-to-three-day surveys of small projects such as well drilling, for environmental impact statements, in northwest New Mexico; James G. Enloe, site survey in New Cochiti Reservoir area. This concluded the morning's field reports.

Following lunch and tours of the Salmon Ruin and the laboratory, field reports continued, moving from the Ramada to the Bloomfield High School. They included Dick [Catadman?] (Office of Contract Archeology, University of New Mexico), reporting further on the Cochiti Reservoir; Dorothy Koster Washburn, analysis of symmetry in ceramic decoration; W. James Judge (National Park Service Chaco Center), review of the past five years of the Chaco Center, including field work by Dennis Stanford, Alden C. Hayes, Thomas Lyons, and Robert Baine, followed by an outline of future research plans; Vorsila L. Bohrer (Eastern New Mexico University), reconstruction of past vegetation of the drainage of the Rio Puerco, northwest of Albuquerque; and Irwin-Williams (Eastern New Mexico University), the archaeology of the Rio Puerco of the East, and a review of the work at the Salmon Ruin to date.

Field reports from Arizona were next called for. They included: E. Jane Rosenthal, Archaic to historic sites on highway rights-of-way in the Papaguería; Donald E. Weaver, Jr. (Arizona State University), the first year of the Cultural Resource Management program, with some twenty small projects, particularly Hohokam and Pima-Papago; Bettina Rosenberg (Arizona State University), archaeological impact statement on hydroelectric plant to be built at foot of Sierra Estrella; Alfred E. Dittert (Arizona State University), field school research in the Tonto Basin; Glendy Garmo [?], analysis of room functions and their social implications in a Pueblo III site in east-central Arizona; Peter Pilles (U.S. Forest Service), progress in protecting forest lands from pot hunters, including aerial surveillance; David Kirkpatrick (Eastern New Mexico University), a nineteenth- and twentieth-century log cabin site [near Cimarron, New Mexico?]; David Doyel (University of Arizona), Salado and Hohokam sites on Pinal Creek; A. Eugene Rogge (University of Arizona), alternatives to Orme Dam at junction of Verde and Salt rivers; Wilcox (University of Arizona), prestabilization research at Casa Grande National Monument; Reid (University of Arizona), the thirteenth season of the field school at Grasshopper; Carol Weed (Southern Illinois University), Central Ecotone Project, thirty-five miles north of Phoenix; Euler (Grand Canyon National Park), survey of park sites, including pueblos, campsites, and lithic scatters; Pamela C. Magers (National Park Service Western Archeological Center), intensive survey of Canyon del Muerto.

Only one report was presented for northern Mexico, by Beatriz Braniff (Instituto Nacional de Antropología e Historia), who said, "Wanted a change from the Olmec and jade so moved to Sonora. Trying to figure out what is going on up here." She also spoke of work by Richard A. Pailes (University of Oklahoma) along the Sonora River, and by Kenneth G. and Marion E. McIntyre of West Vancouver, British Columbia, at a Clovis site near Hermosillo.

Reports on Colorado and Utah came next: Bradley A. Noisat (San Jose State University), water control structures southwest of Hovenweep National Monument; Joseph Winter (San Jose State University), ethnobotanical survey of Hovenweep area; Jerry Bair (National Park Service), review of twenty years of work in the Trinidad Reservoir area; Susan Applegarth (Fort Lewis College, Colorado), survey and excavation of an industrial park area and of a highway project; Breternitz (University of Colorado), site survey by Mesa Verde Research Center, reexcavation at Lowry Ruin, and stabilization at Escalante Ruin; Joy Brown (University of Colorado Museum), further work at Yellow Jacket; Alan Schraedle (University of Utah), field school in Canyon Lands National Park; Craig Harmond (Brigham Young University), field school in Montezuma Canyon; Charlotte Benson (University of Washington and Museum of Northern Arizona), survey of Cedar Mesa; J. Terry Walker (Brigham Young University), excavation for U.S. Forest Service near Monticello; Jim Dikeman (University of Colorado), analysis of Mesa Verde lithic material.

For Texas there was a single report, by Thomas C. O'Laughlin

(Centennial Museum, El Paso), on continuing work on the Jornada Branch, in the Hueco Basin, and on Fort Bliss Military Reservation.

With this the day's field reports ended. A large number concerned cultural resource management, many by contract with federal agencies (particularly NPS) and with industrial organizations. If the format of the 1973 Conference in Tucson had been used—reports grouped into field schools, private research, sponsored projects, and contract archaeology—the trend would be even more noticeable. There was a growing need for carrying out essential archaeological work ahead of destructive activities, with fewer archaeologists undertaking field work unrelated to problems of cultural resource management.

The evening offered the opportunity to see new archaeological films at the Bloomfield High School.

Saturday morning, 16 August, provided more tours of the Salmon Ruin and laboratory operations, and additional reports. Mark A. Grady spoke on the complexities of securing National Register approval for sites. Lipe reported on the SARG meeting of 13 August. Roy Reeves (Inter-Agency Archeological Service Program) spoke of the various congressional acts through the years that had established protection for archaeological resources and in some circumstances funding for research. The agency had field offices in Denver, Atlanta, and San Francisco.

These final reports were followed by the business meeting, which discussed possible places for the 1978 Pecos Conference. The Museum of Northern Arizona, Flagstaff, was chosen, for what would be its seventh time as host institution. Formal notice was taken of the deaths of Donald J. Lehmer, Blair College, Nebraska; Earl H. Swanson, Jr., Idaho State University; and Leslie A. White, most recently of the University of California, Santa Barbara, after forty years at the University of Michigan.

"Understanding the Chaco Phenomenon" was the subject of the Saturday afternoon symposium. By any standard, the archaeological remains in Chaco Canyon are among the most impressive and most studied in North America. For nearly a century a series of ambitious, large-scale investigations had taken place, including those of the Hyde Exploring Expedition with Richard Wetherill and George H. Pepper; Neil M. Judd, sponsored by the Smithsonian Institution and the National Geographic Society; and Edgar L. Hewett of the School of American Research and the University of New Mexico. Nevertheless, questions, disagreements, and unsolved problems remained, and they continued to attract many archaeologists' attention. "The large ruins at Chaco Canyon are the most spectacular evidence of what formerly has been termed the 'Bonito Phase,' and more recently the 'Chaco Phenomenon'" (Lekson 1986: 5). "Much of the innovative research accomplished in the American Southwest within the past decade has focused upon aspects of the Chaco Anasazi regional system" (Doyel and others 1984: 37).

In 1969 a long-term interdisciplinary research program was begun as a joint effort of the National Park Service and the University of New Mexico, carried out through the establishment of the Chaco Center. By 1975 the time was right for a review of what was known about Chaco Canyon and the Chaco Phenomenon and how this vast amount of information should be interpreted. Six years later, at the SAA annual meeting in San Diego (May 1981) the Chaco Center sponsored two symposia on the Chaco Phenomenon, before a larger audience (Judge and Schelberg 1984).

The Pecos Conference symposium papers will be summarized only briefly here, based on Urban's notes:

1. Thomas R. Lyons (Chaco Center): The remote sensing project has provided maps with much archaeological detail, including roads, but follow-up on the ground is essential.

2. Alden Hayes (Chaco Center): About A.D. 1050 major changes occurred in Chaco Canyon—construction of large, symmetrical multiroom structures, elaboration of great kivas, introduction of macaws and copper bells, intensive irrigation, the road system, probably a dual or a ranked society, and architectural innovations from Mexico. "Thought Ed [Ferdon] 'soft in the head.' Now feel that Ed is right (big hand from [Charles] Di Peso)." But there was not an "invasion" from Mesoamerica, only the arrival of small groups.

3. Lonnie C. Pippin (Washington State University): The numerous peripheral Chaco pueblos that lie outside the canyon, such as Lowry, Aztec, Salmon, and Village of the Great Kivas seem to represent a planned, systematic outflow of population from Chaco Canyon.

4. E. Pierre Morenon (Eastern New Mexico and Southern Methodist Universities): The road system should provide clues to which distant areas were important for resources as the immediate Chaco Canyon environment deteriorated.

5. Paul Grebinger (Eisenhower College): Urban has no notes on this presentation. It may have been along the lines of his 1973 paper in *Kiva,* which proposed that in Chaco Canyon "a rank society developed under nearly pristine conditions between A.D. 850 and 1130. The basis for the rank society was differential agricultural productivity" (Grebinger 1973: 3).

6. Charles Di Peso (Amerind Foundation): There are many similarities between Casas Grandes and the Chaco towns—among them planned architecture, complex hydraulic systems, an extensive road network for transporting such goods as shell and turquoise by the "pochteca."

7. Jay Miller (University of Washington): The modern Pueblo descendants of the Chaco population are more likely Tewa or Keresan than Hopi or Zuni.

8. Cynthia Irwin-Williams (Eastern New Mexico University): From a review of the ideas of each of the speakers in turn, the complexity of understanding the Chaco Phenomenon becomes apparent.

9. Steven A. LeBlanc (Mimbres Archaeological Center): Turquoise may have been one of the important materials carried over the Chaco road system, although the Cerrillos mines were not worked until the 1200s. The rise of Casas Grandes was partly the result of the decline of both Chaco and Mimbres.

The final event of the Conference was held at 6:30, a deep pit barbecue and beer party, with both a Western band and a rock band, held at the Salmon Ruins Orchard. This was the first time that the closing evening's music was not Native American. Archaeologists' tastes were changing, and there were now large numbers of younger people at the Conference, who shared less sense of a link between archaeology and today's Native Americans, or perhaps simply new musical tastes.

A general view of the highlights of the Conference has been provided in the Albuquerque Archaeological Society's newsletter (Sundt 1975: 6):

Besides fine food, lots of refreshments and very interesting tours of the Salmon Ruin and the laboratory operations, there were many fine field reports, an excellent movie of the School of American Research's Arroyo Hondo project, and then Sunday a field trip to Chaco Canyon.

KINO BAY, 1976 (THIRTY-NINTH PECOS CONFERENCE)   Although not the first Conference held in Mexico (Nuevo Casas Grandes has that honor), Kino Bay was certainly the warmest location yet and one of the most attractive, the sessions taking place at the Hotel Posada de Mar, Kino Bay, Sonora. The hours of its sessions were an innovation not repeated in subsequent Conferences, 6:30 to 10 a.m. and 5 to 7 p.m. This was a sensible adaptation to the midday temperatures of Kino Bay in August.

Early in April 1976 Beatriz Braniff de Oliveros (program chair) and Patricia Hernández (local arrangements), of the Centro Regional del Noroeste, Instituto Nacional de Antropología e Historia, sent out their first circular, announcing the place and the dates (from the evening of Wednesday, 11 August, to 14 August at Kino Bay, sixty miles west of Hermosillo via paved road), and other program details.

The plenary session on the archaeology of Sonora was planned "to communicate news on the doings and thoughts on this theme . . . [and] informing Southwesterners and Northwesterners about the possibilities that Sonora has to offer and maybe interest others in coming down." The session included seven twenty-minute papers: "The Molina Ranch Site, Survey 1974 and 1976," Kenneth and Marion McIntyre; "Artifacts from Pinacate," Julian Hayden; "Recent Surveys of Tiburón and the Central Coast," Richard White; "The Trincheras Problem," Tom Bowen; "The Rio San Miguel," Beatriz Braniff; "The Sonora River," Richard Pailes; "Sonora and Relations with Casa Grandes," Di Peso; and a talk on Cocóspera, by Arturo Oliveros, was added later.

The second circular letter had a form for preregistration ($8, including coffee, pan dulce, and the Friday Carne Asada). Reservations could be made at the Posada del Mar and the Posada Santa Gemma. The circular also asked for information on who needed transportation from Hermosillo and for the field trip on Saturday to the Baviacora sites, where Pailes was excavating. Details on camping locations were provided, including the fact that fresh water would be brought out daily, and that "beer is available (of course) everywhere you go in Sonora." Advice was provided on documents for crossing the border and for reaching Kino Bay. From Nogales south to Hermosillo, the capital of Sonora, is about 200 miles by road; it could also be reached by air, with the Hermosillo—Kino Bay buses leaving at 7 a.m. and 3 p.m. ("but you will be travelling maybe with chickens, etc.").

At registration a final schedule was distributed, with two pages on Kino Bay history, the Seri, tourism, and archaeology, with the thoughtful reminder:

> Tourism and ignorance have begun the destruction both of archaeological sites and mangroves, and over exploitation of sea products are all undermining the natural environment and future economic possibilities. . . . We must remember that our "beer-can" culture is not the only one in the world, though [it] can boast of being one of the most destructive. . . . Please help us to leave Sonora beautiful and traditional.

The Conference opened Wednesday, 11 August, with registration and cocktails from 5 to 7 p.m. At 7, on the open-air dance floor of the Posada del Mar, a welcome was extended to conferees by Beatriz Braniff de Oliveros and by Arturo Oliveros, as well as by a representative of the governor of Sonora, Alejandro Carrillo Marcor.

Although only eighty names are on the registration list, Braniff mentioned later (memorandum to Stewart Peckham, undated) that "the crowd was small (104) compared to other Pecos Conferences."

Thursday morning "the first session of field reports was held at 6:30 AM in front of the posada's restaurant. Informal presentations on current field work were organized by state. There were seven from New Mexico, and two from the El Paso area of Texas. Meetings were over by 8:30 AM leaving us free to tour the area, sleep, swim, or eat and drink. By the start of the evening sessions, most of us had followed up on all of these options" (Urban, 23 August report).

Thursday evening was devoted to the symposium on recent archaeological developments in Sonora. The session was held on the dance floor of the hotel, overlooking Kino Bay, from 8 to 10:45. Work reported on consisted of the following:

1. Richard White, Jr.'s salvage in the Kino Bay area in sites being eroded by the estuary of the Desemboque, some possibly as early as Armagosa times, and cave sites with abundant organic material.
2. Thomas Bowen, intensive survey and field recording on Tiburón Island, with sites ranging from paleo-Indian to

historic and recent Seri, as well as sites with strong relationships to Hayden's Pinacate material.

3. Rosenthal, reporting on Julian Hayden's Pinacate work—
seventy-one sites divisible into an early, Malpais Phase, and
a later San Dieguito Phase, followed after a long hiatus by
some Papago material.

4. Kenneth MacIntyre, examination of sites on the Rancho
Molina in 1974, where deforestation and gullying are expos-
ing material possibly of Clovis affiliation.

5. Armando Quijada, pictograph sites in Caborca area, including humans, quadrupeds, geometrics, and geometric
blankets.

6. Braniff, research in the San Miguel valley suggesting a
Southwest-Mesoamerican border area of great ecological
variation. Also, the need to define the difference between
Opata and Upper Pima materials.

7. Pailes, work in the valley of the Rio Sonora, which since
1967 has defined the local culture, with links to Sinaloa and
Casas Grandes.

8. Arturo Oliveras, ethnoarchaeological research in the Altar
Valley, and work on the preservation of the Missions of
Dolores and Remedios.

Haury's handwritten notes, headed "4/13/76 Evening on Sonora,"
mention four problems: (1) "dating—estuary, C14, pottery (will take
the best few diagnostics)"; (2) the fragility of the archaeological resources and the resulting need for immediate work; (3) recording
without collecting, as described by Bowen; and (4) publication.

Field reports resumed Friday morning at 6:30, with reports on
Arizona, Colorado, and Nevada. Urban's report continues with an
account of "a first" for a Pecos Conference, the experience of visiting a village of living Indians, not the ruins once lived in by Indians
long dead:

> At 10 AM Tom Bowen was to lead a tour of interested people
> to Punta Chueca, a Seri village about a half hour's drive to the
> north, and to a site or two along the coast. Upon entering the
> village we were inundated by Seri women, and a few men, who
> had carvings, baskets and necklaces to sell. Those of us who
> could speak Spanish were kept busy bargaining until everyone

who was interested in buying an object had made their final purchase.

The business meeting was held beside the wading pool of the hotel—it was in the shade—and it was confirmed that the 1977 Conference, the fortieth, would be held at Pecos National Monument to mark the fiftieth anniversary of the first Conference and that the 1978 Conference would take place in Flagstaff at the Museum of Northern Arizona, which would be celebrating *its* fiftieth anniversary. There was an invitation to meet at the Fort Burgwin Research Center in 1979, although as it turned out the Conference would be in Tucson that year and at Fort Burgwin in 1981. A committee, made up of Haury, Lister, and Leo A. Flynn of Albuquerque, was set up to consider how to make abstracts of Southwestern publications widely available, perhaps through a special section of *American Antiquity*. Unfortunately, this never happened.

The business meeting concluded with a message to Madeleine Kidder, in Cambridge, Massachusetts: "From Kino Bay, the watery frontier of the Greater Southwest, or, the northwestern reaches of Mesoamerica, come warm greetings from the eighty people registered for the Pecos Conference in its 49th year. We expect you to be with us next year at Pecos."

In a letter of appreciation to Braniff and Oliveros (19 August 1976) Haury commented, "The size of the Pecos Conference reminded me ever so much of those we used to have in the 1930s, a manageable number of people. In addition to that, the nature of the discussions was informal and much like it used to be. I fear the conference at Pecos next year will be the exact opposite, and I will predict there will be 500–600 people." He underestimated!

PART THREE
PERSPECTIVE: CELEBRATING THE FIFTIETH AND BEYOND

13
The Golden Anniversary Conference
at Pecos, 1977

From the ruins of Pecos the view northward to the treeless summit
of Pecos Baldy was much the same in 1977 as it had been in 1927. To
the west, sloping down to the Arroyo del Pueblo, piñons and junipers still dotted the grassy expanse. Beyond, at the foot of Glorieta
Mesa, an interstate highway had cut a long slice from northwest to
southeast, as though to emphasize the Pueblo-Plains Gateway theme
of Pecos National Monument. The appearance of the ruins themselves
had changed greatly since A. V. Kidder completed his work there in
1929. The exposure and stabilization of the South Pueblo and the Mission Compound walls, and the footpaths and informational signs for
visitors were the work of the Museum of New Mexico beginning in
1939–40 and of the National Park Service, following acquisition of the
site as a national monument in 1965. Now there was a small museum,
a staff of park rangers, picnic tables, toilets, drinking water, a paved
entry road, and a parking area. But in spite of these changes, Pecos
remained basically what it had been, a vast and complex ruin, the
scene of one of the most careful and long-lasting excavation programs
in the Southwest, and a reminder to all his archaeological successors
of the ways in which Kidder had profoundly changed Southwestern
archaeology.

In 1977 Kidder would have found the work, the language, the aims
and problems, the techniques, and even the funding of Southwestern archaeology fascinatingly different from what he had been familiar with a half century and more earlier. One of the major changes,
of which Kidder could hardly have known much at the time of his
death in 1963, was the New Archaeology. Frank Hole has described
the movement, from the vantage point of his editorship of *American
Antiquity:*

When I became Editor [in 1974], American archaeology was caught in a ferment of controversy over new and explicitly scientific approaches. This New Archaeology had burst forth most expressively in *American Antiquity* while it was guided during four crucial years by my predecessor, Ed Wilmsen. New Archaeology with its ringing calls to sweep out the old and bring in the new was widely, in some cases wildly, heralded as a movement that would simultaneously make archaeology scientific and relevant. Philosophy of science and statistics were called upon to replace analogy and taxonomy. Scientific explanation and explication rather than historical explanation and description; prediction of the past rather than its discovery, were the new goals [Hole 1978: 151].

The beginnings and rise of the New Archaeology have been sketched in chapter 11. Another immense change in archaeology was the development of cultural resource management (CRM), a rather pretentious term for the essential archaeological work that was mandated by new federal and state laws for public lands and for any area where government-financed construction—pipelines, roads, parking lots, buildings, playgrounds—would threaten archaeological sites. CRM archaeology grew rapidly in the 1960s and 1970s, even though many archaeologists at first were unaware or scornful of it.

The transition from little to big archaeology was masked by . . . a coincidental revolution in theoretical paradigms. Fractious debates between the old and new archaeologies were highly visible, center-stage affairs that embroiled virtually the entire profession during the last half of the 1960s and most of the 1970s. . . .
The birth and growth of CRM almost went unnoticed in the heat of the revolutionary clash between theoretical paradigms. The current domination of the discipline by CRM was, in many ways, virtually an accomplished fact before most archaeologists realized what was happening [Rogge 1983: 7, 9].

However, just as the New Archaeology did not wholly replace the old, but supplemented and modified it, cultural resource management, much of which Rogge properly described as "big archaeology," did not displace the smaller variety. It added enormous sums of money, however, through contracts for archaeological work. Rogge quotes an estimate, the best available, that CRM archaeology, by about 1980, had grown to some $300 million a year in funding, with about 6,000 full-time-equivalent practitioners (Rogge 1983: 11). However, an estimated 40,000 of the contracts averaged only about $5,000 apiece, so that small-scale archaeology consumed about 60 percent of CRM funds. The few big archaeology contracts, however, were very big indeed, at $1 million to $2 million each, often for multiple-year projects, but accounting for no more than about 10 percent of CRM funds. The remaining 30 percent of CRM funds went for projects of intermediate size. Archaeology had undergone a gigantic change, with an enormous increase in the number of field projects of all sizes and types and a level of funding that would not have been imagined earlier. Annual CRM money for archaeology was probably on the order of 100 times what was provided by grants from the National Science Foundation, long considered the prime source of funding for archaeological research.

As CRM archaeology grew in importance, there was vigorous, sometimes rancorous, argument as to whether contract archaeology could also be "problem oriented" and not merely "data gathering." Some of this is reflected in the provocatively titled "Digging for Gold: Papers on Archaeology for Profit" (MacDonald 1976). The growing schism is reflected in William K. MacDonald's comment:

> When I began to solicit participation for this volume, I was surprised to find a great deal of apathy and/or timidity among archaeologists. The former attitude was common among those academic archaeologists who seemingly wouldn't soil their hands with contract work; the latter attitude seemed widespread among archaeologists who had contractual or other positions to protect [p. viii].

In the same volume Thomas J. Riley commented that "the well established academic archaeologist . . . often considers contract archaeology to be beneath him, and thus reinforces the dichotomy between academic and professional researchers" (p. 5). MacDonald and Alexander H. Townsend were even more outspoken in a comment on what they termed "corporate archaeology":

> The implications of legal sanctions and competitive bidding for archaeological research are enormous and, moreover, they are in the long run deleterious to meaningful archaeological research.

A situation in which an unwilling client contracts for undesired work to a company [the for-profit archaeologists] which owes its continued existence to pleasing that client is a clear case of conflict of interest when dealing with a public trust [p. 37].

Finally, Steven A. LeBlanc (pp. 79–81) criticized contract archaeology for its poor record in publication, preservation of artifactual material, and communication with other archaeologists—this last, obviously, an issue in which the Pecos Conference could have a constructive role. However, contract archaeology, even from its beginning, was often indistinguishable from any other archaeological research in its quality and its "problem" orientation. The Dolores Archaeological Project in Colorado and the Salt-Gila Aqueduct Project in Arizona can be mentioned as excellent examples of what contract archaeology could accomplish.

Another way to look at the profound changes taking place in Southwestern archaeology between 1927 and 1977 is to scan the titles of books and articles published in the late 1970s. Among the new words, phrases, and concepts that appear are *archaeological traverse, paleoenvironmental and cultural correlates, experimental archaeology, remote sensing, archaeological assessment, interaction sphere, activity patterning,* and *soil chemistry,* to name a few, as well as a new arsenal of chronological techniques. These were not merely new, "fancy" names for old ideas or techniques, but were significant additions to the tools of archaeological research, just as approaches and techniques discussed at the 1927 Pecos Conference were enormous advances over what had been available a half century before that, in 1877.

One of the most impressive indications of growth and change in Southwestern archaeology is that in the late 1970s there were publications on subjects and areas that had scarcely been thought about a half century before. Northern Arizona, which in 1927 had had little more than Fewkes's digging for pots, now was the scene of a large-scale, multiyear research program on Black Mesa, "mitigation" in advance of the Peabody Coal Company's strip mining. In 1976 the first in a series of reports on the work was published, *Papers on the Archaeology of Black Mesa* (Gumerman and Euler 1976). The same year Emil W. Haury published *The Hohokam: Desert Farmers and Craftsmen: Snaketown, 1964–65,* on the second major excavation program (the first was in 1934–35) at Snaketown, a key site in an area specifically noted in 1927 as needing research. The desert area was, in fact, the scene of more research than ever before, including CRM reports such as "Rillito and Rincon

Period Settlement Systems in the Middle Santa Cruz River Valley" by David E. Doyel (1977) and "Desert Resources and Hohokam Subsistence: The Conoco Florence Projects" by William H. Doelle (1976), the latter particularly interesting for including a study of contemporary Papago use of wild plants as a means of understanding past uses of the area. Another new direction for research was in "historic archaeology," which now included places less well known than Williamsburg, Virginia, or Independence Hall in Philadelphia. A good example is "Fort Bowie Material Culture" by Robert M. Herskovits (1978), a study of the nineteenth-century army post in Apache Pass in the southeastern corner of Arizona.

Research at Pecos itself had been revived, particularly on the mission complex at the southern end of the site. NPS excavation disclosed that there had been a succession of churches, not merely the one that today stands so conspicuously beside the convento. In 1974 Alden C. Hayes published *The Four Churches of Pecos,* reporting work begun in 1966 under the direction of Jean M. Pinkley, soon after the national monument was established. Five years later a definitive study of the documentary history of Pecos was published by the Park Service, *Kiva, Cross, and Crown: The Pecos Indians and New Mexico, 1540–1840,* by John L. Kessell, a study that Kidder had hoped could be made as part of his Pecos research but which he had been unable to include.

With all these changes in approaches, techniques, and areal and topical interests since Kidder's time, archaeological research was going ahead vigorously. And in 1977 there was still an annual Pecos Conference, to which any and all could come, still with the traditional short reports on recent research, and with an opportunity for extensive informal exchange of ideas and information. There were still no dues, permanent officers, headquarters, or bylaws—all those "essentials" of almost all annual meetings of organizations. While the 1977 Pecos Conference honored its "Founders" it looked ahead as well as back, celebrating its golden anniversary without pretending to codify past accomplishments or set the limits for Southwestern archaeology's future. An excellent brief retrospective view of the Pecos Conference was published in 1977 by Stewart Peckham.

The fortieth Pecos Conference (not the fiftieth as it was sometimes mistakenly called, in confusion with the fiftieth anniversary) was hosted by the National Park Service, the Museum of New Mexico, the School of American Research, and the College of Santa Fe, and took place 19–21 August at Pecos National Monument, the place of the Conference's creation. As had become essential, there was extensive planning beginning early in 1977. Haury, in a letter to Thomas F. Giles, superintendent of Pecos National Monument (30 March 1977), correctly predicted "that you will have the biggest attendance ever." In February Giles had sent to Haury a sample of the preliminary flyer he proposed to send out, which included announcement of two special events:

> Special invitations are extended to colleagues who were at the First and other early Pecos Conferences. It is hoped that Friday evening, August 19, you will share with us your reminiscences of earlier years in the Southwest and observations on the "state of the art" then and now. . . . The Conference will conclude with a "banquet" of Mexican food prepared by citizens of the nearby town of Pecos. Beverages will be prepared by a well-known brewer.

An appropriate innovation for this special year was the selection of a logo for the Conference, a "capitan" figure, which occurs on Glaze V bowls at Pecos (Kidder and Shepard 1936: 233–237). It was available at the Conference as a pendant or medallion, "made from local clay with local tempers, and the glaze is a total reproduction of the prehistoric types of glaze ware produced here" (Peckham, statement during the Conference).

Marjorie Lambert (telephone conversation with Woodbury, 11 February 1989) suggested that the name "capitan" was probably supplied by one of Kidder's crew at Pecos, but she herself was inclined to view the figure as representing the plumed serpent that came from the south in Pueblo IV times.

In the final program there was the warning:

NOTE: BECAUSE OF THE GREATER THAN USUAL NUMBERS OF PEOPLE WISHING TO GIVE REPORTS, FIELD REPORTS *CANNOT* LAST LONGER THAN TEN (10) MINUTES. PLEASE COOPERATE!

The order in which reports will be given is based on the state in which the reporting institution (not the field work) is located, with the sequence being, tentatively, as follows:

1. California	5. Arkansas	9. Colorado
2. Washington	6. Nebraska	10. Texas
3. Maryland	7. Arizona	11. (other states)
4. Illinois	8. Utah	12. New Mexico

Because of the time factor, the field report session will continue through lunchtime. A barbecue lunch will be available adjacent to the tent so you won't have to miss any reports. See the reverse side of this sheet for menus and prices.

The Pecos Conference had reached a size where not only a gigantic rented tent (striped yellow and white) and a public address system were needed, but also a caterer to provide hundreds of lunches! Although the preregistration list in the Pecos Conference Archives has only 194 names on it, the final figure was about 650, including "late registrants, meal tickets for non-registrant guests from [the town of] Pecos, plus the estimated 'not paid.' "

Details of the Conference were sent out in May in a three-page letter that included a map of Santa Fe and the route to Pecos, via the Glorieta exit from Interstate 285, through the town of Pecos, and south to the monument. Preregistration at $2.50 was urged, and advance payment for the Saturday night "Southwestern dinner of chili, posole, beans, etc., plus soda pop or beer, as taste dictates. The meal will be prepared by citizens of the community of Pecos and for both beverages and food, the price will be $5.00 per person." A bargain, it was generally agreed.

Registration would be at the Laboratory of Anthropology in Santa Fe on Thursday evening and on Friday morning at Pecos National Monument. Field reports would occupy all of Friday and all of Saturday morning, followed by a symposium, "The Rio Grande: Perspective from Its Periphery." Friday evening was to be devoted to reminiscences, an "Old Timers' Session."

Clara Lee (Fraps) Tanner and Hulda and Emil Haury were the only representatives of the "Founders" at the fiftieth anniversary (Fig. 13.1). Haury noted, though, in a letter to Giles (12 April) to give him the sad news of Mrs. Kidder's decision not to attend, that "I find the following who I think are still living: Bob Wauchope, Tulane University (he was a camp helper); Harry Shapiro, American Museum of Natural History; and Erna Gunther (Spier). The ranks are getting lean." None of these had ever been Pecos Conference participants after 1927. Haury overlooked the two Spier boys (Robert, who became an anthropologist, and Christopher), "Judge" Henry Skinner, and Charlotte Gower Chapman.

The Conference opened at 9 a.m. Friday, 19 August, in the big tent near the national monument headquarters, within sight of the spot across the arroyo where the first Conference had been held, under

13.1 "Old Timers" at Pecos in 1977 (left to right): Robert Lister, unidentified, James Hester, Emil Haury, Florence Ellis, Elizabeth Morris, Clara Lee Tanner, Alfred E. Dittert, Hulda Haury, Albert H. Schroeder, Bertha Dutton, Pat Wheat, Arnold Withers, Joe Ben Wheat, Florence Lister, Stewart Peckham, and Charlie Steen. Arizona State Museum negative no. 46054. Photo by Helga Teiwes.

the piñons and junipers rather than a tent (and with few or no fold-ing chairs). After greetings to the assembly the field reports began and continued through the entire day. The summaries of the field re-ports by Sharon F. Urban demonstrate the variety, scope, and vigor of archaeological research in the late 1970s in the Southwest.

First was Dorothy Washburn's study of ceramic design symmetry, currently on "Chaco Canyon and Mesa Verde in relation to outliers of Aztec and Solomon." She was followed by Daniel Wolfman (Arkan-sas Archaeological Society) on dating by "alpha-recoil (mica plate), uranium and thorium traces within pottery . . . needs well dated mica-ceous sherds" (to establish a baseline). From Utah Bruce Waffleton (Bureau of Land Management) had the news that "Moab district lost court case against several groups of environmentalists." The seventeen reports on work by Arizona institutions included the following:

Northern Arizona University. Richard Ambler: Work "in New Mexico in San Mateo (north of Grants), fringe of Chaco and Acoma, Laguna. Survey for uranium company. Found 80 sites with most in the PII range, but Archaic up through Mexican and Anglo occupations."

Arizona State University. Fred Plog: "Much contract work. One a study for Bureau of Land Management of small land parcels. Another project is in the Salt River Valley around Phoenix. Excavation of large sites in the area such as Las Canopas, Casa de Loma, and McClintock site."

Arizona Archaeological and Historical Society. David Wil-cox: The 1974 survey of Tumamoc Hill, on the western edge of Tucson, including "walls, trails, glyphs, ceramics, and the associated St. Mary's site."

Western Archeological Center, National Park Service. James A. McDonald: A survey of Canyon del Muerto which "turned up an additional 125 sites bringing the total up to 650."

Museum of Northern Arizona. Charles Adams: The Walpi Project, which had excavated 100 rooms of the still occupied village, making detailed records on which stabilization and reconstruction could be based. Alexander Lindsay: Excavating some of the 1880s section of Flagstaff, including a house, a brewery, and a saloon—historic archaeology less than a century old. William Marmaduke: Along the right-of-way of a Salt River Project transmission line and railroad, identification of eleven large sites of about A.D. 1150, as well as lithic sites.

Bureau of Land Management. Jean Fryman: Archaeological resources on grazing rights allotments.

Coconino National Forest. Peter Pilles: For the Verde Valley Archaeological Society, excavation of a stratified site near Sedona, and in the national forest a study of the effects of forest fires on sites.

Tonto National Forest. Around Lake Roosevelt new sites had appeared because of low water, including two large Salado sites and a Hohokam site. A new law empowered the Forest Service to cite pothunters on forest lands. Scott Wood worked with timber companies to avoid archaeological sites as far as possible; twenty sites had been located on a 1,700 acre tract.

University of Arizona. David Doyel: The Interstate 19 salvage project near Tumacacori, with Rillito-Rincon phase small sites; corn pollen was found on metates and archaeomagnetic dates were being secured. William Longacre: The fifteenth season of the field school at Grasshopper, including work at the Chediski site a mile to the north, where the pueblo was burned with everything in place. David Tuggle: Survey of Salt Water Draw. Michael Graves: Study of surface deposits.

Amerind Foundation. Charles Di Peso: Mimbres site with five pit houses and three surface rooms exposed so far.

At this point the state-by-state sequence of field reports appears to have broken down, with the remainder of Friday's reports headed "Miscellaneous," although some semblance of grouping appears from time to time.

University of California, Los Angeles. James Hill: Study of subsistence stress on the Pajarito Plateau over a long time span; so far he had "covered 45 tracts of horrid terrain."

University of Colorado. David Breternitz: Completion of the Mesa Verde Survey, with 3,892 sites recorded within the park boundary. Omer Stewart (the only ethnologist reporting at this Pecos Conference): The peyote religion. Joe Ben Wheat: Continuing work at Yellow Jacket, Colorado.

Southern Illinois University, Edwardsville. Theodore R. Frisbie: Study of the abundant mineral resources in the Zuni area that might have been exploited by Chacoans, including alabaster, kaolinite, azurite, galena, hematite, jet, limonite, halite, and petrified wood.

El Paso Centennial Museum. Rex Gerald: Survey of a 180 square mile area east of El Paso.

Southern Methodist University. Pierre Morenon: Bison bones at Pot Creek Pueblo, said by the Taos Indians to be the "source of the last bison hunt." He also said that it "took twice as much energy to build a pueblo than a pit house village."

Zuni Archaeological Enterprise. T. J. Ferguson: The first year of this tribal organization, which had two staff archaeologists, nine field trainees, and one full-time draftsperson, and which was training Zunis "to be archaeologists with some beginning to write reports." Work at Pescado provided dates from the beginning of the site in the twelfth to fourteenth centuries to the early nineteenth century, its long occupation due to the springs close by.

Albuquerque Archaeological Society. Richard Bice: The Cerrillos mine, south of Santa Fe, from which lead for glaze paint was secured, and salvage excavation on land of the Bureau of Land Management.

University of New Mexico. Florence Hawley Ellis: Ethnoarchaeology in the Chama area, using "informants to help determine culture of their own ancestors."

San Juan County Museum Association. Nancy Hewett: A possible astronomical alignment of cobbles near Animas, running in "a north south direction with concentric arches in the east." (Jonathan Reyman suggested a relationship to medicine wheels of the Plains.)

This completed the day's field reports. About 40 percent of the projects reported can be classified as cultural resource management, carried out on contract where archaeological resources were threatened with destruction. Like field work reported in earlier years, each report, though often seeming of small importance, added a little to the slowly growing mosaic of archaeological knowledge and understanding. As the Scots say, "Many a mickle makes a muckle."

The Friday evening celebration of the Conference's golden anniversary was a great success. Haury described some of its highlights in a letter to Madeleine Kidder (29 August 1977):

The "Old Timers" night was well attended, and it turned out to be a most jovial and rewarding occasion. Arny Withers started out to set the tone for the evening by giving an . . . account

(condensed of course) of Pecos history and keying in slides . . .
of early [and] contemporary archaeologists in situations. It was
a hilarious presentation. Bob Lister was M.C., and there were
opportunities for Omer Stewart, Clara Lee Tanner, Scotty Mac-
Neish, Ned Danson, and myself to make some remarks. It was
truly a "fun" evening and you would have enormously enjoyed
that too. Among other things, I was presented with a broken
rusty shovel found on the Harris Site in the Mimbres [Fig. 13.2],
left there in 1934 [the year Haury dug at that site]. It carries an
appropriate inscription. I told Steve LeBlanc, who is now digging in the Mimbres and who presented me with the shovel, that
if he quit digging in my back dirt, he would learn more about
the prehistory of the Mimbres Valley.

The plate on the shovel carries the inscription:

DEPOSITED AT HARRIS VILLAGE
Mimbres, New Mexico, 1934
Returned to "Doc" Haury
Father of the Mogollon
Pecos, 1977

The shovel now reposes in the permanent collections of the Arizona
State Museum, Tucson.

After the Friday evening festivities, the Conference returned Saturday morning to the serious business of additional field reports, which
lasted through the lunch hour. About a dozen people spoke, continuing with New Mexico institutions.

Albuquerque. John Kessell (historian): Completion of his
documentary history of Pecos; he commented that "internal strife
caused the downfall of the pueblo."
New Mexico State University. Pam Megors: Contract research projects, including surveys at White Sands National
Monument and in the Chaco area, and excavation of forty sites
for the Bureau of Indian Affairs in advance of an irrigation
project on the Navajo Reservation. Richard Kelley: Excavation
for the Bureau of Land Management—"BLM wanted a pit house
but one was not found; so one was built." J. R. Grumlack: A
vandalized site, half destroyed by pot hunters.
University of New Mexico. James N. Spuhler (physical

13.2 *Presentation of rusty shovel to Emil W. Haury by Steven LeBlanc, at 50th anniversary festivities, 1977. Arizona State Museum negative no. 46101. Photo by Helga Teiwes.*

anthropologist): Multivariate analysis of skeletal material from several sites. Steven LeBlanc: The Mimbres Foundation's study of human population dynamics from A.D. 1–1400, as well as its research on Mimbres pottery from collections everywhere.

Association for Santa Rita de Abiquiu. Charles Verilla: Study of the partly destroyed Spanish mission, a community project with youth corps help and assistance from Linda Cordell.

School of American Research. Curtis Schaafsma: Survey of the maximum pool area of the Chama Reservoir, with 239 sites.

Museum of New Mexico. James Lind and William Bowman: Survey of State Highway 381 from Crown Point to Farmington.

New Mexico State Planning Office. Michael Marshall: Preservation of murals and excavation of the plaza at San Istilan Rey, Acoma.

Carson National Forest. Mark Henderson: Surveys in the forest.

University of Texas, Austin. James Neely: A large, pothunted Mogollon site of the San Francisco through Tularosa phases.

Brigham Young University. Deanne Gurr: Following work in Canyon Creek Village the previous two years, excavation had moved to Montezuma Canyon where 817 sites had been located.

Arizona Archaeological Society. Don Dove: Survey of sites at Sun City, just west of Phoenix, with a certification program for amateur archaeologists.

In addition, Don Fowler, president of the American Society for Conservation Archaeology, informed the Conference of current legislation of importance to archaeologists, and Dee Green of the U.S. Forest Service urged that archaeologists "get their two cents worth in at the Federal level. Government is making our decisions with no input from us."

Comparing the affiliations of those reporting on field work with those of fifty years earlier reveals a dramatic change. In 1977, in contrast with 1927, more than a dozen of the organizations are neither universities nor museums—the Arkansas, Arizona, and Albuquerque archaeological societies; the U.S. Forest Service (Coconino, Tonto, and Carson national forests); the Zuni Archaeological Enterprise; the New Mexico State Planning Office; the Colorado Highway Department; the Bureau of Land Management; and the NPS Western Archeological Center. Among the universities and museums represented there is also a great contrast with 1927—marked by the presence in 1977 of Northern Arizona University, the University of California at Los Angeles, Southern Illinois University, Brigham Young University, and the El Paso Centennial Museum, among others. In 1927 only a few museums and universities were reporting on field work, including the University of Denver, the University of California, Berkeley, the Southwest Museum, Los Angeles, the U.S. National Museum, the Museum of the American Indian, the American Museum of Natural History, and the Peabody Museum of Harvard University, none of which appear in 1977. Likewise missing in 1977 are reports from the Carnegie Institution of Washington (its archaeology division was discontinued in 1958), the Bureau of American Ethnology (abolished in 1964 and merged with the Smithsonian's Office of Anthropology), and the R. S. Peabody Foundation (its Southwestern research ended with Kidder's last volume on Pecos, in 1958). It is clear that far more of the field work in the Southwest in 1977 was conducted by Southwestern organizations and that archaeologists were employed by a great variety of federal and private organizations not active or even existing a half century before.

With the field reports finally concluded, the business meeting was convened. The deaths of Neil M. Judd and E. B. (Ted) Sayles were observed. A telegram was sent to Madeleine Kidder, at the Sheraton-Commander Hotel in Cambridge: "The more than 600 people attending the Pecos Fiftieth send warm greetings and note Ted's and your role in shaping Southwestern Archaeology. A personal medallion will reach you soon. Special salutations from three who were there in 1927." It was signed "Clara Lee, Hulda, and Emil."

It was confirmed that the 1978 meeting would be held in Flagstaff, where the Museum of Northern Arizona's fiftieth anniversary would be celebrated, and that the 1979 meeting would be at Fort Burgwin, New Mexico. Robert Lister then reported that "prosecuting under the Antiquities Act is not successful," as courts had declared the 1906 rules and regulations unconstitutional, and that Rex Wilson of the National Park Service was supervising a rewriting of the rules and regulations, with the addition of archaeology on the Continental Shelf.

The final session of the Conference was the symposium, "The Rio Grande: Perspective from Its Periphery." The symposium was recorded on tape and a transcript was made by the National Park Service of the invited and volunteered discussions following each paper. This transcript and copies of most of the papers were made available for this history through the cooperation of the School of American Research. Because of the length of the symposium, only excerpts will be quoted or paraphrased here. The full record, however, is a valuable view of the state of knowledge at that time for one major part of the Southwest.

The archaeology of the Rio Grande had been summarized twenty-two years earlier at a Pecos Conference held in Santa Fe, with presentations by Stanley Stubbs on current archaeological knowledge, and by Fred Wendorf on research still needed. Also, in another ten years, with the Conference held at Pecos again, there would be another symposium on the northern Rio Grande (1987). These three sessions reflect the growing interest in the area and the progress made in understanding it during the six decades since Kidder's 1924 characterization of it: "We have . . . a fairly good knowledge of the Santa Fe district, but there are many parts of the Rio Grande drainage as to which we have so far very little information" (Kidder 1924: 86).

Douglas W. Schwartz (School of American Research) chaired the 1977 symposium, and opened the session by saying:

> It's interesting in looking at the history of the Pecos Conference, and especially that first one, the small role that the Rio Grande played in that first conception of Southwestern prehistory; and yet there had been work on the Rio Grande for sixty years prior to that time. So, when the planning committee began to work on this year's symposium, we felt that it would be a good idea, since we're here, to concentrate on the Rio Grande. Yet to simply stick to the Rio Grande seemed to us somewhat limiting in terms of all the developments that had been going on around it and impinge on its understanding. So we decided to develop a symposium looking at the Rio Grande from its periphery.

The first paper, by Richard W. Lang, "The Prehistoric Pueblo Cultural Sequence in the Northern Rio Grande," defined the area as extending from north of Taos to below Albuquerque, plus the upper Pecos drainage. After 4,000 years of occupation "by the carriers of the Oshara tradition," an intrusion of the Cochise tradition occurred at about 1500–1000 B.C. bringing farming, a trend to marked seasonal shifts in subsistence activities, and the introduction of "small hut clusters with storage, cooking, and heating facilities." Pottery appeared around A.D. 400–700, and larger villages developed. Lange traced the steady addition of new and more complex traits from Basketmaker III onward, climaxing with "truly great towns" appearing in Pueblo IV.

Following Lange's paper, Stewart Peckham said that tree-ring dating in the area was still inadequate compared to most of the Southwest. He also observed that there was still too much inclination to look west for stimuli affecting the northern Rio Grande, rather than south and east.

The second paper was by Alden C. Hayes of the National Park Service, "The Rio Grande: A View from Mesa Verde." Hayes said that the Rio Grande area had lagged two or three centuries behind the Four Corners area in its cultural development. "It was not until about 1200 A.D. that the Rio Grande poor relations began to catch up, when large, compact, multi-storied pueblos began to be built." He also discussed the complex population movements involving Mesa Verde, Chaco, and the Rio Grande and pointed out that "after 1300 the Rio Grande's marginal position was completely reversed." With characteristic modesty Hayes added at the end of his paper, "Footnote: Having finished these words, I took down a dog-eared and annotated book from the shelf behind me to learn that Alfred Kidder said most of this in 1924—and of course much better."

In the discussion that followed, Peckham questioned the idea of an "exodus" from Mesa Verde rather than an in situ decline. He was followed by Charlie Steen, who also objected: "I hate to see great masses of Mesa Verde people moving from one area to another." Steen spoke of the ethnocentrism of early Southwestern archaeologists: "each man would stand on his mound and that was the center of the earth, and this attitude . . . still influences our thinking today. We're very prone to think of the San Juan as the place where it all started."

Schwartz then asked Bruce Dickson for his comment. He said that it was incorrect to expect conflict whenever a new group moved into an occupied area, and cited the Okie intrusion into southern California and the Chinese movement to Taiwan after World War II. Next Dorothy Washburn was asked by Schwartz whether she had "anything on the relationship between Mesa Verde and Rio Grande pottery." She replied that she favored "a movement of people," and that there is "definite continuity and structure of the design." Schwartz retorted, "I'm sorry that I let you talk, Dorothy, sorry."

There is, unfortunately, a gap in the record when the microphone was not on while J. Charles Kelley spoke and, apparently, Schwartz disagreed with him. The record then continues with Kelley speaking: "I hate to argue with our illustrious chairman, but how can you possibly ignore the fact that we have ethnohistoric, ethnographic examples of population movement in the Southwest? What about Hano, for God's sake?" He pointed out that arriving groups might not leave clear archaeological evidence of their source: "Is there anything in Hano architecture, Hano pottery, or anything else along those lines, that would tell us if we did not know differently that the Hano people were not simply natives of First Mesa?"

David Brugge added a supporting comment: "Another example is the movement of the Rio Grande peoples as refugees in the Navajo country during the Reconquest . . . in the Dinetah country; not only do you not find Rio Grande kivas; you don't find any kivas. The people up there moved their ceremonies into hogans."

James Judge of the NPS Division of Chaco Research, University of New Mexico, then spoke on "The Rio Grande from the Perspective of the Chaco Basin." The Chaco Project, restudying the Chaco area, had begun in 1971 and would finish in 1980. Already it had modified and refined many previous ideas. A choice could not yet be made between the alternative views of Chaco's development as mainly internal or as Mexican stimulated, but work planned for Pueblo Alto might help resolve the problem. In the late thirteenth century a major population movement from the San Juan to the Rio Grande did take place. Judge reviewed the sequence of events in the Chaco Basin and compared it with concurrent events in the Rio Grande.

There followed a lengthy discussion of Judge's paper by Jan Biella, Richard Chapman, Hayes, Ellis, Albert Schroeder, Curt Schaafsma, Helene Warren, and Kelley (who spoke of merchants going into barbarian countries but carefully concealing their alien nature, and who mischievously concluded, "I might add here a note of warning, for you Southwesterners, that there is a concealed one, a 'hidden one' from Mesoamerica among you").

The next paper was by Di Peso, of the Amerind Foundation, on "The Rio Grande as seen from Casas Grandes." He said that prehistorically only 10 or 15 percent of its bottomlands were used for farming along less than a third of its length, and consequently, archaeologists have tended to concentrate on a small part of it, rather than the entire length of the river. Di Peso then traced the archaeology of the Rio Grande in terms of its relationships with other "Chichimec" groups and by the mid eleventh century a "flow of Mesoamerican religious cults into this portion of the Rio Grande Valley."

Alfred E. Dittert, Jr. (Arizona State University), then presented "The Northern Rio Grande: Views from Acoma-Zuni." He began with details of several prehistoric and recent trade routes from the Puerco of the West and from Acoma to the Rio Grande and then summarized "population displacements" from the eighth century to historic times, some of them of short duration while drought affected certain areas. Most contacts of the Zuni-Acoma area were with the Keresan groups on the southern edge of the northern Rio Grande. He said similarities with the Rio Grande were less, following the Archaic, until "Keresan trade relations resulted in the spread of material culture traits to the Rio Grande from Acoma and from Zuni through Acoma." Rosalyn Hunter-Anderson commented that kin ties might be important in understanding "the mechanisms that allowed people to move back and forth" between regions in the Southwest.

Robert G. Campbell (Texas Tech University) presented "Southern High Plains and Upper Rio Grande Prehistory." He summarized the paleo-Indian, Archaic, and Late Prehistoric cultures and the relation of the last to Plains Woodland. He spoke of the rise of the Panhandle culture and the increase of contacts with the Rio Grande, and the trade in bison remains and Alibates flint from the Plains. He concluded with the observation that "from A.D. 1300 into historic times Athabascan groups appear to displace the Panhandle and Jornada groups."

The next presentation, by James Gunnerson (University of Nebraska Museum), was on relations between the Central Plains and the Rio Grande. He noted the paucity of Plains traits identified in the 1955 SAA symposium and suggested that, as Di Peso had said, northern Mexico was a more likely source for some of these traits, although Southwestern trade sherds were certainly found on the Plains.

The final paper of the symposium was by James Hill (University of California, Los Angeles), an "assessment" of the preceding papers. He first criticized the symposium and then made some constructive suggestions:

> The first thing that I want to say is that I have got a feeling
> that this symposium is premature. I wasn't happy with the
> papers when I read them. And, it may stem from my theoreti-
> cal biases. . . . First of all, the title of the symposium is "The
> Rio Grande: Perspective from its Periphery," and that is wide
> open; it is not even a question. And one of the things I tell my
> undergraduates . . . is that if you don't ask a question, you don't
> deserve an answer. And so what I would like to see is . . . ask-
> ing specific questions such as "Did the people of Mesa Verde or
> Chaco migrate into this area, or did they not?"

Hill then pointed out that there were implicit questions in the papers, of a culture-historical kind, "questions of origins of people, for example, migrations, culture contacts, and influences." But when made explicit they are very difficult questions, for which answers tend to be sought only in pottery and architecture. He said that movements of peoples are extremely difficult to demonstrate and trade sherds not as easy to identify as is often assumed. He suggested that details of the adaptation of each group would help "to pinpoint the points of stress . . . that forced them to move. . . . Presumably they make least cost or optimal solutions to their problems." He also pointed out that identifying an item as traded from elsewhere "doesn't mean much behaviorally" because the context may be wholly different.

In concluding his long and thoughtful remarks, Hill pointed out that "there is always a tendency throughout Southwestern archaeology . . . to explain local developments in terms of outside influences. . . . [to] look at your area . . . and say 'Well, where did it come from?' I am not saying that that is bad . . . [but] the first question should be 'How did it work?' 'How was it integrated into a system?' . . . So, let's start with local adaptations." In addition he observed that the thirteenth-century abandonment of much of the Southwest must have been due mainly to "decreased fertility or birth rates and increased mortality," not to movements of peoples.

With the end of Hill's assessment the symposium was concluded and the conferees adjourned to the final scheduled event of the Conference, "La Cerveza y La Comida—refreshments and a Mexican dinner. Entertainment." Some 650 dinners were served, making this by far the largest assembly of people at any Pecos Conference before or since, and perhaps the most people at Pecos since the seventeenth or eighteenth century. The citizens of the little town of Pecos distinguished themselves that evening by their hospitality and culinary skills. However, there were the usual "free-loaders." "It seems that a number of young archaeologists gave others, who didn't pay, their used plates to go through the line so it would appear they were getting seconds!" The musical entertainment during the banquet was provided by a local Pecos group, guitarists and a violinist, Antonio Ruiz, who had been a member of Kidder's excavation crew in the 1920s. Later, a country-western band provided music for dancing (Albert H. Schroeder, letter to Woodbury, 31 January 1989).

In correspondence just after the Conference Emil Haury made several personal observations on the meeting as a whole. To Harold S. Gladwin he said (letter of 23 August): "The general mood of the Conference was optimistic, and I am particularly pleased that some of the activism that was creeping into the discipline a decade ago has largely vanished. There is, unfortunately, no reduction in the amount of jargon." To Madeleine Kidder he commented (letter of 29 August), "There was an enthusiasm . . . particularly among the younger people, which a number of us felt was unique, refreshing, and holding much promise for the future. The cynicism of a decade ago was missing." On the Rio Grande Symposium he said (letter to Alfred Kidder, 23 August), "A region in which I thought most of the problems had been solved, but it seems to me that people working there are still a long way apart in their ideas." He also wrote Giles, expressing his admiration for the excellence of the arrangements, and commenting, "Apart from the well-laid plans, I thought the Conference had a good bit of substance too. It was a vastly different occasion than we had 50 years ago, but that was to be expected. I can tell you this, that 50 years ago when people spoke, they didn't keep their hats on!"

As much as programs, registration lists, transcripts, and correspondence can tell us of the events at the Conference, they cannot reveal important unscheduled, private discussions. Only rarely is mention made in print of these significant events. One example is the following:

> The need for a conference [on Hohokam prehistory] had existed for some time, but the opportunity had not presented itself. Such a conference finally took on form while five archaeologists interested in Hohokam prehistory were sitting under a shade tree during a break in the 50th [sic] annual Pecos Conference held at Pecos, New Mexico. These discussions resulted in a day-long symposium entitled "Current Issues in Hohokam Prehistory," held at the Society for American Archaeology annual meeting in Tucson, Arizona in May of 1978 [Doyel and Plog 1980: 1].

When its 1977 meeting ended, the Pecos Conference entered its second half century. In many ways it was very different from its beginnings, as Haury commented. But it was continuing with the same central purpose and with the same enthusiastic exchange of information and views that it had begun with. Originally this chronicle was planned to end with the fiftieth anniversary, but it now seems worthwhile to look, at least briefly, at the decade that followed.

14
INTO THE EIGHTIES: THE PECOS CONFERENCE, 1978–88

By the time I'd written the preceding chapter, intending it to be the last year chronicled, the Pecos Conference was well into the next decade and I succumbed to the temptation to add a few more years to this history. However, in spite of the abundance of information available I have attempted to report these recent years quite briefly.

FLAGSTAFF, 1978 (FORTY-FIRST PECOS CONFERENCE)   The forty-first Pecos Conference was held in Flagstaff, 18–19 August. The host was the Museum of Northern Arizona, which was concurrently celebrating the fiftieth anniversary of its founding by Harold S. Colton and Mary-Russell Ferrell Colton. About 350 people attended, one of the largest numbers recorded, except for the Conference's golden anniversary the year before. This was the seventh time the Conference had been held in Flagstaff. This year the interim chairperson was the museum's Marsha V. Gallagher. A large tent for the sessions was erected in the northeast corner of the grounds of the Research Center, across Fort Valley Road from the museum. The weather turned out to be very good—never a sure thing in the season of summer thunderstorms.

In May a letter went out from Claudia Berry, Jeanne Swarthout, and William Marmaduke, all on the museum's staff, proposing a symposium on "The Problem of the Archaic in the American Southwest." It was pointed out that this 8,000-year span had received disproportionately little attention and that recent field work "has generated data which could potentially remedy this situation." They hoped for "regional overviews or syntheses . . . , and paleoenvironmental reconstructions and the status of various Archaic complexes." Unfortunately, this ambitious proposal did not elicit sufficient response to make possible a full-scale symposium.

The first day was devoted to field reports, and their details are excellently summarized in the notes kept by Sharon F. Urban. There were reports from twelve universities and museums and from fourteen other organizations, including the Public Service Company of New Mexico, Archeological Research Environmental Corporation, "HDQ Bio Sci," Human Systems Research, several U.S. Forest Service districts, the Chaco Center and the Western Archeological Center of the National Park Service, and the Bureau of Land Management. From some organizations there were several separate reports, for a total of about fifty-five presentations. Research was heavily weighted to cultural resource management, regardless of what organization sponsored it, continuing the trend discussed in the preceding chapter. Most of the CRM research was directed to significant problems, contrary to the suspicions of some that it was merely "data gathering." Among the reports was one on the Dolores Project, for which $2 million was budgeted for four to five years of work; 700 sites had been located thus far, and five "major problem domains" defined, which would be the basis for analysis of the data. On the White Sands Missile Range petroglyphs of the Jornada phase of the Mogollon (A.D. 300–800) were being studied by Human Systems Research. The Moab Office of BLM was doing a 1 percent sample of a 30,000 acre tract, to be followed by a 10 percent sample, and also a study of visitor impact in the part of Grand Gulch, Utah, set aside as a primitive area.

The business meeting began by noting the recent deaths of Mark Grady, Alfred F. Whiting, Lyndon L. Hargrave, and Alan P. Olson. The question of the next year's meeting place began with a letter saying that Fort Burgwin must withdraw its 1979 invitation but would like to host the Conference in 1980. A meeting at the University of Arizona field school at Grasshopper was not possible, because facilities were inadequate for such a large group. Possible NPS or Forest Service locations were discussed. The University of Arizona was suggested—the last Tucson meeting had been in 1973. Emil W. Haury agreed to transmit the inquiry, which he did, and Tucson became the 1979 meeting place.

As the business meeting proceeded, Haury suggested changing to a meeting every other year, and when needed a smaller meeting with an invited list of participants to consider a particular problem, much like the 1927 meeting called to consider what became the Pecos Classification. These small meetings, however, would not replace the Pecos Conference. He also mentioned the need for a history of the Pecos Conference and, as Haury later described it (letter to Woodbury, 25 August 1978), "Al Schroeder rose up and said he thought you [Woodbury] were doing it. . . . I hope that Al's statement is true." Even if it had not been before that, it now immediately became "true."

The symposium on warfare began with several people describing sites they believed to be defensive. Tumamoc Hill on the edge of Tucson was described by David Wilcox, with its terraces (trincheras) that appeared to be defensive. Donald Weaver reported possible defensive sites along the Verde River, and Robert Euler spoke of "fortified hills, fortified mesa edges" near Prescott. Wilcox then raised the question of how effective the protection from hit-and-run attacks would be at these sites, and who the attackers might be: "Saladoans were too late; Athabascans were not here either. Yumans probably not enough force." This left the Classic Hohokam (Soho Phase) on the Salt and Gila. "This type of community could put lesser sites into a defensive posture."

It does not appear that any consensus was reached on the extent or the causes of warfare in the prehistoric Southwest, but it was an excellent exchange of ideas. It was not quite the first time that the subject had been addressed at a Pecos Conference—that was in 1951 when a session on "Enemy Peoples" was held—but it is probably fair to say that the paucity of discussions mirrors the reluctance of Southwestern archaeologists to consider that the prehistoric Anasazi, Mogollon, Hohokam, or others sometimes engaged in violence, whether attacks, raids, ambushes, or other kinds of hostility. Acceptance was slow for the idea that the archaeological record contained substantial evidence of violence. The ethnographic record as well had often been interpreted with a bias for "peacefulness," as John W. Bennett had said twenty-four years earlier (Bennett 1946). In 1951 Florence Ellis published a detailed examination of warfare and aggression in recent Pueblo society (Ellis 1951), and some years later I briefly reviewed the evidence for Pueblo warfare (Woodbury 1959). There is little in the literature since then, however, to suggest general acceptance of a change in the traditional view of the "peaceful Pueblos."

The 1978 Conference had one other scheduled event, an optional field trip Saturday afternoon conducted by Peter Pilles to visit such Sinagua sites as Elden Pueblo, Winona Village, Ridge Ruin, and Turkey Hill Ruin.

TUCSON, 1979 (FORTY-SECOND PECOS CONFERENCE) The 1979 Pecos Conference met in Tucson on 17 and 18 August, hosted by the Arizona State Museum and the Laboratory of Tree-Ring Research. The Laboratory of Tree-Ring Research planned to hold an open house during the Conference.

The attendance was far below that of the year before, with only 143 names on the registration list, perhaps because southern Arizona temperatures in August were notorious. Also, camping was relatively distant and would not offer the cool nights of Flagstaff's pine forests. A "bring your own bottle" party was planned, however, for Saturday evening in the Molino Basin, through the cooperation of the Coronado National Forest, at a campground more than 2,000 feet higher than Tucson, part of the way up the road to Mount Lemmon in the Catalina Mountains.

At the opening session, Congressman Morris Udall spoke briefly, at the invitation of Haury, who described the occasion (letter to Woodbury, 20 August 1979) as follows: "I was able to persuade Mo Udall to make a personal appearance before the conferees on Friday morning. I felt he should be thanked for his continuing support in Congress in getting legislation important to the archaeological profession."

Field reports were arranged by states, extending through the morning and afternoon sessions of Friday and the morning session of Saturday. A list of reports includes one from Colorado, five from New Mexico, four from Utah, and, not surprisingly, fourteen from Arizona. In addition, Alexander Lindsay gave an "update on recent antiquities legislation," Robert Lister reported on the work he and his wife Florence were doing on Spanish Colonial ceramics, and Bryan Aivazian spoke on "archaeology and public awareness," observing that archaeologists held many conferences to talk to each other but did poorly in letting the public know what was being done with its money and often on its lands; the "lunatic fringe" of archaeology was getting most of the attention.

Following the field reports, at the end of Saturday morning, the business meeting was held, beginning with expressions of appreciation to all who had helped plan and manage the meeting, and a telegram to Madeleine Kidder. The only death noted was that of Frank J. Broilo of Albuquerque. Haury suggested that each Conference address one specific problem, such as the Archaic. "To my knowledge, the concept of the Southwestern Archaic has never been adequately explored or stated, and I thought we might address that problem, which could lead to a published statement, following the model set for us by the First Pecos Conference in 1927" (letter to Woodbury, 20 August 1979). This would have gone beyond the usual symposium on an area or topic, to focus efforts on reaching a publishable consensus on a *problem*. However, the record of subsequent years does not show any achievements in this direction.

The familiar question of where future meetings would take place began with the withdrawal of Fort Burgwin's invitation for 1980. The schedule agreed on was:

> 1980, Black Mesa: George Gumerman, chairperson, Robert Euler and Fred Plog, cochairpersons.
> 1981, Fort Burgwin.
> 1982, Pecos National Monument.
> 1983, El Paso (alternative, Las Cruces).
> 1984, Chavez Pass (Arizona State University, Coconino National Forest, and the Arizona Archaeological Society).
> 1985, "too far in advance."

As it turned out, only 1981 and 1982 followed this plan.

The Saturday afternoon symposium was "Environmental and Cultural Change on the Colorado Plateau." It was described in the information mailed out in June as

> an opportunity for presentation of new information and discussion on a topic of considerable interest. . . . Bob Euler, George Gumerman, Thor Karlstrom, Jeff Dean and Richard Hevly recently completed a paper that has been accepted by *Science* titled "Cultural Dynamics and Paleoenvironmental Correlates on the Colorado Plateaus" [published under a different title, Euler and others 1979]. They have agreed to present their data in more detail at this year's symposium. George Gumerman [Southern Illinois University] will serve as Symposium Chairman.

The first three of these authors had published an earlier version of this paper, "Paleoenvironmental and Cultural Correlates in the Black Mesa Region" (Karlstrom and others 1976). This was part of the ongoing reporting of the extensive work directed by Gumerman on Black Mesa, sponsored by the Peabody Coal Company and the Black Mesa Pipeline Company.

The 1979 symposium opened with Gumerman's observation that there appeared to be correspondences between cultural and environmental change, but the mechanisms behind this were not yet known. Jeffrey S. Dean (University of Arizona) was the first speaker, discussing the use of tree-ring records for paleoclimatic reconstruction.

Richard Hevly (Northern Arizona University) described the factors affecting the types and quantities of pollen from which vegetational changes could be reconstructed. One of the invited discussants, James Schoenwetter (Arizona State University), expressed doubts about population figures Hevly had cited and also spoke of the problem of lack of correspondence between arboreal pollen in a general area and in a particular archaeological site.

The third speaker was Thor N. V. Karlstrom (U.S. Geological Survey) who described the complex relationships of climate to deposition, erosion, and soil formation, and the problems of dating specific soil members or stream terraces. The other invited discussant, Stephen A. Hall (North Texas State University), pointed out the geologic sensitivity of Black Mesa soils and raised the possibility of correlating unconformities at Chaco Canyon and Black Mesa (less than 150 miles apart). Euler (National Park Service) presented a chart of wetter and drier areas of the Southwest. Robert Gasser (Museum of Northern Arizona) pointed out that the data from Black Mesa offered good opportunities for hypothesis testing. He warned that the stress of a drought might be different for a tree and for the crops of prehistoric dry farmers, and also warned that pollen in archaeological sites might reflect the use of certain plants and not the local flora as a whole. This concluded the symposium.

The symposium "was a good move," according to Emil Haury. "It demonstrated the interplay of tree rings, pollen, and geomorphology. But where the program fell short was in relating the archaeological story to the findings of other disciplines" (letter to Woodbury, 20 August 1979). One of the organizers of the program commented privately to me that the symposium was "a dismal failure."

Because I was well started on this history but could not attend the Tucson Conference, I asked Haury to distribute a questionnaire—which he did—asking conferees to indicate reasons for attending Pecos Conferences: what the "greatest value to you" had been, what publications or stimulation to research could be identified as resulting from the Conferences, and a few other similar questions. Response was poor initially, but eventually about sixty questionnaires were returned, partly as a result of mailing out additional copies in 1980. Many of these contained valuable recollections and observations, which have been quoted in earlier chapters or will be quoted in the final chapter.

MESA VERDE, 1980 (FORTY-THIRD PECOS CONFERENCE) Instead of Black Mesa, as expected, the scene of the 1980 Pecos Conference was

Mesa Verde National Park. The presentation of reports and papers was also changed radically from the pattern of field reports and symposium, bringing rather mixed reactions. This should probably be viewed not as a "revolt," such as the one that brewed and partly boiled over in 1970, but as an effort to present information in a format seen by the organizers as more useful for the listeners.

In June a letter was sent out, saying, "We shall not be able to host the 1980 Pecos Conference on Black Mesa. Rather, we have been invited to meet at Mesa Verde National Park on August 14 and 15." The letter also said,

> We feel that this is an ideal time to make long needed changes in the format of the conference. Therefore, the agenda will be as follows:
> August 14—Morning: Symposium on Anasazi developments.
> August 14—Afternoon: Regional and topical reports and field reports.
> August 15—Morning: General session summarizing discussions from the previous afternoon.
> August 15—Afternoon: SARG symposium.

Those who wished to present a field report were told to bring thirty copies of

> a 3–4 page paper succinctly describing the pertinent data and approach and problems you are addressing from your work. . . . An individual from each geographic/topical area will be chosen to summarize all field reports from his or her area and to lead a discussion of them. You should plan to contact that person with your written report upon arriving at the conference. We hope in this way to give the sessions more dynamic value so that all of us may benefit in ways that have not always been present in the recent past.

The concept of the Anasazi symposium is made clearer in a letter (5 July 1980) from Plog and Euler to Linda Cordell (University of New Mexico) inviting her to take part, as one of seven speakers allotted fifteen or twenty minutes each. The symposium was titled "Regional Variation on the Colorado Plateaus," and her topic would be the Rio Grande area. The letter pointed out, "The last decade has seen an enormous growth in theoretical literature on spatial patterns. . . .

and far more specific concepts of the manner in which populations in different areas shared material items." It mentioned recent "provocative hypotheses of major local and demographic shifts in response to changing climatic conditions." The letter closed with a request for consideration of "the boundaries that you feel circumscribe the area of your research . . . and the material criteria that you would use to define those boundaries."

The symposium resulting from this elaborate request is described in a letter by Cordell (to Woodbury, 29 September 1980):

> As the Conference Announcement states, there was an opening symposium on "Anasazi Developments," but as you can see from the letter to me from Plog and Euler, instructions to symposium participants were rather more specific. The papers given on the morning of the 14th were: Art Rohn on the Mesa Verde, mine on the Rio Grande Valley, Jim Judge on Chaco (and the San Juan Basin), Jeff Dean on Kayenta, Joseph Tainter on the Anasazi from Mount Taylor to Gran Quivira and north of highway 66, and T. J. Ferguson on Zuni. I realize [the title of] Tainter's paper sounds absurd, but he just completed an overview of that area for the Forest Service and BLM. I think T. J.'s paper was supposed to provide an "emic" perspective on how regions are defined by the Zuni. I don't think the symposium really worked, although it was fun to do. The main reason that I feel that the symposium didn't work is just that it did not focus ensuing discussions.

Cordell continued, in reference to the rest of the Conference,

> after the symposium field reports were given, and each reporter had to have copies of the field report. In essence, I guess this was viewed as Paul Martin's students winning the point. Note that Fred Plog was one of the organizers. Unfortunately, the papers were given by region (state) and not by topic. One person was appointed to each region to serve as moderator and synthesizer. . . . I think the "state focus" was so ingrained that nobody signed up for a topical session.

The next morning a summary of the states' reports was given: Thomas Windes for New Mexico, David Breternitz for Colorado, David Doyel for Arizona, and Margaret Lyneis for Utah and Nevada.

In a letter to Haury (17 August 1980) Breternitz said that his Colorado "Session began with 65+ persons at Amphitheater; moved to Old Rec. Hall due to rain; 30–40 persons attended to end of papers." He also said, "This year's PC was somewhat of a disappointment, but we did get to see a lot of people; however, not many of the Good Old Boys were there—and we certainly missed you." Cordell (letter to Woodbury, 21 September 1980) commented:

> A number of people, including Al Schroeder, were unhappy
> with the arrangement because one could not personally hear all
> the field reports. The reorganization was an attempt to bring
> meaningful interaction back into the conference context, rather
> than have most fruitful discussions held off under some trees, at
> the same time that papers are being given. Despite some nega-
> tive comments, the group agreed to continue with the basic
> restructuring, although perhaps with some modifications.

The business meeting, at the end of Friday morning, began with a telegram to Madeleine Kidder and expressions of appreciation to the Mesa Verde staff. No deaths were reported. An innovation was the announcement of job opportunities by several contract archaeology companies, as well as the Navajo Nation and the Dolores Project. It was suggested that Conferences be held on a Friday-Saturday pattern, rather than Thursday-Friday, thus avoiding the loss of an extra working day for many. Archaeologists were now punching the time clock.

The final session of the Conference, Friday afternoon, was a report by SARG, which had several times met the day before a Pecos Conference, but as a closed or working meeting (Gaines 1981). This may be the first time its meeting was also a session of the Pecos Conference. Cordell has written (letter to Woodbury, 29 September 1980): "In the afternoon . . . there was a report from SARG. SARG is viewed by many as an 'elitist' outfit and attendance was not very high. Basically, SARG announced that it had obtained some NSF money (not much) and could accept some new participants. Cynthia Irwin-Williams and I joined them, and nobody else had much to say."

As mentioned before, published references to the reports or papers at Pecos Conferences are rare. From the 1980 Conference I have chanced on one: "The Anasazi-Mogollon Transition Zone in West-Central New Mexico" by Joseph A. Tainter is cited by Linda Robertson in her dissertation (1983: 320), a reminder that at least some conference papers have more than transient interest.

FORT BURGWIN, 1981 (FORTY-FOURTH PECOS CONFERENCE)   Planning
for the 1981 Conference began with confusion and misunderstandings, although the schedule for 1981 and beyond had been confirmed
in Tucson in 1979. For a while there was the risk of two rival Pecos
Conferences taking place that summer. Apparently, because the Fort
Burgwin archaeologists from Southern Methodist University were
not at the Mesa Verde Conference, and because at that time Cordell
(University of New Mexico) and Walter K. Wait (National Park Service) were proposed for chairing the program, two planning groups
began work independently in the fall of 1980—Anne I. Woosley for
Southern Methodist University, and Cordell and Wait separately.

Confusion increased as planning proceeded in two directions simultaneously, partly because two locations were now scheduled and
partly because there were two competing views of what kind of program would be most useful. For much of the spring it looked as
though there would be no Pecos Conference at all that year, but a
compromise was finally worked out between the rival groups (more
fully described in Woodbury 1991).

The Conference was held 13 and 14 August at the Fort Burgwin
Research Center. In March program material was mailed with information for preregistration ($15, $10 for students, to include a Thursday evening meal and admission to the Millicent Rogers Museum)
and details on campgrounds, two with no hook-ups and three with
(archaeologists now traveled in mobile homes as well as pick-ups and
Volkswagen minibuses). In addition, breakfasts and lunches would
be served at the Conference, at $2 a meal, because restaurants in Taos
were eight miles away and no fires were allowed in the campgrounds.
The Sagebrush Inn and many other lodgings were listed. Participants
were invited by Art Wolf, director, to an open house at the Millicent
Rogers Museum in Taos, which besides its other exhibits was showing "America's Great Lost Expedition: The Thomas Keam Collection
of Hopi Pottery from the Second Hemenway Expedition 1890–1894"
(see Wade and McChesney 1980).

Woosley (letter to Woodbury, 4 September 1981) said that "our final
count of people either camping or staying at hotels in Taos came to
463. Most everyone seemed to enjoy the sessions, and to have a good
time. . . . All sessions were well attended from beginning to end. We
are working on publishing the Archaic session (looks good)." This
would have achieved one of Haury's expressed hopes—that, as at the
1927 Conference, a significant problem or topic could be discussed
and a consensus reached and published for the guidance of future re-

searchers. Woosley added, "We had a marvelous feast on the evening of the 13th, complete with beer and campfire. I ordered 4 kegs of beer and that was sufficient. We had no problems to speak of at all . . . just happy folks" (ellipsis in original).

Urban's notes (1981) on the Conference record that Cynthia Irwin-Williams opened the Archaic session with remarks on method and theory. She was followed by Fred Niles and Bill Schelly, who spoke on the extensive aeolian displacement of artifacts and disturbance of Archaic sites, often making "reconstruction" impossible. Wait discussed problems of recording and interpreting lithic scatters and the need to understand the environment of the San Juan Basin before a cultural transition at about 5,800 years ago. Dawn M. Greenwald spoke on the ways in which Archaic sites that also contained Anasazi lithic material could be analyzed. The Archaic record for specific regions was then presented: Alan Simmons for the Chaco Canyon region, Bruce Huckell for the Santa Rita Mountains of southern Arizona, John Gooding on high altitude Archaic-like sites in the Rocky Mountains, Van Button and Brian Bilbone on the San Luis Valley of Colorado, and finally Carl Halbirt on the Paunsaugunt Region of southwestern Utah. Unfortunately, these papers on the Archaic were never published (Anne I. Woosley, letter to Woodbury, 5 June 1989). Woosley comments that "today's Pecos Conference participants don't seem to want 'consensus' on any subject."

At the session on Sedentism the speakers included Christy Turner on evidence of violence in Anasazi sites, Stewart Peckham on Chaco outliers, William Lucius and Scott Travis on exchange systems, and Dean Wilson on migration as indicated by nonlocal ceramics. The Friday morning session on lithic technology had six speakers. The session on flora, fauna, and climate included information from Patricia Crown on prehistoric water supply data from the Salt-Gila Project, Susan Fish on interpreting pollen data, Charles Miksicek comparing evidence from pollen and flotation, and Steven Emslie on the study of archaeological faunal material.

At the Friday afternoon plenary session, several large projects were summarized: Breternitz, the Dolores Project; James Judge, the Chaco Project; Lynn Teague and Eugene Rogge, the Salt-Gila Aqueduct Project; Gumerman, the Black Mesa Project; David Doyel, Navajo Nation archaeological projects.

The Conference concluded with the business meeting, attended by fewer than thirty-five people, as would be expected for its end-of-the-last-day scheduling. It expressed thanks to the hosts of the Conference and confirmed a 1982 meeting at Pecos and a 1983 meeting at El Paso, the latter changed subsequently to a very different setting, at Bluff, Utah.

David Brugge (letter to Woodbury, 25 August 1981) has provided some personal observations on the meeting as a whole:

> I am not sure just when the timing was moved back from the weekend [to Thursday-Friday]. . . . It is, I think, an indication of increasing formality and of more people attending as part of their employment rather than on their own. Fort Burgwin did a good job of hosting. There was plenty of camp space. . . . The program was more formal than usual. . . . It was almost entirely oriented to prehistory except for occasional minor references to historic or ethnographic data in a few papers. Many people read their reports. . . .
>
> The crowd was smaller than in some recent years; I would estimate between 200 and 300, which helped make for a more relaxed atmosphere. . . . A lot of the papers were New Archeology, some good, some bad, but fortunately we were spared the detailed statistics in most, which can be as deadly as the old-time post hole dimensions.

The difference between Brugge's estimate and Woosley's count is probably a difference between the number usually present at a session and the total number, including spouses and children, in the campground and motels. The changes in the form of the program, carried over from the Mesa Verde format and a revival of the demands made for the 1970 Conference in Santa Fe, did not continue the next year at Pecos, which returned to informal field reports for the whole group rather than separate concurrent sessions. More important, the threat of a split into two rival conferences in 1981 subsided, and the Conference at Fort Burgwin appears to have proceeded with the traditional friendliness and collegiality.

PECOS, 1982 (FORTY-FIFTH PECOS CONFERENCE) The Thursday-Friday pattern was again followed at the 1982 Conference, 12 and 13 August. The announcement notice quoted Kidder's 1927 statement of purpose, as had been done several times in recent years (but not in the rival 1981 announcements): the intent of the Conference was to "bring about contacts between workers in the Southwestern field to discuss fundamental problems of Southwestern history, and to formulate plans for a coordinated attack upon them; to pool knowledge of facts and techniques, and to lay foundations for a unified system of nomenclature." The announcement went on to say:

> Individual research emphases have changed over the past 55 years, but the essential intent of the first Pecos Conference has been carried on at successive meetings, serving to enrich anthropological studies in the Southwest and neighboring areas, in the manner hoped for by Dr. Kidder. It is in this spirit that the hosts of this year's conference, Pecos National Monument (National Park Service), the Museum of New Mexico, the School of American Research, and the Archaeological Society of New Mexico, invite all Southwesternists to return to Pecos . . . and participate in this now traditional gathering.

Registration began Thursday evening at the Laboratory of Anthropology and continued Friday morning at Pecos National Monument. The total came to 333, down substantially from five years before at the same location. Field reports occupied all day Friday and continued the next morning, grouped into Archaic, Anasazi, Mogollon, Hohokam, ethnology, historical archaeology, and peripheral areas. Such categories, changing year by year, are a clue to the way knowledge is being organized at a particular time. Categories like "Archaic" and "historical archaeology" reflect an expansion of the time period traditionally of concern to Southwestern archaeologists.

To open Friday morning the NPS regional director welcomed the conferees. He noted that Pecos was the scene of some of the first archaeological air photos, taken by Charles Lindberg. John Bezy, superintendent of Pecos National Monument, continued the welcome and added information on messages, telephones, smoking restrictions, and the trail guide for the ruins. The sessions were held under an enormous striped tent, just west of the monument headquarters, and another tent sheltered the extensive book exhibits and sales that had begun in recent years to accompany each Conference. Fortunately no summer rains occurred; instead brisk winds swept through the tents, blowing from everyone's brains the cobwebs that E. B. Danson had referred to in his 1969 plea for outdoor Conferences.

Urban's notes (1982) include forty-two reports, Anasazi having the largest number. First came the Archaic, chaired by Irwin-Williams, with four reports. The Anasazi session was chaired by Frances Joan Mathien and had twelve reports, including an update on SARG by

Sylvia Gaines and five reports on the nearly completed Dolores Project. There were three Mogollon reports with Regge Wiseman chairing.

Haury chaired the Hohokam session, which he introduced with comments on the contrast between 1982 and the 1931 Pecos Conference at Santa Fe, when fifty to sixty people sat around informally and debated and discussed the reports presented. He also commented that Hohokam chronology had become a national sport—there had been a spate of alternative datings proposed in the past few years. The six reports included one by Thomas (Jeff) King on the Gila Heritage Park of the Gila River Tribe, with its replicas including three Hohokam pit houses—117 man-days of work per pit house.

A separate ethnology session was scheduled, the first in many years. It was presided over by Ellis, who reported the loosening of Rio Grande pueblo restrictions on anthropological-archaeological research when of importance for land and water claims. Other reports ranged from the Apache and Comanche to the Salinas area.

Friday evening was devoted to the "Comida" offered by the people of Pecos, with chili, posole, and beans, and a choice of soda or beer. There were 342 tickets sold, and the event was judged an outstanding success.

The next morning, following two reports in the session on historical archaeology, chaired by John Beal, there was a final series of ten rather miscellaneous reports, grouped as peripheral areas, which John Campbell chaired.

The business meeting, presided over by Curtis Schaafsma, began with appreciation expressed to Larry Nordby, the Conference organizer; Bezy, the monument superintendent, and his staff, particularly Verna Hutchinson; and the other organizations hosting the Conference. Raymond Thompson then presented a special appreciation to the people of Pecos, appropriately delivered in Spanish.

A problem arose concerning the next year's meeting place, since Rex Gerald had had to withdraw the El Paso invitation. Edge of the Cedars Museum in Blanding, Utah, was proposed, and it was pointed out that there had not previously been a Pecos Conference in Utah (the comment was also made that beer was sold in Bluff although not in Blanding). There was some reluctance to accept this location, Haury suggesting that Pecos National Monument be made a permanent Conference location, Danson proposing alternate years at Pecos, and Schaafsma supporting this because of the importance of meeting in different regions. This alternating schedule was moved, seconded, and passed unanimously. As it turned out, however, the Conference did not return to Pecos until 1987.

Thompson described some of the efforts leading up to the Antiquities Act of 1906, including reference by New England preservationists to the importance of the Pecos ruin, which they described, in a memorial to their senator, as "even older than Boston." Thompson then observed that not only were Emil Haury, Hulda Haury, and Clara Lee Tanner present at this Conference, surviving "Founders" of 1927, but the Kidders' daughter, Faith Kidder Fuller, was also present. She had climbed a tree and tossed down nuts or pebbles on the 1927 conferees, until she was twice barred from the camp. To commemorate this event of 1927 she was now ceremoniously escorted out of the Conference tent, to mark her third disbarring. Following this bit of history and symbolism, Fuller read from her sister Barbara's moving reminiscences of the Kidder family's summers at Pecos (Aldana 1983). They were followed by a short summary of the history of the Pecos Conference, which I had been asked to present, a few highlights from 1927 and subsequently (Woodbury 1983).

Following lunch the symposium took place, planned and presided over by Schroeder and alliteratively titled in his inimitable way, "Protohistoric Palaver Pertaining to Peripheral Parameters of Pecos Pueblo." Speakers included Larry Nordby, David Snow, Schroeder, Wilcox, Timothy Baugh, and Brugge, all examining various aspects of protohistoric Pecos and its surroundings. Among the observations made was the increasingly defensive nature of Pecos in later prehistoric and early historic times, and the likelihood that it attempted to control the "buffalo market" to pueblos farther west (Nordby); and that the extensive raiding and fighting of the sixteenth century might have been due to stress caused by the sixteenth-century drought as well as the arrival of Athabascans (Schroeder).

This concluded the forty-fifth Pecos Conference, held with a traditional (and not openly protested) program. The symposium papers were published by the Archaeological Society of New Mexico (Fox 1984), thus fulfilling an often expressed hope of many Conference members that symposia be published.

Haury pursued the idea of Pecos as a permanent location for the Conference, and on 30 September Robert I. Kerr, regional director, Southwest Region, National Park Service, wrote with data on costs of the 1982 Conference:

1. The $200 cost of materials included electrical wiring, sign material, bulletin board, Kidder display, banner, flood lights and telephone calls.

2. Personnel service costs also included overtime expenses of $1,480 which otherwise would not have been incurred. Normal salary dollars spent on the conference, of course, were diverted from monument projects that relate directly to the resource or the visiting public.

3. Registration fees brought in approximately $1,665 and a $200 profit was made from the meal. This $1,865 was deposited in the Pecos Conference general fund (checking account) and did not offset monument costs in any way.

I don't agree that we should consider only additional direct costs rather than institutional costs in establishing realistic registration fees, because a small area like Pecos cannot afford to absorb such an amount on an every-other-year basis.

Although it is not stated, the $1,865 referred to may have been used to pay for the 2 rented tents, the portable toilets, and the 200–300 folding chairs. Host organizations had various ways of providing the essentials for a conference, but there were many costs and they had to be met in some way. As the Conference had grown, so had the expense of holding it, and finding places to meet with suitable facilities and the means to manage the costs became more and more difficult. It is testimony to people's dedication that year after year hosts were found and meetings continued to be held.

BLUFF, 1983 (FORTY-SIXTH PECOS CONFERENCE) Long before 1927 Utah occupied an important place in Southwestern archaeology, and it was probably the scarcity of major research centers in the archaeologically "Southwestern" part of the state that explains why it was so long before a Pecos Conference was held in Utah. Institutions in Salt Lake City had, of course, a long record of archaeological activity in the Southwest: Byron Cummings was there, years before his move to Tucson, when he began his annual explorations of the canyon country of southern Utah. A. V. Kidder had cut his archaeological teeth in Utah with Edgar L. Hewett in 1907. Now, on the fiftieth anniversary of J. O. Brew's landmark excavations at Alkali Ridge, in southeastern Utah, the Conference would finally be held in this part of the Southwest.

An announcement was sent out by the Bluff Pecos Committee and the Edge of the Cedars State Historical Monument (in Blanding). The Conference would be held on 11, 12, and 13 August at St. Christopher's Mission in Bluff. The program held to tradition: "In keeping with the informal nature of the Pecos Conference, unwritten presentations are encouraged. . . . Since meetings will be held outdoors beneath tent and ramada cover, there will be no provisions for slide presentations." Field reports were allotted a day and a half.

The Conference began with registration on Wednesday, 10 August, at St. Christopher's Mission and a welcome on Thursday morning on behalf of Bluff City by Ken Ross, who had lived in the Southwest since 1906.

The first session was moderated by Arthur Rohn and began with local archaeological history from Winston Hurst of Bluff, who described the long record of pot hunting in the area, particularly by the Shumway family, who worked with Andrew Kerr, the professor who succeeded Cummings at Utah (see Brew 1946: 23). Hurst said Kerr collected over 2,000 pots in the area in five years. As Kerr had a Ph.D., Shumway assumed that "this was the way it was done," and he thus became a "trained archaeologist." When Julian Steward succeeded Kerr at Utah about 1930 he "changed things and so made pothunters out of the Shumways! This brought on a lot of bad blood. So [the] Shumway family continued on the way they had been," as Urban (1983) reports it.

There were twelve field reports on Anasazi research in the morning session. Because of the large number of Anasazi reports still remaining, it was decided to have the six Hohokam and Mogollon reports concurrently with the Anasazi session. The afternoon Anasazi session, chaired by Winston Hurt, had six reports, including Charles Adams on the first year of the Crow Canyon Campus, near Cortez, a branch of the Center for American Archaeology (a sibling, therefore, of Kampsville, Illinois); Helen Crotty's restudy of the burials and ceramics of the 1932 Rainbow Bridge—Monument Valley Expedition; Jonathan Haas on evidence for tribalization in the Tsegi Phase in the Long House Valley; and Alexa Aldridge on the sixteenth and last year of work on Black Mesa, supported by the Peabody Coal Company. Thursday ended with an open house at the Edge of the Cedars Museum in Blanding.

On Friday morning Anasazi field reports continued. Perhaps the large number was partly due to the location of the Conference, there being many more reports on Utah than in recent years, and partly due to the very large scope of the Dolores Project, the Black Mesa Project, and the Chaco Project, all of which were reported on by one or more people. William E. Davis, director of Abajo Archaeology (a private archaeological contract group in Bluff) moderated this session, which had thirteen speakers.

Before the Friday afternoon symposium began, Bertha Dutton spoke of the recent death of Harry L. Hadlock of Farmington, a dedicated and capable amateur archaeologist.

The symposium, organized and chaired by Paul R. Nickens, was "Current Archaeological Research in Southeast Utah." Nickens introduced it with remarks on the background of current research in the area. Nine papers were given, and it is tempting to paraphrase at length from Urban's detailed notes, but the speakers and titles will have to suffice:

> Frank W. Eddy, Allen E. Kane, and Paul R. Nickens, "The Drainage Unit Concept: The Shortcomings of the Research District."
> Marilyn Swift and Margaret Powers, "Sub-regional Variation in Prehistoric Sites of Southeastern Utah."
> Robert Neily, "Basketmaker Settlement and Subsistence along the San Juan River, Southeastern Utah."
> Joel C. Janetski, "The Nancy Patterson Research Project."
> William E. Davis, "1981 Excavations on White Mesa, San Juan County, Utah."
> William A. Lucius, "An Alternative Speculative History of San Juan County, Utah."
> Bruce D. Louthan, "Elk Ridge [north of Bluff and west of Blanding] as a Refugium during Pueblo I Times: A Reassessment."
> Todd R. Metzger, "Establishing Criteria for the Development of the North Abajo/Canyonlands District: Expansion of the Mesa Verde Anasazi in the Northern Periphery during Late Pueblo II—Pueblo III Times."
> Phil R. Geib and J. Richard Ambler, "Late Pueblo III in the Navajo Mountain Area, Southern Utah."

The three discussants, Ray Matheny, Adrienne Anderson, and Hurst, mentioned the continuing lack of an integrated picture of southeastern Utah, the overdependence on the Mesa Verde ceramic sequence, and the problem of whether the Athabascans' arrival could be recognized archaeologically.

That evening there was a dinner with open-pit broiled steaks pre-pared by the Trail of the Ancients organization of Blanding. Enter-tainment until midnight was provided by a country-western band.

Saturday morning about twenty people attended the business meet-ing, never the most popular event of the Conference. The first ques-tion was where the 1984 meeting would be held, as there was no one present from Pecos National Monument to confirm the hopes of meet-ing there. The consensus was "we'll go to Pecos if they'll have us," but Bruce Anderson of the National Park Service offered to look into the possibility of Wupatki National Monument, forty miles north of Flagstaff, as an alternative. He was also asked to chair the committee for 1984 plans, and Pilles volunteered to assist him.

Alfred E. (Ed) Dittert of Arizona State University announced that the Hohokam Conference would be held at the university in Novem-ber, and also that a Museum Conference would be held jointly by the university and the Heard Museum in October. Schroeder offered formal thanks to Davis and to Bluff for hosting the Conference. Davis, in turn, thanked Edge of the Cedars Museum for its support.

The field trip that followed the business meeting attracted about 100 participants, who visited the Alkali Ridge sites, enjoying the wonder-ful privilege of having J. O. (Jo) Brew and James A. (Al) Lancaster as guides, revisiting the scene of their field work of 1931–33.

Although only 158 names appear on the registration sign-up sheets, attendance was estimated at 220. Again this year publications were on sale. A special T-shirt was designed and sold (for $6) to commemo-rate the Conference, a practice that was rapidly becoming a tradition. Urban's notes close with "All agreed it was a TERRIFIC Conference!"

FLAGSTAFF, 1984 (FORTY-SEVENTH PECOS CONFERENCE) Contrary to the hopes discussed at the 1983 business meeting, it did not prove pos-sible for the 1984 meeting to be held at Pecos National Monument. The Conference would not return to Pecos until 1987, for its fiftieth meet-ing and the sixtieth anniversary of its creation. A meeting at Wupatki National Monument, as had been suggested, did not prove possible either, but several northern Arizona organizations cooperated to hold the 1984 meeting in Flagstaff.

Records for the 1984 Conference are unusually meager, partly be-cause Urban chose to attend the Olympics rather than the Pecos Con-ference(!), and no one else offered to take down a record in her place. However, many details of the plans were mailed out by the cochair-persons of the Conference, Pilles and Anderson. The location would be Flagstaff, with an impressive group of sponsors: the National Park Service, the Coconino National Forest, the Museum of Northern Arizona (where the meeting would take place), the Arizona Archaeological Society, Northern Arizona University, and the Arizona Archaeological and Historical Society. The dates were 9–11 August. A logo was created for the 1984 Conference (including the familiar error of identifying it as the fifty-seventh Conference rather than the fifty-seventh year), with a Hopi symbol of clouds and rain, the San Francisco Peaks, a pueblo ruin (Wupatki), and a variety of pictographs. A special T-shirt was available, decorated with this complicated logo.

The same mailing included a preregistration form ($10 per person) and asked advance payment ($7.50 per person) for the Friday evening dinner of "barbecued beef, beans, bread, potato salad, soda pop or beer." Field reports would be given all day on Thursday and on Friday morning—the same substantial amount of time that was allotted the previous year. This time it proved sufficient, and there were no concurrent sessions. "Informal presentations of about 10 minutes are encouraged," and as the sessions would be held outdoors no slide presentations were possible. Those wishing to give a field report were asked to indicate which of the following sessions it would best fit into: paleo-Indian/Archaic period, Hohokam area, Mogollon area, Anasazi area (Arizona, New Mexico, Colorado, or Utah), "peripheral" areas, ethnohistoric/protohistoric period, historic period, theoretical/ methodological, or other. It was obviously expected that reports on the Anasazi would again dominate. Ethnography was not mentioned. The chamber of commerce handout listed fifty-four places to eat and twenty-seven places to sleep, a remarkable change from the limited choices when the Pecos Conference first came to Flagstaff in 1950.

In addition to a day and a half of field reports, there was a symposium on Friday afternoon, "An Overview of the Prehistory of the Flagstaff Region." Nine twenty-minute presentations were made:

"The History of Sinagua Research and Theories," by Albert H. Schroeder

"Flagstaff as a Microcosm of Southwestern and American Archaeology," by David A. Breternitz

"The Northern Sinagua," by Peter J. Pilles, Jr

"The Anderson Mesa Area," by Sherry Lerner

"The Southern Sinagua," by Paul Fish

"The Cohonina," by Tom Cartledge

"The Sinagua Frontier," by Mike Bremer and Anne Baldwin

"The Wupatki Area,"   by Bruce Anderson
"Sinagua Social Organization,"   by John Hohmann

The symposium publication that was planned has not appeared.
For Saturday, tours were arranged to Wupatki National Monument
and sites in the Coconino National Forest.

SALINAS NATIONAL MONUMENT, 1985 (FORTY-EIGHTH PECOS CON-
FERENCE)   The Pecos Conference continued to be remarkably fortunate in finding new locations at which to meet, where hosts were
both willing and able to manage the logistics and costs. One of the
less known and newest Southwestern archaeological monuments was
the 1985 host: Salinas National Monument, created in 1980 to include the former Gran Quivira National Monument and the Abo and
Quarai New Mexico state parks. These were among the most east-
erly pueblos, separated from the Rio Grande by the Manzano and Los
Pinos Mountains. The area was known to the Spanish as the Salinas
Province and was the scene of missionary activity beginning about
1630, but before the Pueblo Revolt of 1680 it had been abandoned due
to the combination of drought and Apache raids (see Hayes 1981).
    Jim Trott, the NPS archaeologist at the monument, sent out pre-
liminary details, indicating the dates of 15–18 August, and naming
the sponsors as Salinas National Monument, the Museum of New
Mexico, and the Archaeological Society of New Mexico. Preregistration, with a $10 fee, was requested, as well as $7 for the Friday night
dinner. The registration form asked for field reports to be identified
by area. Trott (letter to Woodbury, 9 October 1985) said that of the
1,550 people to which the mailing went, 311 registered and 272 signed
up for the dinner, an excellent attendance for a relatively unfamiliar
location. The mailing and registration figures suggest that 20 percent
of all identified Southwestern archaeologists attended.
    The final program had an impressive innovation: besides listing
each speaker and his or her topic, it included the alphabetized names
of all who preregistered, something never before available at the start
of a Conference. Following the Conference a list of registrants with
addresses was mailed to all who attended, valuable for all who wanted
to follow up reports and conversations at the Conference. Only two
motels could be listed, both in Mountainair, twenty-six miles to the
north. To supplement Mountainair's four restaurants, noontime meals
would be provided at the monument at a nominal cost.
    The Conference was held in front of the main church, San Buena-

ventura, at Gran Quivira under a large blue and white tent. Friday morning Trott welcomed the conferees on behalf of the National Park Service. It was pointed out that the campground nine miles north on the road to Mountainair was private land, so campers should stay within the white flagged area. The dinner would take place in the blue flagged area. The Conference was fortunate to have a camp area, as all land around the monument was private ranch land, not open for such use. But the former maintenance foreman at Gran Quivira, Vernie Wells, would welcome the conferees to his land. Trott also announced that lunches were being provided by the Jubilee Committee of the Mountainair Volunteer Fire Department. A "first" for the Pecos Conference was the request that conferees sign a liability release at the registration desk! The era of possible litigation for any and every reason had arrived.

The first session Friday morning was on the paleo-Indian and Archaic periods, chaired by Dennis Stanford and with seven reports. Nine reports on the Hohokam followed immediately, with Doyel presiding. One was by Christy G. Turner II, on the biological affinity of the La Ciudad Hohokam (Urban comments that "this turned out to be quite a bombshell!"). Turner said that on the basis of dentition the Hohokam's affinities were with northern Mexico, not with the Mogollon, and that the Pima could be grouped with northern groups such as those of Point of Pines and Grasshopper.

In the afternoon the Mogollon session began, chaired by Reggie Wiseman and with seven reports, including the archaeology of White Sands Missile Range, reported on by David Kirkpatrick. Sites on military reservations were at last being surveyed and at least partially protected. Next was the Anasazi session, which Schroeder chaired. There were seventeen reports, ranging from research at the Crow Canyon field school for amateurs, near Cortez, and the seventh and last year of the Dolores Project, to rock art as a communication system, and variations in subject matter of Pueblo IV murals.

When the afternoon's reports were completed, it was announced that the New Mexico Archaeological Council would have "a beer bust at 6:30," and that dinner would be at the campground, north on State Highway 14, with the "Adobe Brothers" band playing bluegrass music.

Saturday morning opened with a session on peripheral areas, presided over by Kate Spielmann. Its thirteen reports were followed by two ethnohistoric/protohistoric reports.

After a break for lunch, there were announcements of the Sunday tours to (1) Pueblo Blanco and Pueblo Colorado, (2) Tenabo, and (3) petroglyphs near Abo. All three units of the monument were open, of course, for self-guided tours. Ten reports on the historic period, in a session presided over by Frances Levine, occupied the first half of the afternoon.

Looking at the field reports as a whole, it is of interest that excavation was reported in less than one-third of the presentations, and about one-fourth reported surveys, with the balance reporting analysis, laboratory study, and archival research. A great deal was being done, but not all of it with the shovel, trowel, and brush.

After a twenty-minute break the business meeting was convened. It began with the presentation of a letter to Governor Babbitt of Arizona expressing concern for the proposed paramilitary and sports complex north of Tucson and the resultant destruction of the Cerro Prieto site. Support by the Conference was moved, seconded, and voted unanimously. A telegram of good wishes was sent to Haury, recovering well from a mild stroke. It was confirmed that the 1987 Conference would be at Pecos National Monument, but a location for 1986 was uncertain. Los Alamos was a possibility but could not be confirmed at the moment. Another possibility was the Arizona State University field school at the Shoofly ruin, near Payson. Tom Lyons asked for a week to check on whether the Conference could go to Chaco Canyon, and Fred Lange suggested the Yellow Jacket ruin in Colorado. Charles Adams pointed out that there should be a five-year list of meeting places, as there had sometimes been in the past. Joe Ben Wheat suggested that whatever confirmation came first should settle the choice for 1986. The preferences appeared to be Payson, Pecos, Yellow Jacket, and Chaco. Dittert reported the death of D. Travis Hudson on 6 July at his home in Santa Barbara. Finally, there were resolutions of thanks to all those who had made the Conference so successful. This completed the business meeting, all in twenty minutes.

The remainder of the Conference was devoted to a symposium, "Salinas Archeology," following the frequent pattern of attention to the archaeology of the area in which the Conference was being held. The symposium was presided over by Alden Hayes, who was editor and coauthor of two of the major publications on the area, "Contributions to Gran Quivira Archeology" (Hayes 1981) and "Excavation of Mound 7, Grand Quivira National Monument, New Mexico" (Hayes and others 1981), both in the series, *National Park Service Publications in Archeology*. Appropriately, Hayes spoke first, on the history of archaeological research in the Salinas area, noting that there was still "more ignorance here per square mile than anywhere else in the Southwest." Hayes was followed by: Joseph Tainter, an overview of the archaeology from paleo-Indian to historic; Stuart Baldwin, details of some of the extensive survey and excavation during the preceding five years; Reggie Wiseman, results of the study of Chupadera Black-on-white by the Albuquerque Archeological Society; Kate Spielmann, evidence for exchange of corn and bison jerky between the pueblo farmers and the Plains hunter-gatherers; K. P. Medlin, the future research plans of the Central New Mexico Research Association, including site surveys, relationships with the Plains, with Zuni, and with the Jornada Mogollon, and the origins of the kachina cult.

Before the discussants were called on, it was announced that there would be a dance that night at the Rosebud Saloon in downtown Mountainair. Discussion was begun by Hayes, who commented on the great ceramic diversity of the area and its distinctiveness from the Rio Grande. David Snow observed that when the Spanish came their demand for corn as well as skins for tribute interrupted the traditional male activities. The relation of the decoration of Tabirá pottery to Jornada rock art was noted by Schaafsma, who suggested looking to the south and southeast for the origins of this new pottery style. Turner said that the Gran Quivira skeletal population was better preserved than that from Pecos, and that there was no evidence for a new group coming into the Salinas.

This concluded the 1985 Conference, except for the optional tours the next morning. In a letter to Woodbury (9 October 1985) Trott adds several details about the Conference that have not been mentioned above. In regard to finances, the planners began with $1,500 "seed money" arranged for by Larry Nordby, of the NPS Southwest Regional Office, which came from the 1982 Conference at Pecos. The Conference cost about $4,300 and took in about $5,430. There were Conference T-shirts printed by the Triticum Press of Pullman, Washington (owned and operated by June Lipe, wife of archaeologist William Lipe); they used the plan of Mound 7, Gran Quivira (see Hayes and others 1981), and 135 shirts were sold at $6.50 each. A shady area was provided with tables for book sales. Among the local groups assisting the Conference were the town of Mountainair (chairs and tables), the Torrance County Historical Society and Torrance County Sheriff's Posse (volunteers to replace the Park Service staff in public areas during the Conference), and the Ghost Riders Bar (beer for Friday night). Trott added, "The weather was perfect with temperatures in the 80's with a light breeze and clear skies."

Payson, 1986 (Forty-ninth Pecos Conference)   The weather in August, 1986, was less kindly than the year before, with a thunderstorm and downpour on the first afternoon, as the barbecue dinner was about to start. But other things went excellently at the Shoofly Village ruin near Payson. The site was being excavated by the Arizona State University field school, which had begun work there in the summer of 1984 under the direction of Charles L. Redman.

The Pecos Conference announcement that Redman sent out in June gave the dates as 7–9 August and the sponsors as Arizona State University, the Tonto National Forest (in which the site is located), and the Arizona Archaeological and Historical Society. It was to be an outdoor meeting, but (fortunately) with a large tent for protection from rain. "In keeping with the informal nature of the Pecos Conference, unwritten presentations of approximately 10 minutes are encouraged." Very prompt reservations at Payson motels were recommended, as the Mogollon Rim (Zane Grey country) is a popular destination for those escaping the heat of Phoenix.

Preregistration was encouraged, with an advance fee of $10, dinner tickets $7.50, and the opportunity to order a Pecos Conference T-shirt and hat. Finally, research report information was requested— "region, culture(?), and subject."

Some 330 people registered, about equal to the larger Conferences of the past decade or two. The Conference opened Friday morning under a big red and white striped tent, placed so that the audience faced "the high escarpment of the Mogollon Rim across the northern half of the Payson basin," a magnificent setting (E. A. Morris, letter to Woodbury, 20 August 1986). After a few announcements the symposium began, on the subject of "Spatial Organization and Integration West of the Continental Divide in the Late Prehistoric Period." It was planned by Wilcox (Museum of Northern Arizona and Northern Arizona University), Pilles (Coconino National Forest), and Weaver (Museum of Northern Arizona). Wilcox pointed out that the area under discussion cross-cut traditional cultural areas, and some of it was being abandoned by 1300, the starting point for discussions. Symposium speakers were: Charles Adams, the Hopi Mesas; Andrew Fowler, the Zuni area; Dittert, the Acoma area; Pilles, Verde Valley, the Flagstaff area, and Anderson Mesa; Shereen Lerner, Lower Verde area; Jon Scott Wood, Tonto Basin; John Hohmann, Globe and Miami area; Doyel, San Pedro area; Henry Wallace, Tucson Basin, Upper Santa Cruz, and Upper Papaguería; Pat Gilman, southeastern Arizona; Richard Ambler, the Athabascan hunters and gatherers who followed the Anasazi; Wilcox, hunters and gatherers who may have been former Anasazis. Although each speaker discussed "spatial organization" for his or her area, each presentation was relatively self-contained, with few connections from one to another. However, as a survey of a large stretch of country in the late prehistoric, it was extremely informative.

The Friday afternoon session began promptly, with Dittert chairing research reports on the Hohokam. He began by remarking that years ago there would be only one or two papers on the Hohokam, and usually a few words by Schroeder and a few by Odd Halseth (Urban 1986). This year there were thirty Hohokam research reports! Topics ranged widely, from identifying agave and corn pollen to "geoglyphs" and intaglios on the Lower Colorado, and included a large number of projects resulting from freeway construction. By 5:12 p.m. the last report had been completed—a remarkable schedule.

At 6 p.m. the barbecue dinner (ribs and chicken, with beer) was to be served at the Shoofly site, catered by Crazy Ed's, which the week before had taken part in a national cook-off contest. A cloudburst and thunderstorm at 5:30 delayed the dinner for an hour or more, but lightning did not strike the Conference tent in spite of its metal frame, and the storm ended with a spectacular rainbow.

Saturday morning began with a half hour of guided tours of the Shoofly site. After that field reports continued, starting with the Payson area and north-central Arizona (after the announcement that Redman had been named Payson's "Good Guy of the Month"). Most of the session consisted of reports on various aspects of the third season of the Shoofly Village excavations. Besides the five-week field school there was a session for amateurs, for certification, and an open house to which 1,600 people came.

The last hour of Saturday morning was devoted to the business meeting. Thanks were expressed to the Tonto National Forest, to the Arizona Archaeological and Historical Society, to the Arizona Archaeological Society, and particularly to John and Linda Hohmann, Paul Minnis, and Pat Gilman. There was an invitation to hold the 1987 meeting (the sixtieth anniversary) at Pecos National Monument, and it was immediately accepted. The Arizona Advisory Commission's voluntary Site Steward Program was reported to have twenty-five volunteers so far, and regional organizers were being sought. A permanent position was reported open for the new state park at Homolovi. Peggy Powers, editor of research news for *American Antiquity,* asked for material, with attention to research goals and interpretations.

The Tucson Basin Conference was announced, for 14–15 October; the Mogollon Conference for 15–16 October; the Anasazi Conference for 24–25 October; and the Hohokam Conference for January 1987 in Tempe. The growth of Southwestern archaeology and the resultant size and complexity of the Pecos Conference was making ever more difficult one of its original central functions—informal, detailed discussions among archaeologists sharing an interest in particular problems or areas. Hence, the more specialized conferences that had sprung up were a valuable supplement to the larger and more general Pecos Conference.

Five deaths were reported: Elizabeth M. Lange of Santa Fe; Garland Jewell Gordon of Concord, California; Arthur Woodward of Patagonia, Arizona; Percy Lomaquahu of Hotevilla; and Ward Weakley, Bureau of Reclamation.

The Conference's final session, Saturday afternoon, was for field reports from the rest of the Southwest, identified in the program as "Above the Rim." Paul Minnis, who chaired the session, announced that there were thirty-three reports scheduled. They included surveys of many areas, the approaching completion of the twenty-year Black Mesa Project, prehistoric farming at Mesa Verde, and warfare and social organization in the Kayenta area, among a wide range of topics.

At 5:35 p.m. Scott Wood closed the final session of the 1986 Conference, asking those who were interested in the Tonto Basin tour Sunday morning to meet at 8. Urban reported that the tour was a great success and included such sites as Rye Creek, Oak Creek, and Cline Terrace.

In postconference comments Elizabeth Morris (letter to Woodbury, 20 August 1986) observed that there was an emphasis on new data and a minimum of models, hypotheses, statistical experiments, and wishful thinking. She also noted how many and varied the T-shirts were, with school, company, and project logos, making for quick identification of the wearers' affiliations. Schroeder, however, wore a T-shirt proclaiming that "age and treachery will overcome youth and skill." Morris's impression was that government and university archaeologists were greatly outnumbered by amateurs, tribal representatives, and contract archaeologists, a contrast to earlier years.

PECOS, 1987 (FIFTIETH PECOS CONFERENCE)   The Conference's return to its birthplace was greeted with enthusiasm as a prospect at the 1986 meeting and as a reality the next year, 13–15 August. The place held a special magic for many participants, perhaps a combination of nostalgia and the splendor of the setting: the view from the rows of chairs in the great red and white tent was not just of the speakers' platform and lectern but also past them, across the valley where the first Conference was held to the escarpment of Glorieta Mesa and the interstate highway that had replaced the wagon ruts of the Santa Fe Trail. The weather was bright and dry, windy but not too hot, and the arrangements were admirable—a big tent for sessions, smaller tents for registration, breakfast and lunch, and book sales. The planning by the National Park Service was as careful and thorough as in previous years, but of course its experience in managing crowds of people without seeming to manage them far surpasses that of most archaeologists.

Larry Nordby, of the National Park Service in Santa Fe, sent out a notice for the sponsors—the Park Service, the School of American Research, the Museum of New Mexico and Laboratory of Anthropology, the Archaeological Society of New Mexico, and the U.S. Forest Service. Multiple sponsorship had become fairly common—in fact, essential—as the size and complexity of the Conferences increased. Nordby included in his announcement the oft-quoted words of Kidder about the purpose of the 1927 Conference, quoted earlier in this chapter.

The preregistration fee was $10, and the Saturday evening dinner was $9 in advance or $11 at the Conference. There was a schedule of field reports and "mini-symposia," an innovation that is described below. Places to stay in Pecos were still almost as few as in previous years—the Inn of Pecos, the Wilderness Inn, the Pecos River Camp, the Hondo Ranch/Camp La Salle, and the Pecos R.V. Campground. The Forest Service campground was also available, just off the road to Glorieta Lookout. Many conferees, of course, stayed in Santa Fe, only about twenty-five miles to the northwest. The list of restaurants in Pecos was also still small; it included the Cactus Flower Cafe, Casa de Herrera, Elsie's Drive In, and Inn of Pecos. The "lunch cart" at the Conference site, however, relieved the problem. The Pecos Conference logo, "Capitan," that had been designed in 1972 was used again.

The Conference began promptly Friday morning, with a welcome by Bezy, the monument superintendent, who mentioned the many changes since the 1972 Conference, especially the handsome Visitor Center, including a large and attractive museum, given by Greer Garson Fogelson and Colonel E. E. Fogelson, longtime friends of the monument. In addition there were a new bilingual trail guide and trailside signs. Bezy added the necessary "housekeeping" information—concerning phone calls, parking, advice about staying on roads and paths, and so on. Nordby, as chairperson of the Conference, announced that there were some sixty to seventy reports scheduled for all day Friday and Saturday, except for three one-hour mini-symposia and a brief business meeting. A Conference innovation was a printed program indicating the precise time for each presentation (for example, 9:10–9:20, Bruce Huckell, Arizona State Museum; 9:20–9:30, Dave Doyel, Pueblo Grande Museum; and so on). There were few no-shows and only a few additional reports squeezed in. Despite the very tight schedule, sessions never got too badly behind, thanks to Nordby's stern warnings and the effectiveness of those chairing the sessions.

There was only one report on the Archaic (none on paleo-Indian), on a pit house discovered when the Tucson sewage plant was digging a trench.

Eight reports on the Hohokam (chaired by Doyel) ranged from irrigation canals and field houses to extensive site surveys, archaeomagnetic dating, pollen studies, and small sites from Colonial to Historic times.

Following a short break—to stand up and stretch, or go for coffee—the miscellaneous method and theory papers were presented, chaired by Nordby. They numbered five and included an experimental training program in field archaeology for the mentally handicapped, experimental maize plots, and several technical topics: archaeomagnetism, tree rings (at Chaco), preservation technology, and remote sensing. During his presentation Judge made the appropriate observation that "we are guests of the past and must respect our host!"

Participants were next allowed an hour for lunch, during which Jim Walker of Brigham Young University had planned to demonstrate the use of a small remote-controlled aircraft for aerial photography, but the wind had come up and was too strong for the tiny plane. The demonstration was rescheduled for 8 the next morning, when he expected it would be calmer.

The Mogollon session then began, with Wiseman chairing. There were eight reports, including updates on Shoofly and Grasshopper field schools, a burial found accidentally near Heber with both hands and feet missing, high altitude shrines, the Casas Grandes northwestern frontier, and a survey along the "Mogasazi Border." Five peripheral area reports, chaired by David Phillips, ranged from Roswell and the Conchas Reservoir in New Mexico to studies of Salado Polychrome. More method and theory reports followed, including trade pottery, Adolph Bandelier's record of sites in the Tonto Basin, the potential of apparently hopelessly disturbed sites, and sampling for survey of a million acres of Lincoln National Forest.

Several announcements ended the Friday sessions, including a warning that the monument gates would be locked at 6 p.m., so "Move your vehicle."

Saturday morning at 8:15 John Cook, the National Park Service regional director, briefly described the Southwest Cultural Resources Center, with its multidisciplinary staff of forty. He commented on the "drive" of archaeologists and their excellent partnership with the NPS in the custodianship of the national cultural heritage.

Schaafsma chaired the first series of reports on the Anasazi and Rio Grande, which reported current work by the Navajo Nation Archeological Department, the third year of survey of the Homolovi ruins, "walking for dollars" (the boundary survey of Grand Canyon National Park), the completion of a seven-year project at Wupatki that yielded 2,764 sites, the change from bulldozing to pot-holing by looters in the Blanding area, and the ongoing study of Glen Canyon.

At 9:35 the first one-hour mini-symposium was presented, "The Northern Rio Grande: Archaic-Developmental Pueblo Transitions." Brad Vierra spoke on "Regional Archaic Mobility Patterns," and Jack Bertram on "Projectile Point Typology and Chronology in the Archaic." There were two discussants: Pat Hicks pointed out uncertainties in the obsidian hydration dating used by Bertram, and Richard Chapman commented on the adaptive stances of the Archaic—why change from a hunter-gatherer to a sedentary life? This and the other one-hour symposia were a welcome change from the long series of brief reports and provided a detailed update of the archaeology of the area in which the Conference was taking place.

Six more reports on the Anasazi followed, which emphasized problems of ruin stabilization, as well as continuing research at Yellow Jacket and at the Crow Canyon Archaeological Center.

At 11:50, only ten minutes behind the printed schedule(!), the business meeting began, chaired by Schaafsma. Thanks were expressed to Nordby and his staff, who prepared and distributed all the information for the Conference, and to Bezy and his staff as hosts for such a fine meeting. Richard Woodbury was asked to summarize briefly the origins and growth of the Pecos Conference. Kit Sargent spoke of the urgency of the petition drive in Albuquerque to impose a quarter cent tax for funds to buy the volcanic escarpment west of town and save its rock art. An invitation to hold the 1988 Conference at the Anasazi

Heritage Center of the Bureau of Land Management, Dolores, Colorado, was promptly accepted. An invitation to meet in 1989 at Bandelier National Monument was also accepted, with the observation that two years' lead time was an advantage to the host organization. Telegram messages of greetings and good wishes were sent to J. O. Brew, Faith Kidder Fuller, Jesse Jennings, Erik Reed, Watson Smith, Charlie Steen, and Arnold Withers.

Following a break for lunch the second northern Rio Grande mini-symposium, "Coalition to Classic Tradition," was held, moderated by Stewart Peckham. Demography and subsistence on the Pajarito Plateau were discussed by Beverly Larson and Nick Trierweiler. Robert Powers described the variation and chronology of sites in Bandelier National Monument, mainly from the twelfth century onward. The changes in this time period in the Albuquerque area were summarized by Jan Biella.

The second session on the Anasazi and Rio Grande followed, with Bruce Anderson chairing. There were five reports: kiva murals, turquoise mining, plans for research at large, late northern Rio Grande ruins, settlement patterns in the Santa Fe area, and the Albuquerque Archaeological Society's ongoing work at a great kiva near Gallup.

The third northern Rio Grande mini-symposium, "Classic to Protohistoric Tradition," chaired by Schroeder, occupied the next hour. There were three papers: "Tano Perambulations" by Peckham, "Coronado's Campsite" by Brad Vierra, and "Pueblos at Contact" by Winifred Creamer. In his discussion David Snow pointed out how much still remains to be known of the northern Rio Grande's prehistoric-historic transition, and how greater use of Spanish documents could help explain why "the present does *not* mirror the past."

The final session of the Conference (protohistoric, ethnohistoric, and historic) was chaired by Jonathan Haas. Its five reports dealt with Pueblo calendar sticks, recent research at Homolovi III and IV, excavation of the 1870s McEwen House in Lincoln County, the unexplained absence of evidence of life-threatening disease in Southwest paleopathology, and the archaeology of the Apache labor camps at Roosevelt Dam.

This concluded the formal sessions of the Conference, but the barbecue at the campground at 6 p.m. was still to come. The Coors truck was on hand, as well as a country-western band, "Distilled Spirits." But the caterer's truck broke down, and there was a wait of an hour before it finally turned up, with the warming equipment for the food not functioning. Despite grumbling at the wait and a very slow serving line, everyone finally got a helping of enchiladas, beans, and roast beef. One diner commented, though, "I warmed my tortilla on the cement slab I was sitting on." However, unlike the year before, the weather remained favorable.

Urban comments that there were often more people outside the meeting tent talking with each other than were inside listening to reports. However, seeing old friends and making new ones, as well as exchanging archaeological and personal news, has always been a feature of the Pecos Conference and meets the felt need to "catch up" informally as well as through the program of reports and papers. There is no official record of attendance but there are estimates that about 350–400 people were present.

Reviewing the program, there were about sixty-five reports and symposium papers. Thirty-one organizations were represented, many with several members reporting separately. There were speakers from seventeen public or private colleges, universities, and museums from California to New York; six cultural resource management organizations; one Native American research unit (Navajo); and seven federal agencies (various offices of the U.S. Forest Service and National Park Service). For-profit, contract research was in a minority (six companies). Archaeology by federal agencies (or at least the reporting of it) was apparently increasing, compared to only a few years earlier. Hence the traditional bastions of archaeology—museums and universities—although still active, were not playing their dominant role of the past. The mini-symposium experiment was successful, with northern Rio Grande archaeology well reviewed. The three one-hour sessions broke up the nine hours of field reports better than a half-day symposium would have done. As with any symposium, some speakers were closer to the central topic than others, and a few papers had no connection with any of the others.

DOLORES, 1988 (FIFTY-FIRST PECOS CONFERENCE) The 1988 Pecos Conference, 18–21 August, was held at a new location, not only in the sense that the Conference had not been there before but also because the Anasazi Heritage Center of the Bureau of Land Management was a new museum just opening that summer. The Conference was sponsored by the Anasazi Heritage Center together with the Crow Canyon Archaeological Center, the San Juan National Forest, and the Yellow Jacket Project of the University of Colorado. Besides continuing the pattern of mini-symposia introduced the year before, a poster session was proposed:

If a summary of your work can be covered with text and graph-
ics that fit in a 4×4 foot space, we encourage you to consider this
medium for your presentation. The poster session will be held
in the multi-purpose room at the Anasazi Heritage Center on
Friday and Saturday. Please indicate on the pre-registration form
if you want to make a poster presentation [advance announce-
ment].

The final program listed ten poster sessions, a good response for an
idea new to the Pecos Conference.

The elaborate Conference announcement that was mailed out also
included information on the Saturday evening pig roast. It also announced that T-shirts could be ordered in advance to be picked up at
the Conference or ordered there for later delivery. The logo was the
most complex yet—a circle with *Cortez* and *Dolores* at top and bottom
and the quadrants labeled: United States Forest Service, with a San
Juan National Forest symbol; Crow Canyon Archaeological Center,
with its symbol; University of Colorado, with a Yellow Jacket Project
symbol; and the Bureau of Land Management, with its Anasazi Heritage Center symbol. All of this was reminiscent of the complications
of medieval heraldry, with the quartering of the arms of four families
for a knight's banner or shield. An innovation this year was a "welcoming Pecos Conference banner . . . made and donated by Mary
Dufur of Dolores. It is intended to travel to other Pecos Conferences
in the future."

The Conference began on the afternoon of Thursday, 18 August,
with a welcoming reception at the Anasazi Heritage Center, which
was exhibiting "Daughters of the Desert," a Smithsonian Traveling Exhibit that had originated at the Arizona State Museum to
honor women who worked in Southwestern anthropology, including
archaeology, between 1880 and 1980. In addition, Ronald L. Bishop
of the Smithsonian Institution gave a lecture on "Anna O. Shepard
and the Development of Ceramic Research." At the same time, at the
Colorado University center in Cortez, E. Charles Adams, Arizona
State Museum, spoke on "Excavations at Homolovi III (Arizona)."

Friday morning the Conference opened with welcoming remarks
by Fred Lange of the University of Colorado and Leonard Atencio of
the Dolores District of the San Juan National Forest. The presentation of field reports on Friday and Saturday followed a pattern similar to the preceding year—sessions for ethnohistoric-protohistoric
(three reports), theoretical/methodological (two), Mogollon (four),

Hohokam (seven), other (seven), and Anasazi area (in four parts, with twenty-four reports). Three mini-symposia had been planned, on large site formation, behavioral analyses of prehistoric cannibalism, and archaeoastronomy. As it turned out, only the first and third of these took place, chaired by Kim Malville and Mark Chenault, respectively, both of the University of Colorado.

The cancellation of the mini-symposium on cannibalism is an occurrence unique in Pecos Conferences and deserves detailed attention. The organizers of the Conference "decided that given the amount of supposedly cannibalized bone that had been found in the past couple of years . . . it would be a good time to re-examine the status of the data base. We also thought that the Pecos Conference would be the best place to do it" (Fred Lange, letter to Woodbury, 4 January 1989). Lange says that one written protest was passed on to him, as well as mention of "phone calls of concern and hints of disruptions, etc. Most importantly, from my perspective, there was a lot of media attention. . . . since we were hoping for a serious discussion and were concerned about sensationalism."

Jonathan Haas, then at the School of American Research and now at the Field Museum of Natural History, Chicago, agrees with Lange's account of the situation, saying (letter to Woodbury, 12 December 1988) that "several Native American groups . . . felt that a special focus on the topic was derogatory to the current image of Native Americans. Lange considered their complaints and decided it was in the best interests of all parties to cancel the session." Nevertheless, Turner, one of those scheduled for the cannibalism session, gave his paper in the session on "other" topics, with the title "Mass Burials," beginning with a comment that he was unhappy at being censored. He cited mass burials at several sites in the Southwest extending over a long period of time, at all of which the bones had clear evidence of being "butchered, burned, and broken" (Christy G. Turner II, letter to Woodbury, 8 December 1988).

During the Conference Turner also met with Jerry Fetterman and Nancy Mayville "to discuss our respective recent mass burial findings. Arizona Republic writer Carle Hodge was present, and he wrote the stories that appeared some time after the Conference" (Turner, letter to Woodbury, 8 December 1988). The first of these stories appeared on the front page of *The Arizona Republic* on 6 September 1988, under the headline "ASU scientist certain of cannibalism in Four Corners area centuries ago." It reported in considerable detail Turner's study of butchered skeletons found in 1893 by Richard Wetherill in a cave near Bluff, Utah; the remains of thirty Hopi killed near Polacca about 1700; a massacre of thirty-five individuals on Leroux Wash near Holbrook, Arizona; and several other finds. Turner expressed doubt that famine was a cause of Pueblo cannibalism and suggested that warfare was a more likely cause than ritual. Hodge's second story (*Arizona Republic,* 11 September 1988) began "Two Indian leaders reacted angrily last week to studies suggesting that ancient Anasazi people practiced cannibalism. 'We are outraged,' Hopi Tribal Chairman Ivan Sidney said, 'by such preposterous and unfounded allegations.'" The second objection came from John Gonzales, of San Ildefonso Pueblo, president of the National Council of American Indians, who said, "I am astounded that in this day and age, so-called educated people can publish such unjustified pronouncements." Hodge reported that "Turner stands by his studies."

Whatever interpretations are made of the cases that Turner cited and regardless of how justified one may consider the reactions of the Indian leaders, the importance of this episode to the history of the Pecos Conference is that never before had a session been canceled due to outside objections or threats. There can be no doubt that the Conference was, year by year, becoming more visible to those outside of anthropology and that it had for some time been an important public forum for exchange of information and ideas, rather than a small, unnoticed gathering of a few Southwestern specialists talking to each other. Also, the time was long past when Native Americans were unaware of or uninterested in the work of archaeologists. The Hopis are reported to feel that it was acceptable to discuss evidence for cannibalism in a scientific meeting but not to report it on the front page of a major newspaper (letter from R. H. Thompson to Woodbury, 18 September 1989). This poses a dilemma for a conference: Should its sessions be closed to the press? to the public? to nonregistrants? to nonanthropologists? There seems little doubt that some future Conference will have to face this problem.

When the mini-symposium on cannibalism was canceled, Lange and the other planners of the Conference substituted a session on the proposed Anasazi National Park, which would combine several large, important sites in the Four Corners Area, including Yellow Jacket, Sand Canyon, and the ruins of the Hovenweep area. Lange introduced Mark Michel of the Archaeological Conservancy, founded in 1980 to preserve endangered sites on private land. Michel in turn introduced the Conservancy's Southwest director, Jim Walker, who said that 48 sites in 11 states had been acquired so far, with the support of 7,000 members and many private, corporate, and governmental donations. He described the continuing looting of some of the major sites in the Four Corners Area, and the need for the protection that national park status would provide. A lively discussion followed, with questions, support, doubts, and detailed suggestions. Although no formal Conference opinion was proposed, conferees were urged to express their support to their senators and congressmen.

The business meeting was unusually brief, with no deaths announced and no resolutions proposed. A date for the 1989 meeting at Bandelier had not yet been set, and no invitation for 1990 had been received.

The Friday afternoon session closed with the announcement that the Austin Lounge Lizards would be playing at the Montezuma County Fairgrounds at 8 p.m., preceded by a local band, "J. D. and the Other Three." Admission was $5 at the door, and refreshments could be purchased. The concert was a benefit for the Colorado University Center in Cortez, the first benefit concert at a Pecos Conference. Both bands performed again at the McPhee Group Campground the next evening for the pig roast (prepared by the Dolores County Search and Rescue), which according to the program followed "Attitude Adjustment" at approximately 6 p.m.

The Conference continued Sunday morning with a symposium on the Dolores Program, with four speakers and two discussants. This was followed in the afternoon by a talk, "Climate, Then and Now," by Ken Peterson. On Sunday there were also tours to major sites nearby, including Yellow Jacket, Sand Canyon, and Crow Canyon.

The complexity of a Pecos Conference and the kinds of generous support it could hope to benefit from are indicated in the final paragraph of the 1988 printed program:

> Thanks to Parducci Winery (Ukiah, California) for donating
> the wine; the Jackson–David Bottling Co. (Durango, CO) for
> donating the soda pop; the Dolores Apple Juice Co. for the apple
> juice, and to all of the volunteers and institutions who worked
> so hard to make the 61st [sic] Annual Pecos Conference a success. Kim Malville provided a fresh LQ-800 [computer printer]
> ribbon.

One participant's comment expresses well the continuing value of the Conference: "The Pecos Conference provides an ideal way for professional and amateur to stay informed on some of the current areas of research and to visit with and share the thinking of some of the foremost archaeologists in the Southwest" (Feagins 1989). William Sundt of Albuquerque had a particularly enthusiastic impression of the Conference (Sundt 1988).

The impressions of Dean J. Saitta (University of Denver), for whom this was a first Pecos Conference, are an appropriate conclusion to this chapter (letter to Woodbury, 5 September 1988):

> It was wonderfully informal, yet what I heard in the way of pre-sentations were well-organized, coherent, and sometimes very intriguing. Of course, the weather was beautiful and I was sky-high about being in Colorado, and this may have colored my perception. Still, I didn't feel I was sitting around listening to "a bunch of contract archaeology folks talk about their work," which is how one conference attendee described Pecos to me. A few people complained that this year's conference was more formal than conferences past, perhaps to a fault . . . but I don't see how it could be any less formal and still hang together as a useful intellectual experience. Nearly everyone I talked to in various bull sessions seemed to be enjoying the conference and getting something out of it.

Sixty-one years before, E. B. Renaud had described the 1927 Pecos Conference with similar enthusiasm as "the best and most interesting and useful anthropological meeting I ever attended."

Although our chronicle ends here, the Pecos Conference gives every indication of continuing vigorously far into the future. The 1989 Conference was at Bandelier National Monument, sponsored by the National Park Service, the U.S. Forest Service, and Los Alamos National Laboratory; the 1990 Conference at Blanding, Utah; and the 1991 Conference at Viejo Casas Grandes, thus continuing the tradi-tion of great geographical and archaeological diversity in its settings. It is especially fitting and pleasing that as of this writing, in its sixty-fifth year, the fifty-fifth Conference is scheduled to return once more to its birthplace at Pecos.

15
RETROSPECT, 1927–88

A. V. Kidder's often quoted 1927 report in *Science* on the first Pecos Conference said:

> The purposes of the meeting were: to bring about contacts between workers in the Southwestern field; to discuss fundamental problems of Southwestern history, and to formulate plans for coordinated attack upon them; to pool knowledge of facts and techniques, and to lay foundations for a unified system of nomenclature.

The last purpose, a unified system of nomenclature, was tackled in 1927 and later improved with the addition and gradual acceptance of such major cultural units as the Hohokam, Mogollon, Sinagua, and Hakataya. But the attempt to define *kiva* was unsuccessful in 1927, and even today a generally accepted definition has not yet been achieved. The binomial system for naming pottery types was considered in 1927 and codified soon after by Harold S. Colton and others. But nomenclature for vessel shapes and design elements, raised in 1927, was not a major focus of interest at subsequent Conferences, and the progress that was made was not a result of Conference discussions, as far as can be determined (see, for example, Shepard 1956 and Washburn 1977). Informal conversations, however, outside the public sessions have always occurred and probably have been the genesis of more progress, planning, and cooperation than we can ever know. The 1927 Conference pointed out the need for research in neglected and peripheral areas, "southwestern Arizona, Sonora, Chihuahua, and eastern New Mexico [and] the Little Colorado in general and the Hopi country in particular." This neglect was remedied in the next three decades, stimulated in part by the 1927 discussions. Besides numerous new sur-veys and small site excavations, there were large-scale programs in hitherto neglected areas—Awatovi, Snaketown, and Casas Grandes, for example.

Kidder proposed more than additions to information on the South-west's "history," by which, of course, he meant all of the past. He hoped "to formulate plans for coordinated attack . . . [on] fundamen-tal problems." There is not, however, much coordination apparent in Southwestern archaeology during the years following 1927. There were many carefully planned individual and institutional efforts and much exchange of information, but coordinated planning among colleagues was virtually absent until 1971, when the Southwestern Anthropological Research Group was formed (Gumerman 1971). SARG was specifically intended to share data among a small group of investigators who were focusing jointly on a single major question, and to assure that their data were recorded in forms that would permit each to use the others' data. SARG continued for some years but then gradually became less active.

Two other purposes stated by Kidder have been achieved by every Pecos Conference—"to bring about contacts between workers" and "to pool knowledge of facts and techniques." These have been the Conference's strength and, on occasion, its weakness. The contacts are invaluable in creating and maintaining working relationships among a large number of people who share many interests but are widely dispersed across the United States. The criticism that at times social contacts have tended to crowd out intellectual interchanges may be partly justified, although few Conferences, even in unofficial evening "sessions," have been the drunken brawl that is sometimes charged. However, in one of the 1979 questionnaires on the Pecos Conferences there is a recollection of "destroying" the women's dorm at the Uni-versity of New Mexico in 1958. And in a conversation on 30 July 1980, Erik Reed recalled an inebriated colleague at one of the Flagstaff meet-ings falling over a boulder in the campground after dark, breaking his leg, dragging himself into the seat of his pick-up and passing out, where he was found in the morning and hospitalized. The high jinks at one of the Fort Burgwin Conferences have already been described. These incidents might be added to, but they characterize a minority of Conferences and relatively few of the participants. Serious but in-formal conversations around a campfire have been more characteristic of the unofficial hours of Pecos Conferences.

The traditional short "field reports" at every Conference have effectively pooled knowledge, but frequently trivial details have crowded out any consideration of interpretation and implications. There is some justification for the frequent complaint that field reports have concentrated on "we found X fireplaces with the following dimensions," or "we found PII sherds in a PII site." In recent years those reporting have been urged in advance to focus on the interpretation of the field work rather than merely its data, but success has been modest.

Although the Pecos Conference has changed through the years, it has changed far less than has Southwestern archaeology. In the 1920s most research was done by a few institutions located far from the area of their field work, in cities such as Los Angeles, Chicago, Washington, or Boston. As was pointed out in chapter 2, the first Pecos Conference had fourteen participants from Southwestern institutions and twenty-seven from distant ones. This was changing, however, even in the late 1920s and early 1930s, with the founding of the Museum of Northern Arizona and Gila Pueblo in 1928, the Laboratory of Anthropology in 1929, and the Amerind Foundation in 1934. In 1927 the University of New Mexico added a department of archaeology and anthropology (the University of Arizona's department, created in 1915, was then the only other such department in the Four Corners states).

In 1927 the Southwest, for anthropologists, was an area of limited extent, functionally hardly more than the Colorado Plateau, although lip service was paid to the existence of prehistoric remains to the south in the mountains and deserts. Even though research was extending to new areas in 1929, William Curry Holden recalls that "the eastern boundary of the Pecos Conference was the drainage of the Pecos River." The situation changed rapidly, first with Harold S. Gladwin's attention to the Hohokam area, and later with expansion of interest in other directions. Eventually, the isolationist attitude of many Southwesternists disappeared, and the region's connections with the Great Basin, the Plains, Mexico, and southern California were respectable topics of inquiry.

Although I have not tried to document this, I suspect that in the 1920s the Southwest was known archaeologically in more detail than any other part of North America. There were, of course, important investigations in many parts of the country, probably none until nearly a century later equaling *Ancient Monuments of the Mississippi Valley* (Squier and Davis 1848), but the Southwest excelled, in the first quarter of the century, in accumulating the detailed information that made the Pecos Classification possible. The Southwest was also the source of major methodological innovations in the 1920s and 1930s. Gordon R. Willey and Jeremy Sabloff (1980) in *A History of American Archaeology* identify six major new ideas of the period they call "the Classificatory-Historical Period" (1914–49): (1) stratigraphy, (2) seriation, (3) typology and pottery classification, (4) culture-classification schemes, (5) the direct historical approach, and (6) area synthesis. The first was introduced almost simultaneously by Manuel Gamio in the Valley of Mexico and Nels Nelson in the Southwest, and the first large-scale application was by Kidder. Seriation was well developed in Europe before 1900, particularly by Flinders Petrie, who influenced its adoption by Max Uhle in Peru, who in turn introduced the concept to A. L. Kroeber, who was the inspiration for Leslie Spier's establishment of it as a major research tool in the Southwest, from which it later spread to the southeastern United States. Of typology, Willey and Sabloff say, "It remained for the archaeologists in the southwestern United States to take the lead again" (1980: 102). A culture-classification scheme first appeared in the Southwest with the Pecos Classification, followed quickly by Gladwin's alternative, and soon after by W. C. McKern's Midwestern Taxonomic Method. Although the first New World area synthesis was by Uhle for the Peruvian area, Kidder's (1924) was the first for North America. It is only the development of the direct-historical approach, in which the Southwest has no important role; credit for it goes to Waldo Wedel and Duncan Strong, who applied it to the chronological problems of Plains prehistory.

The lead of the Southwest in moving American archaeology from descriptive to chronological concerns and from a focus on individual sites to regions disappeared as many other parts of the country caught up with it in scope and intensity of research. This is not the place to try to encapsulate the enormous growth of North American archaeology in the past fifty to seventy-five years, but it can be pointed out that today we have substantial bodies of data with finely tuned chronologies for areas extending from Alaska to Florida. The Southwest has not lagged, but others now match it in the richness of the data base and hence in attractiveness for testing ideas, experimenting with techniques, and reexamining past assumptions.

Through all these changes, the Pecos Conference has functioned well as a means for rapid communication of information and methods and informal testing of hypotheses on skeptical colleagues. Everyone may not speak exactly the same language, but one can quickly learn what archaeological languages others are speaking. The Conference has also been an important annual rite of intensification by which the individual Southwesternist can feel a part of a vaguely defined but important collectivity, responsible, decade after decade, for advancing the understanding of the past. The effectiveness of the annual regional conference is demonstrated in the creation, over the years, of similar conferences for every region of the country, some directly inspired by the Pecos Conference.

As this history reflects, the Pecos Conference, despite its continuity and persistence, has changed with time. In the remainder of this chapter, I will identify some of those changes, consider their probable causes and consequences, and examine the extent to which the purposes of the Conference may have been modified.

FROM SMALL TO BIG (TO TOO BIG?)   It is a strong American tradition that growth is a mark of success. On this basis the Pecos Conference has been highly successful. Although registration totals are missing from some Conferences, it is clear that attendance soon reached about 100 but remained below 200 for many years. By the 1960s and 1970s the number rose well over 200 several times; in the 1980s it passed 300 at least six times. How much of the variation in numbers is due to the special attractiveness of the locations of certain years can be speculated on by the reader. The attendance figures in Table 15.1 are based, as far as possible, on registration rather than dinner or barbecue tickets.

The growth of the Pecos Conference is not altogether a sign of its popularity. Albert H. Schroeder has pointed out (letter to Woodbury, 29 June 1989) that the increase in the size of the Conference is partly due to federal laws and regulations that necessitated a growth in the number of active archaeologists:

> Legislation requiring survey and excavation in advance of construction on federal projects led to an increase in archaeological projects as well as more jobs for archaeologists. Also, Nixon's executive order 11593 not only led to an increase in the hiring of archaeologists by federal agencies other than the National Park Service but also was the beginning of cultural resource management in all federal agencies.

The number of field reports has increased as attendance has grown, yet even with the larger numbers of reports everyone who wished to report has usually been able to do so. Unlike many meetings, the Conferences have not been expanded to fill more and more days, nor

Table 15.1. Pecos Conferences: Attendance and Locations

Conference No.	Attendance	Year	Place	Number of meetings at same place
1	46	1927	Pecos	1
2	65	1929	Pecos	2
3	56	1931	Santa Fe	1
4	?	1937	Chaco	1
5	90	1938	Chaco	2
6	99	1939	Chaco	3
7	140	1940	Chaco	4
8	?	1941	Chaco	5
9	64	1946	Santa Fe	2
10	ca. 100	1947	Chaco	6
11	136	1948	Point of Pines	1
12	81	1949	Santa Fe	3
13	80	1950	Flagstaff	1
14	111	1951	Point of Pines	2
15	152	1952	Santa Fe	4
16	134	1953	Flagstaff	2
17	?	1954	Globe	1
18	115	1955	Santa Fe	5
19	99	1956	Flagstaff	3
20	99	1957	Globe	2
21	140	1958	Albuquerque	
22	ca. 200	1959	Ft. Burgwin	1
23	203	1960	Flagstaff	4
24	60	1961	Nuevo Casas Grandes	1
25	?	1962	Globe	3
26	?	1963	Ft. Burgwin	2
27	135	1964	Window Rock	1
28	109	1965	Trinidad	
29	227	1966	Flagstaff	5
30	246	1967	Tucson	1
31	188	1968	El Paso-Juarez	
32	185	1969	Prescott	
33	ca. 300	1970	Santa Fe	6
34	178	1971	Window Rock	2
35	176	1972	Flagstaff	6
36	238	1973	Tucson	2
37	400+	1974	Mesa Verde	1
38	?	1975	Salmon Ruin	
39	104	1976	Kino Bay	
40	650	1977	Pecos	3
41	ca. 350	1978	Flagstaff	7
42	143	1979	Tucson	3
43	?	1980	Mesa Verde	2
44	463	1981	Ft. Burgwin	3
45	333	1982	Pecos	4
46	158	1983	Bluff	
47	?	1984	Flagstaff	8
48	311	1985	Salinas	
49	ca. 330	1986	Payson	
50	350-400	1987	Pecos	5
51	495	1988	Dolores	
52	513	1989	Bandelier	
53	400-500	1990	Blanding	
54	170-200	1991	Viejo Casas Grandes	2
55		1992	Pecos	6

have simultaneous sessions become the practice, although they have been tried a few times. No abstracts are requested in advance, and reports are not screened for selection or rejection.

Nonetheless, complaints have been heard repeatedly about the Conference being too large. In 1948 Paul Martin protested that a Pecos Conference of 75–100 people would be far too big and said the Conference should be limited to "full-grown professionals." In 1970, after the Santa Fe Conference, which had a larger attendance than any previous meeting, Emil Haury wrote, "It is a matter of some concern that the gathering is getting so big that sheer mass will dictate where and how the meetings can be held." However, large rented tents have made meetings possible in a great variety of locations and weather conditions, and Southwesternists have continued to attend in ever larger numbers. It is amusing to note that in 1968 "the small conference" was discovered by Margaret Mead as "a new social invention . . . a powerful communication form." Her definition would fit the Pecos Conference in its earliest years: "a group small enough to sit around a large table, called together for a specific purpose, for a limited time. . . . All members . . . are accorded participant status; the method of communication is mutual multisensory interchange with speech as the principal medium" (Mead and Byers 1968: 5). It is only fair to add that Mead had in mind "the effort to solve or develop some intellectual task" rather than the exchange of information. Not since 1927 has the Pecos Conference convened with a specific major task as its chief purpose.

In spite of the tenfold growth in attendance (Table 15.1), from about 50 to over 500 (at least twice), one aspect of the Pecos Conference has remained virtually unchanged. From its creation to the present day, it has had no officers, depending instead on ad hoc and interim committees, on a one-year basis; it has no dues, no headquarters, and no memberships except by attendance. Each year a committee is appointed to plan the next year's Conference and a mailing list is passed on to it from the outgoing committee—sometimes only that year's registrants and sometimes that plus the names of all who have attended in recent years. In 1985 announcements were mailed to 1,550 prospective attendees.

In the early years no registration fee was charged, but as attendance grew the costs also grew. With some reluctance but no recorded objections, fees began to be charged to cover some of the expenses involved. In 1951, for the second Conference at Point of Pines, Haury decided to charge $10 a person at registration, to cover the costs of meals. In 1957 the business meeting discussed the pros and cons of a registration fee and approved a $2 fee for future Conferences. Eventually, there often were both a registration fee and separate charges for lunch and dinner tickets. Conferences that ended with a cash surplus often forwarded it to the planners of the next year's Conference as "start-up" money for typing, postage, and incidentals. The ability of host institutions to absorb Conference costs has varied widely, but participants have generally been quite willing to pay fees and buy meal tickets to cover at least some of the costs.

With growth came the feeling on the part of some, at least, that it was becoming impossible to talk informally with colleagues of like interests about their current research or discuss specific areas or problems. Small, concurrent, specialized sessions were tried a few times but were found to be unsatisfactory. Instead, small, independent, specialized annual conferences began to appear: the Gran Quivira Conference (for Spanish colonial studies) in 1972, the Hohokam Conference in 1973, the Jornada in 1979, the Mogollon in 1980, the Anasazi in 1981, and the Navajo Studies Conference in 1986. They are an expectable reaction to the limitations of larger meetings, and these conferences supplement the Pecos Conference rather than compete with it. Large regional or topical conferences are now numerous also, some of them—like the Plains Conference and the Great Basin Conference—inspired by the Pecos Conference, while others, such as the Southeast, the Iroquois, or the Caddo, have other origins (Woodbury 1985a). At the same time, specialists who felt that the annual meeting of the SAA was failing to meet their needs were founding national societies for historic archaeology, underwater archaeology, and other specialties.

At a meeting of the Northeast Anthropological Association in Amherst in March 1980, John M. Roberts (University of Pittsburgh) was speaker at the banquet and chose to address the role of small professional societies and their meetings. He pointed out their advantages, such as greater opportunities for everyone who wanted to get on the program to do so and greater receptiveness to new and divergent ideas than would be found at the meetings of large societies, such as the AAA. He also mentioned that small organizations' meetings paid less attention to status, did not have ten- to twelve-month advance deadlines for submitting titles, and offered greater opportunity for students to meet senior professionals. In addition, he commented on the importance of regional meetings that did not require costly travel across the country. All of this reminded me immediately of advantages many have felt that Pecos Conferences had over the national meetings. The moral appears to be that small is not only beautiful but also more productive.

THE MANY SETTINGS OF THE CONFERENCES   The Conference has met in a variety of settings, returning several times to some and visiting others only once (Fig. 15.1, Table 15.1). The procedure at the annual business meeting for choosing a meeting place has varied from selecting among competing hosts to urging that "someone speak up." Preference is often expressed for a field setting—if not an active dig like Point of Pines, the Salmon Ruin at Bloomfield, or the Shoofly Ruin at Payson, then at least a nonurban setting with archaeological sites close at hand, like Mesa Verde or Salinas. It was certainly not Kidder's intention that Pecos would continue to be the site for the Conferences, since field work ended there in 1929. The selection of Santa Fe for 1931 was logical, as the Conference could be combined with the dedication of the Laboratory of Anthropology, with which Kidder was closely involved. Subsequently, however, Conferences have usually been independent of local events (Albuquerque and Chaco Canyon in 1940 and Bluff in 1983 are exceptions). Urban sites have been rare, only Albuquerque and Tucson, where the Conference was held on a state university campus, and El Paso—Juárez, where it met at both the university campus and the Ciudad Juárez conference center.

The most frequent single location has been the Museum of Northern Arizona, Flagstaff, with eight meetings between 1950 and 1984, but the National Park Service has been the most frequent host, with three Conferences at Globe (the Southwestern Regional Archeological Headquarters and later the Southwestern Archeological Center), two at Mesa Verde, five (sixth scheduled for 1992) at Pecos National Monument, one at Salinas National Monument, and one at Bandelier National Monument. The Conference has met five times in Santa Fe, sometimes with sessions also at Pecos. An almost endless variety of local hosts has made the Conferences possible, sharing such substantial burdens of time and money as program planning, duplicating and mailing announcements, securing space, and arranging for catered meals and, in more recent years, an evening of entertainment. The constant change of location not only spreads the burden but has the attraction of letting attendees see regions and sites they have previously read about. Haury, in proposing a Conference at Point of Pines in 1947, the first one outside New Mexico, argued that Conference participants "should be given a chance to see a new part of the Southwest."

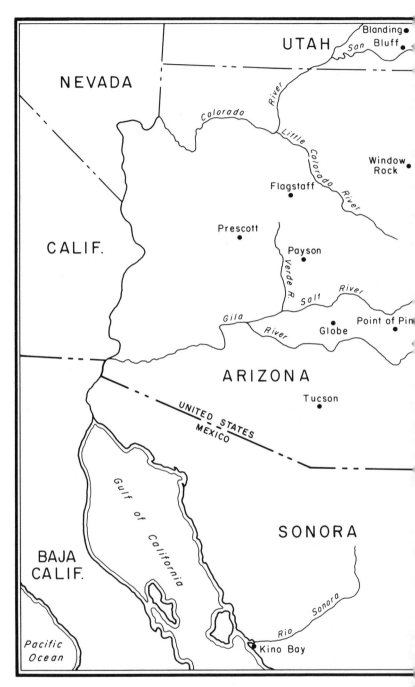

15.1 Map of the Southwest showing locations of Pecos Conferences. Drawn by R. J. Beckwith

COLORADO

• Dolores

• Mesa Verde

• Trinidad

OK.

River

• Salmon Ruin

Chaco Canyon
•

Bandelier
National Monument

• Ft. Burgwin

• Santa Fe

• Pecos

• Albuquerque

Salinas
National Monument
•

NEW
MEXICO

Rio Grande

Pecos

River

• El Paso

Ciudad Juarez

TEXAS

Nuevo
Casas Grandes
•

CHIHUAHUA

Rio Grande

↑
N

0   50   100   150 km

0   50   100 Mi

R. J. BECKWITH

A similar view was expressed by Alfred E. Dittert (letter to Woodbury, 29 May 1989), who said, "Pecos Conferences being held at different places offer the opportunity to broaden one's experiences by exposure to research over a wide area and to summaries of the status of archaeology near the host institution. I had heard about Yellow Jacket, etc., for years but never had an opportunity to see it [until the 1988 Conference]."

The ingenuity of hosts in providing huge tents, catered lunches and dinners, and many other essentials for a large meeting makes urban or campus locations less necessary than was thought a few years ago. Many probably agree with E. B. Danson, who wrote to Robert Euler in 1969, "I have always felt that the most successful Pecos Conferences were those that were held out-of-doors, where people could not show their slides, and where the wind could blow away the cobwebs of one's mind." One response to my 1979 questionnaire included this comment: "I always felt the conferences which were the best . . . [were] held in the field, but these became too big. I never cared as much for those held in cities or towns. People were much more apt to get out of line (drinking), Albuquerque, UNM, a classic example."

Predictions are risky but for future Conferences it seems probable that willing hosts will continue to come forward and that there will constantly be new locations as well as some old favorites.

INNOVATIONS   Although the basic purposes and format of the Pecos Conference have remained remarkably stable, a few notable ancillary innovations have occurred. At least as early as 1959 book sales began, with the Southwestern Monuments Association selling its publications at the Conference, at a 20 percent discount. By 1971, if not earlier, a number of other Southwestern organizations had tables of their publications for sale at Conferences, and Pat Beckett, of COAS Books in Las Cruces, New Mexico, had a large assortment of new and secondhand books, mostly Southwestern. At some recent Conferences the "book tent" has been half as large as the "meeting tent."

Another innovation has been evening entertainment, in association with an outdoor dinner, usually a barbecue of one kind or another. The change is foreshadowed by the difference between Kidder's lecture with slides on the Maya murals recently discovered at Bonampak, Chiapas, in 1948 and the performance by Apache Crown Dancers in 1951, both at Point of Pines. In 1954, at Globe, there was an evening performance by Zuni dancers. When the Conference met in Tucson in 1967 there was a dinner at the Lodge on the Desert, preceded by swimming and cocktails accompanied by a mariachi band. In 1971 Martin Link asked Douglas Schwartz for suggestions for Window Rock's second Conference. Schwartz's detailed reply included the observation on entertainment after the barbecue that "people are really entertaining themselves, but it does help if you have something of an ethnic quality." Link arranged for Navajo dances to follow the barbecue. A high point in evening entertainment was reached at the Salinas Conference in 1985, with the New Mexico Archaeological Council holding "a beer bust at 6:30," following which dinner was served, accompanied by the bluegrass music of the Adobe Brothers. This was equaled, if not surpassed, in 1988 when guests at the evening pig roast were entertained by two bands, the Austin Lounge Lizards and J. D. and the Other Three.

One other innovation deserves mention, the Conference T-Shirt (Fig. 15.2), made possible by the improved technology of silk-screen printing, which has also produced a flood of T-shirts of many other kinds. A special Pecos Conference T-shirt first appeared in 1977, according to the records of Sharon Urban. For the 1983 Conference at Bluff a special T-shirt sold for $6. The next year at Flagstaff a T-shirt with an elaborate logo suitable to the location was available. The following year at Salinas 135 Conference T-shirts were sold at $6.50 each. The new tradition was clearly established. In 1986 there was not only a Conference T-shirt but also a Conference hat, both with a design showing Shoofly Village, where the host institution was digging. For some of the recent years the T-shirts have been produced by June Lipe of Pullman, Washington (whose husband is the archaeologist William Lipe of Washington State University) at her Triticum Press. Who else may have designed and sold T-shirts remains unknown, but the annual Conference T-shirt is another sign of keeping up with the times, like the musical entertainment at the barbecue.

THE CONFERENCE RECORDS   For the earlier years there was no attempt either to record details of the program or to keep notes on its contents, although sometimes quite extensive information has survived in the files of host institutions. At the suggestion of Kidder, Stanley Stubbs began, in the 1940s, a systematic Conference archival record at the Laboratory of Anthropology in Santa Fe. Later Stubbs apparently planned to write a history of the Conference (an undated letter from Kidder to Stubbs refers to this, and from the reference to Stubbs's manuscript on Pindi Pueblo it was probably written in 1950 or 1951). Unfortunately, at the time of Stubbs's death in 1959 he had

**Pecos Conference
Blanding, Utah 1990**

15.2 T-shirt logos made for Pecos Conferences, with appropriate local symbolism. Courtesy of June Lipe and Brian Kenny.

not found the time to write this history. Stewart Peckham took over the responsibility for the Pecos Conference Archives after 1959 and generously provided a great deal of material for this history. He has been succeeded by Willow Powers, the Laboratory's archivist.

For some Conferences a volunteer kept detailed notes of all or some of the sessions, and these have been immensely helpful in putting together this history. The first such record was made by Pat Wheat at Point of Pines in 1948, and she also kept detailed notes of the Conference at Point of Pines in 1951. Elaine Bluhm also recorded two Conferences, those of 1950 and 1956, both in Flagstaff. At Santa Fe in 1953 Lee Correll kept a careful record of most of the Conference. In 1957 in Globe detailed notes were kept on the taxonomy session by Carol A. Gifford and James C. Gifford, with briefer notes on some other parts of the Conference. The meetings in 1959 and 1960 at Fort Burgwin and Flagstaff were taped, almost in toto, by John Champe, as described earlier. Years later these tapes were transcribed with the generous help of Sue Ruiz of the Arizona State Museum. Beginning in 1963 David M. Brugge began taking extensive notes at the Conferences, continuing through 1967, and for some of these years he dictated onto a cassette a fuller version of his notes. Two symposia were taped and transcribed, at Santa Fe in 1970 and in Tucson in 1973. While this book was in press, I learned from Albert Schroeder that tapes of the fiftieth Pecos Conference are on file with the National Park Service in Santa Fe.

In 1975 Sharon Urban of the Arizona State Museum began taking detailed notes on virtually the entire Conference and continued to do so for every year except 1984, when she did not attend. Many other people have had notes on portions of a Conference or lists of field reports and have made them available, particularly Florence Hawley Ellis. For some years a report on the Conference, occasionally fairly detailed, was published in a professional journal such as *American Antiquity* or *Masterkey*. But in spite of all the records mentioned here, information on the Conferences is uneven and for some years very sparse, particularly for some of the Conferences held at Chaco Canyon. This erratic record results in different details being available for different years, making comparisons difficult. Information on many important and interesting events has been lost forever.

The extent of the surviving record should be the focus of our attention, not its unfortunate gaps. It is impressive that a nonorganization—no officers, no memberships, no headquarters—has had the good fortune to accumulate as much of an archive of its history as has the Pecos Conference.

SYMPOSIA   One feature of Pecos Conferences that was foreshadowed in 1927 and has been strongly represented at almost every subsequent meeting is the symposium. This usually consists of several papers focusing on a single general topic, which are invited in advance and are allotted twenty or thirty minutes, as opposed to the ten-minute field reports. Occasionally the roundtable or panel discussion form has been used to increase exchanges among the speakers. Some of these symposia have reviewed the current state of knowledge and understanding of the area in which the Conference was being held. For example, at Point of Pines in 1948 there was a panel discussion of the Mogollon, which was highly appropriate to the location. In Santa Fe in 1955 there was a summary of Rio Grande archaeology. For the 1956 meeting at the Museum of Northern Arizona two symposia were planned, on the archaeology of the Flagstaff area and the archaeology of the Verde Valley, but apparently they were not held, since an entirely different symposium topic appears in the records, the Southwest in the twelfth and thirteenth centuries. When the Conference met at Fort Burgwin in 1959 an appropriate symposium was held, "Plains-Southwest Relationships," and again in 1963 at Fort Burgwin the subject was revived, with emphasis on the historic period. At Casas Grandes in 1961 a roundtable session discussed "Northwestern Chihuahua Pottery Analysis" (originally announced as a somewhat broader topic, "Ceramic History and Technology of Northwestern Mexico and the American Southwest").

The symposium in 1964 at Window Rock was relevant to the capital of the Navajo Nation: "Decline of the Puebloan Pattern and the Expansion of the Rancheria Pattern." The next year in Trinidad there was also a local focus: "Archeological Materials of Southeastern Colorado and Adjacent Regions." Similar local or regional emphasis continued with the following:

> Flagstaff, 1966,   "The Sinagua and Their Neighbors"
> Mesa Verde, 1974,   "Cultural and Environmental Change in the Mesa Verde Area"
> Salmon Ruin, 1975,   "Understanding the Chaco Phenomenon"
> Kino Bay, 1976,   "Recent Archaeological Investigations in Sonora"
> Pecos, 1977,   "The Rio Grande: Perspective from Its Periphery"
> Mesa Verde, 1980,   "Regional Variation on the Colorado Plateau"

Pecos, 1982,   a whimsically titled but effective symposium,
"Protohistoric Palaver Pertaining to Peripheral Parameters of
Pecos Pueblo"
   Bluff, 1983,   "Current Research in Southeastern Utah"
   Flagstaff, 1984,   "An Overview of the Prehistory of the
Flagstaff Region"
   Mountainair, 1985,   "Salinas Archaeology"
   Pecos, 1987,   "The Northern Rio Grande"
   Dolores, 1988,   "The Dolores Archaeological Program"

Although there have been justifiable complaints that symposium
papers were sometimes poorly prepared and dully presented and that
the papers of some symposia bore too little relationship to each other,
the overall result of these sessions was to disseminate new information and interpretations of many regions to their audiences, most of
whom were far from expert on any area but their own. This has been
an important accomplishment of the Pecos Conference through the
years, even though only twenty of fifty-one Conferences have had
a regionally focused symposium. Other symposia have ranged over
an extraordinary variety of topics, from practical or political to theoretical or problem oriented. In 1927 the precedent was established by
following the field reports with discussion of a major topic—the Pecos
Classification. Also, a major problem was identified—areas needing
more research. In place of a symposium on Pecos Pueblo, Kidder conducted a half day tour and explanation of the work accomplished by
the Pecos Expedition. In 1929 there was renewed discussion of the
Pecos Classification from the standpoint of utility and applicability,
and the very recent breakthrough in tree-ring dating was given substantial attention. Thus, from the start, the pattern was set of holding
one or more sessions on a topic regarded as timely and significant.

Only rarely has a symposium had an ethnological, ethnohistoric,
or historical topic. Ruth Benedict and Clark Wissler chaired a session
on ethnological methods and practices in 1931 at Santa Fe; there was
an "enemy peoples" symposium in 1951; in 1954 a session was held on
aboriginal-Spanish contacts; and in 1963 the subject was entradas and
related problems. Indian claims archaeology was discussed in 1958 at
Albuquerque, and there were sessions on Southern Athabascans in
1961 and 1963.

Several times current, practical problems have been taken up: the
interpretation of anthropology in museums, elementary schools, and
colleges, and for the general public in 1950 and again in 1951; the federal government's future relations to anthropology in 1954; needed

changes in the Antiquities Act in 1971; and the proposed Anasazi National Park in 1988.

The more theoretical end of the symposium spectrum is represented by several subjects: Erik Reed's "Northern and Southern (or Eastern and Western) Pueblos" in 1951; the conceptual schemes of Daifuku and of Martin and Rinaldo in 1952; a temporal-spatial synthesis of Southwestern cultural horizons in 1953; current trends in archaeological theory and methods, 1968; "Provenience Concepts: Room-fill and Floor" in 1973. Among the topics proposed for the 1947 meeting in Chaco were the relation of archaeology to ethnology and the drawing of "ethnological" conclusions from archaeological data, including the inference of social organization from floor plans (still a lively topic today). In 1946 in Santa Fe there was a session on "Concepts and Methods of Archaeology."

Not surprisingly, agriculture and its origins have received attention several times, starting in 1952 with the origins of corn in the Southwest, then in 1953 with the origins and dispersal of Southwestern agriculture, and in 1970 with prehistoric water-control systems. Similarly, the relationship of the Southwestern United States to Mexico was examined several times, in 1940, 1947, 1954, and 1959.

In 1955 the Pecos Conference had the privilege of being the first to hear the results of one of the SAA seminars, "The American Southwest: A Problem in Cultural Isolation." The next year, as an experiment, a symposium surveyed the Southwest in a specific time period, A.D. 1100–1300, drainage by drainage. In 1957 four "critical periods" in the Southwest were examined, extending from early ceramic times to Spanish contact. Another experiment, in 1986, dealt with "spatial organization and integration west of the Continental Divide in the late prehistoric period." These were efforts to move away from a review of an area or a specific "problem" (such as relations with Mexico, the origins of farming, or the status of the Mogollon) to topics that would integrate data in new ways, cover large areas, or utilize a variety of theoretical concepts. Whether they were successful is less important than the fact that they moved the Pecos Conference in new directions rather than adhering to a traditional formula.

Several times symposia dealt with advances in archaeological techniques, beginning with tree rings in 1929, then carbon-14 in 1949 and 1951, geochronology in 1954, and archaeoastronomy in 1988. Particular taxonomic questions were occasionally considered: projectile point terminology, 1947; brown wares of west-central New Mexico and east-central Arizona, 1950; and ceramic typology (the unveiling of the ceramic variety and type cluster concept), 1957.

All in all, the initial establishment of a symposium as a standard part of the Pecos Conferences contributed significantly to their usefulness in broadening the sessions beyond presentation of data with little or no focus, synthesis, or sense of problem. Nearly every subject that was seen at the time to be of importance to Southwestern archaeology was taken up at least once. The topics reflect frequent shifts of interest as well as the persistence of older ones. One recommendation, made repeatedly, was rarely followed—that the symposium papers be duplicated in advance and distributed at the Conference, so that more time could be spent discussing the content of the presentations. This shortcoming is probably due to the last-minute preparation of papers, something characteristic of the large, national meetings as well. In spite of frequent urging, symposia were published only a very few times.

STUDENT PARTICIPATION   It is ironic that year after year the question of student attendance and participation should have vexed the Pecos Conference, since in 1927 several students attended. As Odd Halseth later recalled (quoted in chapter 3), "Students who came with their teachers were asked their opinions and were heard and noted for their contributions." On the other hand, Haury recalled that "we [students] were too awed to open our mouths." Five students were at the 1927 Conference: Clara Lee Fraps (Tanner), Charlotte Gower, Emil Haury, Paul Martin, and Robert Wauchope. Those of this group who regularly attended future Conferences came to be revered, along with their elders, as "Founders," regardless of their junior role in 1927.

There were questions about whether Laboratory of Anthropology summer students could attend the Conferences of 1929 and 1931, which were resolved in the students' favor, in view of their fellowship status. When the Conferences in Chaco Canyon began in 1937 after the first three Conferences (Pecos and Santa Fe), students played a different role. They were kept on as helpers during the Conference and "attended" more as observers than participants. However, Clifford Evans, whose letter concerning the 1940 Conference has earlier been quoted at length, commented that there was "no snobbery" expressed toward Kepler Lewis or himself, even though they were students. It is hard to say at this distance how much the attitudes toward students were influenced by the more egalitarian or hierarchical inclinations of individual archaeologists. But it is clear, from the correspondence already quoted, that in 1946 when the Pecos Conference was revived after World War II allowing students to attend seemed a problem to some. As Reed said, "I hate to refuse [Reiter's and Burrows's requests to bring their students], although I don't like the idea very much; maybe they can be there just part of the time." Paul Reiter wrote Haury in 1947 that he told the Chaco field school students who stayed to work at the Conference that "they could 'listen in' but keep still."

The most emphatic objection to student attendance was expressed by Martin, himself a student at the 1927 Conference in 1948, who wrote to Haury: "I think all students and hangers-on should be excluded. Several of my students wanted to come and I told them nix. . . . Can't you restrict this meeting to Southwesterners who hold full time jobs in anthropology." The next year Colton inquired of Stubbs whether students could be allowed at the Conference, and Stubbs replied carefully and in detail. But by 1956, when the registration form asked for "profession" twenty-five out of ninety-nine registrants put down "student." The issue was faced squarely by Schroeder the next year when he issued the final Conference announcement and specifically urged students to attend, noting that "before long they will be the professionals in the field." Robert Lister wrote him in agreement, noting however that Martin still "believes students should not be allowed to attend! Says it clutters up the place." During the subsequent three decades the presence of students seems to have been taken for granted, as far as the record shows. Schroeder was, of course, correct in pointing out that the students of one decade are the professionals of the next, and attending the Pecos Conference and participating in it was and is an excellent way to prepare for the transition.

It may be that the "student issue" evaporated largely because the students became the essential field staffs of large contract projects such as Glen Canyon and before that the rapidly growing highway and pipeline salvage. Still technically students (degree candidates), they suddenly became junior colleagues as well, not merely trainees at field schools or shovel hands. Having been entrusted with significant responsibilities in field work, they could hardly be refused participation in a Conference where their work would be reported and discussed.

INFORMAL VERSUS FORMAL REPORTS   In retrospect it seems as though more emotion than was justified attached to the issue of whether field reports must always be informal, never written out in advance and read to the audience. There had always been some who spoke clearly and concisely without notes and some who preferred a card to remind them of the facts to be presented. From written notes to a written ten-minute report is not a big step, and there were probably always a few prepared "papers" given in the field report sessions. The informal nature of these reports was often stressed in Conference announcements, but the matter seems not to have become a serious issue until 1968, when eight of Martin's students read papers on not only the field work in the Vernon area but also other topics. This combined the "student question" with the question of informal versus formal reports, and also involved the New Archaeology versus the old, as at this time Martin and his students were dedicated New Archaeologists. The next year, after the Prescott Conference, Euler sent out his questionnaire, and the replies included several comments about field reports, including the papers of Martin's students: reports "should not be read verbatim"; "it is valuable experience for the kids to be able to talk about their sites"; reports should tell "what was learned, not what was observed"; there were complaints of "several terrible term papers" and "sophomoric term papers written for x number of college credits," as well as "pedantic students who presume to read long, verbose, and often irrelevant term papers." The issues of presentation format and subject matter were obviously combined in some of these comments.

When Schwartz implemented some of the suggestions of Euler and his respondents in his announcement for the 1970 Conference, he received angry objections from the Martin camp. Mark Leone, for example, wrote that "the ten-minute extemporaneous field report is not an effective medium of communication for complex research. . . . Dictating mode of expression seems outrageous." More details of this controversy have been provided in chapter 11. The upshot was a compromise, with sessions for informal field reports, for a symposium, and for formal papers. The issue subsided after that, with Conference announcements often stressing the informal nature of the field reports but some Conferences also providing for formal, written papers in a separate session, as in 1972, for example. An interesting and relevant observation was made by George J. Gumerman (letter to Woodbury, 22 August 1989):

> I think the conflict between formal papers and field reports has sorted itself out in an interesting way. The Pecos Conference is still the Pecos Conference with all its informality and camping out. The regular and irregular meetings held on the Hohokam, Mogollon, and the Anasazi seemed to fill the gap for more synthetic prepared papers. It seems a good compromise and one that was selected almost subconsciously.

But dissatisfaction with the informal field reports themselves continued. Grouping them by broad cultural units instead of states was an improvement, although used only intermittently. Orienting each field report "to some aspect of cultural process . . . or to the dynamics of culture history" was requested in 1974 for the Mesa Verde Conference, with the alternative of bringing a one-page descriptive summary, to be photocopied and distributed. The next year there was a requirement that descriptive reports would be limited to five minutes, while those that dealt "with the large implications of the field research" could have ten to fifteen minutes. A suggestion in 1977 that reports for each region be "digested" or "collated" and presented by a spokesperson was not attempted, as it seemed impractical because of time constraints. A variation was proposed in 1980, that for the field reports each person bring thirty copies of "a 3–4 page paper succinctly describing the pertinent data and approach and problems"; these would be summarized by someone for each area or state. Each group met separately and concurrently, and the next morning a summary was presented of each group's reports. There was, not surprisingly, some dissatisfaction with this procedure, but a rather complicated modification of it was used the next year at Fort Burgwin. In 1982 at Pecos field reports reverted to the more traditional sequential scheme, although grouped by culture units. A recent (1988) innovation in reporting at the Pecos Conference is offering a poster session. Some informal reports are read, contrary to the rules, but there seem to be few or no objections, and it is possible that the Conference format has settled into a pattern that is generally acceptable, obviously different from that of 1927 but preserving something of its informality.

A strong defense of field reports is offered by Brugge (letter to Woodbury, 25 June 1989):

> There have been many, many archaeological projects through the years that have never reached the pages of published reports, and in some cases not even of manuscript reports filed away in more or less accessible locations. We would forever be . . . totally ignorant that they have been taking place, were it not for the field reports. Knowing even that little, it is possible . . . sometimes to ferret out data from files almost forgotten in dispersed locales.

ARCHAEOLOGY, ETHNOLOGY, OR ANTHROPOLOGY?   A different aspect of the Conferences, and an issue that arose repeatedly, was whether this was an archaeological conference or an anthropological one, including the other subfields along with archaeology. It was sometimes referred to as broadly anthropological, but efforts to include ethnologists, linguists, and physical anthropologists were sporadic and rarely successful. Nevertheless, the desirability of a broad, anthropologically oriented Conference has been expressed repeatedly, although somewhat less frequently in recent years. But the effect has been insignificant. Ethnologists did take part in the Conferences from the very earliest years, and in its report on the 1929 Pecos Conference *Masterkey* called it "a congress of field workers in archaeological and ethnological research." That year there were at least ten ethnological participants, including five Laboratory of Anthropology summer students in ethnology. Ten years later the Conference in Chaco Canyon was called "The Third Annual Anthropological Conference," and the next year Donald Brand's invitation said "all bona fide professional anthropologists are welcome" and asked for discussion leaders for ethnology, archaeology, linguistics, physical anthropology, primitive art, and other specialties.

When the Conference was revived in 1946, Reed and Haury issued invitations to forty-six people, all of them archaeologists, but the next year there were seven ethnologists among the thirty-four registrants, plus a historian and a physical anthropologist. Ethnology's peak was from 1949 to 1952. There were nineteen ethnological and thirty-three archaeological field reports in 1949, and two years later there was an afternoon session solely for ethnology and applied anthropology. Nevertheless, in 1952 W. W. Hill wrote Stubbs to ask if invitations could be sent to ethnologists and included a list of names and addresses. Later that year Evon Vogt estimated there would be twenty-four ethnological reports of about fifteen minutes each, but Stubbs replied that they should be limited to five to ten minutes. On the registration list that year there are eighteen ethnologists, 12 percent of the total, a proportion rarely exceeded in future years.

One factor in ethnological participation expressed by Hill was that attendance required an interruption in the middle of field work, more serious when working with the living than with cultures of the past. In 1951 E. H. Spicer declined to take part in a symposium because he felt that the archaeological emphasis of the Conference made it of little interest to those in other subfields. The small number of ethnologists that usually came to a Pecos Conference also had a negative effect on future participation—one couldn't count on talking with or hearing reports from any substantial number of colleagues, in contrast to the expectations an archaeologist could have. Figures from a few subsequent years indicate the fluctuating role of ethnology: 1954, 8 ethnological and 27 archaeological reports; 1955, 17 ethnologists among 115 registrants; 1957, no ethnologists identifiable; 1958, 12 ethnologists out of 140 registrants; 1960, 6 ethnological and 31 archaeological reports; 1965, 5 ethnological and 37 archaeological reports; 1967, of 246 registrants no more than 15 identified as ethnologists; 1982, a scheduled session for ethnology that had 6 reports; 1988, an ethnohistoric and protohistoric session that had only 3 reports.

Perhaps it is remarkable that ethnologists bothered at all with the Pecos Conference, since they usually played such a minor role. Two factors may help account for their continued presence, even in small numbers. There were some Conference participants who thought of themselves as anthropologists first, with specialization in archaeology, and who therefore urged ethnologists to attend and welcomed them when they did. Also, in spite of increasing subfield specialization in recent decades, there were some ethnologists who were interested in what archaeologists were doing. Even with the modest nonarchaeological participation that the records show, the Pecos Conferences continued to be regarded by some as an important opportunity to hear what others were doing, across the whole spectrum of anthropological specialties, and to exchange ideas with them.

WHAT HAS THE CONFERENCE MEANT TO PARTICIPANTS? One of the questions in the 1979 questionnaire was, "Which was the most successful/significant/interesting Pecos Conference in your view and why?" The fiftieth anniversary Conference in 1977 at Pecos was named most frequently, with such comments as "large participation and good organization"; "special in every way, the people who came to it, the setting, the symposium, the facilities, food and drink"; "a fabulous spirit past/present/future seemed evident [and] especially noteworthy were the reminiscences of the 'older generation'"; "being able to camp gave more opportunity for after hours gathering and discussion"; "listening to Emil [Haury], et al., talk about the early developments and field work in archeology"; "most interesting in that it helped reify my appreciation and understanding of the history and development of the profession . . . too often the 'romance' and history of Southwestern archeology is not felt by new students and this is as important as any other aspect of their training to understand the development of concepts." There was one negative comment, that the 1977 Conference "emphasized the maturity and seriousness of those attending in 1927 and the lack of it on the part of many in 1977."

Many other years were also mentioned enthusiastically, and for many different reasons:

1940,　"brought together Mexican anthropologists and Southwesterners."

1948,　"all the 'greats' in S.W. Arch. were there, including Kidder."

1951,　"Point of Pines symposium; being there with Morris, Kidder, Haury, et al";"[my] first one; I recognized a world where I belonged."

1956,　"Wheat-Gifford-Wasley was consummated on my front porch."

1960 and 1971,　"just happened I was able to make corridor contacts that advanced my work."

1961,　"Nuevo Casas Grandes, well organized with highly topical data"; "just the place, the people, the timing."

1966,　"it helped me develop my ideas about the dissertation . . . ; on the informal side, I was interviewed for the [campus omitted] job the next year at the Tucson conference."

1967,　"best organized symposium; careful choice of subject and participants; weather unspeakable."

1969,　"the proximity of the camp ground and the meeting place led to far greater interaction than has been typical."

1975,　"because the discussion of Chaco and Casas Grandes as major regional centers seemed very important"; "because of the well attended session on Chaco."

1976　(Kino Bay), "because it also included archeological activities in Mexico"; "the contact with Mexican archaeologists."

Also praised were "the 25th at which time we gave A. V. Kidder the silver trowel and where were gathered so many people he loved and we love(d)"; "those [Conferences] at which the problems of a district were discussed and then we could visit the sites being studied (Point of Pines, Bloomfield [Salmon Ruin], Mesa Verde, etc.)." One response was "cannot say—but I enjoyed them less and got less out of them as they became more structured and 'formal.'" Another response was similar: "the Pecos's flow together in a rather pleasant blur in my mind. . . . Now it seems the meetings are so large and unwieldy that I, at least, don't go any more. And, of course, members of our generation are not as frequent, shall we say, as we used to be."

These comments suggest very different expectations and satisfac-

tions from those of the usual professional meeting of a national organization. Many people seem to feel that they are *part* of a Pecos Conference, not merely an audience, and it seems that they perceive it in
differently than the many large, national meetings.

Related to opinions about the significance or interest of any particular Conference is the question of why people attend. Asked on
the questionnaire for their primary reason for attending, people gave
a variety of answers, with the most frequent being to learn what
was going on in the field and, in second place, to renew personal
contacts and enjoy old friendships. Reasons were expressed in many
ways, such as "to see friends, party, hear papers"; "exchange ideas";
"interaction with colleagues"; "discuss problems with others [and]
hear what is happening in specific areas"; "learning what is going on,
both professionally and informally"; "see colleagues/friends, get current professional information"; "to keep up with field investigations
and new interpretations"; "at first to see the big names, then to meet
friends and exchange information." These responses suggest that great
value is placed on informal discussions as well as on the field reports.
It appears that the intellectual and social aspects are almost equally
important.

Another questionnaire query concerned "the nature of your participation," asking that several possible reasons be ranked. "See friends"
barely edged out "confer with colleagues," and "hear reports" was a
close third. Behind these came "give a report."

Varied answers were given to the question, "What has been the
greatest value to you of Pecos Conferences?" The responses generally
confirmed those given to the two previously mentioned questions:
learning what was going on, and seeing friends. Responses included:
"it has helped me from becoming so immersed in my own areas of
research that I become isolated from what is going on among others";
"seeing the Southwest beyond my own research areas, putting faces
to 'big' names"; "the opportunity to 'corner' people I've wanted to
talk with"; "find out . . . what is happening in terms of current research [and] meeting with other archaeologists to discuss research";
"the meetings around the campfire . . . have been invaluable [while]
the formal reports have not been of much help to me"; "personal contacts with other field workers and with old friends"; "find out what
is currently going on in the Southwest in order to keep myself up to
date"; "the *informal* exchange of factual and interpretive information";
"learning about the newest developments and concepts in Southwestern archeology—however, this is accomplished more by talking to

people around the coffee pot or campfire than by listening to 8-minute reports by nervous students who don't know what they're talking about"; "developing and maintaining a network of personal contacts"; "socializing with old and new colleagues, swapping facts and lies"; "you can sound people out and in discussion clarify a lot of your thoughts more easily than in formal papers"; "to talk with colleagues and friends—I met my present wife at the Prescott Conference"; and "be aware of results of field work that might take several to many years to be published." One respondent wrote, "The *tradition* for and behind the Conference; for several years I attended with a feeling of a 'sacred pilgrimage'!" (emphases in originals).

Those who were least satisfied with the Conferences may have failed to return questionnaires, so the answers are in no sense an unbiased sample of all views and opinions. But the negative comments are relatively few, mostly mentioning problems that are all too familiar— dull symposia, the growth of the Conference to hundreds instead of scores of participants, or an occasional complaint about breakdowns in arrangements, particularly a couple of disappointing barbecues. If the responses just quoted reflect the views of most Conference participants through the years, the soul searching and wrangling about format may have been unnecessary. Field reports provide a wealth of up-to-date information, symposia present (usually) a current appraisal of an area or topic, and there is also ample time for the all-important informal exchange of ideas and the renewal of friendships that are so frequently mentioned.

TANGIBLE RESULTS   Although field reports at Pecos Conferences are very different from the longer, more formal papers at many other kinds of meetings, publications have resulted, sometimes directly and sometimes indirectly, from Conference presentations and discussions. The 1979 questionnaire asked about this, and several responses included specific examples. One person wrote, "What I have learned at the conferences has had a very broad and general effect on my thinking and has contributed to ideas I later used in papers." More specifically, the article in *American Antiquity* in 1958 on "ceramic variety" by Joe Ben Wheat, James C. Gifford, and William W. Wasley grew out of discussion and presentation of its ideas at the 1957 Pecos Conference. Another respondent wrote, "My . . . dissertation has material derived from Pecos Conference discussions. . . . [and] the problem investigated by [name omitted] in his dissertation is a direct result of a conversation I had" at a Pecos Conference. Another publication identified as deriving from Conference presentations and discussions is Schroeder's "Hakataya Cultural Tradition" (1957), developed by an unofficial "mini-conference" at the 1956 Flagstaff Conference. His "Hohokam, Sinagua, and Hakataya" (1960) derived in part from this same discussion.

One Pecos Conference symposium—and only one—was published promptly in full, the session on the protohistoric of the Pecos area. It was organized by Schroeder and held, appropriately, at Pecos in 1982 (see Fox 1984 in which the seven papers appear). Several people observed that many published articles have developed from short field reports at Pecos Conferences, although not intended for publication in their initial ten-minute form. One reply emphasized the importance of the informal influence of Conferences on publications, stating, "Virtually all of my own publications contain information, ideas, or clarifications that have stemmed in part from Pecos Conference discussions."

As with other professional meetings, information and ideas are diffused and absorbed and eventually appear in print, their first germination sometimes forgotten. Few Southwesternists publish without interchange with colleagues, and every Conference is an opportunity for this. Many people referred to this on their questionnaires, noting specific projects that had benefited from discussions with others, or topics on which useful information had been acquired at Pecos Conferences. One referred to the stimulation of his research because "of the chance to talk to others about it and to hear what others are doing along the same line." Another wrote, "A great deal of my work in Navajo archeology has been stimulated by Pecos Conference attendance. As an example, a discussion of Anasazi urbanization was important in making me think much more deeply about Navajo settlement patterns."

Publication is only one kind of "result" of conferences. It should not be overlooked that the first Pecos Conference resulted in substantial changes in the way Southwestern archaeologists thought about their data, the Pecos Classification being adopted widely as a framework for their analysis and interpretations. It is doubtful if acceptance and use of such concepts as "Hohokam," "Mogollon," and "Sinagua" would have been as rapid without their discussion at Pecos Conferences.

Less tangible than the Conference's contribution to the progress of information or ideas, from extempore report to publication, but of far greater significance, is its contribution to the position of Southwestern archaeology in North America. In the 1920s many areas were seriously neglected archaeologically compared to the Southwest, and it was partly in emulation of the Southwest that site surveys, pottery classifications, chronological systems, and improved excavation and recording techniques were applied or developed elsewhere. Nevertheless, the Southwest continued to play a leading role as a testing ground for methodological and theoretical innovation, in part because of its unsurpassed body of detailed, well-dated information of every kind. Although it would be difficult to cite evidence for specific contributions by the Pecos Conference to the continuing development of this data base, there seems little doubt that the annual face-to-face communication of so many researchers about their current work and ideas and the immediate expression by colleagues of their doubts or agreements has fostered the accelerating growth and complexity of Southwestern archaeology.

THE YEARS AHEAD   In spite of its growth, and surviving its disagreements about program format and earlier about the role of students, the Pecos Conference has remained remarkably faithful to its tradition of informal field reports and symposia on local or regional archaeology or on topics of general interest. It has not become, as a few have hoped, a regional imitation of the annual meeting of the SAA or AAA. I will not attempt to forecast what the Conference will be like in the years ahead, but will conclude with a few of the comments and suggestions added to the 1979 questionnaire, which may indicate what directions Southwesternists would like the Conference to take.

The suggestion was raised again, as it has been several times in the past, to increase future registration fees substantially, in order "to record the oral reports and business meetings and seminars [symposia] on tapes. Transcribe and print them and send a copy to those that registered." Copies could also be sold by mail and at the next year's Conference. Only two Conferences have been recorded in full (1959 and 1960, and they were not transcribed until 1987). The 1973 session, "Provenience Concepts: Room-fill and Floor," was taped and much later was transcribed, but with many gaps and ambiguities. Parts of the 1977 symposium, "The Rio Grande: Perspective from Its Periphery," were recorded to supplement the written papers, but the transcription is marred by gaps and misheard parts of the discussions. None of these transcriptions has been made generally available. However, today it is possible to make much better quality tapes, and the transcription and printing is a question of dollars, not technology. What it would cost and how much interest there would be in such a complete record will perhaps be given attention by those arranging future Conferences. The incomplete transcript of the 1977 symposium runs to 152 double-spaced typed pages, and the field reports at that meeting might add 200 pages more. A transcript of the tapes made of the 1960 Conference is about 200 pages long. Editing such tapes, duplicating, and distributing them would be a substantial task. Schroeder (letter to Woodbury, 29 June 1989) comments:

> Frankly, I do not think this would be worth the trouble. Most reports are brief progress reports with few observations on significance, relationships, and problem areas. . . . I would prefer a final list, broken down by session, of titles, speakers, and their address[es] so that one could get in touch on points of mutual interest.

This has been done once, at Salinas National Monument in 1985, so it is not impossible, although probably difficult. It certainly gives attendees a convenient reference list for following up Conference reports and contacts.

Another comment (1979 questionnaire) addresses a different set of problems, including the large number of field reports that have to be fitted into a limited time on the program:

> It would seem to me that we need some changes in the format that will accommodate the much larger attendance now. It is possible that the field reports could be summarized by individuals [each] responsible for a particular segment of the S.W. Reports would identify projects, investigators, the problem of each project, and what was encountered, and be based on summaries given to the reporter by the investigators. This would allow people interested in particular districts to get together for discussions.

This has been suggested before, but not yet done satisfactorily. Part of the difficulty, I suspect, is that individuals are reluctant to lose the opportunity to stand before an audience and be heard (and seen). In addition, it is difficult to find people who can effectively read (or hear) and immediately synthesize an assortment of reports in the limited time available for the "regional caucuses."

Another suggestion is that "small sessions (several at one time in different locations) could be devoted to issues or topics of current concern. . . . With small groups, one can hold the group's attention. There are too many distractions when part of a large group is not interested in a presentation." Whether in future years new experiments with simultaneous sessions will be made remains to be seen. There are those who "want to hear everything" and others who prefer to talk with the few researchers with whom they share interests on specific topics. No format can entirely satisfy both.

Changes, reflecting the dichotomy perceived by some between "contract" and "academic" research, are commented on in another questionnaire as follows:

> It seems to me that the enormous growth of contract work in the Southwest has significantly altered the interactions at Pecos Conferences. Specifically, the field reports have become advertising forums for various contract "shops." People are more apt to report the number of surveys they've completed than raise any questions of substance. Away from the structured reports the Conference is, in part, a giant job market for project personnel. I would like to see the Conference return to its original purpose.

Dissatisfaction is also expressed in the observations of another participant, one with a long record of attendance at the Conferences:

> In the P.C.s I have attended I have sensed what seemed to be a regrettable change in the attitude or point of view of participants. In the early Conferences I felt . . . an eagerness to share and to learn. More recent Conferences have frequently left me with a feeling that many participants had been more concerned about making an impression on those around them as regards their own work and status rather than the unity and the good will of the Conference and the profession as a whole. This may have been inevitable as the Conference continued to grow bigger and bigger with the years.

This criticism reflects the profound change in Southwestern anthropology that has taken place in the last sixty years, from the work of a small circle of scholars, many self-trained, and nearly all well acquainted with each other, to an enterprise carried out by many hundreds of people with new and divergent goals and methodologies. The Pecos Conference still provides a meeting place for all Southwesternists, but while they share information and ideas they may feel little or no concern for furthering the discipline as a whole. This is at least partly because professional advancement depends more than ever on producing monographs and scholarly articles, rather than on participation and cooperation with others toward a joint goal.

As archaeology, and indeed anthropology as a whole, has changed from an avocation for a few to a career for many, it has become ever more competitive, as have many other aspects of American life. Nevertheless, the Pecos Conference will continue to stimulate Southwesternists to tackle together the central problems facing the study of the Southwest, just as in 1927 problems then basic to Southwestern research were discussed and argued. And it can continue to provide a forum for reaching new and significant agreements on the most promising ways to better understand the complex and fascinating human story that is the Southwest's past and present.

The Pecos Conference today mirrors our times, as the more leisurely, conversational Pecos Conference of the early years mirrored its times. It is a far cry from the group of friends around a quiet evening campfire enjoying Kidder's ruminations, questions, and anecdotes to the barbecue accompanied by the Austin Lounge Lizards. But the annual exchange of ideas and information, the renewal of friendships, and the forming of new acquaintances that Kidder began continues under the same piñons, even if in modern dress. We are fortunate that Kidder created the Pecos Conference, with a clear statement of its purposes, and that even today it persists in a greatly changed world, an eagerly anticipated annual event with both a symbolic and a practical role, shaping the way Southwesternists view themselves and their profession.

References

Aldana, Barbara Kidder
    1983   The Kidder-Pecos Expedition, 1924–1929: A Personal Memoir. *Kiva* 48(4): 243–250.

Amsden, Charles A.
    1927   The Pecos Conference. *Masterkey* 1(4): 14–18.
    1931   Black-on-white ware. *In* The pottery of Pecos, Vol. 1, Dull-paint wares, by A. V. Kidder, pp. 17–72. *Papers of the Southwestern Expedition* 5. New Haven: Yale University Press for Phillips Academy.
    1934   *Navajo weaving, its technique and history.* Santa Ana, California: Fine Arts Press.
    1949   *Prehistoric Southwesterners from Basketmaker to Pueblo.* Los Angeles: Southwest Museum.

Anonymous
    1929   The Second Pecos Conference. *Masterkey* 3(4): 28–29.
    1938a   Chaco Anthropological Conference. *New Mexico Anthropologist* 2(4–5): 100.
    1938b   Conference of Southwestern anthropologists, Chaco Canyon. *New Mexico Anthropologist* 3(1): 10–11.
    1940a   The Albuquerque and Chaco Anthropological Conferences of the Coronado Congress, August 1940. *New Mexico Anthropologist* 4(3): 39–53.
    1940b   The Coronado Congress. *El Palacio* 47(7): 150–151.
    1940c   Frank Pinkley. *Southwestern National Monuments Monthly Report,* February 1940: iii–vi. Coolidge, Arizona: Casa Grande National Monument.
    1969   1969 Pecos Conference. *Masterkey* 43(4): 131.
    1970   Pecos Conference—1970. *El Palacio* 77(1): 34.

Anthropology Curriculum Study Project
    1972   *Two-way mirror: Anthropologists and educators observe themselves and each other.* Washington: American Anthropological Association.

Bandelier, Adolph F.

1881   Report on the ruins of the Pueblo of Pecos. *Papers of the Archaeological Institute of America, American Series*, Vol 1, Part 2. Boston: A. Williams.

Bartlett, Katharine

1946   Southwestern Archeological Conference. *American Anthropologist* 48(4): 697.

1951a   Notes and News, Southwest. *American Antiquity* 16(3): 288–290.

1951b   Notes and News, Southwest. *American Antiquity* 16(4): 362.

1955   Twenty-five years of anthropology. *Plateau* 26(1): 38–60.

Bartlett, Katharine, and Erik K. Reed

1946   The Santa Fe Conference. *El Palacio* 53(10): 269–276.

1949   The 1949 Pecos Conference. *El Palacio* 56(10): 309–313.

Benedict, Ruth

1934   *Patterns of Culture*. Boston: Houghton Mifflin.

Bennett, John W.

1946   The interpretation of Pueblo culture: A question of values. *Southwestern Journal of Anthropology* 2(4): 361–374.

Bennett, Wendell C.

1948   The Peruvian Co-Tradition. *In* A reappraisal of Peruvian archaeology, assembled by Wendell C. Bennett, pp. 1–7. *Society for American Archaeology Memoir* 4. Menasha: Society for American Archaeology and Institute of Andean Research.

Bezy, John V., and Joseph P. Sanchez, editors

1988   *Pecos, gateway to the Pueblos and Plains*. Tucson: Southwest Parks and Monuments Association.

Binford, Lewis R.

1962   Archaeology as anthropology. *American Antiquity* 28(2): 217–225.

1964   A consideration of archaeological research design. *American Antiquity* 29(4): 425–441.

1972   *An archaeological perspective*. New York and London: Seminar Press.

Binford, Sally R., and Lewis R. Binford, editors

1968   *New perspectives in archeology*. Chicago: Aldine.

Bluhm, Elaine A.

1950   Notes on Pecos Conference—1950. MS, Museum of Northern Arizona Library, Flagstaff.

1956   29th Pecos Conference, notes for K. Bartlett. MS, Museum of Northern Arizona Library, Flagstaff.

Brainerd, George W.
1950   Pecos Conference. *Masterkey* 24(6): 202.

Brand, Donald D.
1938   The Chaco Conference, August 27, 28, 29, 1938. *Clearing House for Southwestern Museums News-letter* 5: 14–17. Denver: Denver Art Museum.
1939   [Untitled announcement in Notes and News] *American Antiquity* 5(1): 71.

Brand, Donald D., Florence M. Hawley, and Frank C. Hibben
1937   Tseh So, a small house ruin, Chaco Canyon, New Mexico, preliminary report. *University of New Mexico Anthropological Series* 2(2). Albuquerque: University of New Mexico Press.

Breternitz, David A.
1967   The eruption(s) of Sunset Crater: Dating and effects. *Plateau* 40(2): 72–76.

Brew, John O.
1946   Archaeology of Alkali Ridge, southeastern Utah, with a review of the prehistory of the Mesa Verde division of the San Juan and some observations on archaeological systematics. *Papers of the Peabody Museum of American Archaeology and Ethnology, Harvard University* 21. Cambridge: Peabody Museum.
1963   James A. Lancaster: Citation for distinguished service. *American Antiquity* 29(2): 230–232.

Brew, John O., and Edward B. Danson
1948   The 1947 reconnaissance and the proposed Upper Gila expedition of the Peabody Museum of Harvard University. *El Palacio* 55(7): 211–222.

Brophy, William A., and Sophie D. Aberle, compilers
1966   *The Indian: America's unfinished business. Report of the Commission on the Rights, Liberties, and Responsibilities of the American Indian.* Norman: University of Oklahoma Press.

Carey, Henry A.
1931   An analysis of northwestern Chihuahua culture. *American Anthropologist* 33(3): 325–374.

Carter, George F.
1945   Plant geography and culture history in the American Southwest. *Viking Fund Publications in Anthropology* 5. New York: The Viking Fund.

Chapman, Kenneth M.
1931   Black-on-white ware. *In* The pottery of Pecos, Vol. 1. Dull-paint wares, by A. V. Kidder, pp. 17–72. *Papers of the South-*

western Expedition 7. New Haven: Yale University Press for Phillips Academy.

1936   Pottery of Santo Domingo Pueblo: A detailed study of its decoration. *Memoirs of the Laboratory of Anthropology* 1. Santa Fe: Laboratory of Anthropology.

1949   The Laboratory of Anthropology. *El Palacio* 56(1): 21–24.

1970   The pottery of San Ildefonso Pueblo. *School of American Research Monograph Series* 28. Santa Fe: School of American Research.

Clark, Grahame

1989   *Prehistory at Cambridge and beyond.* Cambridge: Cambridge University Press.

Colton, Harold S.

1939   Prehistoric culture units and their relationships in Northern Arizona. *Museum of Northern Arizona Bulletin* 17. Flagstaff: Northern Arizona Society of Science and Art.

1945   The Patayan problem in the Colorado River valley. *Southwestern Journal of Anthropology* 1(1): 114–121.

1946   The Sinagua: A summary of the archaeology of the region of Flagstaff, Arizona. *Museum of Northern Arizona Bulletin* 22. Flagstaff: Northern Arizona Society of Science and Art.

1951   The Museum in 1950: The twenty-first annual report of the director. *Plateau* 23(3): 64–72.

1953   History of the Museum of Northern Arizona. *Plateau* 26(1): 1–8.

Colton, Harold S., and Lyndon L. Hargrave

1937   Handbook of northern Arizona pottery wares. *Museum of Northern Arizona Bulletin* 11. Flagstaff: Northern Arizona Society of Science and Art.

Correll, J. Lee

1952   Proceedings of the 1952 Pecos Conference 25th anniversary — 1927–1952, held at Santa Fe, New Mexico, August 11–12, 1952. MS, Pecos Conference Archives, Laboratory of Anthropology, Santa Fe.

Cosgrove, C. Burton

1947   Caves of the Upper Gila and Hueco areas of New Mexico and Texas. *Papers of the Peabody Museum of American Archaeology and Ethnology, Harvard University* 24(2). Cambridge: Peabody Museum.

Cosgrove, Harriet S., and C. Burton Cosgrove

1932   The Swarts Ruin, a typical Mimbres site in southwestern New Mexico. *Papers of the Peabody Museum of Archaeology and*

Ethnology, Harvard University 15(1). Cambridge: Peabody Museum.

Daifuku, Hiroshi

1952   A new conceptual scheme for prehistoric cultures in the Southwestern United States. *American Anthropologist* 54(2): 191–200.

Danson, Edward B.

1954   Report on the Pecos Conference, August 30, 31 and September 1, 1954, Gila Pueblo, Arizona. MS, Pecos Conference Archives, Laboratory of Anthropology, Santa Fe.

1956   Notes and News, Southwest. *American Antiquity* 21(3): 338–339.

1957   Notes and News, Southwest. *American Antiquity* 22(3): 325–326.

Doelle, William H., assembler

1976   Desert resources and Hohokam subsistence: The CONOCO Florence Project. *Arizona State Museum Archaeological Series* 103. Tucson: Cultural Resource Management Division, Arizona State Museum, University of Arizona.

Dorsey, H. W.

1930   Report of the Chief Clerk. *In* Fifty-fifth annual report of the Bureau of American Ethnology, pp. 1–19. Washington: Smithsonian Institution.

Douglass, Andrew E.

1935   Dating Pueblo Bonito and other ruins in the Southwest. *National Geographic Society, Contributed Technical Papers, Pueblo Bonito Series* 1. Washington: National Geographic Society.

Doyel, David E.

1977   Rillito and Rincon period settlement systems in the middle Santa Cruz River valley. *Kiva* 43(2): 93–110.

Doyel, David E., Cory D. Breternitz, and Michael P. Marshall

1984   Chacoan community structure: Bis Sa'ani Pueblo and the Chaco halo. *In* Recent research on Chaco prehistory, edited by W. James Judge and John D. Schelberg, pp. 37–54. *Reports of the Chaco Center* 8. Albuquerque: Division of Cultural Research, National Park Service, U.S. Department of the Interior.

Doyel, David, and Fred Plog, editors

1980   Current issues in Hohokam prehistory: Proceedings of a symposium. *Arizona State University Anthropological Research Papers* 23. Tempe: Arizona State University.

Elliott, Malinda

1987   *The School of American Research, a history: The first eighty years.* Santa Fe: School of American Research.

Ellis, Florence Hawley

1951   Patterns of aggression and the war cult in Southwestern Pueblos. *Southwestern Journal of Anthropology* 7(2): 177–201.

Euler, Robert C.

1982   Ceramic patterns of the Hakataya tradition. *In* Southwestern ceramics: A comparative review. A School of American Research Advanced Seminar, edited by Albert H. Schroeder, pp. 52–69. *The Arizona Archaeologist* 15. Phoenix: Arizona Archaeological Society.

Euler, Robert C., George J. Gumerman, Thor N. V. Karlstrom, Jeffrey S. Dean, and Richard H. Hevly

1979   The Colorado Plateaus: Cultural dynamics and paleoenvironment. *Science* 205(4411): 1089–1101.

Feagins, Jim D.

1989   The 1988 Pecos Conference: The tradition lives on. *Journal of the Kansas Anthropological Association* 9(5–6): 106–107.

Ferdon, Edwin N., Jr.

1955   A trial survey of Mexican-Southwestern architectural parallels. *Monographs of the School of American Research* 21. Santa Fe: School of American Research, Museum of New Mexico.

Fewkes, Jesse W.

1912   Casa Grande, Arizona. *In* Twenty-eighth annual report of the Bureau of American Ethnology, pp. 25–179. Washington: Smithsonian Institution.

1914   Archeology of the Lower Mimbres Valley, New Mexico. *Smithsonian Institution Miscellaneous Series,* 63(10).

Fox, Nancy L., editor

1984   Collected papers in honor of Harry L. Hadlock. *Papers of the Archaeological Society of New Mexico* 9. Albuquerque: Albuquerque Archaeological Society Press.

Freeman, J. D., and W. R. Geddes, editors

1959   *Anthropology in the South Seas: Essays presented to H. D. Skinner.* New Plymouth, New Zealand: Thomas Avery and Sons.

Gaines, Sylvia V.

1981   Current research, greater Southwest. *American Antiquity* 46(4): 931–942.

Gifford, Carol A., and Elizabeth A. Morris

1985   Digging for credit: Early archaeological field schools in the American Southwest. *American Antiquity* 50(2): 395–411.

Gifford, James C.

1960   The type-variety method in ceramic classification as an indicator of cultural phenomena. *American Antiquity* 25(3): 341–347.

Gifford, James C., and Carol A. Gifford

1957   Notes from the Pecos Archaeological Conference, Globe, August 26–28, 1957. MS, Arizona State Museum Library, University of Arizona, Tucson.

Givens, Douglas R.

1992   *Alfred Vincent Kidder and the development of Americanist archaeology.* Albuquerque: University of New Mexico Press.

Gladwin, Harold S.

1936   Methodology in the Southwest. *American Antiquity* 1(4): 256–259.

1943   A review and analysis of the Flagstaff culture. *Medallion Papers* 31. Globe: Gila Pueblo.

1944   Tree-ring analysis: Problems of dating. I: The Medicine Valley sites. *Medallion Papers* 32. Globe: Gila Pueblo.

1945   The Chaco Branch: Excavations at White Mound and in the Red Mesa valley. *Medallion Papers* 15. Globe: Gila Pueblo.

1947   *Men out of Asia.* New York and London: Whittlesey House, McGraw-Hill.

1957   *A history of the ancient Southwest.* Portland, Maine: Bond Wheelwright.

Gladwin, Winifred, and Harold S. Gladwin

1928a   A method for the designation of ruins in the Southwest. *Medallion Papers* 1. Pasadena: Privately printed.

1928b   The use of potsherds in an archaeological survey of the Southwest. *Medallion Papers* 2. Globe: Gila Pueblo.

1929a   The Red-on-buff culture of the Gila Basin. *Medallion Papers* 3. Globe: Gila Pueblo.

1929b   The Red-on-buff culture of the Papagueria. *Medallion Papers* 4. Globe: Gila Pueblo.

1930a   The western range of the Red-on-buff culture. *Medallion Papers* 5. Globe: Gila Pueblo.

1930b   A method for the designation of Southwestern pottery types. *Medallion Papers* 7. Globe: Gila Pueblo.

1934   A method for the designation of cultures and their variations. *Medallion Papers* 15. Globe: Gila Pueblo.

1935 The eastern range of the Red-on-buff culture. *Medallion Papers* 16. Globe: Gila Pueblo.

Gower, Charlotte D.

1927 The northern and southern affiliations of Antillean Culture. *American Anthropological Association Memoir* 35. Menasha: American Anthropological Association.

Grebinger, Paul

1973 Prehistoric social organization in Chaco Canyon, New Mexico: An alternative reconstruction. *Kiva* 39(1): 3–23.

Griffin, James B., editor

1951 Essays on archaeological methods. Proceedings of a conference held under the auspices of the Viking Fund. *Museum of Anthropology, University of Michigan, Anthropological Papers* 8. Ann Arbor: University of Michigan Press.

Gumerman, George J., editor

1971 The distribution of prehistoric population aggregates (Proceedings of the Southwestern Anthropological Research Group). *Prescott College Anthropological Reports* 1. Prescott: Prescott College Press.

Gumerman, George J., and Robert C. Euler, editors

1976 *Papers on the archaeology of Black Mesa, Arizona.* Carbondale and Edwardsville: Southern Illinois University Press.

Guthe, Carl E.

1928 Archaeological field work in North America during 1927. *American Anthropologist* 30(3): 501–524.

1930 Archaeological field work in North America during 1929. *American Anthropologist* 32(2): 342–374.

Hall, Edward T., Jr.

1944 Early stockaded settlements in the Governador, New Mexico: A marginal Anasazi development from Basket Maker III to Pueblo I times. *Columbia Studies in Archeology and Ethnology* 2(1). New York: Columbia University Press.

Halseth, Odd S.

1947 Random notes on the 1947 Chaco Conference. *El Palacio* 54(9): 218–220.

Hargrave, Lyndon L.

1938 Results of a study of the Cohonina Branch of the Patayan Culture in 1938. *Museum Notes* 11(6): 43–49. Flagstaff: Museum of Northern Arizona.

Haury, Emil W.

1936a Notes and News, Southwest. *American Antiquity* 2(1): 48–52.

1936b   Vandal Cave. *Kiva* 1(6): 1–4.

1945a   The archaeological survey of the San Carlos Reservation. *Kiva* 11(1): 5–9.

1945b   The excavation of Los Muertos and neighboring ruins in the Salt River valley, southern Arizona. *Papers of the Peabody Museum of American Archaeology and Ethnology, Harvard University* 24(1). Cambridge: Peabody Museum.

1945c   The problem of contacts between the Southwestern United States and Mexico. *Southwestern Journal of Anthropology* 1(1): 55–74.

1948   Southwestern Archaeological Conference. *American Anthropologist* 50(2): 370.

1949   The 1948 Southwestern Archaeological Conference. *American Antiquity* 14(3): 254–256.

1962   HH—39: Recollections of a dramatic moment in Southwestern archaeology. *Tree-Ring Bulletin* 24(3–4): 11–14. Reprinted in *Emil W. Haury's Prehistory of the American Southwest,* edited by J. Jefferson Reid and David E. Doyel, 1986, pp. 55–60. Tucson: University of Arizona Press.

1976   *The Hohokam, desert farmers and craftsmen: Excavations at Snaketown, 1964–1965.* Tucson: University of Arizona Press.

1988   Gila Pueblo Archaeological Foundation: A history and some personal notes. *Kiva* 54(1): i–ix, 1–77.

1989   Point of Pines, Arizona: A history of the University of Arizona Archaeological Field School. *Anthropological Papers of the University of Arizona* 50. Tucson: University of Arizona Press.

Haury, Emil W., editor

1954   Southwest issue. *American Anthropologist* 56(4): Part 1

Haury, Emil W., Kirk Bryan, Edwin H. Colbert, Norman E. Gabel, Clara Lee Tanner, and T. E. Buehrer

1950   *The stratigraphy and archaeology of Ventana Cave, Arizona.* Tucson and Albuquerque: University of Arizona Press and University of New Mexico Press.

Haury, Emil W., and E. B. Sayles

1947   An early pit house village of the Mogollon culture, Forestdale Valley, Arizona. *University of Arizona Bulletin* 18(4), *University of Arizona Social Science Bulletin* 16. Tucson: University of Arizona.

Hawley, Florence M.

1936   Field manual of prehistoric Southwestern pottery types. *University of New Mexico Bulletin* 291, *Anthropological Series* 1(4).

Hayes, Alden C.

1974 *The four churches of Pecos.* Albuquerque: University of New Mexico Press.

1981 Contributions to Gran Quivira archeology, Gran Quivira National Monument, New Mexico. *National Park Service Publications in Archeology* 17. Washington: U.S. Department of the Interior.

Hayes, Alden C., Jon Nathan Young, and A. H. Warren

1981 Excavation of Mound 7, Gran Quivira National Monument, New Mexico. *National Park Service Publications in Archeology* 16. Washington: U.S. Department of the Interior.

Henning, Dale R.

1980 John Leland Champe, 1895–1978. *American Antiquity* 45(2): 268–271.

Herskovits, Robert M.

1978 Fort Bowie material culture. *Anthropological Papers of the University of Arizona* 31. Tucson: University of Arizona Press.

Hibben, Frank C.

1975 *Kiva art of the Anasazi at Pottery Mound.* Las Vegas, Nevada: KC Publications.

Hinsley, Curtis

1980 The problem of Mr. Hewett: Academics and popularizers in American archeology, c. 1910. *History of Anthropology Newsletter* 7(1): 7–10.

Hobbs, Hulda R.

1938 Conference of Southwestern anthropologists. *El Palacio* 45(9): 52.

Hohmann, John W., and Linda B. Kelley

1988 Erich F. Schmidt's investigations of Salado sites in central Arizona. *Museum of Northern Arizona Bulletin* 56. Flagstaff: Museum of Northern Arizona Press.

Hole, Frank

1978 Editorial. *American Antiquity* 43(2): 151–152.

Hough, Walter

1907 Antiquities of the Upper Gila and Salt River valleys in Arizona and New Mexico. *Bureau of American Ethnology Bulletin* 35. Washington: Government Printing Office.

1931 Jesse Walter Fewkes. *American Anthropologist* 33(1): 92–97.

Jeançon, J. A.

1923 Excavations in the Chama Valley, New Mexico. *Bureau*

of American Ethnology Bulletin 81. Washington: Government Printing Office.

Jennings, Jesse D.
1953   Danger Cave: A progress summary. *El Palacio* 60(5): 179–213.
Jennings, Jesse D., editor
1956   The American Southwest: A problem in cultural isolation. *In* Seminars in archaeology: 1955, edited by Robert Wauchope, pp. 59–127. *Society for American Archaeology Memoir* 11. Salt Lake City: Society for American Archaeology.
Johnson, Alfred E.
1963   Notes and News, Southwest. *American Antiquity* 28(3): 413–416.
Johnson, Frederick, assembler
1951   Radiocarbon dating. *Society for American Archaeology Memoir* 8. Salt Lake City: Society for American Archaeology.
Judd, Neil M.
1924   Report of illegal excavations in Southwestern ruins. *American Anthropologist* 26(3): 428–432.
1926   Archeological observations north of the Rio Colorado. *Bureau of American Ethnology Bulletin* 82. Washington: Government Printing Office.
1930   [Untitled]. *In* Archaeological field work in North America during 1929, edited by Carl E. Guthe. *American Anthropologist* 32(2): 362–363.
1954a   Byron Cummings, 1860–1954. *American Anthropologist* 56(5): 871–872.
1954b   The material culture of Pueblo Bonito. *Smithsonian Miscellaneous Collections* 124. Washington: Smithsonian Institution.
1966   Frank H. H. Roberts, Jr., 1897–1966. *American Anthropologist* 68(5): 1226–1232.
1968   *Men met along the trail: Adventures in archaeology.* Norman: University of Oklahoma Press.
1969   Review of "Earl Morris and Southwestern archaeology" by Florence C. Lister and Robert H. Lister. *American Antiquity* 34(1): 91–92.
Judge, W. James, and John D. Schelberg, editors
1984   Recent research on Chaco prehistory. *Reports of the Chaco Center* 8. Albuquerque: Division of Cultural Research, National Park Service, U.S. Department of the Interior.
Karlstrom, Thor N.V., George J. Gumerman, and Robert C. Euler

1976   Paleoenvironmental and cultural correlates in the Black Mesa region. *In* Papers on the archaeology of Black Mesa, Arizona, edited by George J. Gumerman and Robert C. Euler, pp. 149–161. Carbondale and Edwardsville: Southern Illinois University Press.

Kelley, J. Charles

1960   North Mexico and the correlation of Mesoamerican and Southwestern cultural sequences. *Selected Papers of the Fifth International Congress of Anthropological and Ethnological Sciences, Philadelphia, September 1–9, 1956*, edited by Anthony F.C. Wallace, pp. 566–573. Philadelphia: University of Pennsylvania Press.

Kelly, Daniel T., with Beatrice Chauvenet

1972   *The Buffalo Head: A century of mercantile pioneering in the Southwest*. Santa Fe: Vergara.

Kent, Kate Peck

1957   The cultivation and weaving of cotton in the prehistoric Southwestern United States. *American Philosophical Society Transactions* n.s. 47(3): 455–732.

Kessell, John L.

1979   *Kiva, cross, and crown: The Pecos Indians and New Mexico, 1540–1840*. Washington: National Park Service, U.S. Department of the Interior.

Kidder, A. V.

1916   The pottery of the Casa Grandes district. *In* Holmes Anniversary Volume, Anthropological essays presented to William Henry Holmes in honor of his seventieth birthday, December 1, 1916, by his friends and colaborers, pp. 253–268. Washington.

1919   Review of "An outline for a chronology of Zuñi ruins"; "Notes on some Little Colorado ruins"; and "Ruins in the White Mountains, Arizona" by Leslie Spier. *American Anthropologist* 21(3): 296–301.

1924   *An introduction to the study of Southwestern archaeology, with a preliminary account of the excavations at Pecos*. Andover, Massachusetts: Yale University Press for Phillips Academy.

1927   Southwestern archeological conference. *Science* 66(1716): 489–491.

1928   Southwestern archaeological conference. *American Anthropologist* 30(1): 172.

1930   Conference at Chichen Itza. *Science* 71(1841): 391–392.

1931   The pottery of Pecos, Vol. 1. Dull-paint wares. *Papers of the Southwestern Expedition* 5. New Haven: Yale University Press for Phillips Academy.

1937   Foreword. *In* Excavations at Snaketown, II. Comparisons and theories, by Harold S. Gladwin, pp. vii–x. *Medallion Papers* 26. Globe: Gila Pueblo.

1957   Earl Halstead Morris—1889–1956. *American Antiquity* 22(4): 390–397.

1958   Pecos, New Mexico, archaeological notes. *Papers of the Robert S. Peabody Foundation for Archaeology* 5. Andover, Massachusetts: Peabody Foundation.

1960   Reminiscences in Southwestern archaeology, 1. *Kiva* 25(1): 1–32.

Kidder, A. V., and Anna O. Shepard

1936   The pottery of Pecos, Vol. 2. Glaze-paint, culinary, and other wares. *Papers of the Southwestern Expedition* 7. New Haven: Yale University Press for Phillips Academy.

Kidder, Alfred, II

1978   Bob in New Mexico. *In* Codex Wauchope, a tribute roll, edited by Marco Giardino, Barbara Edmonson, and Winifred Creamer, p. 11. *Human Mosaic* 12. New Orleans: Tulane University.

Kintigh, Keith W.

1985   Settlement, subsistence, and society in late Zuni prehistory. *Anthropological Papers of the University of Arizona* 44. Tucson: University of Arizona Press.

Kluckhohn, Clyde

1949   *Mirror for man: The relation of anthropology to modern life.* New York: Whittlesey House, McGraw-Hill.

Kluckhohn, Clyde, W. W. Hill, and Lucy Wales Kluckhohn

1971   *Navaho material culture.* Cambridge: Belknap Press of Harvard University Press.

Krieger, Alex D.

1946   Culture complexes and chronology in northern Texas, with extension of Puebloan datings to the Mississippi Valley. *University of Texas Publications* 4640. Austin: University of Texas.

Kroeber, Alfred L.

1916   Zuñi potsherds. *American Museum of Natural History Anthropological Papers* 18(1). New York: American Museum of Natural History.

1917   Zuñi kin and clan. *American Museum of Natural History Anthropological Papers* 18(2). New York: American Museum of Natural History.

1928   Native culture of the Southwest. *University of California Publications in American Archaeology and Ethnology* 23(9). Berkeley: University of California Press.

1937   Thomas Talbot Waterman. *American Anthropologist* 39(3): 527–529.

Kroeber, Alfred L., and Thomas T. Waterman

1920   *Source book in anthropology.* Berkeley: University of California Press. (Revised edition 1931, New York: Harcourt Brace).

Lambert, Marjorie

1961   John Leland Champe: A founder of the Plains Conference. *Plains Anthropologist* 6(12): 73–75.

Lambert, Paul F.

1980   *Joseph B. Thoburn, pioneer historian and archaeologist.* Oklahoma Trackmaker Series. Oklahoma City: Western Heritage Books for Oklahoma Heritage Association.

Lange, Charles H., and Carroll L. Riley, editors

1966   *The Southwestern journals of Adolph F. Bandelier, 1880–1882.* Albuquerque and Santa Fe: University of New Mexico Press and Museum of New Mexico Press.

Lekson, Stephen H.

1986   *Great pueblo architecture of Chaco Canyon, New Mexico.* Albuquerque: University of New Mexico Press.

Lewis, Sally

1952   The 1952 Pecos Conference. *El Palacio* 59(10): 328–330.

Lindsay, Alexander J., Jr.

1968a   Current research, Southwest. *American Antiquity* 33(1): 188–122.

1968b   Current research, Southwest. *American Antiquity* 33(3): 409–418.

1974   Current research, Greater Southwest. *American Antiquity* 39(2): 376–380.

Lister, Florence C., and Robert H. Lister

1968   *Earl Morris and Southwestern archaeology.* Albuquerque: University of New Mexico Press.

Lister, Robert H.

1957   Review of "A trial survey of Mexican-Southwestern architectural parallels" by Edwin N. Ferdon, Jr. *American Antiquity* 22(3): 317.

1958   Notes and News, Southwest. *American Antiquity* 23(3): 333–335.

1961   Twenty-five years of archaeology in the greater Southwest. *American Antiquity* 27(1): 39–45.

Lister, Robert H., and Florence C. Lister

1981   *Chaco Canyon: Archaeology and archaeologists.* Albuquerque: University of New Mexico Press.

Longacre, William A.

1976   Paul Sidney Martin, 1899–1974. *American Anthropologist* 78(1): 90–92.

Lowie, Robert H., editor

1936   *Essays in anthropology, presented to A. L. Kroeber in celebration of his sixtieth birthday, June 11, 1936.* Berkeley: University of California Press.

MacDonald, D.K.C.

1962   *How* conferences? *Science* 138(3541): 665–666.

MacDonald, William K., editor

1976   Digging for gold: Papers on archaeology for profit. *University of Michigan Museum of Anthropology Technical Report* 5. Ann Arbor: University of Michigan Museum of Anthropology.

Madsen, David B., and James F. O'Connell, editors

1982   Man and environment in the Great Basin. *Society for American Archaeology Papers* 2. Washington: Society for American Archaeology.

Malouf, Carling

1940   Notes and News, Southwestern area. *American Antiquity* 6(1): 84–87.

Martin, Paul S.

1971   The revolution in archaeology. *American Antiquity* 36(1): 1–8.

1974   Early development in Mogollon research. *In* Archaeological researches in retrospect, edited by Gordon R. Willey, pp. 3–29. Cambridge: Winthrop.

1975   Philosophy of education at Vernon Field Station. *In* Chapters in the prehistory of eastern Arizona, 4, pp. 3–11. *Fieldiana: Anthropology* 65. Chicago: Field Museum of Natural History.

Martin, Paul S., and Fred Plog

1973   *The archaeology of Arizona: A study of the Southwestern region.* New York: Doubleday/Natural History Press for the American Museum of Natural History.

Martin, Paul S., George I. Quimby, and Donald Collier

1947   *Indians before Columbus: Twenty thousand years of North Ameri-*

can history revealed by archeology. Chicago: University of Chicago Press.

Martin, Paul S., and John B. Rinaldo

1950   Sites of the Reserve Phase: Pine Lawn valley, western New Mexico. *Fieldiana: Anthropology* 38(3). Chicago: Chicago Natural History Museum.

1951   The Southwestern co-tradition. *Southwestern Journal of Anthropology* 7(3): 215–229.

Martin, Paul S., John B. Rinaldo, and Ernst Antevs

1949   Cochise and Mogollon sites, Pine Lawn valley, western New Mexico. *Fieldiana: Anthropology* 38(1). Chicago: Chicago Natural History Museum.

McGregor, John C.

1939   Notes and News, Southwestern area. *American Antiquity* 5(2): 161–164.

1940   Notes and News, Southwestern area. *American Antiquity* 5(3): 247–251.

Mead, Margaret, and Paul Byers

1968   The small conference: An innovation in communication. *Publications of the International Social Science Council* 9. Paris and The Hague: Mouton.

Meighan, Clement W.

1955   Great Basin Archaeological Conference. *American Antiquity* 20(3): 308–312.

1958   Notes and News, general. *American Antiquity* 24(1): 97.

Meighan, Clement W., David M. Pendergast, B. K. Swartz, Jr., and M. D. Wissler

1958   Ecological interpretation in archaeology, Part 1. *American Antiquity* 24(1): 1023.

Miller, Jimmy H.

1991   The life of Harold Sellers Colton: A Philadelphia Brahmin in Flagstaff. Tsaile, Arizona: Navajo Community College Press.

Morgan, Lewis H.

1881   Houses and house-life of the North American aborigines. *Smithsonian Contributions to Knowledge* 4. Washington: Smithsonian Institution.

Morris, Ann Axtel

1931   *Digging in Yucatan.* New York: Doubleday, Doran.

1934   *Digging in the Southwest.* New York: Doubleday, Doran.

Morris, Earl H.

1939   Archaeological studies in the La Plata district, southwestern Colorado and northwestern New Mexico. *Carnegie Institution of Washington Publication* 519. Washington: Carnegie Institution of Washington.

Nelson, Nels C.

1919   The archaeology of the Southwest: A preliminary report. *Proceedings of the National Academy of Sciences* 5: 114–120. Washington: National Academy of Sciences.

Nusbaum, Jesse L.

1956   Introduction. *In* Pipeline archaeology: Reports of salvage operations in the Southwest on El Paso Natural Gas Company projects, 1950–1953, edited by Fred Wendorf, Nancy Fox, and Orian L. Lewis, pp. i–vii. Santa and Flagstaff: Laboratory of Anthropology and Museum of New Mexico.

1980   *Tierra Dulce: Reminiscences from the Jesse Nusbaum Papers*. Santa Fe: Sun Stone Press.

Peckham, Stewart

1977   Pecos Conference returns home for golden anniversary. *El Palacio* 83(2): 46–47.

Penniman, T. K.

1976   Beatrice Mary Blackwood, 1889–1975. *American Anthropologist* 78(2): 321–322.

Perret, William R.

1974   The president's letter. *Albuquerque Archaeological Society Newsletter* 9(9): 2.

Reed, Erik K.

1946   The distinctive features and distribution of the San Juan Anasazi culture. *Southwestern Journal of Anthropology* 2(3): 295–305.

1947a   The 1947 Pecos Conference. *El Palacio* 54(9): 217–218.

1947b   Southwestern Archaeological Conference. *American Antiquity* 12(3): 198.

1948   The Western Pueblo archaeological complex. *El Palacio* 55(1): 9–15.

1949a   The significance of skull deformation in the Southwest. *El Palacio* 56(4): 106–119.

1949b   Sources of Upper Rio Grande culture and population. *El Palacio* 56(6): 163–184.

1950   Eastern-central Arizona archaeology in relation to the Western Pueblos. *Southwestern Journal of Anthropology* 6(2): 120–138.

Reed, James S.

1980   *Clark Wissler: A forgotten influence in American anthropology.* Doctoral dissertation, Ball State University, Muncie. Ann Arbor: University Microfilms.

Reiter, Paul

1946   Notes and News, Southwest. *American Antiquity* 12(1): 69.

1948a   Notes and News, the Southwest. *American Antiquity* 13(3): 270–274.

1948b   Notes and News, the Southwest. *American Antiquity* 14(1): 72–74.

1949   The 1948 Southwestern Conference. *American Antiquity* 15(1): 77.

Roberts, Frank H.H., Jr.

1929   Shabik'eschee village: A late Basketmaker site in the Chaco Canyon, New Mexico. *Bureau of American Ethnology Bulletin* 92. Washington: Government Printing Office.

1930   Early pueblo ruins in the Piedra District, southwestern Colorado. *Bureau of American Ethnology Bulletin* 96. Washington: Government Printing Office.

1931   The ruins at Kiatuthlanna, eastern Arizona. *Bureau of American Ethnology Bulletin* 100. Washington: Government Printing Office.

1932   The Village of the Great Kivas on the Zuñi Reservation, New Mexico. *Bureau of American Ethnology Bulletin* 111. Washington: Government Printing Office.

1935   A survey of Southwestern archaeology. *American Anthropologist* 37(1): 1–35.

1937   Archaeology in the Southwest. *American Antiquity* 3(1): 3–33.

Robertson, Linda B.

1983   *Achiya: Dekyap'bowa: Alliance and polity in the development of Cibola.* Doctoral dissertation, Brown University, Providence. Ann Arbor: University Microfilms.

Rogge, Allen E.

1983   *Little archaeology, big archaeology: The changing context of archaeological research.* Doctoral dissertation, Department of Anthropology, University of Arizona, Tucson. Ann Arbor: University Microfilms.

Rozaire, Charles

1960   The Pecos Conference. *Archeological Survey Association of Southern California Newsletter* 7(4): 5.

Russell, Frank
1908   The Pima. *In* Twenty-sixth annual report of the Bureau of American Ethnology, pp. 3–389. Washington: Smithsonian Institution.

Sayles, E. B.
1945   The San Simon Branch: Excavations at Cave Creek in the San Simon Valley. I: Material culture. *Medallion Papers* 34. Globe: Gila Pueblo.

Schmidt, Erich
1928   Time-relations of prehistoric pottery types in southern Arizona. *American Museum of Natural History Anthropological Papers* 30(5). New York: American Museum of Natural History.

Schroeder, Albert H.
1956   Comments on "A trial survey of Mexican-Southwestern architectural parallels." *El Palacio* 63(9–10): 299–309.
1957   The Hakataya cultural tradition. *American Antiquity* 23(2): 176–178.
1960   The Hohokam, Sinagua, and Hakataya. *Archives of Archaeology* 5. Madison: Society for American Archaeology and Wisconsin University Press.

Schwartz, Douglas W.
1957   Climate change and culture history in the Grand Canyon region. *American Antiquity* 22(4): 372–377.
1981   Four exceptional men. *In* Collected papers in honor of Erik Kellerman Reed, edited by Albert H. Schroeder, pp. 251–273. *Papers of the Archaeological Society of New Mexico* 6. Albuquerque: Albuquerque Archaeological Society Press.

Seltzer, Carl C.
1944   Racial prehistory in the Southwest and the Hawikuh ruins. *Papers of the Peabody Museum of American Archaeology and Ethnology, Harvard University* 23(1). Cambridge: Peabody Museum.

Senter, Donovan
1937   Tree rings, valley floor deposits, and erosion in Chaco Canyon, New Mexico. *American Antiquity* 3(1): 68–75.

Shepard, Anna O.
1956   Ceramics for the archaeologist. *Carnegie Institution of Washington Publication* 609. Washington: Carnegie Institution of Washington.

Smith, Robert E., Gordon R. Willey, and James C. Gifford
1960   The type-variety concept as a basis for the analysis of Maya pottery. *American Antiquity* 25(3): 330–340.

Smith, Watson

 1952a Kiva mural decorations at Awatovi and Kawaika-a, with a survey of other wall paintings in the pueblo Southwest. Reports of the Awatovi Expedition, No. 5. *Papers of the Peabody Museum of American Archaeology and Ethnology, Harvard University* 37. Cambridge: Peabody Museum.

 1952b Excavations in Big Hawk Valley, Wupatki National Monument, Arizona. *Museum of Northern Arizona Bulletin* 24. Flagstaff: Museum of Northern Arizona.

 1969 *The story of the Museum of Northern Arizona.* Flagstaff: Museum of Northern Arizona.

 1990 *When is a Kiva? And other questions about Southwestern Archaeology,* edited by Raymond H. Thompson. Tucson: University of Arizona Press.

Spier, Leslie

 1917 An outline of the chronology of Zuñi ruins. *Papers of the American Museum of Natural History* 18(3). New York: American Museum of Natural History.

Spinden, Herbert J.

 1913 A study of Maya art, its subject matter and historical development. *Peabody Museum of American Archaeology and Ethnology. Harvard University Memoir* 6. Cambridge: Peabody Museum.

Squier, E. G., and E. H. Davis

 1848 Ancient monuments of the Mississippi Valley: Comprising the results of extensive original surveys and explorations. *Smithsonian Contributions to Knowledge* 1. Washington: Smithsonian Institution.

Steen, Charlie R.

 1964 The archaeologist reports: News from around the state. *El Palacio* 71(4): 39–41.

Steward, Julian H.

 1937 Ecological aspects of Southwestern society. *Anthropos, Internationale Zeitschrift für Völkerkunde und Sprachenkunde* 38(A): 87–104.

Steward, Julian H., and Frank M. Setzler

 1938 Function and configuration in archaeology. *American Antiquity* 4(1): 4–10.

Stickney, Francis

 1968 The Pecos Conference—1968. *Midland Archeological Society Newsletter,* September [unpaged].

Stocking, George W., Jr.
  1982   The Santa Fe style in American anthropology: Regional inter-
           est, academic initiative, and philanthropic policy in the first
           two decades of the Laboratory of Anthropology, Inc. *Journal
           of the History of the Behavioral Sciences* 18: 3–19.

Strong, W. Duncan
  1936   Anthropological theory and archaeological fact. *In* Essays in
           anthropology presented to A. L. Kroeber in celebration of
           his sixtieth birthday, June 11, 1936, pp. 359–370. Berkeley:
           University of California Press.

Sundt, William M.
  1974a   From the Pecos Conference—1974. *Albuquerque Archaeological
           Society Newsletter* 9(11): 4–5.

  1974b   More from the 1974 Pecos Conference. *Albuquerque Archaeo-
           logical Society Newsletter* 9(12): 5–7.

  1975   1975 Pecos Conference. *Albuquerque Archaeological Society
           Newsletter* 10(9): 6–7.

  1988   "A good time was had by all at the Pecos Conference."
           Awanyu: Albuquerque Archaeological Society Newsletter 16(4): 2–3.

Taylor, Walter W.
  1948   A study of archeology. *American Anthropological Association
           Memoir* 69. Menasha: American Anthropological Association.

  1954   Southwestern archeology: Its history and theory. *American
           Anthropologist* 56(4): 561–570.

Thompson, Raymond H.
  1983   Introduction. *In* The Cochise cultural sequence in southeast-
           ern Arizona, by E. B. Sayles, pp. 1–5. *Anthropological Papers
           of the University of Arizona* 42. Tucson: University of Ari-
           zona Press.

Titiev, Mischa
  1944   Old Oraibi: A study of the Hopi Indians of Third Mesa.
           *Papers of the Peabody Museum of Archaeology and Ethnology, Har-
           vard University* 22(1). Cambridge: Peabody Museum.

Turner, Christy G., II
  1963   Petrographs of the Glen Canyon region: Styles, chronology,
           distribution, and relationships from Basketmaker to Navajo.
           Museum of Northern Arizona Bulletin 38 (*Glen Canyon Series* 4).
           Flagstaff: Museum of Northern Arizona.

Urban, Sharon F.
  1975   Pecos Conference—1975, Farmington, New Mexico. MS,

Arizona State Museum Library, University of Arizona, Tucson.

1976   49th [39th] Annual Pecos Conference, Bahía Kino, Sonora, Mexico, August 11–14, 1976. MS, Arizona State Museum Library, University of Arizona, Tucson.

1977   50th [40th] Pecos Conference, Pecos National Monument, Pecos, New Mexico, August 19–21, 1977. MS, Arizona State Museum Library, University of Arizona, Tucson.

1978   51st [41st] Pecos Conference, Flagstaff, Arizona, August 18–19, 1978, Museum of Northern Arizona. MS, Arizona State Museum Library, University of Arizona, Tucson.

1979   52nd [42nd] Pecos Conference, Tucson, Arizona, August 17–18, 1979, Arizona State Museum & Laboratory of Tree-Ring Research. MS, Arizona State Museum Library, University of Arizona, Tucson.

1980   53rd [43rd] Pecos Conference, Mesa Verde, Colorado, August 14–18, 1980. MS, Arizona State Museum Library, University of Arizona, Tucson.

1981   54th [44th] Pecos Conference, Ft. Burgwin, Taos, New Mexico, August 13–14, 1981. MS, Arizona State Museum Library, University of Arizona, Tucson.

1982   55th [45th] Pecos Conference, Pecos, New Mexico, August 13–14, 1982. MS, Arizona State Museum Library, University of Arizona, Tucson.

1983   56th [46th] Annual Pecos Conference, Bluff, Utah, Aug. 11th & 12th, 1983. MS, Arizona State Museum Library, University of Arizona, Tucson.

1985   58th [48th] Annual Pecos Conference, Salinas Nat'l Mon., Mountainair, N.M., August 15–18, 1985. MS, Arizona State Museum Library, University of Arizona, Tucson.

1986   59th [49th] Annual Pecos Conference, Payson, AZ, August 7–10, 1986. MS, Arizona State Museum Library, University of Arizona, Tucson.

1987   60th [50th] Annual Pecos Conference, Pecos, N.M., August 13–16, 1987. MS, Arizona State Museum Library, University of Arizona, Tucson.

1988   61st [51st] Annual Pecos Conference, Dolores, CO, Aug. 18–21. MS, Arizona State Museum Library, University of Arizona, Tucson.

Vivian, R. Gwinn

1990 *The Chacoan prehistory of the San Juan Basin.* New York: Academic Press.

Wade, Edwin L., and Lea S. McChesney

1980 *America's great lost expedition: The Thomas Keam collection of Hopi pottery from the Second Hemenway Expedition, 1890–1894.* Phoenix: Heard Museum.

Washburn, Dorothy K.

1977 A symmetry analysis of Upper Gila area ceramic design. *Papers of the Peabody Museum of Archaeology and Ethnology* 68. Cambridge: Peabody Museum.

Wasley, William W.

1961 Notes and News, Southwest. *American Antiquity* 26(3): 455–459.

Wauchope, Robert

1965 Alfred Vincent Kidder, 1885–1963. *American Antiquity* 31(2): 149–166.

Wauchope, Robert, editor

1956 Seminars in archaeology: 1955. *Society for American Archaeology Memoir* 11. Salt Lake City: Society for American Archaeology.

Webb, George E.

1983 *Tree rings and telescopes: The scientific career of A. E. Douglass.* Tucson: University of Arizona Press.

Wendorf, Fred

1953 Archaeological studies in the Petrified Forest National Monument, Arizona. *Museum of Northern Arizona Bulletin* 27. Flagstaff: Northern Arizona Society of Science and Art.

Wendorf, Fred, Nancy Fox, and Orian L. Lewis, editors

1956 *Pipeline archaeology: Reports of salvage operations in the Southwest on El Paso Natural Gas Company projects, 1950–1953.* Santa Fe and Flagstaff: Laboratory of Anthropology and Museum of Northern Arizona.

Wheat, Joe Ben

1954 Crooked Ridge Village (Arizona W:10:15). *University of Arizona Bulletin* 25(3), *University of Arizona Social Science Bulletin* 24. Tucson: University of Arizona.

1955 Mogollon Culture prior to A.D. 1000. *Society for American Archaeology Memoir* 10. Salt Lake City: Society for American Archaeology.

Wheat, Joe Ben, James C. Gifford, and William W. Wasley

1958   Ceramic variety, type cluster, and ceramic system in Southwestern pottery analysis. *American Antiquity* 24(1): 34–47.

Wheat, Pat

1948   Notes on Southwestern Archaeological Conference, August, 1948. MS, Pecos Conference Archives, Laboratory of Anthropology, Santa Fe.

1951   Pecos Archaeological Conference, August 14–17, 1951, held at the University of Arizona Archaeological Field School, Point of Pines, San Carlos, Arizona. MS, Pecos Conference Archives, Laboratory of Anthropology, Santa Fe.

Wilcox, David R.

1987   Frank Midvale's investigation of the site of La Ciudad. *Anthropological Field Studies* 19. Tempe: Arizona State University Office of Cultural Resources Management.

Willey, Gordon R.

1967   Alfred Vincent Kidder, October 29, 1885–June 11, 1963. *National Academy of Sciences Biographical Memoirs* 39: 292–322. New York: Columbia University Press.

Willey, Gordon R., and Philip Phillips

1958   *Method and theory in American archaeology.* Chicago: University of Chicago Press.

Willey, Gordon R., and Jeremy Sabloff

1980   *A history of American archaeology.* 2nd edition. San Francisco: W. H. Freeman.

Woodbury, Nathalie F. S.

1991   Past is Present: "Dear Elsie"—news from the field. *Anthropology Newsletter* 32(6): 4,6.

Woodbury, Richard B.

1959   A reconsideration of Pueblo warfare in the Southwestern United States. *Actas del XXXIII Congreso Internacional de Americanistas, San José de Costa Rica, 1958* 2: 124–133. San José de Costa Rica: La Editorial Lehmann.

1973   *Alfred V. Kidder.* Leaders in Modern Anthropology Series. New York: Columbia University Press.

1983   Looking back at the Pecos Conference. *Kiva* 48(4): 251–266.

1985a   Regional archaeological conferences. *American Antiquity* 50(2): 434–444.

1985b   The small conference as personal network. *In* Southwestern culture history: Collected papers in honor of Albert H. Schroeder, edited by Charles H. Lange, pp. 251–258. *Archaeo-*

logical Society of New Mexico Papers 10. Santa Fe: Ancient City Press.

1991   Southwestern archeology as seen through sixty years of the Pecos Conferences, 1928–1988. MS on file in the Arizona State Museum Archives, University of Arizona, Tucson, and in the Pecos Conference Archives, Laboratory of Anthropology, Santa Fe.

Wormington, H. Marie

1947   Prehistoric Indians of the Southwest. *Colorado Museum of Natural History Popular Series* 7. Denver: Colorado Museum of Natural History.

1957   Ancient man in North America. 4th edition. *Denver Museum of Natural History Popular Series* 4. Denver: Denver Museum of Natural History.

Wyman, Leland C.

1970   *Blessingway*. Tucson: University of Arizona Press.

INDEX

Bernal, Ignacio, participant, 243
Bertram, Jack, report, 355; speaker, 418
Bice, Richard, report, 377
Biella, Jan, speaker, 419
Big Bend, 8, 126
Bilbone, Brian, report, 399
Binford, Lewis R., publication, 307
Bishop, Ronald L., lecture, 421
Black, Robert, report, 295
Blackwood, Beatrice, career, 77
Bliss, Wesley, at Chaco Conference, 131; field work, 199, 265
Bloom, Lansing, biography, 56
Bluff, Conference at, 404–7
Bluff Ruin, 147
Bluhm, Elaine, recordings, 196, 234
Bohrer, Vorsila, report, 355
Borbolla, Rubín de la, address and report, 141; affiliation, in citation, 140
Borhegyi, Stephen, speaker, 184
Bowen, Thomas, paper, 360; report, 361
Bowman, William, report, 380
Boyd, E., speaker, 279
Bradfield, Wesley, biography, 75; field work, 8
Brainerd, George, publication, 204
Brand, Donald, lecture, 131; letters to Emil Haury, 136, 138–39, 139–40
Braniff, Beatriz, paper, 360; reports, 356, 362
Breternitz, David, field work, 267; publication, 296; reports, 285, 288, 352, 356, 376
Brew, J. O., career, 171; field work, 127, 148; opinion, 181; speaker, 184, 227
Brew, Alan, report, 285
Broilo, Frank, report, 355
Brook, Vernon, report, 285
Brown, Jeff, report, 293
Brown, Joy, report, 356
Brown, Ralph, career, 253–54
Brown, Ralph S., student, 117
Brugge, David, conference notes, 274, 279, 286, 288, 297; letter to Richard Woodbury, 425; participant, 384; reports, 286, 355
Buckles, William, paper, 289
bull sessions, 186

Bullard, William, field work, 199
Bumpus, Herman C., career, 13
Bureau of American Ethnology, personnel, 8
Burgh, Robert, career, 156
Bussey, Stanley, report, 355
Button, Van, report, 399

California field work, 344
Campbell, Robert, papers, 289, 385
Canadian River, 126
cannibalism as a topic, 422
Canyon Creek, 126
carbon-14, announcement of, 190; report on, 156
Carey, Henry, 274
Carlson, Roy L., speaker, 279
Carnegie Group, the, 53–56, 122
Carnegie Institution, field work, 16
Carter, George, publication, 148; report, 229
Casa Grande, 9, 50
Casas Grandes, 8
Cassidy, Francis, field work, 199
Caywood, Louis, report, 293
ceramics, problems in, 133, 204, 237–40, 245, 248; scholar of, 4–5; sherd collections, 8–9; sherd conference, 122
Chaco Anthropological Conferences, 129–46, 156–66
Chaco Canyon, as a topic, 357–59; sites of, 7, 39, 126, 127
Chaco Center, the, 355, 358
Champe, John, 252, 263; participant, 256; speaker, 279
Chapman, Kenneth, biography, 21, 23; career, 13
Chapman Richard, speaker, 418
Chenhall, Robert, paper, 305
Chicago Natural History Museum, field work, 149
Claflin, William, field work, 102
Colorado archaeology as a topic, 288–89; field work, 6, 102, 344, 356, 399. See also Dolores and Mesa Verde
Colorado Museum of Natural History, field work, 102; personnel, 10
Colorado River Storage Project, 243

Colton, Harold S., biography, 23; career, 12, 295; field work, 126, 147, 293; publication, 133; speaker, 218
Colton, J. Ferrell, 23
Colton, Mary, 23
conferences, other regional and topical, 204, 220, 407, 415, 434
contract archaeology, 226, 345, 355, 369–70, 457. *See also* salvage archaeology
Cook, John, report, 418
Cooley, Maurice, speaker, 312
Cordell, Linda, letters to Richard Woodbury, 396, 397
corn. *See* maize
Correll, J. Lee, career, 215, 285
Cosgrove, Cornelius B., biography, 25; career, 7; field work, 8, 102
Cosgrove, Harriet, biography, 25; publication, 148
costs, management, and logistics reviewed, 169–70, 330–31, 403–4
Creamer, Winifred, paper, 419
Crotty, Helen, report, 405
Crow Canyon Campus, 405
Crown, Patricia, speaker, 399
cultural relationships as a topic, 154. *See also* problems of classification, general cultural
cultural resource management (CRM), 357, 368–69; as a topic, 390
culture-classification in review, 430. *See also* problems of classification, general cultural
Cummings, Byron, biography, 25, 29; career, 9; field work, 10, 102, 126, 127
Cutler, Hugh, comment, 272; speaker, 275
Cuyamungue Pueblo, 217

Daifuku, Hiroshi, publication, 215
Davis, John M., address, 227
Day, Sam, III, address, 285
Dean, Jeffrey, paper, 393
death notices, 196, 225, 233–34, 269, 278, 295, 308, 312, 353, 357, 381, 390, 392, 406, 411, 415
Depression, the, field work and, 128–29;

relief work in archaeology, 137, 147
d'Harnoncourt, René, speaker, 141
Dick, Herbert, field work, 286; panelist, 257, in citation, 256; reports, 219, 254; speaker, 279
Dickson, Bruce, speaker, 383
Dikeman, Jim, report, 356
DiPeso, Charles, papers, 359, 360, 384; reports, 230, 243, 376
direct-historical approach in review, 430
Dittert, Alfred E., Jr., paper, 384; reports, 254, 355
Dobie, J. Frank, participant, 104
Dobyns, Henry, participant, 338, 341; reports, 234, 267
Dolores, Conference at, 420–25; Dolores Project report, 390
Douglass, Andrew E., address, 97; biography, 29, 31; career, 11, 267
Douglas, F. H. (Eric), speaker, 141, 218
Dove, Don, report, 380
Doyel, David, reports, 356, 376
Dozier, Edward, report, 294
Dutton, Bertha, 276–77

early man, as a topic, 154, 229, 234–35; noted sites for, 10
ecological problems as a topic, 312
educational materials as a topic, 154, 201–4, 217
Eggan, Fred, opinion, 135; recollection, 162
Ellis, Bruce, reports, 209, 229
Ellis, Florence H., conference notes, 220, 310, 325; letter to Richard Woodbury, 307–8; presentation, 211; recollection, 307; reports, 209, 216, 234, 377, 402. *See also* Hawley, Florence
El Paso Archaeological Society, field work, 308; report, 285
El Paso-Juarez, Conference at, 303–8
Emerson, Raymond, field work, 102
employment opportunities, 243, 284, 397
Emslie, Steven, speaker, 399
Enloe, James, report, 355
Ennis, George, field work, 193

environment and archaeology, 248; changes and culture as a topic, 393–94

ethnobotany file, 286

ethnographers listed, 191. *See also* ethnology

ethnologists, the question of attendance by, 213–14, 448–50

ethnology, early, 37, 58, 62, 68; methods, 122; presenters and reports listed, 141, 164, 177, 191, 201, 209, 216, 217, 221, 229, 234, 267, 286, 288, 294, 325, 402; symposia reviewed for, 443

Euler, Robert, career, 219; letters to Edwin Ferdon and William Robinson, 301, to colleagues, 312–13; participant, 391, 394; publication, 237; reports, 234, 254, 267, 276, 356

Evans, Clifford, letter to Nathalie and Richard Woodbury, 143–45; student view, 143–45

excavations, a list of early, 102

expert witness, 199

Ezell, Paul, field work, 199, 267; participant, 338, 341

Farmer, Malcolm, career, 173, 196, 219; report, 134; speaker, 201

Ferdon, Edwin, publication, 259; recollection, 164

Ferguson, T. J., report, 377

Ferguson, Wesley, report, 267

Fewkes, Jesse W., biography, 74

field and laboratory techniques as a topic, 220

field reports, listed, Chapters 1–15, passim; review of role of, 428–29, 446–48

field work. *See separately by individual and state*

Figgins, Jesse D., field work, 10

financial support for archaeology, 137

Fish, Susan, speaker, 399

Fisher, Reginald, field work, 102

Flagstaff, AAAS Conference, 128; Pecos Conferences at, 192–204, 219–25, 233–37, 263–72, 290–96, 337–42, 389–91, 407–9; review of research near, as a topic, 408

Flannery, Regina, student, 117

Forestdale, 137, 168

Forked Lightning Ruin, 80

Fort Burgwin, Conferences at, 251–62, 278–81, 398–400; Research Center at, 253

Fowler, Don, report, 380

Frank, Paul, student, 117

Fraps, Clara Lee, biography, 66, 373

Frisbie, Theodore, report, 376

Fritz, John, report, 293

Fryman, Jean, report, 376

Fuller, Faith Kidder, biographical note, 403

Fulton, W. S., field work, 13, 14, 137

Gallagher, Joseph, report, 355

Gasser, Robert, participant, 394

geochronology as a topic, 230

Gerald, Rex, reports, 254, 377

Gifford, James C., publication, 248

Gifford, James C., and Carol A. Gifford, 242–43

Gila Bend, 260

Gila Pueblo, Caucus at, 114–15; establishment, 12, 113; research, 147. *See also* Globe

Gillen, John, student, 117

Gilpin, Laura, presentation, 122

Givens, Douglas, publication, 41

Gladwin, Harold, biography, 75; career, 12, 113; field work, 9, 101, 127, 147; publication, 166

Glassow, Michael, presentations, 288, 305

Globe, Conferences at, 226–30, 238–45, 276–78; Gila Pueblo Caucus, 114–15

goals reviewed, 428, 443

Gooding, John, report, 399

Gower, Charlotte, biography, 66, 68

Grady, Mark, report, 357

Graves, Michael, report, 376

Great Basin Archeological Conference (GBAC), beginnings, 227–29, 230–31

Grebinger, Paul, paper, 359; report, 306

Greenwald, Dawn, speaker, 399

Griffin, James, report, 219; speaker, 288, 289

Griffin, William, publication, 274
Grigg, Paul, report, 355
Grumlack, J. R., report, 378
Guadalupe Mountains, 126
Guernsey, Samuel, biography, 74; field work, 8
Gumerman, George, letters to Richard Woodbury, 318, 447; presentation, 393; recollection, 318
Gunnerson, James, paper, 385; presentation, 280; speaker, 279
Gunther, Erna, biography, 62
Gurr, Deanne, report, 380
Guthe, Carl, biography, 75; career, 13; publications, 101–2, 126

Haas, Jonathan, 422; report, 405
Haile, publication, 216
Hakataya, designation of the, 237
Halbirt, Carl, report, 399
Hall, Dorothy, participant, 338, 341
Hall, Edward T., publication, 148; report, 217
Hall, Stephen, participant, 394
Halseth, Odd S., biography, 31; field work, 102, 126; letters to A. V. Kidder, 103–4, to Mrs. D. B. Heard, 109, to Herbert Dick, 278; presentations, 177, 272; publications, 162, 165; recollection, 102; speaker, 184, 201
Hammack, Laurens, report, 293
Hammond, George, lecture, 131
Hargrave, Lyndon, field work, 10, 102, 126, 255, 293; paper, 306; publications, 133, 152
Harmond, Craig, report, 356
Harrington, Mark R., biography, 33; career, 6; field work, 102, 127
Harris, Arthur, paper, 306
Harvard students, 4, 9, 51, 53
Haury, Emil, biography, 68, 70; career, 9, 373; comment, 344; field work, 10, 126, 127, 137, 147, 148, 168; letters to Harold Gladwin, 123–24, to Richard Woodbury, 68, 84, 93, 110, to Paul Martin, 158, 173–74, 174–75, 208, to Arnold Withers and Stanley Stubbs,

204–5, to A. V. Kidder, 245, to Erik Reed, 151, to Paul Reiter, 158, 169, to Douglas Schwartz, 329, to Martin Link, 336, to Madeleine Kidder, 377–78; opinion, 181, 344; publication, 259; recollection, 123; report, 293; speaker, 184, 217, 218, 271
Haury, Hulda, letter to Richard Woodbury, 82
Hawley, Florence, biography, 77; field work, 102; lecture, 131; publication 133; speaker, 191. See also Ellis, Florence H.
Hayden, Julian, comment, 301–2; field work, 147; paper, 360; publication, 254
Hayes, Alden, letter to Richard Woodbury, 131–32; papers, 358, 383; publication, 371; recollection, 131; reports, 254, 293; speaker, 352, 411
Heerden, Jaap van, recording, 252
Henderson, Mark, report, 380
Hester, James, letter to Edward Danson, 281; paper, 280; report, 275
Hevly, Richard, paper, 397
Heye, George C., field work, 14
Hewes, Gordon, report, 229
Hewett, Edgar Lee, biography, 33, 35; career, 4, 129; field work, 127; lecture, 131; letters to A. V. Kidder, 103, to Jesse Nusbaum, 124; mention of, 124; recollections on, 88–89
Hewett, Nancy, report, 377
Hibben, Frank, field work, 249; presentation, 191; reports, 216, 249
Hicks, Pat, participant, 418
Hill, Ernest, presentation, 177
Hill, James, paper, 385; report, 376
Hill, W. W., letters to Emil Haury, 175, to Stanley Stubbs, 213–14
historical archaeology, 371; review of the direct-historical approach, 430
Hodge, Frederick, biography, 75
Hohokam, designation for the, 115, 123; field report of note on, 410. See also problems of classification, general cultural
Hoijer, Harry, mention, 221
Holden, William Curry, field work,

Holden, William Curry (*continued*)
126; letter to Richard Woodbury, 107;
participant, 107
Hough, Walter, biography, 37
Howard, Edgar, field work, 126
Huckell, Bruce, report, 399
Hughes, Jack, presentation, 289
Hunter-Anderson, Rosalyn, participant, 385
Hurst, Winston, presentation, 405
Huscher, Harold, speaker, 279

Indian tribal claims, 196, 199, 229, 267
Irwin-Williams, Cynthia, comment,
348; paper, 359; reports, 254, 353, 355;
speaker, 353

Jackson, Earl, publication, 254
Jackson, Percy, biography, 57
Jeançon, J. A., career, 77
Jelinek, Arthur, report, 267
Jenks, Albert, field work, 102
Jennings, Jesse, letter to Richard Woodbury, 227–28; publication, 250; recollection, 227; reports, 211, 250
Johnson, Alfred, report, 254
Johnson, Frederick, publication, 156
Johnson, R. Roy, paper, 306
Juárez-El Paso, Conference at, 303
Judd, Neil M., biography, 37, 39; career,
7; field work, 101; publication, 7
Judge, W. James, paper, 384; report, 355

Karlstrom, Thor, paper, 394; speaker, 353
Kellar, W. J., report, 230
Kelley, J. Charles, report, 217; speaker,
259, 260–61, 383
Kelley, Richard, report, 378
Kelly, Daniel, award to, 328
Kelly, Marsha, participant, 338
Kelly, William, career, 227, 338
Kent, Kate Peck, publications, 248, 254
Kerr, A. A., career, 6, 405
Kerr, Robert, letter to Emil Haury, 404
Kessell, John, publication, 371; report, 378
Kewanwytewa, Jimmy, 295

Kidder, Alfred V., 3–77 passim; address,
122; biography, 39, 41–44, 278; field
work, 10; letters to A. E. Douglass, 3,
to Clark Wissler, 15, to Earl Morris,
16, to Odd Halseth, 16, to Charles
Amsden, 116, to Joe Ben Wheat, 238–
39 presentation, 178; publications, 5,
115, 128; speaker, 184, 201, 219
Kidder, Alfred II (Alfie), 44
Kidder, Madeleine, 39, 44
Kimball, Solon, student, 117
King, Dale, career, 50; participant, 154;
presentation, 229; student, 117
King, Thomas (Jeff), report, 402
King's Ruin, 126
Kinishba, 167
Kino Bay, Conference at, 360–63
Kinsey, Mark, report, 355
Kintigh, Keith, research, 9
Kirkpatrick, David, reports, 354, 410
Kluckhohn, Clyde, career, 162; presentation, 177; publication, 166
Krieger, Alex, panelist, 256; publication, 257
Kroeber, Alfred, biography, 57; field
work, 8; publication, 115
Kunitz, Stephen, reports, 295, 325

Laboratory of Anthropology, establishment, 12–13; field work, 102, 104;
history, 115, 121, 188, 190
La Ciudad, 9
Lambert, Marjorie, letter to Fred Wendorf, 252; recollections, 219, 280;
report, 265
Lancaster, James, award to, 258
Lang, Richard, paper, 382
Lange, Fred, 422; address, 421
Larson, Beverly, speaker, 419
LeBlanc, Steven, paper, 359; reports,
355, 380
Leech, Milton, address, 304
Lehmer, Donald, panelist, 178; student, 131
Leone, Mark, career, 319; letter to
Douglas Schwartz, 319–20; paper, 305;
report, 327

Leopold, Luna, 342
Levy, Jerrold, career, 286; reports, 267, 294, 327; speaker, 312
Lind, James, report, 380
Lindsay, Alexander, field work, 265; reports, 375, 392; speaker, 272
linguistics, 221
Link, Martin, 330
Lipe, William, speaker, 352
Lister, Robert, career, 156; letter to Douglas Schwartz, 241; publication, 272; recollection, 131; reports, 254, 261, 381, 392
Long, Boaz, address, 215, 216
Long, Paul, report, 254
Longacre, William, report, 376
Los Muertos, 148
Lowell Observatory, 11
Lucius, William, speaker, 399
Luebben, Ralph, report, 276
Lummis, Charles, biography, 76
Lyons, Thomas, paper, 358

MacCurdy, Winifred, 113
MacGregor, Gordon, report, 217
MacIntyre, Kenneth, report, 362
maize, as a topic, 142; discussions on corn, 219, 271–72
Marmaduke, William, report, 375
Marquina, Ignacio, presentation, 140, 141
Marshall, Michael, report, 380
Martin, Paul Sidney, biography, 70; field work, 127, 137, 149, 267; letters to Emil Haury, 173, 174, 207, to Douglas Schwartz, 320–21; publication, 183; recollection, 87
Martin, Paul Schultz, report, 255; speaker, 312
Mason, J. Alden, field work, 101, 126
McCown, T. D., speaker, 184
McDonald, James, report, 375
McGregor, John, field work, 10, 126
McIlwraith, Thomas, biography, 58
McIntyre, Kenneth G., and Marion E. McIntyre, field work, 356; paper, 360
McKee, E. D., career, 219

McKinney, Lewis, career, 145
McNair, Robert, career, 217; report, 209
Medallion Papers, 113
Medlin, K. P., speaker, 412
Megers, Pamela, reports, 356, 378
Meighan, Clement, publications, 229, 248
Mera, Harry P., biography, 44–45; field work, 126; report, 134
Mesa Verde, as a topic, 352; Conferences at, 349–53, 394–97
method and theory as a topic, 154, 343; theory and application as a topic, 304–7; theory in review, 444; method in review, 430; publications, 247, 306; research list cited, 150
Mexican-Southwestern relationships as a topic, 140–42, 154, 240, 258–62; publications list, 259. *See also* Mexico
Mexico, Conferences in, 138–42, 272–76, 360; field work in Sonora, 8; reports, 140–42, 217, 243, 274, 356, 362; Southwestern relationships, 140–42, 154, 240, 258–62
Michael, Mark, 423
Miksicek, Charles, speaker, 399
Miller, Carl, student, 177
Miller, Jay, paper, 359
Mimbres, early research, 7–8, 25, 102. *See also* problems of classification, general cultural
mini-symposia, 418, 419
Mitvalsky, Frank (Midvale), biography, 76
Mogollon, as a topic, 296–97, 299; designation of the, 123, 136–37; panel discussion, 178, 181, 183; research, 147, 390, 410, 417; researchers listed in citation, 150
Moore, Harvey, field work, 209
Morenon, Pierre, paper, 358; report, 355, 377
Morley, Sylvanus G., biography, 53; career, 16, 41
Morley, Frances Rhoads, 53
Morris, Ann Axtell, 45, 46
Morris, Earl H., biography, 45; career,

Morris, Earl H. (*continued*)
6, 16, 156; field work, 102, 126; role in origin of the Conference, 94–95
Morris, Elizabeth Ann, 46
Morss, Noel, biography, 76; field work, 9, 102
movements of people as a topic, 209; population movements as a topic, 383–86. *See also* warfare
Mummy Cave, 126
Museum of New Mexico, establishment and personnel, 48
Museum of Northern Arizona, ceramic seminars, 133; establishment, 12; history, 192–93, 219; personnel, 193, 219, 389; projects, 147, 286
Museum of the American Indian-Heye Foundation, personnel, 6, 14

Naco site, 217
naming the Conference, 160–61, 192
National Geographic Society, 11
National Park Service, archaeology of the, 122, 164, 217, 225–26, 265; as Conference host, 435
Navajo archaeology as a topic, 134, 142; research, 164, 177, 209, 217; researchers listed, 150; tribal claims, 196. *See also* Window Rock
Neely, James, report, 380
Nelson, Nels, biography, 74; career, 5; field work, 8
Nesbitt, Paul, field work, 8, 102, 127, 137
Nevada, field work in, 6, 102, 127
New Archaeology, The, 148, 306–7, 311, 367–68
New Mexico, field work in, 7–8, 102, 126, 127, 148–49, 293, 344, 354–55, 357–59, 378, 380, 399; research center, 12
New World occupation, 10; early man as a topic (Archaic period), 234–35, 399
Newman, Stanley, report, 221
Niles, Fred, speaker, 399
Noguera, Eduardo, career, 140; presentation, 141
Noisat, Bradley, report, 356
Nuevo Casas Grandes, Conference at, 272–76

Nusbaum, Deric, field work, 126
Nusbaum, Jesse, biography, 48; career, 12, 13, 116; field work, 157, 199; letters to Frank Roberts, 118, to A. V. Kidder, 119; presentation, 155

Oklahoma, research in, 64, 65
O'Laughlin, Thomas, report, 356–57
Oliveros, Arturo, report, 362; speaker, 360
Olson, Alan, career, 285; reports, 254, 265, 285
Opler, Morris, student, 117
Osborne, Douglas, report, 254

Pailes, Richard, field work, 356; paper, 360; report, 362
Paloparado, 230
Patayan, designation of the, 152; researchers listed for, 150. *See also* problems of classification, general cultural
Payson, Conference at, 413–15
Peabody Museum, field work, 102, 148; personnel, 9, 55, 64, 171
Peckham, Stewart, paper, 419; participant, 383; reports, 254, 267, 285, 354; speaker, 399
Pecos Classification, viii–ix, 90–95, 114–15
Pecos Conference, xviii, xxi–xxii; evaluated, 98–100; Odd Halseth on 85–86
Pecos Ruin, Conferences at, 14–17, 73–74, 79–100, 100–110, 367–87, 400–404, 415–20, 433; history of ownership, 216; Kidder at, 4; protohistoric Pecos as a topic, 403; the churches of, 371
Pendergast, David, report, 265
Penner (Haury), Julda, biography, 70
Perret, William, 350, 352
Peterson, Ken, speaker, 424
Phillips Academy, personnel, 4, 10
Phoenix City Museum, personnel, 31
photographic record of the Southwest, 64
Pilles, Peter, reports, 356, 376

Pinkley, Frank, biography, 48, 50
Pinkley, Jean, career, 50; report, 286
Pippin, Lonnie, paper, 358
Plains-Southwest relationships as a
topic, 255–58, 278–80; protohistoric
Pecos, 403
planning the Conference, examples, 14–
17, 116–21, 138–39, 149–52, 157–60,
169–76; restructuring, 312–23
Plog, Fred, papers, 305, 327; report, 375
Point of Pines, Conferences at, 167–68,
204–12; the site, 148, 168
popular publications, 35, 46, 256; as a
topic, 154, 166
population estimation as a topic, 272
population movement as a topic, 383–86;
movements of people as a topic, 209.
See also warfare
population question as a topic, 142
poster presentations, 420
Pottery Mound, 249
pottery, the revival of Pueblo, 23
Powers, Robert, speaker, 419
Prescott, Conference at, 308–18
problem identification discussed, 152; for
Mexico, 362; reviewed as a goal, 443
problems of ceramic terminology, 133,
204, 237–40, 245, 248
problems of classification, of artifacts,
178; general cultural, 83–84, 90, 95,
114–15, 123–24, 128, 136–37, 152–53,
154, 178, 181, 183, 209–211, 215, 218–
19, 223, 233, 240, 243–44, 247. *See also
separately by culture*
provenience as a topic, 346–49
publication of proceedings, in review,
439–41, 453–56; mentioned, 83, 104,
133, 136, 141, 142, 152, 161–62, 175, 190,
204, 215, 231, 237, 242, 263, 274, 297,
381; published papers, 403; published
references to papers, 397; published
summaries of reports, 135; recordings
of proceedings, in review, 455;
mentioned, 251–52, 263, 346
Pueblo culture and American civilization as a topic, 97
Pueblo culture and Rancheria expansion
as a topic, 286

Pueblo Grande, 126, 127
pure sites, defined, 7

Quijada, Armando, report, 362

Rancheria expansion as a topic, 286
Ray, Verne, report, 209
Reagan, Albert, field work, 127
recorded proceedings, in review, 455;
mentioned, 251–52, 263, 279, 346. *See
also* publication of proceedings
Redman, Charles, field work, 413
Reed, Erik, letters to Emil Haury,
149–50, to Gordon Vivian and
Bertha Dutton, 277; presentation/
publication, 154; reports, 217, 286;
speaker, 218
Reeves, Roy, report, 357
regional variation as a topic, 395–97
Reid, J. Jefferson, reports, 348, 356
Reiter, Paul, field work, 126; letters to
Emil Haury, 151, 157, 158–59, 159–60,
160–61, 169–70
relief archaeology, 137; CCC field work,
147; report, 217
Renaud, Etienne B., biography, 50–51
research centers, 12–14, 429
resolutions of note, on the Antiquities Act, 335–36; on preservation of
historic documents, 235
restoration as a topic, 133
restructuring the Conference, 312–23
Richert, Roland, career, 68
Ricketson, Edith, biography, 55
Ricketson, Oliver G., Jr., biography, 55
Rinaldo, John, panelist, 178; speaker, 218
ring chronology. *See* tree ring dating
Rio Grande archaeology, 35, 126; as a
topic, 231, 382–86, 418, 419
Roberts, Frank H. H., Jr., biography,
51; career, 7; field work, 8, 10, 102,
126, 127; letter to Jesse Nusbaum,
117; presentation, 141; recollection,
123; role in origins of Pecos Confer-
ence, 94
Roberts, Henry, field work, 102
Roberts, John, field work, 209
Roberts, Linda B., 51

Robinson, William J., letter to Emil Haury, 299; speaker, 312
Rodeck, Hugo, report, 216
Rogers, Malcolm, biography, 75; letter to Odd Halseth, 75–76
Rogge, A. Eugene, report, 356
Rohn, Arthur, report, 254; speaker, 352
Romney, Kimball, report, 221
Rosenberg, Bettina, report, 355
Rosenthal, E. Jane, reports, 355, 362
Roth, George, participant, 338, 341
Rozaire, Charles, reports, 263, 269
Ruiz, Antonio, 386
Ruiz, Sue, 252
Ruppé, Reynold, report, 219
Ruppert, Karl, biography, 77
Russell, Frank, publication, 115

S.A.R.G. *See* Southwestern Anthropological Research Group
Saitta, Dean, letter to Richard Woodbury, 425
Salinas Archeology as a topic, 411–12
Salinas National Monument, Conference at, 409–12
Salmon Ruin, Conference at, 353–59
salvage archaeology, as a topic, 230; development of, 48; pipeline, dams and archeology, 156–57, 265, 267; project summaries list, 399. *See also* contract archaeology *and* relief archaeology
San Diego Museum of Man, foundation and personnel, 8, 35; publication, 175
San Juan River archaeology, 6
Santa Fe, Conferences at, 115–25, 149–56, 187–92, 213–19, 231–33, 318–30. *See also* Laboratory of Anthropology
Sapir, Edward, students of, 104
Saxe, Arthur, paper, 305
Sayles, E. B., field work, 127, 168
Schaafsma, Curtis, participant, 412; report, 380
Schelly, Bill, speaker, 399
Scherer, James, biography, 58
Schiffer, speaker, 346
Schmidt, Erich, biography, 76
Schmitt, Karl, presentation, 191

Schoenwetter, James, participant, 394; report, 285
School of American Research, field work, 102, 103; personnel, 48
Schraedle, Alan, report, 356
Schroeder, Albert H., field work, 157, 217; letters to Woodbury, 341–42, 431, 456, to Florence Ellis and Edward Danson, 240, to Frank Hibben, 248–49; presentations, 191, 275, 286, 338; report, 225–26; speaker, 184, 272, 289
Schulman, Edmund, recognition for, 250
Schwartz, Douglas, letter to Martin Link, 330–32; participant, 382; publication, 248
Scott, Donald, career, 148
Scovill, Douglas, 332; letter to Martin Link, 332–33
sedentism as a topic, 399; settlement as a topic, 271–72
Seltzer, Carl C., career, 72
Seminar on the American Southwest, 232
Senter, Donovan, participant, 131
seriation, review of use of, 430
settlement as a topic, 271–72; sedentism as a topic, 399
Setzler, Frank, field work, 126, 136
Shapiro, Harry, biography, 72; career, 6
Shepard, Anna O., biography, 76; field work, 126
sherd collections, 8–9; sherd conference, 122
Shiner, Joel, report, 254
shovel, inscribed, 378
silver trowel presentation, 217
Simmons, Alan, report, 399
Simpson, Ruth, report, 229
Sinagua as a topic, 295–96; publication on, 147
Sjoberg, Andree, report, 276
Skinner, Henry, biography, 60–61; letter to Clark Wissler, 60
Sleight, Fred, report, 217
Smiley, Terah (Ted), report, 237; speaker, 184, 227

Smith, Elmer, career, 156
Smith, Jack, career, 352
Smith, Victor, field work, 8
Smith, Watson, letter to Emil Haury, 171; publication, 148
Smithsonian Institution, personnel, 10, 35, 39
Snaketown, 127
Snow, David, participant, 412, 419
Snowflake, 193
Society for American Archaeology (SAA), beginnings, 41; presentation, 232, 272
Southwest Museum, Los Angeles, field work, 8, 9, 269; personnel, 58
Southwestern Anthropological Research Group (S.A.R.G.), as part of the Conference, 397; formation of, 428; personnel, 349, 354
Southwestern National Monuments, origin and activities of, 225, 229
spatial organization as a topic, 413–14
Spicer, E. H., career, 184; field work, 209; report, 276
Spielmann, Kate, speaker, 412
Spier, Leslie, biography, 61–62; lecture, 131; publication, 9
Spier, Robert, 62
Spinden, Herbert, biography, 64; participant, 142
Spuhler, James, recollection, 134; reports, 221, 378
stabilization, 226
Stallings, William (Sid), field work, 126
Starkweather Ruin, 127, 137
Steen, Charlie, career, 50; publication, 284; speaker, 383
Stephenson, Robert, letter to Richard Woodbury, 145–46; recollection, 145
Steward, Julian, field work, 127
Stewart, Omer, presentation, 286; report, 376
Stirling, Matthew, publication, 129
Stocking, George, publication, 125
stratigraphy, the concept, 5, 41, 430
Strong, W. Duncan, career, 252
Stuart, David, report, 355

Stubbs, Stanley, field work, 126, 127, 156, 199, 255; panelist, 178; presentation, 231
students, in attendance, 66–73, 84–85, 104, 187–88, 241, 287; the question of attendance by, 117–19, 131, 151, 214, 241, 445–46; reports by, 304; role (participation) of, 142–45, 170–74, 233, 304, 317
Studer, Floyd V., participant, 107
SU site, 137, 149
Sundt, William, publication, 352
Sunset Crater, 294, 296
surveys, a list of early, 101–2, 127, 128. *See also* contract archaeology
Swartz, Don, 186
symposia, in review, 442–45; the start of selected, 186–87
synthesis, as a direction for the Conference, 155, 231–33, 247, 248; in review, 428, as a topic, 221, 223; early regional, 5; a thesis on, 225; publications, 125, 126; review of use of area synthesis, 430

Tainter, Joseph, publication, 395; speaker, 412
Tanner, Clara Lee, 66, 67, 373
Tax, Sol, student, 117
Taylor, Morris, paper, 289
Taylor, Walter, publication, 148
Tello, Julio, lecture, 131
Teocentli, 6, 64
Texas, field work in, 8, 101, 107, 126, 148, 253, 356
Texas Tech University, field work, 253
theory and application as a topic, 304–7; review of symposia on, 444. *See also* method and theory as a topic
Thieme, Frederick, publication/presentation, 220
Thoburn, Joseph, biography, 64–65
Thompson, J. Eric, lecture, 131
Thompson, Raymond, report, 403
Titiev, Misha, publication, 148; report, 294

Trager, George, panelist, 258; presentation, 280
Travis, Scott, speaker, 399
tree ring dating (ring chronology), 11, 29, 31, 39, 55, 101, 267
Trierweiler, Nick, speaker, 419
Trinidad, Conference at, 287–89
Tucson, Conferences at, 296–302, 342–49, 391–94; discussion of Mogollon, 137
Tuggle, David, report, 376
Turner, Christy G., II, participant, 412; presentations, 267, 422; reports, 254, 410; speaker, 399
Turney, Omar, field work, 9
Tuthill, Carr, career, 14
Twin Buttes, 193
typology, review of the use of, 430

Udall, Morris, address, 392
Underhill, Ruth, panelist, 201; presentation, 191
Urban, Sharon, 342, 354, 390
U. S. Coronado Cuarto Centennial, 138
U. S. Geological Survey, 342
U. S. National Museum, personnel, 7, 37, 39
University of Arizona, field school, 167; personnel, 9; students, 14
University of Colorado Museum, personnel, 6
University of New Mexico, field school, 129, 145; field work, 148–49
University of Utah, personnel, 6
Utah, field work in, 6, 127, 148, 344, 356, 390, 399; review of archaeology in, as a topic, 404–6

Valkenburg, Sallie Van, publication, 254
Ventana Cave, 147
Verilla, Charles, report, 380
Vidal, Federico, presentation, 177
Vierra, Brad, paper, 419; speaker, 418
Viking Fund, 187, 190
Vivian, Gordon, 277
Vivian, Gwinn, report, 285
Voegelin, Carl, report, 269

Vogt, Evon, 209; letter to Edward Dozier, 214–15

Wade, William D., speaker, 312
Waffleton, Bruce, report, 375
Wait, Walter, participant, 399
Walker, J. Terry, report, 356
Walker, Jim, 423
Walnut Canyon, 126
Ward, Albert, report, 354
warfare, as a topic, 209, 391, 423
Warren, Hamilton, speaker, 201
Washburn, Dorothy, comment, 383; reports, 355, 375
Wasley, William, 263; publication, 248; reports, 254, 260, 293; speaker, 218
water-control systems as a topic, 327–28; report on, 267
Waterman, Thomas, biography, 65–66; role in the Pecos Classification, 92, 94
Wauchope, Robert, biography, 72; career, 232
Weaver, Donald E., Jr., presentation, 391; report, 355
Wedel, Waldo, career, 68; presentations, 280, 289; publication, 220; speaker, 279
Weed, Carol, report, 356
welcoming banner, 421
Wendorf, Fred, field work, 193, 199, 217, 230, 253, 254, 265; presentation, 231; publication, 183; speaker, 218
Wesley, Clarence, address, 177
West Texas Historical and Scientific Society, 8
Western Branch of the AAA, organization, 178
Wetherill, Ben, field work published, 217
Wheat, Joe Ben, letter to colleagues, 238; publication, 225, 248; reports, 229, 254, 265, 272, 293, 376; speaker, 304
Wheat, Pat, 175, 208
Wheeler, Richard, report, 254
White, Cheryl, report, 293
White, Richard, Jr., paper, 360; report, 361